BEATRIX

The Gardening Life of Beatrix Jones Farrand

1872–1959

JANE BROWN

VIKING

VIKING
Published by the Penguin Group
Penguin Books USA Inc., 375 Hudson Street, New York, New York 10014, U.S.A.
Penguin Books Ltd, 27 Wrights Lane, London W8 5TZ, England
Penguin Books Australia Ltd, Ringwood, Victoria, Australia
Penguin Books Canada Ltd, 10 Alcorn Avenue, Toronto, Ontario, Canada M4V 3B2
Penguin Books (N.Z.) Ltd, 182–190 Wairau Road, Auckland 10, New Zealand

Penguin Books Ltd, Registered Offices: Harmondsworth, Middlesex, England

First published in 1995 by Viking Penguin, a division of Penguin Books USA Inc.

1 3 5 7 9 10 8 6 4 2

Illustration credits appear on page 252.

LIBRARY OF CONGRESS CATALOGING IN PUBLICATION DATA
Brown, Jane.
Beatrix: the gardening life of Beatrix Jones Farrand, 1872–1959/Jane Brown.
p.   cm.
Includes bibliographical references and index.
ISBN 0-670-83217-0
1. Farrand, Beatrix, 1872– .   2. Landscape architects—United States—Biography.
3. Landscape architecture—United States—History.
4. Gardens—United States—History.   I. Title.
SB470.F37B76   1994
712´.092—dc20
[B]   94-1271

This book is printed on acid-free paper.

Printed in Singapore
Set in Bembo and Florens
Designed by Kate Nichols

ACKNOWLEDGMENTS

At the outset I want to mention that the benevolent ghosts of my earlier books, Miss Jekyll and Edwin Lutyens, Vita Sackville-West and Lanning Roper, all helped me on the journey to find Beatrix Farrand. One or another of them seemed to go before me into every unfamiliar room, into every gathering of unknown faces, as I encountered America. For this I am grateful.

The inner life of this book began on the first weekend of October 1987. I arrived in the way of ordinary mortals from Kennedy Airport, via a taxi through Queens and the Long Island Expressway bus, into an extraordinary world that I don't suppose I shall ever find again. It was, of course, Beatrix Farrand's world, which can still be found on certain days and in certain lights, like Brigadoon, along the leafy inlets of Long Island's North Shore. We walked among Quaker graves on Shelter Island, explored the tangled box parterres of Stanford White's garden, and took tea in proper style in Junius P. Morgan's drawing room. Two days seemed to span two hundred years; they were crowded with delights, but not untouched by modern tragedies, and they were made possible by the kindness of many distinguished Americans, and the particular grace of one exiled Englishman, Valentine Lawford. But to everyone I met that weekend go my thanks for the true inspiration for this book.

In New York I would particularly like to thank Mac Griswold, Fred Seidel, Pamela Lord, Paula Deitz, Olivia L. Gilliam and The Myrin Institute, Ngaere A. Macray and Sagapress, Messrs. Cadwalader, Wickersham & Taft, the New York Public Library, the New York Historical Society library, and Suzanne S. Stroh.

For introducing me to Mount Desert Island and Maine, my thanks go to Sarah Broley and her remarkable family and friends, to the Bar Harbor Museum, and to Patrick Chassé. In the Berkshires, I would like to thank Scott Marshall and Carole Palermo-Schultz at The Mount, Lenox, the Lenox Library, Melanie Simo, and for much kindness and laughter and a memorable picnic at Tanglewood as well as serious advice, Mike and Elsa Bakalar. In Connecticut my thanks to Katharine Warwick at Hill-Stead Museum, Farmington, and to Mrs. Anson P. Stokes III. In Massachusetts, mostly around Boston, an area particularly significant in Beatrix's early and late career, Nan Sinton and her many friends and John and Judith Tankard have given me particular help, but I would also like to thank Sheila Connor Geary, Peter del Tredici, and the director and staff of the Arnold Arboretum, Linda Jewell, then chairman of Landscape Architecture at the Harvard Graduate School of Design, many others at the Graduate School, and especially the staff of the Frances Loeb Library, at Harvard's Houghton Library, especially W. F. Dailey, curator of the Theodore Roosevelt Collection, Walter Punch, librarian of the Massachusetts Horticultural Society, Diane Kostial McGuire, Cynthia Zaitzevsky, Eleanor M. McPeck (who sent me her entry on Beatrix from *Notable American Women*, 1980), Michael Durr (who identified *Forsythia* "Beatrix Farrand" for me), Mr. Walter Hunnewell at Wellesley, Rolf Diamant, the Superintendent of the Frederick Law Olmsted National Historic Site, Mrs. Ralph P. Engle Jr., John and Sue Reed of Cambridge, and last but hardly least, Harvard University, for appointing me a Visiting Scholar in Landscape Architecture 1990–91.

In Washington, my inestimable debt to Laura Wood Roper and her friends is recorded in my introduction, but I would also like to remember the late Louise Graves. Otherwise my many visits to Washington were enlivened by the company of Harry and Sarah Broley, Michael Boudin and his friends, Frances Lumbard of George Washington University, Ann Satterthwaite, Adrian Higgins, and many people at Dumbarton Oaks, especially Annie Thacher, associate librarian in the Garden Library. I am also grateful to Suzanne K. Miller, who generously lent me her researches into the National Cathedral archives.

For her knowledge of Oberlin College and investigations on my behalf, my thanks to Pleasaunce Crawford; for similar generosity concerning Smith College, repeated thanks to Paula Deitz and to the college archivist, Margery N. Sly. My gratitude also goes to Elaine Engst, archivist at the Department of Manuscripts and University Archives at Cornell, to Carol Szymanski at the Firestone Library, Princeton University, to Robert Fagles, the Marks Professor of Comparative Literature at Princeton, to the staff of the Beinecke Library at Yale, and to Suzanne Carter Meldman and Richard C. Bumstead, the university planners, both of whom organized my visit to the campus and library (Department of Special Collections) at the University of Chicago. To my friends at the Chicago Botanic Garden I am grateful for several fascinating visits, even though, despite the help of Roy Klehm and the American Peony Society, we were unable to locate the peony named "Beatrix Jones" in time for publication. If "she" is known to any American gardener who may read this, I would love to hear.

In England, the treasures of the Elmhirst Centre Archive at Dartington Hall were revealed to me by Mary Bride Nicholson and her successor as archivist, Maggie Giraud. I would like to add my thanks also to Miranda Seymour, author of *Ring of Conspirators*.

And, finally, in California—for there would be no Beatrix book at all without their continued kindness, patience, and generosity—my thanks to Stephen Tobriner, Michael Laurie, Margaret Kabalin, Caitlin King, and Lisabeth Chester. (I hope these last three, former students who worked so hard looking after the Documents Collection in the library of the College of Environmental Design at the University of California, Berkeley, are now all on their way to successful landscape and architectural careers.) For their hospitality and friendship in Berkeley, my warm thanks and regards to Bill and Elly Bade, Joan Mirov, and Steve Sugarman and Karen Carlson.

The gulf between my work and the book's final reality has, in this instance, been emphasized by the Atlantic Ocean. I want to record my appreciation of the editorial and production skills of Kathryn Court and her colleagues at Viking, perhaps particularly singling out Kate Nichols, the designer. I hope they feel that *Beatrix* is equally their achievement.

CONTENTS

ACKNOWLEDGMENTS

V

LIST OF ILLUSTRATIONS

XIII

Introduction

HOW THIS BOOK CAME
TO BE WRITTEN

1

Chapter 1

THE ELUSIVE FREDDY AND
THE SPIRITED MARY

7

Chapter 2

DIVORCE! AND SOLACE IN
AN EARTHLY PARADISE

17

Chapter 3

BEATRIX AND THE BRAHMINS

31

Chapter 4

THE HUNT FOR BEAUTY:
EUROPE, 1895

46

Chapter 5

EARLY WORK AND A PLACE
IN HER PROFESSION

59

Chapter 6

AUNT PUSSY, MISS NIMROD,
AND OLD CELIMARE

74

Chapter 7

THE WHITE HOUSE
CONNECTION, 1903–12

88

Chapter 8

BEATRIX AND THE SON
OF THE MORNING

103

Chapter 9

BEATRIX AND THE AMERICAN WAY
OF GARDENING

125

Chapter 10

TRANSATLANTIC FELLOWS: DUMBARTON OAKS
AND DARTINGTON HALL, 1931–37

149

Chapter 11

MANY HAPPY AND SAD RETURNS: 1937–59

169

Chapter 12
Beatrix Jones Farrand, 1872–1959:
Her Legacy, and What Has Become of It
191

List of Commissions
203

Appendices
217

Notes
222

Sources
244

Index
246

Illustration Credits
252

LIST OF ILLUSTRATIONS

page nos.

Frontis.	Beatrix Jones, c. 1900
9	George Frederic Jones, by J. W. Ehninger
9	Frederic Rhinelander Jones, about nine years old, by J. W. Ehninger
11	Lucretia Rhinelander Jones in a family group, c. 1884
18	Beatrix, studio portrait, c. 1880
20	Rotch & Tilden fireplace detail, Reef Point, 1882
21	Beatrix at Reef Point, c. 1886
23	John Lambert Cadwalader, by John Singer Sargent
29	Early planting plan, Reef Point
32	Beatrix, c. 1890
35	Professor Charles S. Sargent, by John Singer Sargent
36	Jackson Thornton Dawson at the Arnold Arboretum
38	Professor Sargent and his family
39	Holm Lea, the Sargent house in Brookline
39	Holm Lea, the extensive gardens
43	Fairstead, Brookline, F. L. Olmsted's home and office
48	Mary Cadwalader Jones, c. 1895
52	Gertrude Jekyll at Munstead Wood
54	William Robinson
55	The bridge over the Kent at Levens Hall, 1895
60	Beatrix at the outset of her career
61	W. R. Garrison's garden, Tuxedo Park, 1896
62	W. R. Garrison plan, design for a boathouse
63	Chiltern, Bar Harbor, designs for seats in wood, 1906
63	Chiltern, Bar Harbor, seats and table designs

64   Woodburne, Lansdowne, summerhouse design, 1908
66   Designs for simple headstones
70   Crosswicks, Jenkintown, Pennsylvania, presentation details, 1903
71   Crosswicks, a second presentation drawing
76   Mary Cadwalader Jones in middle age
81   The Mount, Lenox, c. 1905
83   Brick House, Darien, design for the garden, 1902
84   Henry James and Howard Sturgis at The Mount
85   Easton Lodge, Essex, England, by Harold Peto
86   Montevideo, Simsbury, fan trellis details
91   Edward F. Whitney residence, Oyster Bay, seat design
91   Edward F. Whitney residence, Oyster Bay, trellis detail
92   Town garden design for Dr. James Markoe, 1909
93   Crosswicks, the flower garden
93   Crosswicks, detail of walls and piers
94   Clarence Warden residence, Haverford, spring garden
94   Harston, Chestnut Hill, ornamental details
96   Roland Park, Baltimore, Women's Club garden
97   Design for a suburban garden, 1910
97   Pergola for a suburban garden, 1910
97   Gateway for a suburban garden, 1910
104   Professor Max Farrand
107   Willard D. Straight house, Elmhurst, Old Westbury
109   New York Botanical Garden sketches for rose garden
110   Professor F. W. Williams home, garden in New Haven
112   Glenmere, New York, details of garden basket
112–113   Glenmere, New York, wall details, 1916
115   Eolia, New London, north entrance design
115   Eolia, New London, paving detail
116–117   Eolia, New London, Brett & Hall's planting plan
118   Eolia, New London, Beatrix Farrand's planting plans
127   Percy R. Pyne III residence, Long Island, garden design
130–133   Oakpoint, Bayville, Long Island, planting design
134   Oakpoint, Bayville, Long Island, the rock garden
135   Oakpoint, Bayville, Long Island, pool garden
135   Oakpoint, Bayville, Long Island, Chinese trellis detail
136   Satterlee garden, Great Head, Bar Harbor, planting plan
140   Traquair House and pavilions, Scotland, 1906
144   Beatrix Farrand, c. 1925
145   The Hill School, Pottstown, garden design
152   Dartington Hall, the courtyard
156   Dumbarton Oaks, plan by Rudolph Ruzicka, 1935
160   Thirlestane, Bar Harbor, the rose garden
164   Beatrix on her last visit to William Robinson
165   Mary Cadwalader Jones, c. 1922
167   Dartington Hall, Dorothy Elmhirst gardening
170   Mildred and Robert Woods Bliss at Dumbarton Oaks
172   Max and Beatrix Farrand at Reef Point
173   Reef Point from the air

174–175	Reef Point Gardens, plan
176	Beatrix Farrand, c. 1937
177	Professor Max Farrand, c. 1937
183	Arnold Arboretum, Meadow Road planting
183	Arnold Arboretum, plan for Meadow Road planting

COLOR ILLUSTRATIONS

1	Crosswicks, Jenkintown, Pennsylvania, presentation details
1	Botanical study by Mary Robeson Sargent from a family album
2	The East Colonial Garden, the White House, 1913
2	Elmhurst, Old Westbury, Long Island, perspective of walled garden
4	Harston, Chestnut Hill, Pennsylvania, the sunken garden
4	Wingwood House, Bar Harbor, Maine, design for the garden
5	Great Head, Bar Harbor, Maine, the Satterlee ravine garden
5	The Haven, Northeast Harbor, Maine, the Milliken garden
6	The Farm House, Bar Harbor, Maine, Miss McCormick's garden
7	The Eyrie, Seal Hardor, Maine, the Spirit Path
7	The Eyrie, Korean tomb figure
7	The Eyrie, tomb figure in woodland
8	The Eyrie, flower garden as it is today
8	The Eyrie, the flower garden in the 1940s
9	The Eyrie, the "bottle" gate
10	The Eyrie, the garden entrance
10	The Eyrie, the pink-washed wall
11	The Eyrie, the Moon Gate
12	Rock Creek Park, Washington, D.C., the bridge
12	Rock Creek Park, the stream and waterfall
13	Rock Creek Park, another detail of watercourse
13	Rock Creek Park, details of pebble ornament
14	Dumbarton Oaks, Washington, D.C., a garden house
15	Dumbarton Oaks, tribute to Beatrix Farrand's friendship
15	Dumbarton Oaks, Green Garden terrace
16	Dumbarton Oaks, inside the pergola
16	Dumbarton Oaks, the Wisteria Pergola
17	Dumbarton Oaks, details of pergola interior
17	Dumbarton Oaks, the Wisteria Pergola
18	Dumbarton Oaks, the Box Terrace
18	Dumbarton Oaks, entrance facade
19	Dumbarton Oaks, the Swimming Pool Terrace
20	Dumbarton Oaks, the Beech Terrace
20	Dumbarton Oaks, garden seat
21	Dumbarton Oaks, terraces above Lover's Lane Pool
22	Dumbarton Oaks, the Box Walk
23	Dumbarton Oaks, the Path End
23	Dumbarton Oaks, the North Vista
24	Dumbarton Oaks, the Perennial Border
24	Dumbarton Oaks, Lover's Lane terraces

❧ FAMILY TREE ❧

Showing Some of the Relatives
of Beatrix Cadwalader Jones

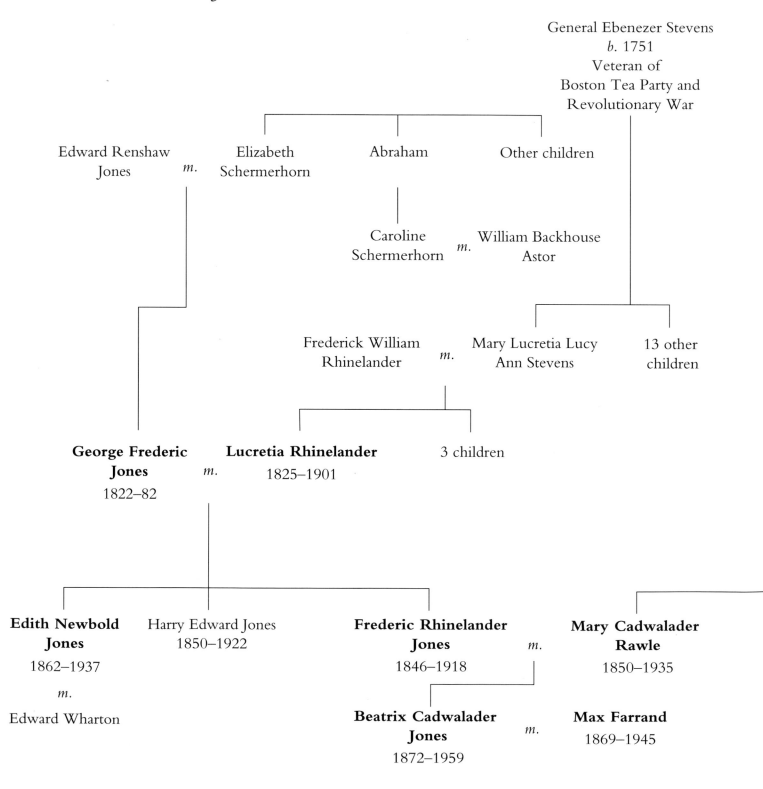

General Ebenezer Stevens
b. 1751
Veteran of
Boston Tea Party and
Revolutionary War

Edward Renshaw
Jones   *m.*

Elizabeth
Schermerhorn

Abraham

Other children

Caroline
Schermerhorn   *m.*   William Backhouse
Astor

Mary Lucretia Lucy
Ann Stevens

13 other
children

Frederick William
Rhinelander   *m.*

**George Frederic
Jones**
1822–82   *m.*

Lucretia Rhinelander
1825–1901

3 children

**Edith Newbold
Jones**
1862–1937

m.

Edward Wharton

Harry Edward Jones
1850–1922

**Frederic Rhinelander
Jones**
1846–1918   *m.*

**Mary Cadwalader
Rawle**
1850–1935

**Beatrix Cadwalader
Jones**
1872–1959   *m.*

Max Farrand
1869–1945

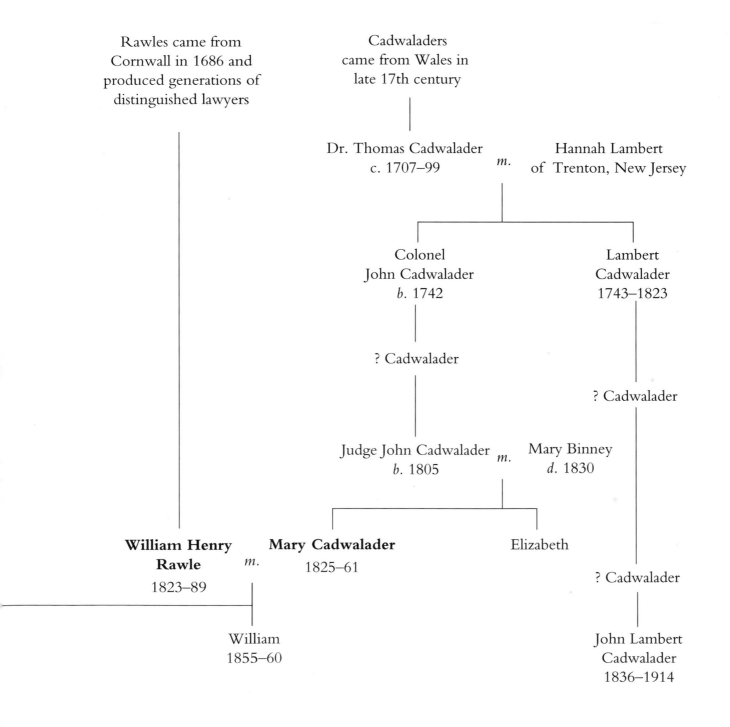

Rawles came from
Cornwall in 1686 and
produced generations of
distinguished lawyers

Cadwaladers
came from Wales in
late 17th century

Dr. Thomas Cadwalader
c. 1707–99   *m.*

Hannah Lambert
of Trenton, New Jersey

Colonel
John Cadwalader
b. 1742

Lambert
Cadwalader
1743–1823

? Cadwalader

? Cadwalader

Judge John Cadwalader   *m.*
b. 1805

Mary Binney
d. 1830

**William Henry
Rawle**   *m.*
1823–89

Mary Cadwalader
1825–61

Elizabeth

? Cadwalader

William
1855–60

John Lambert
Cadwalader
1836–1914

BEATRIX

The Gardening Life of

Beatrix Jones Farrand

1872–1959

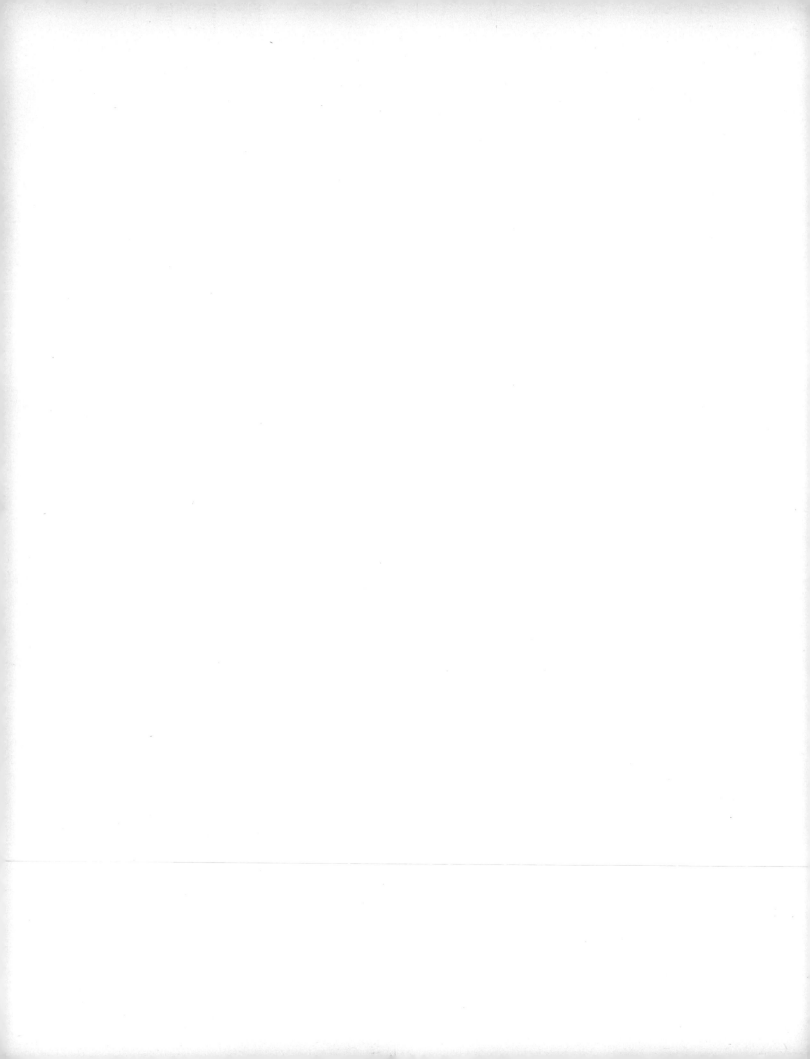

Introduction

❧❧❧

HOW THIS BOOK
CAME TO BE WRITTEN

*T*o many people who open this book the name of Beatrix Farrand will be familiar. She is, almost, the female equivalent of America's most well known landscape architect, Frederick Law Olmsted, the maker of Central Park. Her equivalent for Central Park is one of America's most distinguished gardens, that of Dumbarton Oaks in Washington, D.C. It is also usually remembered that Beatrix Farrand contributed a great deal to the Ivy League campuses of Yale and Princeton, and that she worked for Morgans, Rockefellers, Whitneys, McCormicks, Otto H. Kahn, and Edward S. Harkness, and at the White House. She is invariably thought of as a gilt-edged lady dabbling in gardens for the denizens of the Gilded Age. Is this an accurate impression? This is the first of many questions that have inspired this book.

The suggestion that I, an Englishwoman with no American connections but friends, should write Beatrix's story was made by my friend Mac Griswold. She and Eleanor Weller were hard at work on their vast study of America's garden history from 1890 to 1940, *The Golden Age of American Gardens,*[1] and clearly Beatrix, when seen among her contemporaries, revealed an English restraint in her tastes. Did she merely copy what she had seen in England and Europe and foist it off on the richest Americans?

Beatrix Farrand had first come into my life because she was instrumental in saving Gertrude Jekyll's drawings from certain destruction in an England which had war, and little else, on its mind. The Jekyll drawings ended up, along with Beatrix's own drawings, books, and other archival material, in the Documents Collection of the College of Environmental Design at Berkeley. I first went there in 1979 to research the Jekyll material for my book *Gardens of a Golden Afternoon,*[2] the story of the Lutyens and Jekyll partnership in garden making. I suppose that I was so grateful at finding the Jekyll drawings safely preserved that I brushed aside the disorientation that arises from studying a wholly environmental subject among surroundings that are alien to that subject. My research trips to California were exhilarating, but I did not at first recognize that the reason as to why Beatrix Farrand's legacy was in California was of vital importance. It is the question that dominates the end of this book. However, back in 1979, on my Jekyll foray, I could not resist looking into some of the Farrand folders. They were fascinating, for here was the work of an accomplished, inventive professional, as opposed to the Jekyllian image of the hardworking, artistic amateur.

Some nine years and five books after Lutyens and Miss Jekyll, I returned to Berkeley to lecture, with the idea of Beatrix in my mind. I had received permission to use the Documents Collection again, but there were others who had rights to Beatrix too. As an outsider, I trod warily. Ngaere Macray's Sagapress had published a pioneering and notable book, a collection of papers on Beatrix's work, *Beatrix Farrand's American Landscapes: Her Gardens and Campuses,* in connection with an exhibition initiated by The Wave Hill American Garden History Program in 1985.[3] Fate conspired to my meetings with the three scholars who had written these papers, Eleanor McPeck, Diana Balmori, and Diane Kostial McGuire, who all generously gave me their support and allowed me to benefit from their work.

Then to Georgetown, and the wisest of my American friends. My books include *Lanning Roper and His Gardens,*[4] written at the request of his friends after Lanning's death in 1983. His gardens are some of the loveliest made in England since the war, but Lanning was of course American. Writing about him had brought me to the house that became my American "home," the yellow house with green shutters on O Street and Thirty-fourth in Georgetown, the residence of Mrs. W. Crosby Roper, Jr., Lanning's sister-in-law, also known as Laura Wood Roper, the biographer of Frederick Law Olmsted.[5] Laura drafted her distinguished friends to my aid. I have a vivid memory of that doyen of Olmstedians, Frederick A. Gutheim, sitting with ramrod-straight back, interviewing me from Laura's blue silk sofa, enumerating the salient points that I should attend to: what is there about that gold-plated lady that we need to know? How did she relate to other landscape architects? What does she add to our awareness of our environment? She was a woman in a man's world—look at the way feminists were trying to take over Edith Wharton—I would have to watch that one.[6] Finally this courteous, quiet American shrugged his shoulders and got up to leave. "Well, she's just been sitting here, waiting for you, hasn't she?" he said.

From that moment, Beatrix took over. There always is a point up to which one plays with a subject, considers it from every angle, feeling completely in control. Then, suddenly, the subject takes over, dragging the protesting biographer across thousands of miles and hundreds of thousands of words.

Beatrix, of course, being such a lady, merely ushered me by the elbow, but it was a firm ushering, and there was no escape. At such a moment, panic ensues. I remember as a particular nightmare one celebrity-studded, very crowded and noisy book party in New York at that time, when I surveyed the dazzling company, not knowing a single one (the one I had arrived with having been swept off into the melee), and suddenly longed for the delights of the JFK departure lounge and the flight to Heathrow. How could I even consider competing with this? And then a friendly human being disentangled himself from the alien crowd; it was Robert Grant Irving, an American who had written a fascinating book, *Indian Summer*,[7] about two Englishmen, Lutyens and Herbert Baker, working in New Delhi. I knew him, he was enthusiastic about my idea, and I thank him for that moment which saved me from cutting and running there and then.

Beatrix played her last card at Dumbarton Oaks. It snowed, and Washington was confounded; antique Georgetown had become young and pretty overnight. The supreme capital of the Western world, reduced to an apologetic standstill by two inches of overnight snow, inspired easy time-traveling. I walked up to Dumbarton Oaks through Christmas-card streets, enjoying a slipping and sliding camaraderie with perfect strangers: I spent the afternoon deeply immersed in the correspondence between Beatrix Farrand and Mildred Bliss, both aging and ailing, with ailing husbands, Max Farrand and Robert Woods Bliss, devoted all to each other and especially to the "no longer fledgling" garden, the thing of beauty that they had created. That was the 1940s. I switched off the reader, left the library, and came down the stairs. This was the 1980s, but there it was—the North Vista, that stepping, narrowing, intriguing vista, most difficult of all problems for the designer, most favorite idea of Mildred Bliss, seen through the window, chanced upon the stair, as it was planned to be, flecked in fresh snow and washed in pale golden winter sunlight: Beatrix's living picture, created with all the assurance and vision of a painting by Monet or Claude.

I set out in search of the substance of Beatrix Farrand's life. She and her husband, Max Farrand, had no children. She was an only child, as was her mother,[8] and her father's brother and sister were also childless. Max Farrand's brothers had only "acquired" Beatrix when she married Max, at the age of forty-one, so they knew little of her early life. In fact, there were no family members to treasure her as part of their past. She had written two pages of autobiography, unnervingly in the third person so that it reads like her own obituary, which in fact she intended it to be.[9] In it she masks the important people and events in her life in anonymity, referring to "her grandmother," "her friends," and a series of "fortunate meetings." There are few clues and many questions arise. It was not an auspicious start.

Her gift to the University of California, the Reef Point Collection,[10] included 2,700 volumes of her library books, 1,786 herbarium specimens from Reef Point gardens, her labeled and cataloged collection of Gertrude Jekyll's drawings, and her own collection of drawings from her life's work. There is a smattering of correspondence and a collection of her own Kodak snapshots of her gardens in progress. The collection is overwhelmingly related to her work. As such it had formed the basis for the research done on her, before I came along with the intention of putting her work into the context of her life. The remnants of her life are not in the library at Wurster Hall on the Berkeley campus; they are in a modest collection of battered cardboard boxes, still in the university store in the old industrial area down by the Bay, where they had lain, occasionally looked at, but largely as they had come from Reef Point, for a very long time. The contents of those boxes form much of the substance of this book.

There was not a great deal of material on which to reconstruct a life. One treasure had already been removed to the Documents Collection, her handwritten student's notebook of the 1890s, which recorded her earliest interests and her visits to the World's Columbian Exposition at Chicago in 1893, the Olmsted office, and the Arnold Arboretum, under the wing of Charles Sargent. There was nothing else of obvious significance; it was a motley collection of envelopes and folders, diaries and notebooks and some treasured objects, the fragment of pink mosaic from Ravenna, a lock of her own auburn hair cut when she was fourteen, shooting records from the grouse moors at Millden in Scotland, a nonsense rhyme handwritten and tied with red ribbon, and lists of the Christmas presents she received in 1912. Why she had kept these things was perhaps of more interest than the objects themselves. At the bottom of one of the boxes was a folded sheaf of papers, which turned out to be something I had not expected to find, for they recorded her parents' divorce.

Beatrix's parents' separation and divorce was the deep shame of her life, and she simply did not wish it to be known or discussed. It hangs like a storm cloud over her story, and yet it explains a great deal about the mainspring of her life and work. Before I had gone much further in my research, especially into the papers of Henry James in the Houghton Library and those of Edith Wharton in the Beinecke, two people who were particularly close to Beatrix and her mother, Mary, it became perfectly clear that she had intentionally destroyed most of the evidence about her personal life because of that divorce. It explains why Beatrix and her mother play such minuscule roles in books written about James and Edith Wharton, when in fact they were Edith's closest and most beloved relatives and in constant touch with her, and why there are enormous gaps in the record of Mary's friendship with Henry James, when this must have been one of the most remarkable friendships of his life.[11] After her mother's death in 1935, Beatrix painfully and ruthlessly destroyed most of her family's papers. She burned almost everything, making a token gesture of "clean" letters to the relevant libraries and literary posterity.

Luckily there are two places where her private shame was irrelevant, but where she had long-standing friendships that were more than professional relationships. The correspondence that survives at the Arnold Arboretum was invaluable; perhaps it was a good omen—it was certainly encouraging—that the second place was in England, at Dartington Hall. Here the Elmhirst Centre Archives preserve most of the story of her friendship with Dorothy Whitney Elmhirst, which lasted from 1912 until the end of Beatrix's life. At the end of her life it was Dartington that filled Beatrix's musings and dreams, and it was to the Elmhirsts, in her last years, that she revealed most of her warmth and feelings, and her unflagging brilliance in her professional judgments, even though she was hampered by the physical failings of age.

It is not for me to say that I *know* Beatrix Farrand from writing this book about her life and work. But I have formed a tremendous admiration for "dear brave Trix," as Henry James called her, not only for her professional brilliance, which I trust is unquestioned, but for her courageous and indomitably stylish journeying. I hope she will forgive me for "digging up" the divorce, and realize that there is for us no shame, only perhaps sadness. And I trust that my living American friends will forgive me when I say that my last reason for writing this book is to divert their rose-tinted eyes from English gardens to a marvelous heritage of their very own.

Dogmersfield
March 1, 1993

Chapter 1

❧❧❧

THE ELUSIVE FREDDY AND
THE SPIRITED MARY

*B*eatrix Cadwalader Jones was born on June 19, 1872, at 21 East Eleventh Street, her parents' New York town house. Her birth was registered on June 22 by her father, Frederic Rhinelander Jones, who, for the first and probably the one time in his life, listed himself with an occupation, that of a "manufacturer." He owned a "grand Miscellaneous Shop,"[1] importing and selling decorative items, lamps, mirrors, and ornaments for smart New York homes.

Beatrix's mother was a twenty-two-year-old Philadelphian, Mary Cadwalader Rawle. Frederic and Mary had been married in March 1870, and after a summer-long wedding trip to Europe, they had returned to New York for the fall season. Now, some twenty-one months later, their first baby arrived in the early summer heat wave of a city that most of their friends had already left. So as soon as they could, when Beatrix was three weeks old, they took her to Newport, to Pencraig, a rambling cottage on Harrison Avenue, the summer home of her Jones grandparents.

Perhaps they journeyed too soon, for the baby became ill and was baptized in emergency on July 19 at Pencraig, with her parents as her only sponsors. She was named Beatrix (though the certificate of baptism spells it Beatrice) after her mother's first remembered heroine, the spirited Beatrix Esmond of Thackeray's novels.[2] Despite that early alarm, Beatrix grew into a sturdy child. She spent the summers of her babyhood at Pencraig, which brought her close to her Jones grandparents and her young aunt, Edith Newbold Jones, just ten years her senior, who grew up to be the novelist Edith Wharton.

Beatrix inherited a great deal from the Jones side of her family; her handsome looks and her tall and stately bearing were from her father and grandfather, and the social connections that came with the Jones name were to be a great asset to her. Despite her later opinions to the contrary, the Jones banking fortune also gave her a very privileged and comfortable upbringing.

She was, in later life, most proud that she came from "five generations of gardeners,"[3] and the Joneses played their part in that. Aunt Edith certainly became a passionate gardener and both Jones and Rhinelander forebears were of a breed that took the bounty of well-stocked greenhouses and an efficiently run garden for granted. Beatrix's earliest gardening memory was of her grandmother Lucretia Jones's rose garden at Pencraig. Here she remembered being "conscious of plants" and in "helping" with the deadheading she experienced that early respect and familiarity that only comes when the plants are larger than oneself. She also remembered how she amused her elders, especially the nongardening ones, by chatting about "Marie van Houtte" and "Baroness Rothschild" as if they were people she had spent the afternoon with; she was four years old.[4]

Beatrix's father, Frederic Rhinelander Jones, was born in 1846, the elder son of George Frederic and Lucretia Rhinelander Jones. A second son, Henry Edward, known as Harry, followed in 1850, and their little daughter, Edith, came twelve years later. Freddy was always to be his mother's favorite; Harry, in turn, was adored by his younger sister.

Lucretia Jones was not the stuff of loving motherhood. She was rather more preoccupied with and confident of her place as "*The* Mrs Jones" of New York society. She was more than comfortably ensconced in the upper echelons of The Four Hundred, and the ballroom into which Ward McAllister, who coined the term, reputedly fitted them belonged to George Frederic's first cousin, Caroline Schermerhorn Astor. On her father's side, for certain, Beatrix was not short of distinguished forebears.

One of the most colorful was Freddy's great-great-grandfather on his mother Lucretia's side, General Ebenezer Stevens. He could trace his New World ancestors to the 1630s, and he was born in 1751. He helped tip the tea into Boston Harbor in December 1773 and fought the British from Bunker Hill to Yorktown. He prospered in the East India trade (allegedly carrying government agents), and he fathered fourteen children from his two marriages, most of whom married well. His youngest child, Mary Lucretia Lucy Ann Stevens, married Frederic William Rhinelander, of the third generation of a Huguenot family who had come to America in 1686, and became rich dealing in New York property. Frederic William and Mary Lucretia's first child, Lucretia, was born in 1824; there were three more children and then their father died, still only in his thirties. The Rhinelander brothers continued to amass their fortune, but seemingly forgot their widowed sister-in-law and her small daughters, who were left in what to them was shaming poverty. When Lucretia came out "she wore a home-made gown of white tarlatan, looped up with red and white camellias from the greenhouse, and her mother's old white satin slippers; and her feet, being of

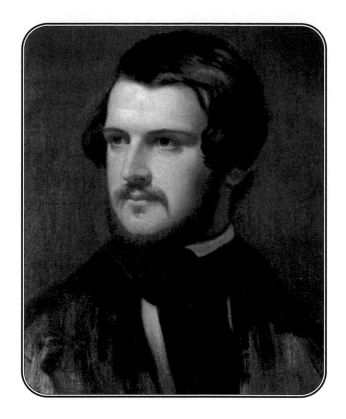

a different shape from grandmamma's, she suffered martyrdom, and never ceased to resent the indignity inflicted on her, and the impediment to her dancing."[5] This was to be the last martyrdom to what she felt was Rhinelander oversight in Lucretia's "starved, cramped, touching little life" that far, and she was determined to escape.[6] Fortunately, there was a suitor to hand, the rich and indulged George Frederic Jones, who, on being forbidden to marry a poor Rhinelander girl, was determined to do so. Their courtship, in which much was achieved by the means of a rowing boat with a sail made of George Frederic's bedcover, is featured in Edith Wharton's story "False Dawn."

Beatrix's paternal grandfather, George Frederic Jones, was the youngest child of Edward Renshaw and Elizabeth Schermerhorn Jones. A graduate of Columbia, he was amiable and art-loving; but with no particular purpose in life, he chose to enjoy his family fortune rather than add to it. His bent was toward poetry and literature, but this was firmly quashed by Lucretia. George Frederic's elder brother, Edward Jones, was made of sterner stuff; a physician, he became part of the liberal influence at Columbia in the 1850s and 1860s with George Templeton Strong and Lewis Rutherford.

Lucretia and George Frederic had married on October 17, 1844, and after a wedding trip to Cuba, they settled in Gramercy Park (80 East Twenty-first Street), where Freddy was born in January 1846. Lucretia had not nearly enough, however, of the good things that George Frederic's money could buy, and soon they were off to Europe, gallivanting from city to city with other fashionable New Yorkers, regardless of the poor baby carted in their wake.

LEFT: *George Frederic Jones, Beatrix's paternal grandfather, from a portrait by John Whetton Ehninger.*

RIGHT: *Freddy Rhinelander Jones, about nine years old, from a portrait by John Whetton Ehninger.*

George Frederic confided to his diary just how "awful a thing it is to travel in Europe with an infant of twenty months."[7] Freddy was thus imbued with his parents' (and particularly his father's) passion for Paris above all other places. The Joneses were in Paris when revolutionary war broke out in February 1848, and when they could safely leave, they returned to America. They bought Pencraig, their house at Newport, and there Harry was born in May 1850.

While Lucretia, fitted out with the contents of endless trunks and parcels from the Paris fashion houses, concentrated on becoming the best-dressed woman in New York society, her sons Freddy and Harry were confined to the nursery and schoolroom ritual of the day. The most they saw of their parents was when they escaped to peek down the stairs at the endless stream of visitors being received for the winter round of dinners and receptions. In summer they were rather more of a family, riding, sea fishing, wildfowl shooting, and sailing their catboats at Newport, while Lucretia tended her summer garden. Into this well-regulated life the late arrival of Edith, when Freddy was sixteen and Harry was twelve, caused confusion (as well as turning their domestic life into literary history).[8]

Edith was born in January 1862. She later wrote that she was too young to remember the Civil War, but that it came as a profound shock to her family. George Frederic and Lucretia decided to let both their houses and move to Europe, where the living was cheaper and the uprisings could be observed as the difficulties of others far away. They set sail in November 1866, taking Edith and Harry with them. It was arranged that Harry should finish his education at Trinity Hall at Cambridge, studying civil law. Freddy, in his twentieth year, was left at home, ostensibly (at least according to Edith's later recollection) at Harvard. He left little mark of his presence there,[9] though rather surprisingly he was remembered by Henry James, who was three years his senior and had recently finished at the Law School. They can have had little in common, except perhaps the same society and a love of Paris. James's yearning for old Europe would have found a fellow feeling in Freddy that would have been rare at Harvard. But Freddy certainly had no studious or literary or even legal ambition, and was merely content to have a good time.

Though his Harvard years are shadowy, Freddy makes a certain appearance in the summer of 1869 on board a ship en route to Europe to be reunited with his family. It was on board the *Scotia* that he met Mary Cadwalader Rawle for the first time; she was known to his traveling companions, his Newbold cousins. They met again briefly in Switzerland, and when Mary returned to Philadelphia Freddy turned up there to see her in the fall of 1869. Henry James returned from Europe in early 1870 and went to Newport to catch up on everyone's life; there he was surprised to hear of Freddy's engagement to Miss Rawle of Philadelphia. So surprised was he that immediately upon leaving the ferry in New York, he made straight for the elder Joneses' house to see

Family photograph c. 1884, with Lucretia Rhinelander Jones, center, in black; her daughter, Edith, top right; and Edward Wharton in front of Edith. It was probably taken to mark Edith's engagement to Teddy Wharton.

Freddy. He found him absent, but was told that Miss Rawle was next door. Although James was "not particularly presentable for a first call," his curiosity was imperative. He thought Miss Rawle, if she "had any soul at all,"[10] would understand, so he called on her, and of course she did. Henry James was certain, from that brief encounter, that he had found a friend in Mary, but their friendship was not to develop for some time. What is worth noting from the story is James's *surprise,* for he clearly had little confidence in Freddy's suitability for marriage to a lively, intelligent girl.

Beatrix's mother, Mary Cadwalader Rawle, was a lady of consequence; high-spirited, a firecracker, a thoroughbred, these are the adjectives she inspired (and I suppose it is a symbol of her time that these are the adjectives that we would sooner apply to a horse). She was a Philadelphian and immensely proud of it. It was the city where her Cadwalader and Rawle ancestors had played honorable and prominent roles in the making of America. She was patriotic, and thrilled to be able to write that she was born in the last days of 1850 into a city where men were still alive who had heard the windows "clack open" that joyous night the watchman called "Past twelve o'clock of a cloudy night and Cornwallis is taken."[11]

Mary's mother's family, the Cadwaladers, had come from Wales at the end of the seventeenth century. Dr. Thomas Cadwalader, born in Philadelphia in about 1707, was noted for his pioneering use of the inoculation against smallpox in the early 1730s. He was also a bookish man, a friend of Benjamin

Franklin, and involved in the founding of the Philadelphia Library, the hospital and the Academy.[12] Dr. Thomas married well, to Hannah Lambert, the daughter of a rich landowner from New Jersey, and they had two sons, John, born in 1742, and Lambert, born the following year. They became soldiers, rich enough to be members of the elite private infantry "the Silk Stocking Company" and courageous enough to acquit themselves well in the Trenton campaign through the bitterly cold Christmas and New Year of 1776–77. Lambert Cadwalader was taken prisoner by the British and when eventually released, retired to Greenwood, his estate near Trenton, which he inherited from his mother. Colonel John Cadwalader soldiered on during 1777 to Brandywine and Germantown; he became General Washington's aide and staunch supporter, and usually enters the history books for fighting a duel with Colonel Conway, leader of the Conway Cabal which questioned Washington's leadership.

These cavalier brothers, John and Lambert, sired a complex cousinage of Cadwaladers who mostly became eminent lawyers. Lambert's great-grandson, John Lambert Cadwalader, born in 1836, was to become one of the most influential men in Beatrix's life in the absence of her father. Colonel John's grandson, also John Cadwalader, born in 1805, became one of Philadelphia's most distinguished judges; in 1825 he married Mary Binney, the daughter of another Philadelphia family, and they had two daughters, Mary and Elizabeth. Mary Binney Cadwalader died while the girls were still small, and the aspiring lawyer married again and sired a second family. He found his little daughters inconvenient, so they were parted, and sent one to each set of grandparents, Mary to the Cadwaladers, Elizabeth to the Binneys. At her grandmother's house, Mary eventually met a young lawyer friend of her uncle's, William Henry Rawle, and they were married in 1849, when she was nineteen. Beatrix's mother, Mary, was their first child, born the following year, on December 12, 1850, into a world that was seemingly privileged and secure, but where in truth the heartless rejection, separation, and consequent loneliness inflicted upon her mother's own childhood was to have a profound effect on her future.

Mary's father, William Henry Rawle, was the product of even more generations of lawyers than the Cadwaladers could muster. The Rawles, sincere Quakers, had come from Cornwall—from the rugged north coast, with its gigantic breakers, and from St. Juliot[13] in the land of Lyonesse near Tintagel, to join William Penn in 1686.

Francis Rawle from Cornwall, who was around thirty when he arrived in Philadelphia, married Martha Turner in 1689 and they had six sons and four daughters. He was what may be dubbed a conscientious colonist, for he wrote a treatise on *Ways and Means for the Inhabitants of Delaware to become Rich* (1725).[14] Several of his sons were lawyers, and one of them was a William, and a string of Williams leads down the generations. One William Rawle was a law student at the time of the Revolutionary War and he returned to England to study, going back to Philadelphia after the war to set up his law firm, which lasted until 1925. His son, William, was first president of the History Society of Pennsylvania, a constitutional lawyer who published *A View of the Constitution of the United States* in 1825. *His* son, William Henry Rawle (1823–89), Mary's father, edited *Smith on Contracts* (1853) and wrote other books on property law.

These are her proud and dutiful ancestors as Mary recalled them in her book *Lantern Slides,*[15] with additional information from the annals of the great and good where so many Cadwaladers and Rawles are to be found. Only men are mentioned, of course, for the women merely made it all possible and kept their places, or were pushed aside if inconvenient like the two little daughters of Judge Cadwalader's first marriage. It comes as little surprise, therefore, to learn that William Henry and Mary Cadwalader Rawle were deeply disappointed that their firstborn was a daughter; she was named after her mother but called Minnie throughout her childhood (as she will be throughout the rest of this chapter).

Mary Rawle had little time for her daughter, and concentrated upon conceiving the longed-for son, who was eventually born in 1855. Little Minnie's life revolved around her nurse, a part-Irish, part-Northumbrian woman named Eliza Black who was beloved by her small charge. Minnie was also devoted to her dog, a lazy cocker spaniel named Hadji; for the rest of her life she felt it essential to have a dog sleeping at the foot of her bed.

With the rest of the household preoccupied with baby William, Minnie filled her mind with a scene that stayed vivid in her memory. In the snowy New Year of 1856, her father was visited by the kindly William Makepeace Thackeray. Thackeray was on a tour for his newly published *History of Henry Esmond,* and listening to tales he put later into *The Virginians.*[16] In his concern for his own daughter (Minny) left at home, he made a tremendous fuss of little Minnie Rawle, who, for a rare moment, was the center of attention in her own home. The name of Thackeray's heroine was on everybody's lips, and Beatrix Esmond must have lodged herself in Minnie's brain.

When Minnie was not in Eliza Black's care, her chief companions, even from an early age, were grown men. On Sundays she was taken to Old Saint Peter's by her Binney grandfather, and sat on a pile of hassocks so that she could see over the high box pews. She was allowed no ordinary books on Sundays, only Bible stories or *Pilgrim's Progress;* on other days she read voraciously from whatever was at hand, including her father's *Punch* and *Illustrated London News.* On Saturdays she rode, sometimes with her bachelor uncle, William Cadwalader, and sometimes, most joyously, with her father. Father and daughter were very much alike, sparely built with delicate features and dark hair, and generous amounts of physical and mental vitality. Minnie treasured her Saturday rides with her father only second to poetry readings with him.

Mary Rawle's obsession with her son had been heightened by the difficulty of conceiving him, and then by his delicate health. When he died from diphtheria at the age of five, she was totally broken. Minnie only remembered her mother as a lovely young woman in a blue gown with dark hair curled about her ears, who turned almost overnight into a sickly, aging recluse after little William's death. Mary herself died from consumption in 1861, in her thirtieth year.

After her mother's death it was up to Minnie, aged eleven, to become her father's constant companion and support. She accompanied him to Washington, to visit President Lincoln at the White House, and also to meet her famous uncle, General George Cadwalader at the Willard Hotel. The year was 1863, and at the end of June she was left at the hotel while her father calmly went out to take part in the Battle of Gettysburg (July 1–3). In the spring of 1865 she went with him to Charleston, to be present at Fort Sumter for a ceremony recalling the beginning of the Civil War four years earlier. The day, April 14, 1865, was also of course the day that John Wilkes Booth shot President Lincoln; the news eventually reached the Rawles on board the *Mary Sanford,* creeping down the coast of Florida to the safety of Havana.[17]

During Minnie's teens, life for father and daughter was very comfortably centered in their new home, above the lawyer's office in Walnut Street, where peaches and apricots grew in the garden. She became knowledgeable about wine and entertaining generally, and they enjoyed an easy and pleasant social life of small parties and a few dances. They would ride out most afternoons (such was the leisurely life of a prominent lawyer in those days), and they took diversionary trips to New York and summer holidays at Long Branch, New Jersey. But Minnie grew only too aware that this could not last, for her father, still only in his early forties, was so eligible. She admitted that to have a "marriageable father is a greater responsibility than a marriageable daughter,"[18] implying—as would be in keeping with her experience and that of her mother—that her happiness, her rightful enjoyment of her admirers, must take second place to her father's prospects. Undoubtedly, if Minnie was courted by gallants of Philadelphia (and her friends later remembered that she was much courted), her father was hotly pursued, and her role was to keep house for him and defend him. So, by the time she was nineteen, her opinion of men was firmly fixed by the roles of friend and companion that her grandfather, uncle, and father played. In *Lantern Slides* she goes to some lengths to establish "that the most natural friendships are those between men and women."[19]

It seems that when William Henry Rawle decided he would marry again he at least took care for his daughter's feelings. In announcing his intention to marry his late wife's cousin, Emily Cadwalader, of whom Minnie was very fond, he softened the blow by treating his daughter to her longed-for first trip to Europe in the summer of 1869. They sailed from New York in the paddle wheel Cunarder, *Scotia,* holder of the Atlantic Blue Riband. Of shipboard life

Minnie gleefully observed the good company, hearty "English" food, a jolly salt of a captain, that the hot water arrived in small brass cans, and that there was "an obliging moon."[20] The first and last memories may have been connected with the presence on board of friends of her father's, the Newbold family, who were traveling with their handsome cousin Frederic Rhinelander Jones.

Freddy was soon forgotten as Minnie allowed herself to be enchanted by the rituals of Victorian London, particularly the befeathered girls of her own age, guarded by dowagers, stout coachmen, and powder-bewigged footmen, who made their way to drawing rooms at Buckingham Palace. At her first dinner party she recorded finding herself next to "a raw-boned and red-faced" gentleman who questioned her as to whom she most wanted to meet in England. "Oh, Professor Owen, of course," she replied, "because he knew what dinornis was like from just a bit of bone."[21] Her dinner companion turned out to be the great scientist, and he took her to the Regent's Park zoo and to the British Museum (where he was superintendent of natural history) and put a skeletal fragment of the apteron bird into her hand. The Rawles also went to one of the Owens' famous Sunday gatherings at the house Queen Victoria had given the professor, Sheen Lodge in Richmond Park, famous for its lovely garden.[22]

After touring England, Minnie and her father went to France and Switzerland, and there met Freddy again. They returned home in a September gale, on the *Scotia,* and William Rawle and Emily Cadwalader were duly married in Philadelphia in late autumn.

Emily's relationship with Minnie was good, and she surely did everything to help Minnie adjust; but no home can have two mistresses, and Minnie was sensitive about being "in the way." After nine long, tender years, her home was no longer her kingdom and her father now had another, closer companion.

Young Freddy Jones arrived and pressed his suit; he was tall and very good looking, amusing and lively company, extremely rich and related to the best New York society. In obligingly falling in love with him, Minnie may not have noticed that her bookish passions were not his, and that he, so unlike the men she was used to, lacked any ambition for himself. They were married quietly on March 24, 1870, "in our own house, as was frequently the custom with us and farther south," she recalled.[23] It was just six months since she had come home from Europe.

They returned to Europe on their wedding trip, first to Paris so that Minnie could be introduced to Freddy's family, to his mother and father and her new sister-in-law, "a clever child, with a mane of red-gold hair, always scribbling stories on any paper." In early June the couple left on a long walking tour, "an idyll," Minnie called it, "it was all new to me and I was young and in love with life."[24] That she was "in love with life" was the most reliable of her opinions about herself; it sums up the vitality that she never lost.

The walking tour was a marvelous adventure. Freddy showed her what she called "Christmas tree Germany." They took a river steamer up the Rhine, they "chanced" upon the first performance of *Der Valküri* in Munich, discovering a shared passion for Wagner's music, they saw the Oberammergau Passion play and collected wildflowers in the Dolomites. Free from encumbrances, deliciously free from dressing for dinner and drawing rooms, they started out at eight each morning and walked till noon, making their way into northern Italy. Minnie ends her account, "After a glorious October in the Umbrian hill towns we found my husband's family in Florence . . . and I began to feel like Miss Flora McFlimsey, that I had nothing to wear."[25]

Chapter 2

✥✥✥

DIVORCE! AND SOLACE IN AN EARTHLY PARADISE

*T*he most settled background to Beatrix's earliest life was the house where she was born, 21 East Eleventh Street. It is the end one of a row of pretty Greek Revival houses built in the 1840s for a family named Isaacs, just a short step from Fifth Avenue.[1] No. 21 faces south; it is built of warm bricks that glow deep rose-red in the afternoon sun. It is a tall house, with an elegant iron guardrail curving beside a flight of eleven steps, a wide front door, and full-height windows to the main rooms. These were the "dear old Empire rooms"[2] long remembered with affection by Henry James. Beatrix had a sunny nursery upstairs, which was later converted to her workroom.

It would seem that the first ten years of her life were spent in an unruffled nursery regime. Mary Jones was well practiced at running a household; Beatrix was well cared for and Mary and Freddy played a full part in the social round, being seen for lunches at Delmonico's, endless dinners with the cousinage, at the New York Academy of Music and as regular attenders at the Patriarch's Balls after they were instituted in 1873. At first Freddy was busy with his shop enterprise, but this could not have lasted long; perhaps the 1873 stock market panic affected business, perhaps he got bored with it, but it is never mentioned again. Mary, on the other hand, was not made for idleness and needed to be useful. By the time Beatrix was three or perhaps four years old, Mary was involved in her lifelong campaign on behalf of New York City Hospital school. She began as a charity worker for the mission on Blackwell's Island in the East River, where the city hospital and asylums were horrifying places.[3] She realized that the staff, as well as the patients, had to contend with appalling conditions, and she turned her energies to the cause of the nurses,

*Beatrix, a fashionable studio
portrait at about eight years old.*

for their better education, status, and working conditions. It was typical of the firebrand Mary to take on such a difficult crusade, but she had the energy, and she was perfectly used to the company of formidable and influential men, so she was hardly afraid to tackle those most likely to help her. In this way she soon formed friendships with Henry Adams and Brooks Adams, Henry Cabot Lodge, and the Theodore Roosevelts, father and son.

This made her a formidable and unusual young lady in society, and perhaps very soon this aggravated her pleasure-loving and unambitious husband. Her closest friend at the time was Florence Lockwood, who later described Mary as being like "a high-bred, high-strung Arab horse, among an equally well-bred but quite different herd. She probably broke some of the New York conventions, I am sure that she had done so in Philadelphia, but no one ever suffered from what she did except perhaps herself."[4] One thing is certain, that breaking of conventions would have been an anathema to her mother-in-law, Lucretia Jones.

How long it took for the Freddy Joneses to consciously recognize their incompatibilities cannot be known, but their marriage, at least on the outside, seemed to remain intact for the first ten years of Beatrix's life. Her vivid memory of her grandmother Lucretia's rose garden in Newport was probably heightened by a change in their routine, when in 1879 Freddy took them to Bar Harbor for the first time. Mary had never liked Newport, and long stays at Pencraig with Lucretia could not have been getting any easier. Mary's father and step-mother, William and Emily Rawle, had "discovered" Bar Harbor, which was already nicknamed "Philadelphia by the sea," and rented a summer cottage. Freddy and Mary were immediately captivated, and Freddy was quick to take action; he bought a plot of land on the Shore Path, close to the village center, and commissioned Arthur Rotch, the Boston architect, to build him a cottage.[5] The first plans for the cottage were prepared for Freddy, and feature "Mr Jones's Bedroom," but was it too quiet, too unsophisticated for him? When Henry James visited the newly completed cottage, now named Reef Point, in August 1883, there is no mention of Freddy's presence: he had, in fact, made the deeds of the property over to Mary the previous March, just six months after he bought it.[6]

Beatrix was always tremendously proud that her family were among the first wave of summer visitors to appreciate Mount Desert Island. She treasured a memory of "the jingle of the stage coach harness as it drove up next door to the Des Isles cottage which we then occupied."[7] Just as she was firmly rooted in old New York society, so it was important to her that she belonged in Bar Harbor before the ostentatiously rich cottagers arrived. There is a photograph of her at about this time, enduring wintry conditions at the newly built Reef Point; she looks a cheerful, sensible little girl with laughing eyes and a firm jawline.

At some time after Beatrix's tenth birthday, June 19, 1882, Mary and Freddy finally parted company. The actual separation must have caused ripples of shock among their relatives and friends. Presumably the end of Freddy's only known business enterprise and his consequent, and assumed, lack of interest in doing anything else only aggravated their differences. While he lived for pleasure and the social round, quite usual among his class and time, the young Mrs. Jones was making an ever grander adventure of her life, rushing out to endless committee meetings and hospital visits, returning to fill her dinner table with the artistic company she loved, and which was to make her reputation as a literary hostess. She was determined to have her own way, because that was what she was used to, and was probably outspoken in her criticism of Freddy's idle hours. On his part Freddy must have found himself with a largely absentee wife, always busy, too busy to wait around for his pleasure and comfort, so he decided to seek such things elsewhere. Family gossip (by which I

Rotch
and
Tilden
Archts
Boston
Mass
1882

Sketch of Fire Place
on Landing
F. R. Jones Esq

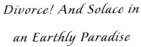
Divorce! And Solace in

an Earthly Paradise

Beatrix at Reef Point, with the earliest and smallest version of the house behind her, c. 1886.

mean the story current among present generations) is that Freddy went too far, by flaunting his mistress at a window table at Delmonico's. I think the reasons were, and would have needed to be, far more serious than that, but the emotional implications can only be surmised and it might be more practical to look at the financial aspects of marriage and divorce for Freddy and Mary Jones.

Freddy did not have to make money nor apply himself strenuously to keeping it. It just fell into his lap. His father, George Frederic Jones, long ailing, had died in Cannes in March 1882, just before Beatrix's tenth birthday. From his father's will, Freddy—along with Harry and Edith—inherited $20,000 each outright, and a further share of the remainder (an unknown amount) after other bequests. Lucretia Jones was left books, pictures, and furniture from their joint home, and not more than $30,000 to buy a house for herself and $600 a year allowance. Lucretia was also very rich in her own right by this time, from various Rhinelander bequests.[8] (These sums can be multiplied by twenty for present-day values.)

As her favorite, Freddy was always sure of his mother's indulgence, and eventually her fortune. In the meantime, his father's comparatively early death

FACING PAGE: *Reef Point: the only surviving Rotch & Tilden sketch for a detail in the house, dated 1882, for Frederic Rhinelander Jones, Esq. This drawing, and a plan referring to "Mr Jones's bedroom," are the evidence for Freddy's brief, early interest in Reef Point.*

gave him further expectations, which were realized in the summer of 1888. A cousin, Joshua Jones, a recluse, who lived and died in his apartment in The New York Hotel, left a vast number of shares in the Chemical Bank of New York (formerly the Jones and Mason family bank), which meant "upwards of $120,000 each" for Freddy, Harry, and Edith.

Could the Joshua Jones windfall, or even its prospect, have been the impetus for Freddy to depart for France with his mistress? He could have so easily afforded to leave Mary and Beatrix with their homes in New York and Bar Harbor, and with an allowance (Mary also had an allowance of her own), and run for his freedom with a fortune that, especially in terms of Paris living, ensured that he would be more than comfortable for the rest of his life. His moment of departure can perhaps be narrowed slightly further. Freddy and Mary were together at the Patriarch's Ball of February 1884[9] and possibly at the marriage of Edith to Teddy Wharton in New York on April 29, 1885. What is absolutely certain is that Freddy was well settled in Paris by the autumn of 1893, when his mother, Lucretia, made her last certain appearance in Newport before leaving for Europe to join her favorite son.

Lucretia Rhinelander Jones died in Paris in June 1901, at her home, 50 avenue du Bois de Boulogne. Her love for her children was clearly apportioned in her will. She left $95,000 to Freddy, $50,000 to Harry (also now married and living in Paris), and the remainder in equal shares to Freddy, Harry, and Edith. Freddy and Edith met in London that year, presumably to discuss the will and perhaps hand over the $45,000 that he gave to Beatrix out of his mother's money.[10]

To understand the impact of divorce on this society, and perhaps some of its implications in Beatrix's story, we have to move on to 1920 and the publication of *The Age of Innocence*. Edith Wharton portrayed her mother, Lucretia, as Mrs. Welland in the novel, and it seems most likely that in writing of the subject of divorce, she used not only her own much too raw and recent (and dissimilar) experience, but the earlier case in her family memory. Divorce! "The word had fallen like a bombshell in the pure and tranquil atmosphere of the Archer dining-room—Mrs Archer raised her delicate eye-brows in the particular curve that signified: 'The butler . . .' and everyone changed the subject. . . ." What was actually under discussion was the right of a woman to have a divorce, "a continuation of life"[11] should her husband choose to live with harlots.

Freddy and Mary's divorce case was heard on March 4, 1896, in the New York County Court.[12] Quite simply, Mary Cadwalader Jones petitioned through her lawyers, Parsons, Shepard & Ogden of 111 Broadway, against Frederic Rhinelander Jones, represented by George V. N. Baldwin. On March 11 they were adjudicated divorced, the decree was filed on March 16th, and it was all completed in just over two weeks, by March 21. The grounds were obviously desertion and adultery, but no mention of such details has surfaced and Beatrix always avoided the subject.[13] She was, after all, a product of the society in the Archer dining room.

John Lambert Cadwalader,
by John Singer Sargent.

The role of unofficial guardian and adviser to Mary and Beatrix was as-sumed by Mary's cousin, John Lambert Cadwalader: Henry James called him a "gallant, unblemished, really *original* gentleman and friend."[14] He was fourteen years older than Mary, a bachelor, a distinguished and successful lawyer in practice with Charles E. Strong,[15] and he was president of the Board of New York Public Library.[16] Cadwalader was kindly, but rather dour; not an easy man, he could be sarcastic, cold and overly fastidious, ". . . he had not the an-imal spirits which carry a man along exhuberantly and in easy relations with all sorts of men."[17] But undoubtedly Mary had had enough of "animal spirits" and her cousin was a suitable adviser, smoothing her path on financial and le-gal matters and leaving her to the life she wished to lead. She was now deeply involved with the welfare of her nurses. She was chairman of the Advisory Board of the Nursing School, and she certainly did not confine her duties to committee meetings; she supervised the choice of students, inspected their working and living conditions, and took the battle for their professional recog-nition to the politicians.[18]

Mary's devotion to her nurses was carried out quietly and unobtrusively, and clearly it was not a duty confined to office hours. But she also needed to fill her life and her home with literary and artistic people to whom she could talk; one of the earliest habitués of no. 21 was the novelist Francis Marion Crawford, then in his late thirties and working frantically to produce 5,000 words a day, feeling very alone in New York because of his Italian upbringing. Mary and Freddy had met his widowed mother, Louisa Ward (married to the sculptor Thomas Crawford) at Palazzo Odescalchi on their wedding trip, and Mary and Louisa remained friends. Francis Marion Crawford was the first of many writers to find a refuge in Mary Cadwalader's comfortable home, and his memories allow a warm glimpse of Beatrix growing up. He would arrive after Mass and stay for the famous Sunday lunch—often finding John La Farge, Augustus Saint-Gaudens, or John Singer Sargent at the table as well. Crawford was a "domestic" helper; he kept a carpenter's kit in the house to do odd jobs, calling himself "the umbrella-mender," and in the evenings he helped Beatrix with her Greek.[19]

On the opposite side of East Eleventh Street lived Frederick and Lucy Whitridge, and their son Arnold.[20] Arnold was a boy in the 1890s, and Mary was one of his favorite people: he remembered "whenever I crossed the threshold of that house I was happy . . . knowing I was going to have a good time—that here was life as it ought to be lived. Mary invariably sat at her desk, surrounded by books and magazines; she had quick, sympathetic eyes, with a 'whimsical twinkle'—she radiated a love of life, she met it more than half way, she was interested in a thousand things, both old and new, and she was very skilful at encouraging a young person to have a point of view."[21]

Another of their Sunday lunch visitors, Maud Howe Elliott, Francis Crawford's cousin, remembered the drawing room that never changed . . . "the imposing mahogany doors leading to the dining room, polished like dark mirrors, reflected a bowl of roses on the table, a watercolour by La Farge on the wall, the books on the shelves . . . those doors must presently open, showing the table with its fine linen cloth, sparkling crystal, ancient silver. . . ."[22]

Beatrix's New York winters were made up of these pleasant Sundays after church in the morning, and weekdays with her tutors, shopping, and the usual social round. They made regular visits to Mary's family in Philadelphia and to the Whartons in Newport, but more and more of their time in summer was spent at Bar Harbor. By the time she was fifteen they had adopted a regular pattern, leaving New York in May and staying at Reef Point until mid-October. Bar Harbor became the backdrop for half her life and she soon came to regard it as her true home.

Reef Point itself had soon grown into "the epitome of a summer place" as they enlarged it for their longer stays. It rambled comfortably beneath its shingled roof, with a small tower, several balconies and verandas wreathed in summer flowers, and many small dormers and what Beatrix called "eye-winker" windows. The lower walls were of smoothed logs, a design feature of Rotch's that Mariana van Rensselaer praised as "a simple enough expedient, but pretty, and appropriate to the thickly wooded site and the modesty of the structure, while expressive of much greater solidity than would have been the unmixed use of shingles."[23] Reef Point was pretty and it fitted into its setting with a vernacular grace, sitting on a rocky ledge well back from the sea and sheltered by the thick growth of white spruce. Mary had bought the adjacent plot, which gave them four acres of garden; a footpath which led from the end of Hancock Street to the Shore Path was moved beyond this boundary (where it runs still) and they had complete privacy.

Beatrix later credited both her parents with the wise decision to work with the native plants and the natural conditions of the garden, rather than clearing everything "to make smooth and level lawns" as most of their neighbors had done.[24] She helped her mother as she learned what would grow in their boggy patch and in the mainly peaty soils with rocky outcrops. The island boasted a fabulous native flora as walks in the woods and on mountain scree slopes revealed: trilliums, wild iris, native lilies which grew among ferns, violets, roses, and asters, dwarf cornel, viburnums, rhodora, clintonia, and, of "surpassing loveliness," the spring blossoms of the wild plum, *Amelanchier canadensis.* With all this as their basis and inspiration they gradually cultivated different and suitable habitats, and discovered that azaleas loved the sea mists and heathers grew well, but that for vegetables and special flowers the topsoil had to be carefully built up and shelter provided.

But gardening was just one of the activities that occupied the long summer days. There was a constant stream of visitors, tea and tennis parties, cycling and walking expeditions, picnics, sailing, riding, and golf. Mary, being Mary, soon became involved with Bar Harbor life, the Village Improvement Association, the Mount Desert Island Hospital, the Island Mission, and church life.

One of their most regular visitors was their faithful "umbrella-mender," F. Marion Crawford. In 1894, Crawford published a novella called *Love in Idleness: A Bar Harbor Tale,* and in it he leaves us a vivid portrait of Bar Harbor life, and of Beatrix as the young woman she had become. It is a light-hearted but sharply observed tale. It begins with the hero, a young artist, Louis Lawrence, on board the island-bound steamer contemplating his visit to the young lady he loves. "The picture is beautiful, and some people call it grand . . . there is something fiercely successful about the color of it, something brilliantly self-reliant. It suggests a certain type of handsome woman, of the kind that need neither repentance nor cosmetics, and are perfectly sure of the fact, whose virtue is too cold to be kind, and whose complexion is not shadowed by passion, nor softened by suffering, nor even washed pale with tears."[25] Our hero recovers from his bitter reverie and observes his goal; Bar Harbor with its cluster of gigantic hotels, pinnacled and helmeted like "an evil dream of medievalism" and then "behind all and above all rise the wooded hills . . . an endless green-ness" of white pines, pitch pines, black and white spruce "there drops the feathery larch by the creeping yew, and there gleam the birches, yellow, white and grey; the sturdy red oak spreads his arms to the scarlet maple, and the witch hazel rustles softly in the mysterious forest breeze. There, buried in the wood's bosom, bloom and blossom the wild flowers and redden the blushing berries . . . ,"[26] violets, wild iris, strawberries, raspberries, blueberries and blackberries, wild rose, blue bells, red lilacs, goldenrod and clematis—presumably not all at one moment, but still a magical harvest indeed!

Lawrence is met at the busy harbor landing by Fanny Trehearne, the nineteen-year-old heroine, straight and tall "with a quiet business-like way of moving, as though she never changed her position without a purpose," who handles her "smart little turnout" with characteristic confidence. "It was part of her nature to fix her attention upon whatever she had in hand." Fanny possessed an air of "superior smartness," with a healthy complexion tanned to a golden brown, and she was dressed in navy serge and a nautical hat with the veil turned up. In an early conversation she pronounces the long-standing rusticator's disdain of Bar Harbor's *arriviste* smartness as much too civilized. "I'm beginning to hate it!" But, offers the tentative Louis, isn't the beauty of the place your reason for coming here? "You think it's my mission to beautify landscapes?"[27] Fanny spiritedly replies.

The pair arrive at their destination, which has clearly not been far, and it (the Trehearne house) bears a strong resemblance to Reef Point: it was large, built in a big lot which stretched from the road to the sea, bought at a time when land was cheap. It has a comfortable library with plain dark woodwork and big leather chairs, "the comforting backs of books" and a deep veranda. The story line continues through summer days of boating, tennis, walking, and riding, and poor Louis fails at every turn, always outdone by the sporty summer visitors, as well in verbal skirmishes with his adored Fanny. "It's rash to care for only one man," she bursts out in self-defense. Louis admits, "She had a harsh way of saying things which, spoken with a smile, could not have given offence. . . ."[28] But all ends happily. Louis, a failure at everything, rescues Fanny when her horse bolts. He proposes, and in the heat of the moment, she accepts.

It is irresistible to suggest that the kind and grateful Crawford was painting Beatrix—her looks and spirit, her sharp wit and stern independence. That giveaway outburst, "You think it's my mission to beautify landscapes?" identifies her for certain. How could Crawford have dropped in such a telling phrase if he had not heard it, and where else could he have heard it other than from Beatrix? Her future must have been the subject of much discussion, and though John Lambert Cadwalader usually gets the credit for suggesting that she extend her interest in gardening to a professional level, it was more likely that the idea originated with Mariana van Rensselaer, who was well known to Mary as well.[29] Mrs. van Rensselaer had been advocating landscape gardening as a suitable profession for women for several years but in Beatrix's society this would still have been unusual, and many of her friends would not have known what it really meant. "My friends look upon my studies at first as sort of mild mania,"[30] she was to tell a reporter from the *New York Sun* just a few years later. Much later Beatrix wrote that the key to her decision about her profession was her meeting with Professor Charles Sprague Sargent, who allowed her to study at the Arnold Arboretum, which she always thought of as her alma mater. It was actually Mrs. Mary Sargent that she met, and it was undoubtedly through Mary Sargent's kindness that Beatrix gained this privilege. But it seems certain that the subject was much in the air during those Bar Harbor summers of the early 1890s, otherwise why would F. Marion Crawford have brought it into his fictional conversation?

Beatrix had grown up loving and needing the beautiful Mount Desert landscape in a way perhaps she did not quite understand herself. She had acquired her landscape "eye," her ability to understand the quality of a place, which could never have been learned in New York, and without which she could not have progressed. "No one should attempt the profession who has not by nature a quality which corresponds to the musician's ear for music," she was to tell future aspirants. "No one can be a landscape gardener who has not an eye any more than a musician can be made from a person who has no ear."[31]

She spent the summer of her twenty-first birthday, 1893, reading, observing, photographing, and noting down the details of her beloved island: "I noticed a pretty grouping of trees on the side of a hill. They backed against a rail fence . . . and looking at them from below they seemed to be in a close mass." She propped up her bicycle and investigated further. "Looked at from the side and from the same level though the effect was quite different. . . ."[32] The layout of the trees that made such an effect was paced out and sketched; they were spaced out in a roughly triangular form, an irregular row of white pine, white and yellow spruce against the fence, with a loosely spaced trio of birch, a yellow and a white spruce in front, and, at the very front, a tight threesome of white spruce. She had learned an elementary lesson of nature—it was best to plant in tight, unevenly numbered groupings and make a contrast with looser gatherings.

One of Beatrix's favorite places on the island was Oldfarm, the Dorr family home at Compass Harbor, south of Bar Harbor. Charles F. Dorr, who had made his money out of textiles in New England, prided himself on the first really well built house on the island, with its base of granite boulders split out from the adjacent gorge and shingles of California redwood. Mrs. Mary Ward Dorr, a friend of Beatrix's mother, in turn prided herself on the first formal garden in Bar Harbor. Undoubtedly the garden attracted Beatrix, but there was also the Dorr family talent for sympathetic knowledge of the natural habitats and virtues of their island, epitomized by their bachelor son, George Bucknam Dorr.[33] George Dorr was always to be Beatrix's friend and adviser. She watched his campaign for the island's conservation with interest and one day, when she was a distinguished practitioner of her art, she would repay his early kindnesses.

From the first approach Oldfarm inspired her. "The trees along the Oldfarm waterfront are quite tall so that one cannot see [the] coastline. This seems to give the effect of quite a big drop, that is, it looks as though the trees were on top of a cliff and so gives the hill on which the house stands [a feeling of] more height. The middle distance is blue water—Point d'Acadie on left and Round Porcupine with its black cliffs on R. This is carried on to the 3 next Porcupines, and on the horizon to the Gouldsboro' Hills [on the Schoodic peninsula]." She sums up—"The view is not seen all at once, and the lines of the foreground are as irregular as those of the hills in the distance." Oldfarm's prospect was shared—at a slightly different angle—with Reef Point. Beatrix trimmed and planted, and photographed the view to the end of their own garden and beyond, with its careful reiteration of the Oldfarm lessons of framing a view, concealing some things and revealing others, and imitating the natural forms to emphasize atmosphere. She had learned, by observation at Oldfarm, Frederick Law Olmsted's second principle of landscape design, ". . . creation of designs that are in keeping with the natural scenery and topography; respect for, and full utilization of, the genius of the place."[34]

Beatrix found a lot to admire and emulate in Mary Ward Dorr's garden—that the fashionable eulalia, lyme grass, if planted in a sheltered spot would survive the island winter; that a generous planting of hollyhocks and larkspur looked wonderful against the "solid background" of the arborvitae (*Thuja occidentalis*) hedge; that "splendid" *Solidago sempervirens* came from seed, and that garden varieties of other island natives, lilies (*Lilium tigrinum* and *L. speciosum*) and asters (*Aster novae-angliae* and *A. ericoides*) made splendid showings in the late summer garden. She noted a "pretty scarlet trumpet honeysuckle" over Mrs. Dorr's porch, and more of the planting around the house. She "[t]ried to get a Kodak of grouping of shrubs in front of Oldfarm. Two small round lilac bushes on *either* side of the front door, an Arbor-vitae standing back in a corner made by the L, backed by two or three large white spruce. A large lilac by the kitchen turn and a *Pyrus japonica* [*Chaenomeles*] on the right of the approach. Two magnolias out of key but a good *Pinus mugo* very effective. . . ." She had quickly learned to be critical of exotics in her island setting, as Mrs. Dorr's "unfortunate" weakness for magnolias made clear; further disapproval was cast on the garden of the Morrill family, at Redwood, farther south along the Shore Path from Reef Point. "I noticed how entirely out of place a couple of catalpas and a magnolia looked against a background of white and black spruce." But she also noted how attractive the veranda around the house could be when a low wall was built around the edge and nasturtiums were planted to flower over the wall and fall to ground level on the outside. When "the Canary-bird vine was planted with the nasturtiums" a lovely contrast was created between them and the vine's delicate green leaves of "fluttering grace" and its butterflylike flowers.[35] Another idea which caught her eye was a *Clematis paniculata* in full flower trained on a wire frame half-wreathed around a window.

At Birch Point, the home of Bar Harbor's first wealthy summer resident, Alpheus Hardy (next door to the Mount Desert Reading Room, the elite men's club), Beatrix checked on old white birches being felled. She did ring counts—"as high as 60 on one" but it had a rotten three-inch heart; another also went up to over sixty and was healthy all the way through. She measured standing trees with a girth of three to four feet, four feet from the ground—very large specimens. And she acquired further sound practical knowledge. "*Poa pratensis* (Kentucky blue grass) makes the best turf for a lawn in this part of the country, though it takes three years for it to become thoroughly estab-

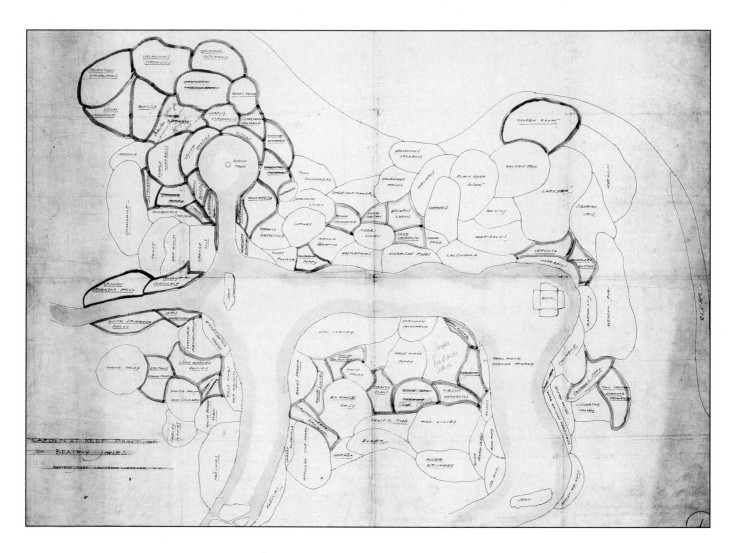

lished; sown half and half with *Agrostis canina* (Rhode Island bent) it makes sod sooner. . . . (*A. canina*) is a little finer than *A. vulgaris* var. *alba* . . . and flourishes in poorer ground than the blue grass likes. . . ."[36]

Beatrix undoubtedly had access on the island to almost anywhere she wanted to go. She must have known nearly everyone. She was immensely proud of her chosen profession, and the fact that this clearly well-to-do and attractive young lady had such determination to become a landscape gardener must have broken down any opposition to her progress. From her gathering grounds on the island, she brought home her knowledge to the garden at Reef Point. By the time Beatrix was twenty her mother had clearly relinquished control of this particular territory. In October 1893, according to her notebook, she chose plants to go around the house, which was her first real impact on Reef Point's garden—honeysuckles to climb the porch (*Lonicera tatarica, L. fragrantissima, L. grandiflora*), roses (*Rosa rugosa alba* and *R. rubra, R. multiflora, R. rubiginosa*), berberis, weigela, lilacs, *Rhus cotinus,* and *deutzias,* with a big bed of fifty tiger lilies—"to be planted 8″ apart." Her first, hesitant, and impractical garden plan was made for this planting and instructions were left for the planting to be done in late October. The embryo landscape gardener

An early planting plan of Reef Point by Beatrix Jones shows her first attempt at organizing planting by colors, incorporating existing plants and natives. Predominant yellows and golds (daisies, day lilies, roses, and lilies) drift along the border and around the birch tree clearing, where she has introduced touches of blue and purple. Pink and white flowers are kept separate in the lower part of the plan.

couldn't carry out the plan herself. She had an appointment to keep, the most significant appointment of her life so far.

The quotations of the last few pages, the proof of Beatrix's acquiring her landscape "eye," come from only one surviving notebook that she kept for always. There must have been a reason for this. She was much too conscientious only to have filled one notebook; did the others not illustrate a suitable accomplishment? Or was this one so significant, that she treasured it forever? Her island summers, her gardening prowess, the admiring remarks of her friends and visitors, her sharp observations of other people's gardens and the composition of landscapes, the more public declarations of Mrs. van Renssalaer advising on the suitability of landscape gardening as a career for young ladies, and her own private convictions were all sending her on her way. She was taking her precious notebook for scrutiny by demanding eyes, perhaps by the imperious Charles Sprague Sargent himself; but she was also taking it with her to add further entries, as her diary of events that marked her entry into her landscape life. As she left her island that mid-October day of 1893 bound for Boston, she noted one more image seen from the train . . . "On top of a hill, bare hill, around one side was a sort of garland of trees—white pines coming down to deciduous (poplars, birches) with 1 or 2 specimen hemlock at the river's edge." She had truly adopted her landscape life; from now on no observation would be wasted. No doubt she was following instructions from Professor Sargent and the notebook was her "homework," but it also marks her real commitment to her profession. For a life in landscape design is more than a job—like the island of Mount Desert, it is perhaps more of "an addiction" that must become a way of life. From this moment on, Beatrix's life was full of certain things to be done, certain places to be seen: to a landscape designer hardly any experience of the world is to be wasted. She was embarking on a profession that demanded artistic and technical skills. She had to learn about architecture, freehand and engineering drawing, some theoretical engineering and surveying, mathematics and designing, let alone the techniques of planting and the Latin names of plants as well as their characteristics and uses. And all her learning must be rounded off with an exhaustive study tour of Europe to observe the best examples in the world.

Chapter 3

❧❦❧

BEATRIX
AND THE BRAHMINS

*B*eatrix traveled to Boston from Bar Harbor on October 13, 1893, and then out to the Sargent home, Holm Lea, at Brookline.

For the rest of her life she regarded knowing Professor Charles Sprague Sargent as the key to her success, and the reasons for this are entwined in the social history of this particular corner of Massachusetts.

From the date of Harvard's founding, 1636, it seemed that events conspired to create its late nineteenth century supremacy in natural sciences and humanist philosophy. The fortunes of the Brahmin families had been made and could now be dutifully applied to good works, gathering an impressive roll call as the century had progressed: the Massachusetts Historical Society was founded in 1791, the Boston Athenaeum in 1807, the Massachusetts Horticultural Society in 1829, the Boston Society of Natural History in 1830, and the Boston Public Library opened in 1854 and the Museum of Fine Arts in 1870. Charles William Eliot had begun his reign of forty years as president of Harvard in 1869[1] and one of his first actions had been to found the Bussey Institution for agriculture and horticulture, and to appoint his friend the historian Francis Parkman as professor of horticulture in 1871.[2] Parkman, in poor health and with failing eyesight, found solace in his garden overlooking Jamaica Pond in Brookline, tending his roses and lilies. He had published *The Book of Roses* in 1866 and his garden, along with the estates of Colonel Perkins and Thomas Lee, had inspired Andrew Jackson Downing's accolade: "The whole of this neighbourhood of Brookline is a kind of landscape garden, and there is nothing in America of the sort, so inexpressibly charming, as the lanes which lead from one cottage, or villa, to another. No animals are allowed to

Beatrix, c. 1890.

run at large, and the open gates, with tempting vistas and glimpses under the pendent boughs, give it quite an Arcadian air of rural freedom and enjoyment."[3]

Professor Parkman soon found his additional role too much. After just a year he was succeeded as professor of horticulture by Charles Sprague Sargent. Sargent had graduated from Harvard, almost bottom of his class of 1862, served in the Union army, then disappeared for a three-year tour of Europe. At the age of twenty-seven he had come home to Holm Lea, to manage his father's estate. Obviously relieved that he showed an interest in something, namely horticulture and botany, Sargent's relatives and friends encouraged him. His cousin Henry Sargent, who had a fine garden on the Hudson, introduced him to Downing, the "father" of American landscape gardening. Another relation, Horatio Hunnewell, making his own garden in Wellesley, became a close gardening colleague. For Sargent the professorship seemed at first just further encouragement, but it turned out to be rather more.

Harvard's professor of natural history, Asa Gray, was also head of the university's botanic garden in Cambridge. Gray had long hoped for more land for an arboretum and he had been negotiating with the trustees of James Arnold, who had left a bequest for some horticultural or philosophical project of which his friends, the trustees Messrs. Dixwell, Emerson, and Parker, might approve. They were all prepared to approve of trees, and at some inspired moment scented by cigars and port, it was decided that the Arnold money should be used to fund an arboretum, for the study and culture of trees, on the Bussey farmland which Harvard already owned at Jamaica Plain. Sargent, the professor of horticulture at the Bussey Institute, who had already won Professor Gray's approval for enthusiastic application to the management problems of the Botanic Garden too, now found himself also director of the new Arnold Arboretum. The appointment was made on November 24, 1873. Two days later Charles Sprague Sargent married Mary Robeson of Boston, and thus two commitments "that were to become lifelong devotions" were made almost simultaneously—"one to trees and the Arnold Arboretum and the other to an enduring family life at Holm Lea."[4]

Tall and impressive, with the Sargent family good looks (he was a cousin of John Singer Sargent), and in his mature years bearing a strong resemblance to the Prince of Wales (later Edward VII), Sargent was a man of few words. Certainly the possessor of an "aloof Boston soul"[5] he could be terse and intimidating. The plant collector E. H. Wilson, who was to climb the roof of the world and tramp miles for treasures to bring home to the Arnold, "voted him autocrat of the autocrats" but soon realized that he was—when one shared his passion—"kindliest of the autocrats."[6] He was also the hardest of workers, happiest at his desk, in the herbarium or among his trees. Though he was a Harvard professor for fifty-four years he never gave a lecture, and he hated public speaking. He reveled in getting things done, usually doing them himself, and he set to work with a will to turn the "worn-out farm, partly covered with natural plantations of native trees nearly ruined by excessive pasturage"[7] into a scientific garden, the "greatest collection of trees and shrubs of the Northern Hemisphere."[8] To accomplish this, he had less than $3,000 a year!

Sargent's first step was to commission Frederick Law Olmsted, the designer of Central Park who was already working on a park system for Boston, to design the road system for the Arboretum. Together Olmsted and Sargent found the way that made the future certain. With the help of President Eliot they persuaded Boston City Council to administer the Arboretum as part of the park system—and thus pay for the construction and maintenance of the roads and paths—in return for the admission of the public "provided they behaved themselves."[9] As Stephanie Sutton, historian of the Arboretum and biographer of Sargent, has written, it "was almost like asking Congress to let Imperial Russia administer Alaska as a playground,"[10] but it worked. Boston gained an extra "park" and Professor Sargent was free to consider his trees, while Olmsted had the money for the design and construction of the roads, which began in 1883.

At this time Olmsted too settled in Brookline, at 99 Warren Street, which he chose because the architect H. H. Richardson and Sargent were his closest neighbors.[11]

Beatrix first visited the Arnold in late 1890 or early 1891, just at the end of the major grading and road building period. For the young Arboretum as she saw it, the closest description comes from an article in *Garden & Forest,* the magazine Sargent "conducted." The observer of progress is Mrs. J. H. Robbins of Hingham. "Here 150 acres are devoted entirely to the cultivation of woody plants, that is, trees, vines shrubs . . ." and it is well "to realize that this beautiful spot is still in its infancy, that it is slowly growing to perfection, and that all that is unfinished and unsightly about it now is but the deep-laid foundation of a great and enduring monument. . . ." Sargent's first plantings were now seventeen years old. ". . . There is a wonderful charm in these groups of Firs and Spruces in endless variety of form and color—stout little Spruces from the Rocky Mountains, the stately fast-growing Douglas Fir, the beautiful Blue Spruce of Colorado, the Black Spruces from Maine and the White Spruces from Canada, all flourish here. . . ." Mrs. Robbins noted Olmsted's broad driveway "admirably graded . . . (leading) by a gentle ascent to the higher ground, bordered throughout its large, gracefully sweeping curves by masses of native shrubs. . . ." These include the "more than 500" forms of lilac, the forsythias, magnolias, philadelphus, and thorns that were impressed firmly on Beatrix's mind's eye so that she became famous for her drifts of blossom (and it is forsythia, one of the giant-flowered hybrids raised at the Arnold in the 1940s, that bears the name "Beatrix Farrand"). Mrs. Robbins's description goes on, "Creepers run from the bushes to veil the edges of the road, and the mass behind leads gradually up to the groups of trees, which are arranged in botanical order . . . first, on the right, come the Beeches, with their spreading branches and serrated leaves. . . . They have been started here from seed or

*Professor Charles Sprague
Sargent, by his cousin John
Singer Sargent.*

bud, and, of course, are still comparatively small . . . beyond them the oaks, hornbeams, chestnuts, hickories, butternuts and black walnuts. Then the road makes a serpentine curve upon itself, and comes gently rising to the summit of the hill" with its view of the surrounding country. "Here at your feet lie the groups of Birches, Elms and Ash-trees, with Catalpas on a rising ground behind. . . . Nor must you go until you have climbed to the top of the Hemlock Hill and rested in the shadow of its mighty giants and learned what centuries can do for trees. . . ."[12]

As Mrs. Robbins kept saying, it was so easy to learn in this beautiful place. Every plant was labeled and seeing them in their families made it possible to compare and contrast virtues of form, flower, size, and general effect. Beatrix with her note pad had a marvelous time in this living encyclopedia; she spent happy hours on her own in the Arboretum, but on occasion Sargent offered to take her around. On one such outing on June 10, 1894, a Sunday, she wrote: "Mr Sargent took me over to the Arboretum. On the way we stopped and looked at Mr Parkman's collection of shrubs. It was awfully dreary—house and grounds taken by the Park Commission, house being torn down." (Parkman had died the previous year.) "Only a year ago the grounds were under cultivation and now they look as if they had been deserted for years, paths overgrown and long grass springing up everywhere. St Bruno's Lily in full bloom—*Azalea calendulacea* still fine too, *Magnolia macrophylla* not flowering yet—the largest in the neighbourhood. *Aruncus spirea* in bed 'quite handsome' altho' a little coarse. . . . Jamaica Pond is lovely—or at least must have been lovely before Parkway took it—Mr S is trying to make the Commission give up the plan for the road along the shore in one of the loveliest spots."[13]

BEATRIX

The Gardening Life of

Beatrix Jones Farrand

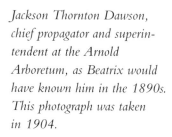

Jackson Thornton Dawson,
chief propagator and superin-
tendent at the Arnold
Arboretum, as Beatrix would
have known him in the 1890s.
This photograph was taken
in 1904.

Beatrix later wrote that the formidable Sargent became interested in her because she loved trees and flowers. He also appreciated a well-dressed and handsome woman, and there was the hint of a gleam in his eyes "so well disguised that only the most imaginative people perceived it."[14] On Beatrix's part it must be remembered that she was brought up to be perfectly at ease with distinguished older men, and would have chatted brightly, quite unperturbed by his preoccupations and aloofness. Her notebook entries make evident his part in the conversation—the largest specimen of azalea, his efforts with the Park Commission, were his gruff asides. Beatrix continued at his heels. "In the Arboretum itself a great deal of work has been done, especially behind the building [Horatio Hollis Hunnewell paid for the laboratory which was built in 1892] where the Magnolias are to begin."[15] She noted *Magnolia parviflora* in bloom, though a small bush, and *Magnolia glauca* to be perfumed almost like a rose. They went on to the roses—*Rosa spinossisima* in bloom, also *R. nitida, R. lucida, R. setigera, R. multiflora,* and the Austrian briar were all noted for future use. Other shrubs which caught her eye were the hydrangeas, stuartia, *Viburnum molle* and *V. dentatum* in bloom and *Fothergilla gardenii,* just beginning to fruit. All were tucked away in her memory.

If Professor Sargent was busy Beatrix was almost better off, for she could search out the Arnold's superintendent and chief propagator, Jackson Thornton Dawson. Dawson was a gem. A jovial, warm, good-natured Yorkshireman, he, like Sargent, was born in 1841, and brought to America by his widowed mother. He was apprenticed to a nurseryman, served in the Civil War, and then employed by Parkman as head gardener at the Bussey Institution. When Sargent took over, he took over Dawson too, and they were a perfect partnership. Dawson was passionate about his plants and their daily care. He knew the personal history of every plant in the Arboretum. In his own time he was devoted to his family, and to his roses; he worked for years to successfully hybridize *Rosa multiflora* to achieve a multicolored hardy climber—which he did—with bright pink flowers, and named after himself. In complete contrast to the reclusive director, Dawson was the Arboretum's character—everybody knew him and he was friendly with plant collectors and botanists from all over the world. His trademark, the gift of his loving wife, was his fresh white boiled shirt, clean every morning, worn with waistcoat and tie. To clean his plant labels he would wipe them on the lily-white shirt-front, often making his visitors shudder!

In later years, when Beatrix herself was distinguished, she carried on a friendly correspondence with the Arnold's later directors or chief propagators, which has survived. Everything in her personality and Dawson's would suggest that they were firm friends too; she was never averse to getting her hands dirty in order to learn, and she probably spent a great deal of time watching and helping him.[16]

On days when she could not go to the Arboretum there was plenty to amuse and educate her at Holm Lea itself. The house was enormous and rambling, sited on a knoll overlooking a lake and its large garden, or small park, filled with trees and shrubs, the lake spectacularly edged with the Professor's rhododendrons. The house itself contained an endless stream of comfortable rooms, replete with polished mahogany, bowls of flowers, chintz-covered chairs, velvet-tasselled sofas, foot stools, side tables, comforting Victoriana, and many pots of exotic and exciting plants. Holm Lea's most remarkable feature was its surrounding wide paved piazza or terrace, which was tented over in summer to shelter the massed flowers, tender azaleas, camellias, and scented pelargoniums from the hottest sun. Staying at Holm Lea in June must have been like living in a flower show tent.[17]

Guests at Holm Lea, including a regular like Beatrix, were also assured of being marvelously looked after. Mary Robeson Sargent managed everything to perfection. She served the most wonderful meals, entertained all the Professor's guests—who often arrived at a moment's notice—superbly, and also kept the house quiet while he was working. Besides all this, she reared their five children and she painted—patiently and quietly, in the small telephone room. She gathered and then painted the wildflowers of Holm Lea, delicate watercolors, which she bound into large leather-bound volumes embossed in gold "C S Sargent from M R S" and presented to her husband, and, as a real labor of love, she drew and painted the flower, fruit, and leaves of each one of Sargent's collection of the woods of America.[18]

Springs and summers at Holm Lea were busy and sociable, with constant

The Sargent family at Holm Lea: Charles Sprague Sargent and his wife, Mary Robeson Sargent, are seated in the center, surrounded by their grown-up children.

FACING PAGE, TOP: *Holm Lea, the Sargent house in Brookline, as Beatrix would have known it and where she was a regular and frequent visitor after her first meeting with Charles and Mary Sargent in 1890.*

FACING PAGE, BOTTOM: *Holm Lea, the gardens of which Charles Sargent was so proud, and where he entertained and instructed a constant stream of visitors during the spring and summer, especially during rhododendron flowering.*

parties of visitors to-ing and fro-ing to admire the flowers. Sargent was very proud of his own collection of native and exotic rhododendrons, carefully planted to avoid clashing of colors—the magentas, purples, crimsons, and white predominant and away from pinks and flame colors, his magnolias, flowering cherries, and kalmias. Beatrix noted how the enormous house was almost covered in honeysuckles in flower in June, and the great drifts of yellow water iris glowed at the edge of the lake. Regularly the house party went off to Wellesley so that Sargent and Horatio Hollis Hunnewell could compare notes: "June 11 Rhododendrons, if possible, finer than ever! All agree there is no shrub to compare with them for grand effect. Those in the lattice tent are much admired, —the foliage under the lattice shade being very dark green, equal to any in the English climate, owing to the partial shade they get under the lattice, . . . very similar to what they have in the cloudy English climate. Had many visitors to-day: . . . Thayers, Mrs F L Ames, Mrs Montgomery Sears, Sargents, Miss (B) Jones, Charles Adams, Merriams Howlands. . . ."[19]

Undoubtedly during her Holm Lea visits of 1892 and 1893 Beatrix heard many dinner table discussions on the progress of the World's Columbian Exposition site in Chicago, and the Sargents had promised her a visit; at last, on October 19, 1893, she saw what it was all about, and noted many details for her future reference. Creating the Exposition had been something of a saga: New York had refused to host the celebration of Columbus's discovery of America because it would "spoil" Central Park, nicely coming along after twenty-years-a-growing, and in the ensuing scramble Chicago won the honors. The decision was made in April 1890, and Olmsted's firm was appointed landscape designers and consultants the following August. They had just two-and-a-half years, considerably less with those freezing Chicago winters, to convert 500 acres of swamp, scarcely above the level of Lake Michigan, into a showground, a summer-long garden, the 1890s version of Disneyland. Being privy to many discussions of the project (Sargent made frequent visits to the site and his nephew, Harry Sargent Codman, was Olmsted's partner-in-charge) as well as reading about it, gave Beatrix a sobering insight into the profession she wanted to join, and taught her salutary lessons that would surface again and again in her career.

Firstly, that the landscape architect would always be expected to provide a summer-long garden out of a swamp, *instantly.* Olmsted had already worked on the Exposition site as a park project for Chicago. He was keen to keep the site's integrity, its relationship to the mighty lake (the most interesting scenery that Chicago possessed), and create lagoons, with the buildings on the intervening built-up ridges. Circulation around the site would be by both land and water. For the second lesson, Beatrix would have learned that what Olmsted called "the slow, conscious development of a sound landscape design" did not match everyone else's vision of a splendid, crowded, bustling Beaux Arts spectacle of axial planning, white palaces, and formal gardens. This of course sounds like an architect's vision, and it was, that of the consultant architect and director of the site development, Daniel Burnham, who—partly because of his own skill and personality, and partly because of Olmsted's flexibility and gentleness—held the whole concept together, letting every designer and artist feel that some battle of principle had been won. Olmsted's victory, for the third lesson, was that he kept one large natural-looking lagoon and a wooded island free from formality, as the base for cramming as much good greenery into the site as possible, to give visitors to the fair some visual relief from the "sensory overload" of the enormous glistening white temples of commerce.[20] The island, a mix of park, garden and contrived wilderness, also gave the eye a chance to rest. It was a triumph: "Wooded Island illuminated was the most striking scene of the whole Exposition. Ten thousand different colored cups containing a candle capable of burning an hour were strung along the ways and set amidst the flowers and trees making a scene not surpassed even in fairy land."[21]

By the time Beatrix went to Chicago, almost at the end of the fair, she was well aware that she would be seeing the planting, done in atrocious conditions, at its best. For at least a week she wandered at leisure, investigating everything carefully, noting that the island planting was indeed beautiful. There were lovely beds of peonies, phlox, and columbines, and a handsome snapdragon "Madame Crozy" in the gardens, wonderful cannas outside the great glass Horticultural building. Inside it she encountered something that puzzled her, which she thought was "a poor representation of a Japanese garden" with miniature trees, deformed and strange-looking. "What did root raising mean?" she asked in her note. She was seeing bonsai, surely the earliest in America, as the idea was not to reach the Arnold Arboretum for another ten years and Larz Anderson's notable collection in Brookline was not started until 1913.[22]

For her final lesson Beatrix undoubtedly used prowling around the Exposition to accustom her eye for details, for so much of the quality of landscape design comes down to attention to detail. She noted and sketched "a very good fence" of painted wooded slats and posts around the Massachusetts State Building (Peabody and Stearns's old colonial house "of the better class") and also an arch of Lombardy poplars, planted about eight feet apart with the tops bound together "exceedingly pretty and effective." But her conclusions, as she wandered the site, must have been on the miracle of transformation that the teamwork of artist, architects, engineers, and landscape architects could produce. Perhaps a "mission to beautify landscapes" was not so inaccurate a description of her future after all. Certainly at Chicago in that autumn of 1893 she was in the very best place to see both the challenges and rewards of her chosen profession. And she was no longer on the outside. She was one of the "few" who, as Sargent had thundered in the *Garden & Forest* editorial marking the Exposition opening could realize "that the harmony of the scene and the perfection and convenience of the whole scheme of arrangement were due to the genius of one man, Frederick Law Olmsted."[23]

*B*eatrix was back at Holm Lea in February of the following year, for another exciting expedition with the Sargents, this time to Biltmore in North Carolina, where Olmsted had been working miracles for George Washington Vanderbilt since 1888. The party, which included Olmsted, Mary Cadwalader Jones, and several others, traveled in Vanderbilt's private railroad car, the "Swannanoa," which carried them, via a length of private track, to the gates of Biltmore. From there it was a three-mile carriage drive, three "magical miles" through the ravines and wooded valleys ornamented with pools, waterfalls, and streams, of Olmsted's masterfully "natural" contrived and concealed approach. Suddenly the visitors passed "with an abrupt transition into the enclosure of the trim, level, open, airy, spacious, thoroughly artificial Court"[24] and thus into the overwhelming presence of Richard Morris Hunt's enormous château. Of this château, almost complete when Beatrix saw it, only superlatives have been written: "The château is beginning to hum" wrote the architect to his wife, "The mountains are just the right size and scale. . . ."[25] Henry James, a later visitor, wrote famously of the interior measuring by leagues; the main rooms were cathedral-like, and there were twenty bathrooms. Outside there were acres of gravel and lawn, formal pools, and four acres of walled gardens, all set on the sliced-off top of a mountain, affording a breathtaking view over fields, woods and hills to the Great Smoky Mountains.

The main purpose of the trip was for Olmsted and Sargent to discuss the progress on Vanderbilt's great arboretum and tree nursery project, where it was planned to raise eleven million young specimens for American woodlands. Sargent had been spirited away from his beloved Arnold Arboretum to encourage Vanderbilt, and his clever, Yale-educated forester Gifford Pinchot, into the management of hundreds of thousands of acres of the Biltmore land as America's first commercial forestry experiment. It was a cause close to his heart, and Olmsted's, in which they were both inspired by their friend George Perkins Marsh's call for the conservation of forests and soils; they knew only too well his warning in *Man and Nature* that one of the causes of the fall of the Roman Empire was a failure to look after their forests and soils.[26]

The kindly Sargent had probably thought the expedition would interest Beatrix, but she might have arranged it all for herself, for George Vanderbilt was a summer resident of Bar Harbor (and Olmsted was working for him at his estate Point d'Acadie, on the coast south of Reef Point, next to the Dorrs' Oldfarm) as was the family of Gifford Pinchot. Her interest in the proceedings was made clear, for Olmsted remarked her presence rather grumpily to his nephew, John Charles Olmsted, at home in Brookline and that she was "in some way inclined to dabble in Landscape Architecture."[27] Despite Olmsted's grumpiness, the following June, when Beatrix was next at Holm Lea, she was invited to visit and inspect the office at 99 Warren Street.

"June 5 1894 Mr Olmsted's place

"The entrance is quite charming, a lych-gate covered with *Euonymus radicans* both the plain and variegated, and quite bushy on top. The road goes around a tiny island with shrubs planted on a high mound and completely shutting out the gate."[28]

She noted the rocky dell to the right of the entrance, with five or six stone steps down into it, and a mass of ferns, with Virginia creeper, *Rosa multiflora,* and honeysuckle running riot over the rocks. "It is said that the *multiflora* grows much faster if it is trained upwards, is this true?" she asked. On the opposite side of the house was the lawn, with shrubs, which she thought were "rather badly arranged . . . there are two azalea bushes which jar fearfully in colour, one a bluish pink and the other a bright orange. The fern plantation, to my mind, comes too far out [and is] too little graded into the lawn. . . . Also two brilliantly white and evidently cultivated spireas in a quasinatural shrubbery seemed rather out of place. A yellow-leaved spirea was quite bad too. . . ."[29] Most of her criticisms can be easily imagined in the garden today, and pose problems for the conservators. Olmsted's garden was his experimental ground, the subject of many changes of mind and alterations, and also

Fairstead, Brookline, Frederick Law Olmsted's home and office, 1894. Beatrix visited Fairstead on June 5 of that year.

a trial field for plants he was interested in—perhaps the out-of-place spireas belonged to this group. He also tried, in a very small space, to carry out perhaps too many of his six principles: the fern plantation came under the category of "bays and headlands" to create a feeling of spaciousness; the contrast between the rocky dell, the lawn and its shrubs and the wooded "indefinite boundary" were all in accordance with his "scenery" rule—"The design of passages of scenery and a liberal use of plants, even in the smallest spaces and in areas with the most active use."[30] But, whatever was wrong with it, Beatrix had certainly cultivated her critical eye; she had also apparently been thoroughly drilled by Sargent on the question of clashing colors, which is particularly interesting since Gertrude Jekyll was not to publish her bible of color rules, *Colour Schemes for the Flower Garden,* for another fourteen years. It seems that Beatrix had already devoured William Robinson's *The English Flower Garden,* with its brief essay on color by Miss Jekyll. Her color sense was clearly inculcated from the very earliest days.

However, the real purpose of the visit to Olmsted's was to see just how the office worked. She studied everything she was shown and avidly noted down every detail: "The office was interesting. The survey of a piece of ground is taken by the local engineers of the place, marking one foot contour lines and the principal landmarks, such as big trees, rocks . . ." and streams. "The sketches are then made free hand over the survey, of course on tracing paper." She examined the card catalog of trees and shrubs, which noted where it could be found, available sizes, prices, and each plant's requirements and suitability. (The office plant finder was a classic way of doing this which held good for half a century.) "The planting plans are made . . . first the plantations are indicated in the sketch . . . size and shape." Then the "shape" is adapted and "filled" with plants that will suit the soil and site, exposure of the position, and give the best effect. The plants were keyed in by number, related to a list on the side of the plan, with another number of plants required. "The scale is usually 20-40-60 feet to one inch."[31]

Such details of surveys and planting plans, which may seem pedestrian, represented the excitement of work in progress to the would-be landscape designer. Charles Eliot's apprenticeship in the office had consisted of making sketches, enlarging and reducing these plans, calculating earth-working volumes and areas, and making preliminary studies for designs that were subject to "repeated re-consideration and revision" by Olmsted himself.[32] This was how one learned, although Beatrix did not have that chance; but the visit to the office to see how it was done intrigued her. She found a series of rooms, each dominated by the huge drafting tables, around which the apprentices were hunched on high stools, drawing under low-slung lamps; the tables were very bright but the rest of the room was gloomy and dark. There was a photograph room, where every job was recorded, with endless pockets of filing cards holding records of people and plants. Everywhere, on shelf and cupboard top, were the ever-increasing rolls of discarded survey drawings, soon dusty, and even more rolls of the almost unintelligible "blueprints."

The Olmsted office was the elite haven of a very high art; but would Beatrix really have wanted to work there? On the face of things, with her philosophical outlook, her interests and enthusiasm, she had much in common with the likes of Charles Eliot or Harry Sargent Codman, and to work in the office would have been a challenge. But would the spirited Beatrix have tolerated long hours in a drab and dusty office? Eliot and Codman had been through college and had their corners rubbed off, but she was expected to remain at a distance, elegant and effortlessly so, simply because she was a young lady. It was this combination of social demands and femininity that kept her apart; she was so deeply conscious of this that it fired her independence. She would never have *asked* to join the office milieu, even if Olmsted might have considered it kindly, for his opinions of female abilities were far in advance of his time.[33] Beatrix's independent pride, the product of her upbringing, consigned her to her lonely, difficult road into her profession.

She stayed on a little longer at Holm Lea that summer. She visited the public gardens in Jamaica Plain, noting with disgust "the warts of pansies and daisies stuck all around the lawns" and the ornamental beds of forced roses "which will probably fade in a few hot days."[34] Then by her birthday, June 19, she was at Reef Point, back to the summer occupations and pastimes of her garden and her beloved island community. How she would have hated to be confined to a dusty office! She had plans, and plenty of planning to do for the next stage in her education, a long study tour of Europe.

Chapter 4

❧❧❧

THE HUNT FOR BEAUTY:
EUROPE, 1895

*B*eatrix had plenty of advice on the planning of her tour, from the Whartons, her mother, John Lambert Cadwalader, John La Farge, and probably Crawford. On the professional side, Charles Eliot gave her several introductions and suggested places to visit, including the English Lake District, the Royal Parks, and Kew, Chatsworth, and Cambridge, all of which he had found useful. Sargent would certainly have recommended that she see as many kinds of plants in their native habitats as possible, and she quoted him afterward as exhorting her to look at great landscape paintings and "learn from all the great arts as all art is akin."[1]

She was also aware, if at one remove, of Olmsted's rather more egalitarian advice given to William Platt, when he had set out on a European landscape tour with his brother Charles in 1892; "I am afraid that I do not think much of the fine and costly gardening of Italy," Olmsted wrote. "I urge you to hunt for beauty in commonplace and peasant conditions; rustic stables, sheds, wine presses, tileries, mills, pergolas and trellises, seats and resting-places . . . and all of such things as are made lovely by growths that seem natural and spontaneous . . . especially vines."[2] If William Platt, who wanted to be a landscape architect, heeded the great man we shall never know, for poor William drowned later in the summer. Charles Platt, however, found the Italian gardens of dazzling appeal to his aesthetic sensibilities, and came home to write vivid articles about them; the articles became his book on the subject, which Beatrix owned, and had sparked a controversy, of which she was aware.[3] Charles Platt saw the Italian gardens as beautiful for their own sake, and appropriate models for the American designer to follow, because of their unity and harmony with both their houses and their landscape settings. He had been harshly criticized in Sargent's *Garden & Forest* for most of these sentiments: "beauty for its own sake" denied "inner meaning," and such contrived beauty could not appeal to the nobler part of our natures, as natural scenery did, Platt was told.[4] Charles Eliot (who did not go to Italy on his grand tour) dismissed Platt's book as unsatisfactory for its lack of scholarship, plans, and details. This despite Platt's closing note to his critics saying that his chief purpose was to illustrate the gardens as they were today. Scholarship he was prepared to leave to others, but, he concluded, "with the general interest that undoubtedly exists in the subject of gardening today, it is hoped that this work may be of value towards a more thorough understanding and appreciation of the reasons which led to the formal treatment of the gardens."[5]

It was of immense value to Beatrix to be aware of the Platt controversy before she went to see Europe for herself. Was there to be no middle ground in gardening in America between Olmsted and Sargent's beliefs in picturesque natural beauty re-created ever closer to people's homes, and the vast spreads of embroidered French-style parterres outside Newport châteaus? Seeing that there were such wonderful landscape opportunities in America—as Platt said, "a great similarity in the character of the landscape in many parts of our country with that of Italy," perhaps America could use the Italian influence?[6] Platt certainly had started something, just as he had hoped, and a spate of books—including Edith Wharton's *Italian Villas and Their Gardens* (1904)—would shortly follow, making it unlikely for any young designer to escape their influence.

The Platt controversy paralleled the battle of the styles that Beatrix knew was raging in English gardening circles. Two important books, John Dando Sedding's *Garden Craft Old and New* (1891) and Reginald Blomfield's *The Formal Garden in England* (1892), had vigorously revived the idea that architects should design gardens in the old, seventeenth-century formal style, with walled "rooms" out-of-doors, straight paths, and plenty of architectural ornament and detailing. The opposing stance had been assumed by an outspoken Irishman, William Robinson, who was the champion of plants, well grown in their optimum conditions, as the most essential ingredients of any garden.[7] Robinson was always to be one of Beatrix's heroes and she had already made plans to meet him, and two other important English gardeners, Mrs. Theresa Earle[8] and Miss Gertrude Jekyll.[9] All three figured largely in Robinson's *Garden* magazine, to which she subscribed. These threads all came together in her grand tour plan; with their Baedekers and the Murray guidebooks, as well as Mariana Starke's *Travels in Europe,* she and her mother set out.[10]

Mary and Beatrix arrived in Gibraltar on March 18, 1895, after a stormy crossing. Beatrix was immediately aware of the foreignness of it all, the old, steep and narrow streets, the strange smells and faces—Moorish, Spanish, and English—and of tourists with "eyes popping out of their heads."[11] She was determinedly a *traveler.*

On the following day, a Tuesday, they landed in Algiers and found a car-

Mary Cadwalader Jones,
c. 1895.

riage to drive them around the bay ("a dreadful journey")[12] to the Jardin d'Essai, a large garden started in 1832 to raise subtropical plants for export. Beatrix
was amazed at an avenue of *Ficus roxburghi* and other avenues of palms, bamboos, and magnolias. She felt her visit was far too short and rushed back to the
boat with great regrets.

Next day they sailed along the Sardinian coast—"the weather delicious
and the lights and shadows on the mountains beautiful." They landed at
Naples and set off for Rome, where they were installed at the Hotel d'Italie. A
week's pottering in sunshine and among flowers helped them recover from the
journey, and then Saturday, March 23, was spent with Edith and Teddy Wharton on their first serious sight-seeing. It was a busy day: to the Casa Respiglia
to see Guido's *Aurora* ("shamefully repainted"), to the Palazzo Colonna to see
the painted flowers by Mario de Fiori, where Beatrix was entranced by the
rose brocades, tattered by the decay of ages, and to the Forum Romana. After
a good lunch they visited Villa Medici on the Pincian Hill, voted "a triumph"
and noted by Beatrix for its spacious terrace "giving a very good foreground
for the beautiful facade of the villa."[13] This was later called Medici's "most
striking" characteristic by Georgina Masson.[14]

Beatrix reveled in her feast of these fabled gardens; at last she was looking at the reality of Platt's paintings, and at the living, sun-drenched, rounded embodiments of Percier and Fontaine's plans in their Beaux Arts bible, *Choix de plus célèbres maisons de plaisance de Rome et ses environs*[15] to which she constantly referred. Reality was often puzzling: her imagined low box hedges turned out to be four feet high. Not all Medici's axes had culminations, and there was no artificial perspective. Her notes and observations are apt and to the point. She was having a marvelous time being fully alive to the scale, geometry, landscape settings, and delight in ornament and water at play that these wonderful gardens reveal, rarely to more appreciative eyes than hers. She followed Olmsted's advice in hunting for beauty in ordinary "commonplace and peasant conditions" and spent hours wandering back alleys, peering through gateways and exploring fearlessly off the beaten tourist tracks. For, as Edith Wharton wrote in her book, many of the gardens were not easily seen, and perhaps could not be seen at all. There were always the frustrations of the artful young "guides" and cheeky urchins who posed as "ornaments" for money.[16] Her trip, a day excursion, to Frascati was bedeviled by a young guide, named "Amerigo," who set out on the well-worn tourist track through the grounds of Villa Aldobrandini to Villa Ruffinello and the ruins of Tusculum. Beatrix persuaded him to begin at Villa Torlonia, where she enjoyed her anticipated artificial perspective, measuring the terrace stair to find it narrower at the top than at the bottom and noting the trick of slanting landings. Then Amerigo took them the standard way, coming out halfway up Aldobrandini's water stair and so missing the Nymphaeum. It must have been in bad condition: no water, and decaying twisted columns, all exposed to the relentless sun. "Where did the Italians sit in hot weather?" she asks in her notebook, clearly having missed the enchanted grotto, which had delighted John Evelyn, with hydraulic organs and singing birds, made to work by the water. She pursued the question of shade up through the ilex groves to Villa Ruffinello, but the remains were "not worth the steep and stony climb,"[17] and then more happily to the smallest Frascati villa, Lancelotti, where clipped aerial hedges flank the parterre.

On an early April Tuesday Beatrix and Mary took a train to Viterbo, and drove to Villa Lante. This was still, in 1895, the home of the Duke of Lante, and his children were playing in the garden. It came totally up to Beatrix's expectations. Photographs of that time illustrate the romance of what she saw: the slightly moth-eaten but beautifully clipped box hedges, the moss-patterned stone, and the thymes and ivies wreathed along paths and under steps. Here the water was abundant, and she stood on the terrace between the pavilions of the villa and committed to her memory forever the "square enclosure jutting out into the vale below, with high green hedges, sweet *broderies* of box bordered by flowers, and in the midst a broad water-garden leading by balustrated crossways to an island fountain which rises like a mount to four great figures of sombre-tinted stone."[18] George Sitwell's incomparable description goes on, "Water gushes from the points of a star which the naked athletes uplift, from the mouths of the lions by their side, from the masks on the balustrade, from the tiny galleys in which vagrant cupids are afloat. . . ."[19] Lante's enchantment raised Beatrix's own prose to a pitch that would not have disgraced her aunt. "The place had an air of refinement . . . one felt more and more that some moonlight nights in May . . . the ghosts of the people who once lived there must come back. Again their long dresses trailed rustling over the walks and the sound of their voices laughing, for no one could cry in such a garden, became confused with the rippling of the fountains."[20]

Villa Lante was the highlight of the gardens for her. On another carefully arranged day she went into the Vatican gardens, but found them overpoweringly interconnected spaces, which were too crowded except for the "gem," the elliptical court, *giardino segreto* of the Villa Pia, the garden-house, "the most perfect retreat imaginable for a midsummer afternoon."[21] This answered her question about shady retreats again; the stone banquettes, the vases raised against hedge and wall, the paving pattern, the alcoves, all influenced her greatly.

Between garden excursions Beatrix and Mary rested at Villa Odescalchi at Bassano di Sutri (where the garden has fine vases and statues similar to the monsters of Bomarzo). They also went on a week-long sailing expedition down the coast via Sorrento, Capri, Amalfi, Salerno, and the Gulf of Policastro. They had picnics on the beach, explored caves and ruins galore, including Paestum, and returned "on a splendid breeze"[22] which must have been soft indeed to sailors from the coast of Maine.

Of course they went to Florence, to the Boboli Gardens, and to Villa Gamberaia on its ridge overlooking Settignano. The villa was still a "lodging house" when Beatrix was there, and roses and vegetables filled the plots around the fishpond, but the structure of the garden was sound, a mysterious (nothing is known about its designer) and intriguing masterpiece, with the wonderful spaces—the fishpond garden, the grotto, secret *ilex boschi,* eight garden rooms held together by a unifying green *allée.*

They saw the falls at Tivoli, and the gardens of Villa d'Este. They drove to Hadrian's villa, where the view over the Vale of Tempe made most impact on Beatrix. They looked at the Borghese gardens "so squalid as to be melancholy."[23] They went northward to Milan, where Beatrix admired the public gardens and delivered a letter from Professor Sargent to the Rovelli brothers, whose azaleas and rhododendrons were just past their best. She saw Isola Bella, a little overdone for her taste, and thought Villa Carlotta at Cadenabia on Lake Como the most exquisite villa she saw. Their last journey gave them a halt at Verona and Beatrix time enough to try and see Guisti. Her last glimpse of Italy was that ravishing view: "When the heavy entrance doors are swung back, an enchanted vista . . . the deep, refreshing green of an avenue of cypresses leading to a precipice crowned by the foliage of a higher garden . . ."[24]

Beatrix had visited over twenty gardens. She had missed Villa Madama, Albano, Palazzo Chigi ("though we rang long and loud"), and Mondragone. She had had to spend some "painful" society mornings with the American colony in Rome. She had seen Palazzo Reale at Caserta, the "swansong of the

Italian baroque"[25] which she was told was the Italian Versailles. She replied that she had not seen Versailles, so she could make no comparison—but that would soon be changed.

However, their next stop was to be Munich, and the baroque of Germany. In Germany, or rather the princeling states of the 1890s, she was to see the repeated realities of *rond-point* and *patte d'oie,* parterres and *bassins* and *bosquets* in the great baroque gardens inspired by Versailles after the Thirty Years War ended in 1648 and overlaid by the English landscape style in Munich, Dresden, and Berlin. Their first garden, at the end of a two-hour drive out of Munich, was the elector of Bavaria's Nymphenburg, where F. L. Sckell had designed a fine landscaped park around the formal parterres and canals on the garden front of the palace. Beatrix wrote long notes about the formal and landscape features; she was most impressed.

They also spent a good deal of time at the Grosser Garten, the great and elaborate park at Dresden, where again Beatrix was intrigued by the mix of seventeenth-century baroque and a later landscape garden.[26] They took a river steamer to Pillnitz and saw Carl F. Bouche's ornamental gardens and the great collection of conifers that had been started in 1874. In Berlin for the festival of Whitsun Beatrix spent a good deal of time in the enchanting Tiergarten, seeing the Charlottenburg Palace, and making the trip to Potsdam, to Sans Souci and the Charlottenhof Park. She took Charles Eliot's introduction to the "very kindly"[27] Dr. Carl Bolle, who took them to his island plantation, Schwarfenberg, in the River Tegel and talked endlessly about his trees.

Most of Beatrix's tour of German gardens was at Charles Eliot's suggestion, and it gave her an interesting preparation for the French baroque and English parks to come: but she found even the summer coloring of the German landscape "poor and thin compared to the blue of the Italian air." Her deepest disappointment was the garden statuary, for which she had now conceived a passionate interest—"the statues are the worst defect we noted in Germany, they are always so overblown, and have not even the refinement given by having all their features gently worn away, so that their smiles are less distinct and their hands less encumbered with fingers."[28]

Perhaps the heat of Berlin in early June exhausted her, for Beatrix ceased her notebook entries here. Her mother's list of their crowded schedule from June 2 (the Tiergarten) through to their last day in Paris at the end of September is the only evidence for the rest of their tour.

During the second week of June Beatrix encountered London for the first time, and they were settled into the comforts of Symonds' Hotel in Brook Street which was to become their regular London base. Beatrix's first target was Battersea Park, across the river from the Houses of Parliament, an emphatically non-royal park which was popular for its vast rock and tropical gardens, besides being where the (younger) "cream of society" took morning bicycle rides.[29]

Their first excursion out of London (they went everywhere by train) was to Clandon station in Surrey, bound for Newlands Corner, the home of St. Loe

BEATRIX

The Gardening Life of
Beatrix Jones Farrand

Gertrude Jekyll, a photo-
graph taken in her garden at
Munstead Wood when she was
in her eighties. Beatrix visited
her in 1895, some thirty years
earlier. Although their acquain-
tance did not continue through
letters and further meetings,
as with William Robinson,
Beatrix's admiration of Miss
Jekyll's books was constant.

Strachey, owner and editor of *The Spectator*. Here, in rural and easy comfort, with spectacular views from Kipling's "Merrow Down" across the Surrey Hills, Mary Cadwalader Jones renewed many of her old literary contacts.[30] Cecil Spring-Rice, sometime ambassador to Washington, took them to Knole, the Sackville home in Kent; perhaps he showed them the galleries, the ballroom, the King's Bedroom, with the help of a particular friend of his, though she was only a precocious three-year-old, Vita Sackville-West, the baby of that great house.

With considerable astuteness Beatrix had arranged to see three gardeners, whom we now know to be the most influential of their day, but in 1895 they still largely had these reputations to make. On Wednesday, July 3, they took a train to Godalming in Surrey, where they were met by a pony and trap and driven through Godalming's narrow High Street up the hill to Munstead. Here she met for the first time the portly, bespectacled figure of Gertrude Jekyll, who was fifty-two years old, full of what the young Edwin Lutyens called her "rotundities" and good humor. In the summer of 1895 Miss Jekyll had not long taken to gardening; for the first time she was living in her garden at Munstead Wood, in the small summerhouse and studio, The Hut, which Lutyens had finished building for her the previous year. Her garden was over ten years old and well organized. Beatrix quickly learned that the Surrey sand had much in common with her soil at Bar Harbor, and both the Jekyll countryside and Miss Jekyll's woodland garden sported familiar heaths, ferns, and "whortleberry," gentle coverings of sphagnum moss and the bracken that covered most of her woodland. "No other manner of undergrowth gives to the woodland in so great a degree the true forest-like character" she wrote in *Wood and Garden*.[31] But there were also flowers to be admired, with which Beatrix was also familiar, the delphiniums, yuccas, alstroemerias, eryngiums, hydrangeas, and the "flower of this month"[32] the scented Clove carnations. The Munstead delphiniums made the proudest display "in two main groups in the flower border, one of them nearly all of the palest kind—not a solid clump, but with a thicker nucleus, thinning away for several hundred yards right and left."[33] White and pale yellow flowers were added here, with maize grass and hosta foliage. The deeper blue delphiniums were grouped with yuccas and silvery globe thistles at the western end of her long border. As a Munstead finale the *Lilium giganteum* were beginning to flower majestically at the edge of the wood. However, they only stayed for the morning (Miss Jekyll was strict with her working timetable), and then they drove toward Guildford to see the romantic Elizabethan house, Loseley.

Two days after Miss Jekyll's, Beatrix and Mary visited Mrs. Theresa Earle in her rather smaller garden at Woodlands, at Cobham, farther north in Surrey. Mrs. Earle was a comfortable lady of almost sixty, a gardener with a great interest in good food and travel and the magical mixture of all three.[34] She published her first *Pot-Pourri from a Surrey Garden* in 1897 and Beatrix collected three volumes of these very popular books. But I suspect that Mrs. Earle was rather too charming and diverse in her interests, too much of the talented English amateur for Beatrix, who was in rather a hurry to become a professional.

Undoubtedly her most influential English contact was William Robinson, with whom she had corresponded—and it was almost certainly Robinson who suggested that she should see what Miss Jekyll and Mrs. Earle were doing. After a week or so of seeing London sights, including the Royal Parks, and making excursions to Cambridge and to Wiltshire, Beatrix and Mary went to spend an August weekend at Gravetye Manor, Robinson's estate in Sussex. Robinson, who started as an apprentice gardener in Ireland in the late 1850s, had become a very rich man from his publishing.[35] He had bought his Gravetye estate in 1885 and was extremely proud of his thousand acres of rolling woodland that sheltered the source of the river Medway, which flows out through Kent to join the Thames at Rochester. When Beatrix visited he was in the throes of grand-scale landscaping, damming the stream (the young Medway) that filtered through the meadows below his windows to make a series of lakes. On the garden front he had leveled and planted his famous parterre (that belied his fierce criticism of formal gardening) filled with roses, pinks, and lavenders, and on the banks behind the house there were walks through scented shrubs and fine trees. Beatrix had to make an exhaustive tour of Gravetye's wonders; Sunday and Monday mornings were devoted to long walks in the woods. For many people Robinson's profound planting knowledge and fund of ideas were hidden by his crustiness and failure to suffer fools gladly. For Beatrix she just had another version of Professor Sargent to cope with, and they must have got on splendidly. Robinson's influence, through her personal admiration for him (and she visited him many more times) and through his books, which she studied thoroughly, was almost as great as Sargent's and will reverberate through this book.

Apart from this triumvirate of embryonic gardening gurus, Beatrix's English ambitions were to experience the English landscape (walking and playing golf figures largely in their schedule) and encounter the spirit of Elizabethan and Tudor houses and gardens, the best examples from Reginald Blomfield's *The Formal Garden in England*. No great eighteenth century landscape parks or picturesque gardens were included in her schedule. It seems that from the very start, she had worked out her priorities and decided to tread, warily, the middle way. At home there was the Platt versus Olmsted controversy, and she had followed both; she had expended a great deal of energy to make the most of the Italian villa gardens but was not too blinded by enchantment to analyze their uses to her—their Mannerist tricks of perspective, the influence of the

William Robinson, the most influential gardening writer and editor in England, when Beatrix arranged to meet him on her first visit in 1895. She made many more visits to him at Gravetye Manor in Sussex over the years and they remained friends until the end of his life.

The bridge over the River Kent at Levens Hall, Cumbria, England. The photograph was taken by Beatrix in 1895 and was used to illustrate her first published article.

landscape and light, their provisions for shade, sun, and flowers. Perhaps, most of all, they gave her a sense for fine statuary and ornament that she would never lose. But she had also done as Sargent and Olmsted suggested, she had absorbed the details of ordinary places and studied great varieties of planting. So did she dare discuss the formal versus natural controversy while walking in the woods with William Robinson? The question remains unanswered; I suspect she was wise enough to let Robinson's enthusiasm for trees and plants and how they grew in southern England teach her as much as possible. And then she went on her way, to see Longleat, Ham House, and north to Levens Hall, which added to Penshurst and Knole, and a day of exploring Windsor and Eton, gave her the feel of Shakespeare's England—which Mary Cadwalader Jones enjoyed most of all as well.

She had a great curiosity to find out what English topiary was all about (Robinson called it "cruelty") and so Levens Hall, exactly as drawn by F. Inigo Thomas in *The Formal Garden in England*,[36] was a priority and they made a diversion to see it en route from London to Edinburgh in early August. The quaint image of the aged topiary was tucked away in her mind, and captured with her Kodak, but then Levens brought her something else, material for her first piece in *Garden & Forest:* "In the home grounds the gently flowing river is bordered by tall grasses, the large leaves of the coltsfoot and great tufts of purple loosestrife . . ." and here also "the simple lines and quiet colour of this ivy draped bridge . . . are what make it satisfying to the eye . . . the native plants grow about it as familiarly as though it were a boulder playfully deposited there by Nature in the Ice Age."[37] She was perfectly determined to show the commonplace faction at home just how appreciative and observant she was. Her short piece, her first published work, was accompanied by her own photograph of the ultra-vernacular stone bridge that illustrated Olmsted's virtues of the commonplace so well.

In Scotland they spent days walking and golfing at Loch Earn, west of Perth, then moved farther north to Millden Lodge in Glen Esk, north of Brechin. John Lambert Cadwalader rented this shooting lodge every August for years and Beatrix greatly enjoyed following the guns for miles on foot or on a pony over moors with romantic names—Black Moss, Fernie Bank, Berrie Hill, and Dalhastrie. She also visited the Lindsay garden at nearby Edzell Castle many times and loved it deeply.

From Scotland they came south speedily, collected their belongings in London and headed for Paris. This was going to be difficult, for Freddy was living in Paris and the tension of these times is betrayed in Mary's brief notes, only ten entries to cover the period from August 21 to September 29, when they left for home.

Beatrix had the Paris parks and Versailles to occupy her while Mary was involved in difficult negotiations with Freddy and the lawyers over their impending divorce. Beatrix absorbed herself in explorations. She haunted Versailles for several days, studying and photographing the courts and allées around the palace from every angle. She walked in the Bois de Boulogne, visited the Trianons, and, according to Mary's note, made a special Sunday visit for the playing of the fountains, Les Grandes Eaux. She began her special study of Le Nôtre, delighting in "his bluff and simple personality" and in the "keen, earnest face, nervous in its modelling around the mouth, and with fine, frank, wide-open eyes" of his marble likeness in the church of St. Roch. She warmed to his sense of humor, and later related the story of how he laughingly declined the King's offer of a coat-of-arms, saying that he had one already—"three snails surrounding a spade and surmounted by a cabbage leaf."[38] Most importantly she discovered his work, and "his peculiar magic of infinite perspectives."[39] He was much more approachable than the shadowy forms of Della Porta, the Sangallos, and Crivelli who created d'Este, Aldobrandini, the Vatican gardens and Isola Bella.[40] And he was supreme, the best designer to learn from. He had "carried the art of garden design to the highest point of development it had ever reached," wrote Reginald Blomfield, "and this by no violent reform or blundering originality, but by profound thought on the lines laid down by his predecessors."[41] Beatrix was, as usual, taking the best examples, starting at the top where she meant to continue.

As to the Paris parks, Robinson had written enough in his early books[42] and Charles Eliot and Professor Sargent had recommended them highly, for Beatrix to be intrigued. Parc Monceau and Buttes-Chaumont, representing the work of Barillet-Deschamps[43] and Alphand,[44] were the admired peak of French sophistication in nineteenth-century design. Alphand's Les Buttes-

Chaumont was the picturesque transformation of an old quarry, a dramatic combination of rocks, water, and exotic planting; Parc Monceau, on the other hand, *un pays d'illusion,* was "solely for the pleasure of the senses and amusement of a licentious society"[45]—a collection of pavilions, windmills, waterfalls, ornaments, and baubles, but again among exotic, subtropical plants that were equally entertaining. Robinson thought the great waving fronds of *Musa ensete,* the Abyssinian banana, en masse worth making a journey to see and the collections of wigandias, cannas, giant grasses, and bamboos and dracaenas and aralias, must have made an amazing company.

Beatrix clearly thought it all too much for the New World; she wrote a short piece on parks, "City Parks" for the New York magazine *Municipal Affairs,* in which she politely declines the imitation of European fashions: "It must be remembered that parks in European cities are intended for the use of a homogeneous population, accustomed for generations to obey authority and respect public property, where as with us they are for the use of people gathered from all parts of the world, many of whom have been brought up under conditions in which there was nothing artistic. . . . Details of the parks in Europe have to be altered to suit our needs . . . for instance . . . the large pebbly gravel which is so ornamental abroad . . . will surely be thrown all over the grass."[46] She felt American cities, certainly New York, needed small spaces of formal design for direct paths, tough play areas for children, and most of all a green linkage, a system of open spaces, however small some of them may be, to provide walking or cycle ways through the urban heartland, just like Boston's Emerald Necklace, and the "wildlife corridors" we appreciate so much now, a hundred years on. Right from the start, she was very advanced in her thinking.

Beatrix's Grand Tour was of immense value, both in her personal and landscape education. She heeded almost all the good advisers: for six and a half months she had examined subtropical and Mediterranean plants in their own habitats, she had hunted for beauty in the details of ordinary life, visited endless galleries, museums, ruins, and historic sites, paced out the gigantic parterres of Caserta and the Nymphenburg as well as Versailles, and enjoyed the mountains of Bavaria and seascapes of Italy. She had amassed a large collection of photographs, made many rough sketches and notes, and these all contributed to her repository of design styles and ideas. From the Italian gardens in particular she had learned enduring lessons—the finest proportions of a balustrade were ever impressed on her mind's eye, but she had also completely absorbed the feeling of the gardens, how by design, texture of materials and color and planting they fitted into their landscape settings. It would be also true to say, contrary to the idea that Beatrix was influenced by her aunt Edith, that it was more likely the other way around. When Beatrix arrived in Rome with her list of gardens to be visited in April 1895, Edith was still only contemplating *The Decoration of Houses,* which she wrote with Ogden Codman and was published in December 1897. Edith's interest in the villas and their gardens, as a subject for articles, surfaced much later (specifically when she was making her own home at The

Mount in 1901), and Beatrix's determination to understand the techniques be-hind their design must have been perfectly new to her.[47]

There remains, at the end of Beatrix's grand educational tour, the question about her drawing ability. She knew that the historical presumption was to-ward landscape designers as artists, and vice versa, and William Kent and Humphrey Repton were obvious examples. She also knew that Olmsted felt that an artist, however brilliant, might well lack the practical application and tenacity to see the job done. What was required was a confidence to sketch an attractive semblance of a completed scheme—because people in general found it impossible to understand technical plans—and also the ability to make the necessary technical working drawings. The hesitant and amateurish sketches in her 1893 notebook are all that survive from her earliest years of study, and they do not indicate a natural flair. This did concern her; throughout her long tour she made copious notes and took many photographs; there were a few sketches, but no fat sketchbooks filled with inspired artistry. Nor did she spend hours with watercolors at an easel capturing the mood of the English land-scape. Was there more than a measure of self-support in her careful description of Le Nôtre's "failure" in this aspect, and was this another reason for making him her hero? "There is a legend that he painted two or three landscapes of great promise, which have since disappeared," she later wrote, though, "the boy cannot have shown real aptitude for painting," because we know that he was still young when he became his father's assistant in the parterres of the Tuileries.[48]

Characteristically Beatrix sought a practical solution. It is perfectly possible to learn technical drawing skills and from them work by softening the end re-sult by overdrawing freehand and adding washes, to produce an attractive per-spective. By the time she came to the end of her tour this is what Beatrix resolved to do, and on her return to New York in October 1895 she set about finding people to help her. Her family's Columbia connections[49] led her to Professor William Ware's architectural course at the School of Mines, at the corner of Fiftieth Street and Fourth Avenue, where she may have been able to attend the classes in architectural drawing and construction which were open to draftsmen from city offices. She kept some large Beaux Arts detail drawings of buildings, and in late life she often referred to her serious study of technical matters with the best tutors. As her work will soon show, she became adept at scale plans and elevations and at the surveying and engineering work necessary to construct a driveway. It seems certain that her "best tutors" were from the School of the Mines, who were the best of their day, and that she learned from them quickly and with complete understanding exactly what she needed to set her on her way.[50]

Chapter 5

❧❧❧

EARLY WORK AND A PLACE
IN HER PROFESSION

*R*ight from the start Beatrix attracted attention, and she knew how to turn
publicity to her own advantage. An early interview in the *New York Sun* is titled "Miss Beatrix Jones's Vocation—She does landscape gardening of all kinds
from the ground up." She was quoted upon a practical point: "I always wear my
bicycle suit for business. It is conventional, quiet looking and is not in the way."
There was no photograph, so the story of over a dozen column inches concluded: "Miss Jones is 25 years old and comely. She is tall and slight, and her
beauty is of the majestic kind that defies description. Although fond of tennis
and golf, and in love with her profession, she yet finds time for society."[1]

She gave the interview at Reef Point in early October 1897. At the time
her tally of jobs included draining a 25-acre swamp and putting it "in trim for
cultivation," clearing a 40-acre forest plot in Bar Harbor and transforming it
"into a pleasing grove," and laying out the small cemetery in Seal Harbor. The
first of these jobs was for Mrs. William Bliss[2] and the second was that found
for her by Professor Sargent, perhaps for the Bostonian C. M. Perry at his
summer home. The work at Seal Harbor cemetery included the design of a
romantic timbered lych-gate in the English tradition, and a small tool house.

Rather more significant were her early connections at the resort development of Tuxedo Park, an hour north of Manhattan by train. The development
had been planned in the mid-1880s by James Smith Haring and the Boston
landscape architect Ernest W. Bowditch, for Pierre Lorillard, in the Picturesque manner, making the most of the natural beauties of the hilly and
wooded 7,000 acres. House plots had been carefully fitted into the contours
around Tuxedo Lake and two smaller lakes, with large areas of woodland and

*The newly professional land-
scape gardener Beatrix Jones at
the outset of her career, in her
late twenties.*

game preserves buffering the select community from the outside world. The first houses were shingle-style "cottages" with decorative bargeboards and many gables, on stone foundations which tied them to their setting (much like Reef Point). The architect Bruce Price designed several of them, and he also designed the rugged stone entrance lodges, with lookout towers, which still guard the park. Beatrix was asked to do some screen planting at this entrance in 1896 (which still survives). It was a small but effective softening of the impact of the necessary domestic development at the gates—cottages and a school for estate workers, and the commuter station of the Erie Valley Railroad.

Clearly the residents of Tuxedo Park liked it so much that they wanted to live there all year round, so the later houses were more substantial than summer cottages. Beatrix worked for prominent resident William R. Garrison on his classical, stucco villa designed by William A. Bates, set on a large buttressed terrace, facing the lake. The site, according to the survey provided by the civil engineers, was a small, rounded valley of sweeping contours between West Lake Road and the lake's edge. The house was set in the center, on its leveled terrace platform. It was very splendid, a prime site, and numbered "1." Beatrix's ink on blue linen watercolored plans (she used the expensive blue linen for important clients) are for natural planting keeping well with the integrity

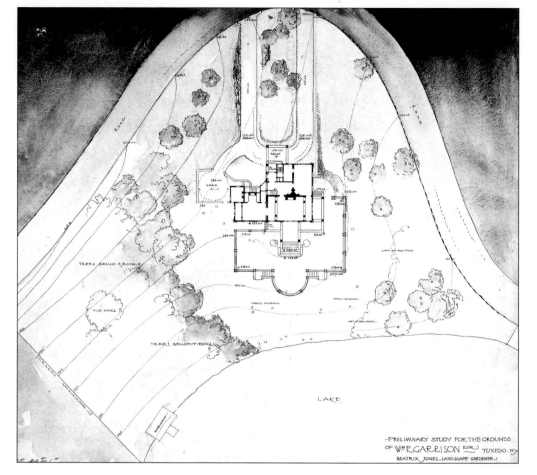

William R. Garrison's garden
at Tuxedo Park, New York,
1896. Beatrix's presentation
layout features the double drive,
her planting around the house,
and the natural setting for the
whole garden.

of the site and retaining the best of its native covering of hickory, oak, maple, and birch. A double drive in from West Lake Road was carefully planted to enhance the front portico, and to screen service wings, with big groups of old shrub roses, glossy green viburnums, and cornus, spirea, and chaenomeles. The house door occupied a scented niche among lilacs, shrubby honeysuckles, and the low, trailing Prairie Rose, *Rosa setigera*. Beatrix chose roses with great sensitivity to the site—*Rosa harrisonii,* "Harrison's Yellow," raised by George Harrison of New York in 1830, *Rosa lucida* or *virginiana,* the deep-lilac-colored and spicy *Rosa cinnamonea,* and semi-evergreen classic *R. wichuraiana.* Altogether Mr. Garrison's planting was a sympathetic and simple collection of classics, from a beginner who had done her homework well.

The *New York Sun* interview prompted a number of inquiries. There was a neat little scheme for the Village Improvement Association of Greenfield, Connecticut, for planting flowering shrubs around their schoolhouse. Beatrix marshaled the Tuxedo Park rose species again, plus magnolias, kerria, viburnums, the shrubby honeysuckles (*Lonicera tatarica*), *Deutzia gracilis* and three young tulip trees, liriodendrons, which virtually set the schoolhouse in a flowering grove. The drawing that survives for this job is not by Beatrix, and indicates the arrival of her first assistant into the large, sunny office, converted from her old nursery, that overlooked East Eleventh Street. For another early

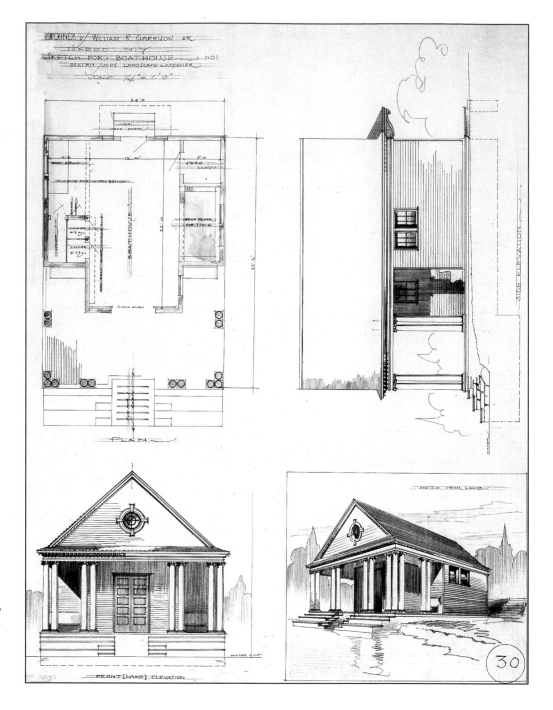

Another Garrison plan, 1896, shows elevations and a perspective of a classical-style boathouse on the lake shore, drawn by Beatrix.

client, Trenor L. Park of Harrison, New York (958), she redesigned a terrace and sketched her first arbors.

But it was when New York was abandoned for the summer at Bar Harbor that the kindness and encouragement of friends and neighbors came into full play, showing just how well disposed the world could be to a spirited young adventuress. Many—perhaps most—of Beatrix's early commissions are on Mount Desert, the product of long summer gardening days. But, upon close examination, it becomes clear that though her friends were full of good intentions, many of them obviously did not know what she did, or wanted to do, or perhaps what a landscape gardener did at all! She did a small garden for

SKETCH OF SEAT

IN GARDEN OF

EDGAR SCOTT ESQ

BAR HARBOUR

BEATRIX JONES, LANDSCAPE GARDENER

Perspective etc a shade hazy
but something like this would
be good . . . It should have a lower shelf

Beatrix's work for Edgar T. Scott, Chiltern, Bar Harbor, Maine: designs for garden seats in wood c. 1906.

Mary Cadwalader Jones's friend and colleague on the board of Mount Desert Island Hospital, Dr. Edward K. Dunham on Sea Cliff Drive, Seal Harbor. This was simply a weathered stone path (on the foundations of an old stable) through the summer flower borders to a rustic seat. For another of the many medical men who summered on the island, the eminent New York surgeon, Dr. Robert Abbe, who was a passionate amateur archeologist and supporter of George Dorr's idea for Acadia National Park, she did something rather more technical. In one of her many collaborations with the civil engineer Edgar I. Lord, Beatrix designed a new double drive and a bridge over the Duck Brook (the house was called Brook End). The garden was not large, and in between

ABOVE LEFT: *Chiltern: designs for two seats, one in wood and one to be molded in concrete, and a small garden table. The note reads, "Perspective etc. a shade hazy but something like this would be good . . . It should have a lower shelf." (The writing is not Beatrix's and is probably the client's.)*

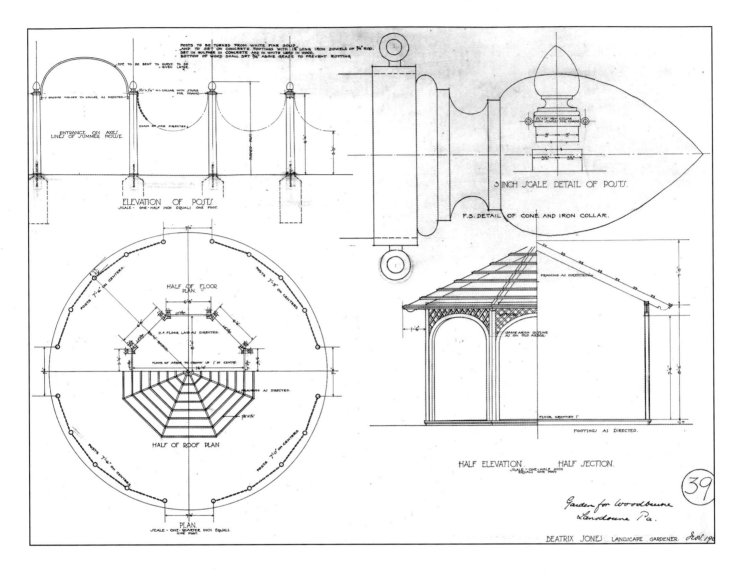

Drawing labels include:

POSTS TO BE TURNED FROM WHITE PINE SOLID
AND TO BE SET ON CONCRETE FOOTINGS WITH 18" LONG IRON DOWELS OF ¾" ROD.
SET IN SULPHUR IN CONCRETE AND IN WHITE LEAD IN WOOD.
BOTTOM OF WOOD SHALL SET ½" ABOVE GRADE TO PREVENT ROTTING

PIPE TO BE BENT TO CURVE TO
¶ GIVEN LATER

ENTRANCE ON AXES
LINES OF SUMMER HOUSE.

ELEVATION OF POSTS.
SCALE - ONE-HALF INCH EQUALS ONE FOOT.

3 INCH SCALE DETAIL OF POSTS.

F.S. DETAIL OF CONE AND IRON COLLAR.

HALF OF FLOOR PLAN.

HALF OF ROOF PLAN

PLAN.
SCALE - ONE-QUARTER INCH EQUALS ONE FOOT.

HALF ELEVATION. HALF SECTION.
SCALE - ONE-HALF INCH EQUALS ONE FOOT.

FOOTINGS AS DIRECTED.

39

Garden for Woodburne
Lansdowne Pa.

BEATRIX JONES LANDSCAPE GARDENER. Nov. 190

Woodburne, the Edgar T. Scott home in Lansdowne, Pennsylvania, 1908: a sheet of details for the design of an octagonal summerhouse surrounded by a circlet of posts and chains and hoops for roses. This drawing is not by Beatrix Jones, but by one of her office staff. Posts and chains for roses was an idea revived by Gertrude Jekyll.

the two drive entrances she planted a natural rock and flower garden, using natives as well as summer garden flowers. She seemed to like nothing more than to tackle the difficult rocky slopes of the Bar Harbor area, and draw up and supervise the making of a smooth, correctly profiled drive.

Perhaps she even came to be something of a fashion, for she certainly encountered many of the summertime celebrities. She did some planting suggestions for the Fabbri house, Buonriposo, a rather Moorish style villa on Eden Street, facing the sea. It was the home of Ernesto Fabbri, a research physiologist at the American Museum of Natural History in New York, and a Bar Harbor legend as an amateur radio operator. For one of the most celebrated houses, La Rochelle, designed by the Boston architects Andrews, Jacques & Rantoul, for George S. Bowdoin, she went to considerable efforts, which are not revealed by the single surviving drawing. She told the *Sun* reporter: "I am at work now on grounds up on the West Shore Road. I have been up there three times this week. It will be a charming place when done. See, here is the plan . . . I have made some changes in the entrance gate since this was drafted, and am going to arrange for lanterns in place of those ornaments, but the boundary wall is to have just those panels, and there will be large trees where those dark spots are, and shrubbery in the lighter places."[3]

She designed the driveway for another celebrated cottage, Chatwold, for Robert P. Bowler; Chatwold became famous when his widow, Louise, sold it to the flamboyant publisher, Joseph Pulitzer. Pulitzer became a leader of the island's highest-flying set, which included Dr. Silas Weir Mitchell (Edith Wharton's consultant and John Lambert Cadwalader's brother-in-law), and the three presidents, Eliot of Harvard, Seth Low of Columbia, and Daniel Gilman of Cornell. The Mitchell connection brought her several jobs for medical men and others in the Philadelphia area, and she walked perfectly easily in the company of such luminaries. Mary Cadwalader Jones, whose upbringing chiefly in the company of distinguished older men had given her ease in such company, had passed this skill on to her daughter. It meant that Beatrix would manage J. P. Morgan, Theodore Roosevelt, and John D. Rockefeller Jr., and their kind with perfect grace.

*B*ut in her belief that surroundings deserve to be the solace of the poor more than the playground of the rich, Beatrix wanted to do something for the benefit of the less fortunate.

Beatrix was increasingly aware that her skills were of most benefit when used in conjunction with the skills of others—architects, engineers, planners—as part of a team. Her second contribution to *Garden & Forest* was the furtherance of the latter cause. In the issue of April 7, 1897, she published her edited version of a paper given to a meeting of the Royal Institute of British Architects in London by the "well-known landscape-gardener" Henry Ernest Milner, whose book *The Art and Practice of Landscape Gardening* had been published in 1890. Milner had addressed a lively gathering on February 15 and Beatrix, having received the paper, felt it deserved a wider audience. His subject was "The Garden in Relation to the House." In the formal versus the natural debate of Blomfield and Robinson, Milner had drawn the ire of both by trying to walk the middle way; now he had his chance to speak of the "happy mean where the art of both schools should go hand in hand," with the architect designing the terraces, walls, and steps and the landscape gardener taking charge of "the arrangements of verdure and composing the wider picture."[4] Beatrix liked his suggestions about choosing the site and approach to a house: "His recommendation of a hillside rather than a hilltop for the location . . . is one we would do well to take in heart." (Did Biltmore with its sliced-off mountain come to mind?) And there was her favorite subject of driveways: "The approach . . . should always appear to be direct, and any deviation from such directness should not only arise from, but should also be made to arise from, some decided obstacle. By direct is not meant straight." A straight approach is artificial, may be used for an imposing building, but in general a curved road is preferable, "following within limitations the natural undulation of the ground."[5]

In these ways Mr. Milner skillfully gave the landscape gardener his field of operations. The "terrace" was not merely the level extension of the house but the whole "of the ground that forms the base or setting of the building"; no two places could be alike and to copy another "design" was inadmissible; the landscape gardener must find an original solution to all these problems, from the entrance gates as a symbol of refuge from the hurly-burly of the world, to the view from the house, "the broader treatment beyond."[6] Beatrix added that "Mr Milner's interesting paper recalls to us the prime necessity for remembering that the arts of architecture and landscape gardening are sisters, not antagonists." She felt that there was still "too little of this collaboration and too little sympathy between" the two professions, and she looked forward to a wider appreciation of the necessity for a "broad landscape treatment" as part of the artistic whole.[7]

In submitting this plain speaking, or rather plain writing, to *Garden & Forest* Beatrix could not fail to be noticed. She may even have appeared remarkably farsighted and level-headed in the eyes of her more timid fellows. Her

Some designs by Beatrix Jones for simple headstones, using colonial motives.

SOME DESIGNS FOR SIMPLE HEADSTONES
AFTER COLONIAL MOTIVES
BEATRIX JONES LANDSCAPE GARDENER

direct personality and deep sense of vocation found it irksome to be button-holed by well-meaning homeowners who just wanted her to solve some trivial garden problems, to enlarge a terrace, provide prettier flowers, and yet they failed to realize the possibilities of her role. From the start she was a person of serious vision. She was not one to sit around and wait for the world to change, she was prepared to go out and find her opportunities.

Everyone in the landscape world, from the elite Olmsted office through to every civic authority, was concerned with the provision of parks. She had studied enough parks in Europe to have more of a vision than most of her fellows. During 1897 and 1898, after the appearance of her *Garden & Forest* piece, she worked on plans and suggestions for American parks. She submitted notes on replanting in Augusta State Park[8] and she sent in to the New York Parks Department plans and suggestions for improvements, which did not have quite the result she expected.

Her opinions about New York's open-space provision, or lack of it, eventually found an airing in a special "municipal aesthetics" issue of the *Journal of the Committee on Municipal Administration* in December 1899.[9] She demonstrated that it was not too late for New York to acquire a system of small parks, a mixture of "open air gymnasiums," i.e., play-parks for the children, and green oases where older people might find an illusion of the countryside that they so rarely see. She was against emulating the "costly paintings and ornamental fantasies" of London or Paris parks, because such things were too expensive, and also unsuitable to the melting-pot society of urban young America. She concluded that neither the proud achievement of Central Park, nor the difficulty of acquiring new land in such a crowded city should deter an attempt to fulfill at least something of Frederick Law Olmsted's concept of the 1860s, that Central, Riverside, and Prospect Parks were only the beginning.[10]

Beatrix's name and ideas, in their journey from submission to publication, passed across the desk of the city parks superintendent, Samuel Parsons Jr.[11] Almost certainly, being Beatrix, she followed up with a visit, and presented herself in exactly the right place at the right time. For, apart from his day-to-day problems, Parsons was struggling to persuade his fellows in the landscape world to form a professional association. For complex reasons he was meeting a lot of opposition, based upon apathy and suspicion, for the profession Beatrix was so proud to join was in a state of crisis. While she had been educating herself and finding her vocational feet, it had suffered a series of "staggering reverses" during the 1890s.[12] Frederick Law Olmsted had founded the profession out of his remarkable but tattered life; his office was both fount and pinnacle, it was the "grand professional post-graduate school" he had vowed it would be.[13] And yet, there were those tragedies of the nineties: Harry Sargent Codman, Charles Sargent's nephew, whom he had escorted around half the world to nurture his career, had died of complications after an appendectomy, aged twenty-nine, in early 1893. Calvert Vaux, Olmsted's alter ego, and the creative force behind Central Park, was found drowned in New York harbor on a November morning in 1895. Charles Eliot, the brightest hope of all, died in the autumn of 1897 just before his thirty-ninth birthday. The editor to whom Sargent had entrusted *Garden & Forest,* William A. Stiles, died at about the same time, so the voice of the landscape world was stilled at the end of that year. And finally after a last trip to his beloved England to try and revive his spirits, Olmsted himself was brought home sunk into depths of senility and confined to a mental hospital in September 1898.[14]

In the face of all these tragedies, the only thing was to pick up Charles Eliot's fallen banner, for he had suggested a "general association" for all who "desired the advancement of landscape art" at a meeting of the American Park and Outdoor Art Association in summer 1897. The idea had been popular, and undoubtedly Eliot would have carried it through successfully. Samuel Parsons was, good-naturedly, trying to carry on, but he had encountered hostility from the Olmsted office, partly founded in long arguments over his management of Central Park and tendency "to aim at garden as distinguished from landscape effects."[15] There was too, stemming from the Olmsted/Platt philosophical differences over gardens that were beautiful for their own sakes versus the ennobling virtues of the wild landscape, a rift which had polarized into gardens versus landscape. The Olmsted office, the "grand post-graduate school,"[16] now inherited by John Charles Olmsted and Frederick Law Olmsted Jr., with the support of the "graduate" Warren Manning, was jealous of their elevated professional status. It saw the proposed association as an opportunistic effort on behalf of the "barrow boys" (those who had trained as gardeners and found making private gardens a profitable business). There was, of course, more than a little snobbishness in this rift; the postgraduates looked down on Parsons, the son of a nurseryman who had been apprenticed in Central Park.

Samuel Parsons persevered and had called several meetings during 1898, and Beatrix attended at least one of them. However, by the time she returned to New York from Bar Harbor toward the end of October, she and Mary had already planned to spend the worst of the winter in the Mediterranean. They were to leave before Christmas with a party of friends, and celebrate the new year in Palermo. John Charles Olmsted wrote to his adored wife, Fidie, on the evening of January 4, 1899: "I am going to another of Parsons' meetings of landscape architects called to form a national society. I am not enthusiastic about it and doubt if there will be enough desirable members to make it a success. However, as Parsons is evidently bound to get up a society any how and as he would get himself elected president thereof largely for the sake of the advertizing he could get out of it, Manning and others think they would rather be in it and have me president than to stay out and let Parsons run it."[17]

The meeting turned out to be "pleasant"—perhaps because John Charles had his way and *was* elected president of the new American Association of Landscape Architects. Nine charter fellows were present; they planned to invite seven more without further investigation of their qualifications (Beatrix must have been one of the seven) and to investigate a further six. By the time the first printed version of the transactions of the new association appeared, the first eleven[18] were listed as charter members and fellows. Beatrix, as Robert Patterson was to write in her obituary sixty years later, always felt "undeserving of the honor of becoming a charter member or fellow."[19] Though a real modesty was very much a part of her honest personality, perhaps this had rather more to do with the fact that she was not actually present at the founding meeting!

However, there she was, one woman among a select gathering of men, though a few months later the association proudly announced its first woman fellow as Elizabeth Bullard. Miss Bullard, a painter, was elected because Olmsted had confidence in her as a successor to her father, Oliver Bullard, to carry out his park project at Bridgeport, Connecticut.[20]

In the new association the Olmsteds naturally had their place. But John Charles regarded his role as president, as he had written, rather as a necessity than to great purpose. His neatly penned letters to Fidie repeatedly give the impression that the long meetings in Parsons's office were just more duties away from home that he could do without. He thought a dining club would have been better, more enjoyable, and doubtless it would have excluded any women.[21]

In Frederick Law Olmsted Jr., the fledgling ASLA had a useful connection. The following year, 1900, he was appointed as head of the first Harvard course in landscape architecture, set up by President Eliot in memory of his son. Frederick and Beatrix were frequent allies in the cause of educational standards in the years to come. Another founding fellow was Warren Manning, who had worked in the Olmsted office and at Biltmore and was now in practice on his own account, with many commissions around Bangor and Rockport, Maine.[22]

The first secretary of the association was a young garden designer, Daniel W. Langton, but he had to give up after a year because of failing eyesight. Downing Vaux, Calvert's son, became secretary after Langton and supported the ASLA loyally until his death in 1926. Samuel Parsons and his young partner, George F. Pentecost, were also founding fellows.

The remaining three charter fellows were a little more heavyweight. Charles Nassau Lowrie was a civil engineer with a large New York practice specializing in parks. He was to be consultant to the Hudson County of New Jersey Parks Commission for the next thirty years. Nathan Franklin Barrett was the one of whom the Olmsted faction were most doubtful.[23] He was a planner and had entered the landscape world via his layout for the industrial complex of the Pullman Carriage Company on the shores of Lake Calumet in the Chicago suburbs. His model layout for employees' housing could not escape the dominating proportions of a railway carriage; housing blocks, public "squares," and open spaces were uniformly, and rather comically, long and

Plans for Crosswicks, the Clarence B. Newbold estate in Jenkintown, Pennsylvania, 1903: Beatrix's presentation drawing of gate and wall treatments with a half plan of paving to the exedra.

narrow. Barrett was a jolly, pipe-smoking character who was careless of niceties. He made the beginnings of Joseph H. Choate's Naumkeag at Stockbridge in the Berkshires, where Olmsted had said a garden was impossible, and his own half-acre plot in New Rochelle boasted colonial, Japanese, English, Moorish, *and* Roman influences.[24] The final charter member was Ossian Cole Simmonds, a Michigan man, and another civil engineer, who was superintendent of Graceland Cemetery and a Michigan/Illinois native plants and parks man.

The experience, which qualified Beatrix as a charter fellow, was, in comparison with Lowrie, Barrett, Simonds, Manning, and the Olmsteds, smaller but perhaps of better quality—Tuxedo Park, Seal Harbor Cemetery, Greenfield schoolhouse, the Bliss swampy field, the 40-acre forest lot, and some other small jobs. But her prospects were good, for she was beginning a majestic garden for her Newbold relatives at Crosswicks, Jenkinton, Pennsylvania, and, most exciting of all, according to the pocket biography of her in *Municipal Affairs* in December 1899, working on the site for the National Cathedral

in Washington, D.C. Had she but known it, she had been recommended to Bishop Henry Yates Satterlee, the first bishop of Washington, as "the most skillful landscape gardener in America."[25]

So, at the age of twenty-seven—in the summer of 1899 after the founding of the ASLA—and less than four years after her debut in her profession (which she dated herself as July 1895),[26] Beatrix could count herself equal with the other fellows. Simply by being a charter fellow of the American Society of Landscape Architects she was ensured a certain place in her world.

But the minutes of the ASLA show that she was neither overly enthusiastic nor careless of the company the society promised her; she was discriminating, but conscientious. There were two further meetings in 1899, neither well attended, and things only seemed to brighten with the first annual dinner on January 9, 1900, at the Hotel Martin in New York, which Beatrix attended, and which made a column of report in the local newspapers.[27] The following

Crosswicks: a second presentation drawing, treatments for walls, gates, and piers in brick stone and trellis. These delicately watercolored drawings were prepared for exhibition at the American Society of Landscape Architects.

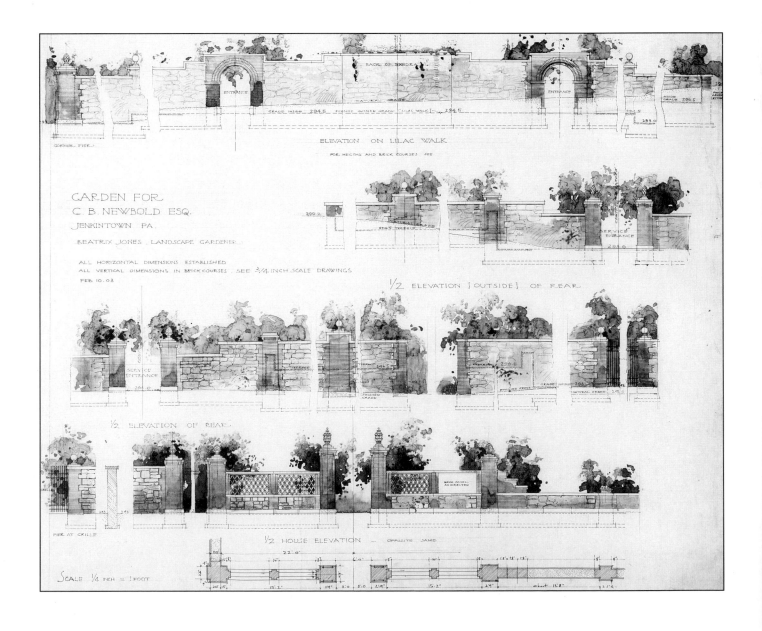

month she was appointed to the executive committee, whose meetings were not recorded. The surviving printed report of the first ten years of the ASLA is brief and hardly earthshaking: after discussions and letters in support of the preservation of the Palisades, of Riverside Park and Drive, and a mass-participation in the design of a park for Yonkers, matters dwindled to the usual gossip, the trivia of choosing sites for monuments, holding exhibitions, discussing interprofessional relationships, and the design of a society seal.

For two weeks in the spring of 1902 the society held its first annual exhibition. Beatrix exhibited her design for the Anson Phelps Stokeses' Brick House at Noroton Point, Darien, and (or very soon afterward) her impressive plans for Crosswicks.

Beatrix assiduously attended the annual meetings and dinners (except for 1903 and 1904) from 1900 until her marriage in 1913, but rarely any lesser meetings unless they were of special interest. On March 14, 1905, she went to hear a paper on large tree planting and the following month, on April 18, there was a talk on Italian gardens. She took part in a lively discussion after each lecture.

The American Society of Landscape Architects was to play very little part in her life or her progress. She never approved of the term "landscape architect" and refused to use it; her notepaper was always printed "landscape gardener." This requires a further historical explanation, for to Beatrix and to many since her time this is more than a matter of mere words.

Frederick Law Olmsted regarded himself as a landscape *architect,* but he had acquired the term, not willingly, from Calvert Vaux, in the early days of their partnership.[28] Vaux in turn had learned it, along with its intimations of landscape design as an art, from England. The English had in their turn learned it from the Scots.[29] The first use of the term has been attributed to a friend of Walter Scott's, Gilbert Laing Meason, who published a book in 1828 titled *On the Landscape Architecture of the Great Painters of Italy.* Though Humphrey Repton (like Capability Brown) regarded himself as a landscape *gardener,* John Claudius Loudon picked up the architectural connotation when he edited, in 1840, *The Landscape Gardening and Landscape Architecture of the late Humphrey Repton, Esq., being his entire works on these subjects.* In 1849 William Andrews Nesfield, former fan painter turned parterre designer, signed himself "Landscape Architect" in presenting a scheme for very grand gardens on the new east front of Buckingham Palace for the approval of Prince Albert, possibly to impress the consort.[30] Andrew Jackson Downing had brought the term to America from the Loudon influence, inserting a section called "Landscape or Rural Architecture" in his *Treatise on the Theory and Practice of Landscape Gardening, adapted to North America* in 1844 and in many subsequent editions. It was of course Downing who had met Calvert Vaux in England in 1850 and persuaded him to return to America and practice.[31] Vaux was convinced that landscape design should be thought of as an art, and its practitioners as artists: "I think it is the *art* title we want to set art out ahead . . . and make it *command* its position—administration, management, funds . . . and everything else. Then we have a tangible something to stand on: as administration with art attached the thing is the wrong shape," he wrote in correspondence with Olmsted in the 1860s.[32] Olmsted was less sure: "I love beautiful landscapes . . . better than anybody else I know. . . . But I don't feel strong on the art side. I don't feel myself an artist . . . and it would be rather sacrilegious to post myself at the portals of art."[33] Thus over the next thirty years of practice Olmsted adopted the term *landscape architect* as sufficiently visionary to apply to the team leader, the designer who saw the possibilities and harnessed the many specialist technologies in the achievement of the pleasing whole. Such a visionary overview protected the landscape from the enthusiasms of the engineer (too many straight roads and ducted watercourses), the architect (too many buildings and ornaments), and the horticulturalist (too many exotic plants). But of course each specialist resented the landscape architect's pose as a kind of heaven-assisted supremo. Adopting the term *architect* because both *artist* and *gardener* were insufficient is a pity, for we have spent the ensuing century in many hours of debate obsessed with semantics.

Beatrix thought, as many others did, that architects built buildings, and that their priorities were entirely different. She believed completely in generous cooperation, as she wrote in *Garden & Forest*.[34] As the term landscape *gardener* had been good enough for Repton, so it was good enough for her.

Chapter 6

꧁꧂

AUNT PUSSY, MISS NIMROD,
AND OLD CELIMARE

*H*er second European tour, in 1899, which caused Beatrix to miss the wholly unspectacular launch of the American Society of Landscape Architects, may be regarded as the finishing of her landscape education, as well as an escape from the New York winter. She was never to travel again in quite this eager frame of mind. The almost annual trips to Europe made with her mother over the next twelve years were social and cultural rituals, and though it was never possible for Beatrix to travel without her "landscape eye," it was visits to her friends, rather than making pilgrimages to places, that set their itineraries. Beatrix kept records of only the 1895 and 1899 trips, so all her later excursions have to be seen through other eyes; luckily the two people who kept their eyes firmly on her, and wrote down most of what they saw were her adored Aunt Pussy, Edith Wharton, and Henry James, whose own lives have been documented in minute detail. The Master christened her Miss Nimrod when he visited the shooting lodge in Scotland . . . "a house of bloody shooters, & even Trixy's hands are imbrued," where she had enjoyed part of every August during these twelve years.[1] Both her Aunt Edith and Henry James loomed large in her life during this time, until she finally won her freedom with her marriage.

Their 1899 trip is detailed in Mary's diary, which Beatrix kept. They spent the New Year in Palermo at the Grande Hotel des Palmes, in lively company with the American and English contingent of visitors and residents. Sicily was becoming extremely popular, soon to be dubbed "the new winter resort" by Douglas Sladen.[2] During January Beatrix and Mary saw the fashionable gardens of the English community, including the Whittaker family gardens at

Sperlina, Marsala, and Malitano, and that of the redoubtable Canon Skeggs, and—of most interest—the old island gardens, which in some way made up for her never seeing the Moorish gardens of Spain. By a strange quirk of history the Norman invaders of Sicily in the twelfth century had made gardens in the manner of their Islamic predecessors, who had conquered the island three hundred years earlier. In the Benedictine cloisters of Monreale Cathedral Beatrix found what Mary's friend Maud Howe likened to "some supremely beautiful Andalucian patio," a cloister surrounded with slender paired columns, some twisted, some inlaid, and some plain alabaster with fretted capitals, with carved acanthus foliage and lions' and men's heads. In this court was the Arab Fountain, made of topaz-colored marble, with the lion-heads dripping "a slow soft shower of diamond drops" from their mouths.[3] Even in January there were carpets of Parma violets and later the court was planted with yellow wallflowers, white stocks, purple flag iris, and lavender mauve hyacinths.

Mary and Beatrix also visited the Duc d'Orleans's Parco Aumale, with its lemon groves and rose avenues, the Villa Tasca on the road to Monreale, and the Hon. Albert Stoppard's garden in an old monastery court at Taormina. They spent long and happy hours wandering in Palermo's Botanic Garden, with its famous tropical water garden, and also among the Villa Giulia's avenues of Portuguese laurel and laurustinus. Beatrix snapped and sketched and made notes. Spurred on by William Robinson's *The Subtropical Garden,* as well as Professor Sargent's advice,[4] she was particularly conscious of a rare chance to see exotic plants in their native habitat. Mary Cadwalader "mooned about contentedly" as she recorded in her diary on what was at least their fourth visit to La Favorita on January 18. They also saw much more of Sicily, visiting the places they had only glimpsed briefly on their sailing expedition from Naples in 1895—Syracuse, Salerno, Paestum, and Messina (before the devastating earthquake of 1908).

At the end of January they moved to Rome, and Beatrix was able to see the gardens of Villa Madama and Villa Albani, which she had missed before. They rested up at Villa Odescalchi, then toured northward to Siena, Bologna, and Venice, feeling themselves to be "almost the only people in Venice"[5] at the tail end of February. From there they went north to Geneva, where Beatrix had an appointment to meet M. Correvon, the famous plantsman and rock garden expert. She saw his rock gardens on calcarous and granite soils and heard of his interest in *formes architecturales,* the plants to become beloved of landscape architects—fatsias, ficus, acanthus, ivies, and spearleaved grasses.

From Geneva they went on to Paris, to the Hotel Balzac, with trips to the theater, seeing Sarah Bernhardt as Delilah ("dull! much too old for the part," commented Mary) and to the Easter services. (Perhaps Beatrix paid a call on her father; more assuredly she made return trips to Versailles and Chantilly.) Then, at the beginning of April the travelers arrived thankfully at Symonds'

Mary Cadwalader Jones in middle age. This photograph, one of a series of passport photographs that have survived, emphasizes the strength and determination of her personality, which in reality was softened by her vitality, sense of humor, and kindness.

Hotel in Brook Street, London, to their now "usual" suite. They took in London theaters (*The Belle of New York,* Irene Vanbrugh in *The Gay Lord Quex*), and made trips to Canterbury in Kent and Glastonbury in Somerset. This was for Beatrix's cathedral research. She had come with a letter from Bishop Satterlee to Mr. and Mrs. Stanley Austin, who owned the beautiful, ruined former Glastonbury Abbey, asking for stones from the ruins to build a "cathedra," a stone chair, for the future Washington Cathedral.[6] With the stones promised, they boarded the *Bremen* at Southampton on April 16, for a smooth crossing which landed them at home on the twenty-sixth, to find two new jobs awaiting Beatrix.

But this trip had served a purpose for Mary Cadwalader Jones too. She had been able to finish her book, *European Travel for Women,* which was published by Macmillan in London and New York, the following year. This slim and popular volume reads very typically of Mary, full of lively perception and practical tips: "heroines in novels are always described as bewitchingly lovely at sea, but to more ordinary mortals it is decidedly trying . . ." So be sure to take warm underclothes and an extra shawl. A cheap, stiff fan, a thick gauze veil, a portable rubber bathtub, and a small bottle of brandy or ginger would all come in handy for coping with the shocks and deprivations of European cities, and a folding silver fruit knife would be a luxury! She urged her feminine readers to make the most of their travels by reading beforehand and *looking* hard. And all-pervasive was her sense of the proprieties—a party of ladies could go to a respectable London theater without a gentleman—also in London, as at home, a woman bows first in the street, but don't forget the reverse is true for the Continent. It was so typical of Mary's unselfish love of her daughter that she could occupy herself so well, while Beatrix was immersed in her gardens and plants.

In May of 1899 Beatrix visited Washington to report to Bishop Satterlee.[7] Mary resumed her social round.

The bishop had put great faith in Beatrix. His great work was to build his cathedral. He had decided on the site on Mount Saint Alban, with its expansive view over Georgetown to the distant obelisk of Washington's Monument, and had bought the land in 1896. The first building was to be the national Cathedral School for Girls, built with funds from Mrs. William Randolph Hearst, and Beatrix and Robert W. Gibson, the architect, had been asked to report on the best site for the school, which was in effect the best site for the cathedral itself. Bishop Satterlee recorded that their report, which had been adopted unanimously by the Cathedral Committee in 1898, stated that the "best site for the Cathedral was on the southern portion of the grounds, with the axis or transepts in line with 36th Street and the nave with Harford Street. This position would leave the whole east front to be seen with unobstructed views from all points. The chancel and towers will be visible from every part of Washington, for the ground will slope down from 80 to 120 feet on the east side of the Cathedral. So also it is with the south. The slope of the ground between the south transept and Massachusetts Avenue is beautifully adapted for parking. Thus, the east, south and west of the Cathedral will always be free and open, with no building . . . to obstruct the view, while the north of the Cathedral will (as it should be) be covered by 'quads' of educational buildings."[8]

The site was delineated in this way, with twelve marker stones at the angles of the proposed cathedral; the Cathedral School for Girls was at the northwest corner of the site, and other buildings followed. In 1900 Bishop Satterlee appointed Beatrix "landscape architect" to the Cathedral Park Board, a group of fifteen ladies—the president was Constance Satterlee, the bishop's daughter—who were to look after the grounds. She drew construction sections for the Mount Alban roadways (but her delicate contours have been long lost under layers of tarmac). Whether she was able to do any planting with the Cathedral Park Board is not certain.[9]

Upon Beatrix's return from Washington she went to Bar Harbor. Mary, having hired, as usual, a couple to look after 21 East Eleventh Street, followed with their maid and cook at the end of May. She stopped off in Boston, meeting Beatrix for a visit to the Sargents at Holm Lea, which included a rhododendron garden party, a drive around the Arnold Arboretum, and a visit to Mrs. Harry Quincy at Dedham (this last in connection with the Quincy Hospital which Mary visited with John La Farge at the end of June). After a ladies' luncheon to celebrate Beatrix's birthday on June 19, the rest of the summer was pure holiday—full of long, lazy Bar Harbor days, tennis and tea gatherings of old friends and neighbors, the Dorrs from Oldfarm, the Amos Pinchots[10] and Edgar Scotts. For the Scotts Beatrix was tackling the alteration of the entrance to their house on Main Street, south of Bar Harbor Centre, where Cromwell Harbor Brook enters the sea. Main Street had been realigned to a new bridge, and the new drive allowed her to plan a lovely dell garden, as well as prepare lots of designs for seats and terrace details. The Scotts became useful friends and clients, for there was also work on their garden at Woodburne in Lansdowne, Pennsylvania, where she must have spent hours on the planting for a large layout of fifty-two beds, for a two-season flowering—springtime tulips, narcissus, forget-me-nots, aquilegias, iris, and hyacinths with thymes followed by a summer progression of peonies, *Iris germanica*, phlox, roses and *Chrysanthemum segetum*.

Beatrix returned to New York in early October. Mary and the household followed later in the month, and social life at no. 21 was soon revived. Edith Wharton was in their party for Thanksgiving, and the First Assembly was at the Astoria on December 14 (Mary "saw to everything" but did not attend because of the death of Mrs. Theodore Roosevelt Sr.). Christmas lunch included Edith and Teddy Wharton and Berkeley Updike of the Merrymount Press. Edith was in sparkling form over her newest enthusiasm, her plan to buy land and build a summer cottage in the Berkshires, which she had "discovered" the previous September. Edith's building of her house was to be of pivotal importance to Beatrix's burgeoning career, but her aunt had already been helping her with small introductions.

Edith had married Teddy Wharton in 1885 when Beatrix was fifteen. Her affection and like-mindedness with her sister-in-law, Mary, which dated from their first meeting, remained constant throughout Mary's separation and divorce, and was intensified when difficulties began in Edith's own marriage. Edith and Mary were a mutual support against the formidable Lucretia Jones, and Mary and Beatrix were frequent visitors to Land's End, Edith's home at Newport, rather than enduring the chilly correctness of Pencraig. For Beatrix, Aunt Edith was the only member of her father's family who played any part in her life (Uncle Harry paid occasional visits and sometimes remembered her birthdays), and Mary increasingly felt Edith to be "closer than a sister of my own blood."[11]

Among Beatrix's earliest jobs were sketch designs for a garden for the J. J. van Alens at Newport (they had taken the Whartons for a long Aegean cruise a few years earlier), and for another of Edith's friends, Mrs. Elizabeth Hope Slater, she sketched a classical Beaux Arts pergola set on grass terraces, sloping to the sea. She had surveyed the site herself.

When Edith finally tired of Newport, feeling it encouraged a lingering depression, she fled to rest in Mary's care at Reef Point. (It was here that she met Dr. Silas Weir Mitchell, the famous neurologist who treated her depression, who happened to be John Lambert Cadwalader's brother-in-law).[12] Edith was wise enough to see that Bar Harbor was not for her. She needed invigorating surroundings in which to work well, and it was the search for such a place that took her to Lenox. In the summer of 1901 the Whartons completed the purchase of Laurel Lake Farm, and she chose Ogden Codman, her coauthor of *The Decoration of Houses,* as her architect. Codman's elaborate treillage arbor, made for the garden at Land's End, was moved to Lenox, but this turned out to be his only contribution, for he and Edith soon parted company.[13] Edith's tastes had veered from the French to the English, and she chose Francis L. Hoppin as her architect to build a house modeled on Belton in Lincolnshire, which was reputedly the work of Christopher Wren.[14] The Mount, as she called it, was finished quickly, by the late summer of 1902, and the Whartons were installed on September 20.

Beatrix was working at the Mount from the beginning. Edith's first priority was her kitchen garden, for which Beatrix's design drawing is dated July 14, 1901. This was sited on the left of the entrance drive, just beyond the gatehouse; it was an enormous rectangle, 250 feet long by 175 feet wide, which was divided in half and each half was quartered to a central circular crossing in traditional style. At each end, north and south, there were raised terraces; a grape arbor faced south and there was a pear arbor at the stable end. Edith reveled in her "big kitchen garden with a grape pergola" and it was being cultivated before the house was finished. She wrote to Sara Norton in June: "It's great fun out at the place, now too—everything is pushing up new shoots—not only cabbages & strawberries, but electric lights and plumbing."[15]

A few days after designing the kitchen garden Beatrix produced her next drawing, for the driveway; this shows her now proven knowledge of roadway construction, which she enjoyed, with a well-engineered convex surface draining to earth gutters. The progress down the drive fell carefully into three sequences: firstly, passing the kitchen garden, an almost straight avenue of sugar maples led from the road (the junction of Plunkett Street and what is now Route 7) to a second curving section, which Beatrix carefully cut through a small copse of sugar maples and pines. Finally, there was a generous left-hand sweep into the walled court of the house.

By the time Beatrix had accomplished this domestic aspect of the work, Edith had finished inside her house and was eager to tackle her own formal garden. Having veered from the French to the English in design terms, she now alighted on Italy; it was actually more than that, for the beginning of The Mount's formal garden coincides with Edith's negotiations with Richard Watson Gilder of *Century* magazine, for the first of her articles on Italian villas and their gardens.[16] Edith, having decided to turn the subject into literary art, also decided that she knew exactly what she wanted, and Beatrix knew her aunt too well, and loved her too much, to interrupt her in full flight. The Mount's garden was born from Edith's assumptions about Italian gardens, made *before* she researched and wrote her articles, and Teddy Wharton's later "constant amusement" in the opening of vistas and planting of trees and wildflowers.[17] It was no less than a designed disaster, and Beatrix must be absolved from anything to do with it.

Perhaps she should have braved her aunt's anger, though I don't imagine it would have been easy for her to change Edith's mind. But poor Edith had to tolerate some feline remarks about her garden. Ambassador Choate from Naumkeag at Stockbridge, who knew a good deal about gardening and European gardens, apparently stepped onto her terrace and remarked, "Ah, Mrs Wharton, when I look about me I don't know if I'm in England or in Italy."[18] He undoubtedly meant that if he were in England the grass would lap the terrace walls, offering serpentine vistas through the trees to the distant lake; but if he were in Italy he would expect elaborate, falling terraces at his feet, with beds of bright flowers, plopping fountains, gamboling stone cherubs, ranks of potted geraniums, all surrounded by thick evergreens, which framed the view of the lake. The Mount owns a mixture that is neither: the enclosed, formal gardens floated in the middle distance, to the right and left of the view, as if stretched on a rack. They teeter at the end of a seesaw, which is the Lime Walk that tentatively connects them across the line of sight to the lake.

Despite this design aberration, Edith enjoyed The Mount: "for over ten years I lived and gardened and wrote contentedly," she recalled in *A Backward Glance,* and at least it gave her some happy memories for the rest of her life spent in Europe.[19]

And she continued to forward Beatrix's career. She smoothed the path for her to work for their cousin Clement B. Newbold, at Crosswicks, Jenkintown, in Pennsylvania. This was discussed for a long time, and Beatrix's first confident plan, for another rectangular walled garden, this one 300 feet long by 200 feet wide, is dated July 24, 1901, when she was also working on The Mount's. Crosswicks' becomes a more elaborate affair, with raised walks all around, a sunken garden in the center, and a large terrace at one end. Over a long period—she worked for the Newbolds at various times until 1916—Beatrix designed every kind of detail and ornament, gates, gate piers, seats, steps, the pergola, latches and bolts, a sundial, and flower baskets. She planned and planted an evergreen garden, a curving grass walk between banks of mainly rhododendrons (species *R. grandiflora, R. caerlescens, R. purpurea elegans,* and *R. atro-sanguineum*) and her fondly remembered hybrids: "Henrietta Sargent," "H. W. Sargent," "F. L. Ames," "Mrs. C. S. Sargent," "Lady Grey Egerton," and "Mrs. Harry Ingersoll."

Another cousin, Tom Newbold, gave Beatrix a little work at his Hyde Park home, a design for a garden and summerhouse in 1912. Yet another commission came from a regular visitor to The Mount, Edith's colleague on a small insurgent group who were dissatisfied with the work of the Society for the Prevention of Cruelty to Animals, Mrs. Gordon Bell. For Mrs. Bell Beatrix designed a garden seat for her garden in Ridgefield, Connecticut.

And the Lenox grandees, who owned the most palatial cottages, invariably found a little garden work for Edith's clever niece, whom they encountered at dinner, and rather vied with each other to patronize. The first was Emily Vanderbilt Sloane. The Sloanes (Emily's husband was the carpet manufacturer

W. D. Sloane) lived in the ninety-four-room Elm Court, originally built in the mid-1880s by Peabody & Stearns with an impressive miniature park of lawns and shrubberies designed by Frederick Law Olmsted. The entrance front of the house displayed an enormously wide gravel sweep around a circular lawn, where ranks of greenhouse exotics, pots of cannas, red pelargoniums (geraniums), cycads, and *Musa ensete* (banana ferns) were set out for the summer. When Emily Sloane encountered Beatrix she clearly had a passing enthusiasm for a gentler kind of gardening. In 1908 Beatrix designed a large, many-bedded flower garden, with subtle mixes of flowers—dark red carnations with the white dianthus "Mrs. Sinkins"; pink and white cornflowers with santolina (cotton lavender); pink Japanese anemones with *Lilium longiflorum*. There were beds filled with roses, a single variety to each bed, and all Gertrude Jekyll's recommended favorites. Four beds of "Mrs. John Laing," a rosy pink, vigorous hybrid perpetual; "Victor Hugo," the brightest of crimsons; "Prince Camille de Rohan," crimson maroon; and "Paul Neyron," with enormous rich pink flowers, were opposite four beds of crimson "Gruss an Teplitz"; pink "Caroline Testout"; "Frau Karl Druschki," with its perfect buds of pure white, tinted green; and "Mrs. W. J. Grant," another rosy pink. These were a mix of hybrid teas and hybrid perpetuals. The rose beds were to be further ornamented with pots of white pelargoniums and pillar roses.

Mrs. Sloane tired of the idea of flowers, for the drawings are unfinished and Beatrix was passed on to another of the great cottages, Eastover, the home

Edith Wharton's residence, The Mount, in Lenox, Massachusetts: the garden photographed c. 1905. The drive approach and the kitchen garden at The Mount were designed skillfully by Beatrix in 1901, but Edith and Teddy Wharton made the flower gardens more to their own tastes.

of Harris C. Fahnestock, where it seems she did considerable work which has been entirely lost. Eastover was built by Francis L. Hoppin and his firm Hoppin & Koen, architects of The Mount, and was illustrated immaculately finished in *American Architect & Building News* in October 1913. These photographs of the south front, with the awnings out over the loggia, show a balustraded terrace leading down to a sunken garden, divided into four beds around a sundial and four columnar yews. The planting can be identified from the photographs as beds of salvias, mignonette, and heliotrope around the sundial, with taller roses, double hollyhocks, and day lilies at the sides. Beyond the flower garden are lawns with restrained flower borders. Beatrix's drawings show all this to be her design. In January 1910 she was consulted by Francis L. Hoppin on the grading for the entrance and whole layout, and the siting of large trees, and she designed the entrance court, the balustrades, steps, a pool, and fountain, but apparently not the planting, which was the realm of the Fahnestock gardeners. Eastover was a remarkable tribute by Hoppin, presumably on the basis of his admiration for her approach at The Mount, and it was a triumph for her classical Beaux Arts detailing.[20]

The Lenox connection also led to Giraud Foster's magnificient Bellefontaine, which had been built by Carrère & Hastings. What Beatrix did is not clear; she was sent a blueprint of the design for the splendid Italianate layout, which presumably Tommy Hastings had designed himself, perhaps for planting suggestions. It was an important professional link with Hastings, who appears again later on. And a final Lenox connection with far-reaching implications was a meeting with Anson Phelps Stokes of Shadowbrook. After the loss of a leg as a result of a riding accident, Mr. Stokes reluctantly sold Shadowbrook, and for consolation Mrs. Stokes found him a most beautiful place for a house, on the tip of Collender's Point, at Noroton, Connecticut. Their son's firm, Howells & Stokes, built Brick House, for which Beatrix designed the garden.

Henry James visited The Mount for the first time in the late summer of 1904, at the beginning of a lecture tour. Edith prized his visit, and certainly did not share it with her female relatives; James, however, was frequently only too relieved to escape the "gorgeous vortex" of Edith's company—his "radiant, omnipotent and beneficent" Edith was most desirable in small doses.[21] It was always to Mary's that he fled for undemanding comforts. She had made a deep impression on him at that first glimpse in 1869, when she was Fred's intended (when calling on the Joneses would have revealed a merely seven-year-old Edith!). James frequented Mary's Sunday lunches in the 1870s, finding 21 East Eleventh Street "the great good place" full of warmth and welcome during his many unhappy times in New York,[22] and he had seen her briefly at Reef Point in August 1883 shortly before he sailed for England. It was Mary who engineered the renewal of their friendship, when knowing Edith's frustration over two near meetings with him, she sent him *Crucial Instances,* Edith's short stories, and *The Touchstone,* and told him of Beatrix's career and their im-

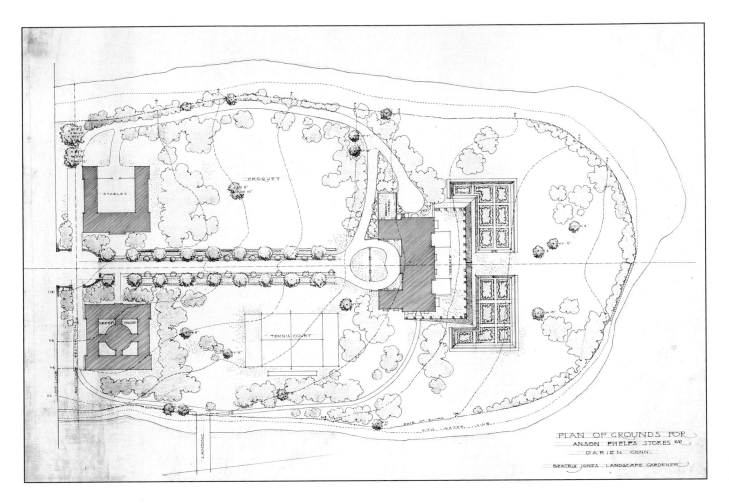

Brick House, the home of Anson Phelps Stokes, Noroton, Darien, Connecticut, 1902: Beatrix's simple and beautiful design for the layout of the house that the Stokeses built after leaving Shadowbrook in Lenox, Massachusetts. The terrace has low formal flower beds right and left, with the central vista remaining clear for the view out to sea.

pending arrival in England in the summer of 1902. His response meant that he was a presence in all their lives until the ending of his own.

From that first visit in July 1902, Beatrix and Mary were regularly lodged at Lamb House, Rye, despite his warnings of the "low and longitudinal Aberdeen terrier" (Mary adored all dogs) and that "Miss Beatrix was not to look at his untidy garden."[23] Beatrix, once wrapped in the Master's fond and rather garrulous embrace, had little choice but to hear his views on gardening, that he wanted "as much vernal beauty as possible" in his private acre. He paid 20 shillings a week to his gardener George Gammon for it, and himself remained "densely ignorant," not knowing "a dahlia from a mignonette."[24] He had also acquired a tender gardening virago, Susan Muir-Mackenzie,[25] a friend of Gertrude Jekyll's, whom he praised and serenaded. James was afraid of becoming fascinated, "Would the garden become a trap for his hours (which were full) and for his purse (which was empty)?"[26] And, like so many nongardeners, he saw gardening as miracle-working, and regarded Beatrix with some wonderment. She was attentive, sending him notes and presents that amused and touched him, which brought forth a stream of picturesque praise—"My dear, brave Beatrix" he called her, Trix "the Earthshaker," rejoicing for "Trix in her big field." Their priorities were very different, and theirs was a relationship of blissfully affectionate misunderstanding, not unlike

Henry James and Howard
Sturgis at the Mount.

many a fond father and daughter; and certainly Beatrix found in her "dear old Celimare" an indulgent patron.[27]

For the Master had more gardening friends than he would care to own, and from Beatrix's first visit to Lamb House in the summer of 1902 she was launched into a network that lasted through all her English visits. Susan Muir-Mackenzie smoothed the way to further visits to Munstead Wood and other gardens that Miss Jekyll was working on.[28] From Lamb House Beatrix made excursions to Hever Castle and Penshurst Place. Whenever the occasion arose everyone from Lamb House migrated to Windsor, to Howard Sturgis's[29] house, Queen's Acre, on the edge of the Great Park. Qu'acre, as it was called, was convenient for Cliveden, where Beatrix's Kodak captured Lady Astor on the terrace looking over her parterre beds packed with small tea roses and ribbons of tufted pansies.[30]

From Windsor it was a short trip to another regular haunt, Stocks at Tring, the home of the art critic of the *Times* of London and his redoubtable novelist wife, Mrs. Humphry Ward.[31] Mary Augusta Ward was one of Mary Cadwalader's closest friends; she was the cousin of Lucy Whitridge on East Eleventh Street, and they were both granddaughters of the great Dr. Arnold of Rugby School. While both Marys talked about literary matters, Beatrix used Stocks as a jumping-off point to examine nearby gardens, including Sir Francis Bacon's own garden at Gorhambury, and also a much newer garden which was a strong influence on her, that at Luton Hoo, made for the "Randlord" Julius Wernher (cr. Baronet 1905) by Romaine-Walker & Besant, in a grand Beaux Arts manner. Beatrix may also have seen the garden called Romaine-Walker's magnum opus, Danesfield[32] at Medmenham in Buckinghamshire—a new Tudor-style house overlooking the Thames valley, with splendid terraces, flower parterres, topiary, fountains, and balustrades all in flourishing Beaux Arts crossed with baroque style, a taste that pleased a particular breed of new-money clients.

The designer who successfully walked the tightrope between such baroque flashiness and lichen-covered restraint was Harold Ainsworth Peto.[33] Peto was an architect and had been in partnership with Sir Ernest George, one of the "fathers" of the Arts and Crafts movement, before he abandoned architecture for garden design in the 1890s. But Peto had also been to America, had a tremendous respect for Charles Platt, and was himself passionate about all things Italian. Beatrix saw Peto's own terrace garden filled with exquisite Italian ornaments tucked away in the valley of the river Frome at Bradford-on-Avon, but the work that influenced her most, the garden which foreshadows her garden architecture to come, was at Easton Lodge, Dunmow, in Essex.

Easton Lodge, Essex, England. The garden, designed for the Countess of Warwick by Harold Peto, was the only one in England where Beatrix could have seen the French-style pergolas that inspired many of her later designs. Photograph from Country Life, *1907.*

This belonged to Daisy, Countess of Warwick, a famous beauty of the Prince of Wales's set, who had taken to gardening; she had set up her own College for Lady Gardeners at Studley in Warwickshire, and at Easton, which was her own inheritance, she commissioned Peto to design this formal garden around the lodge which was inspired by Bacon's essay "On Gardens." To the north of the lodge there was a lawn corresponding to Bacon's "green"; next, an old croquet-lawn was bordered on two sides by arched pergolas evoking Bacon's "covert alley upon carpenter's work" and displaying Peto's knowledge of wood construction. Their central treillage domes derived from seventeenth-century French patterns, and their timber arches were covered with jute netting and wreathed in climbing plants, creating galleries of green architecture. The sunken water garden north of this "agreed with Bacon's fountain. . . . it had a central balustraded pool over a hundred feet long, resplendent in summer with water-lilies and surrounded by broad grass walks."[34]

The Owen F. Roberts home, Montevideo, Simsbury, Connecticut, 1920: a detail of construction for a fan trellis of cypress or white pine strips painted to match the wall, attached by expanding bolts to allow for growth of the vine stems.

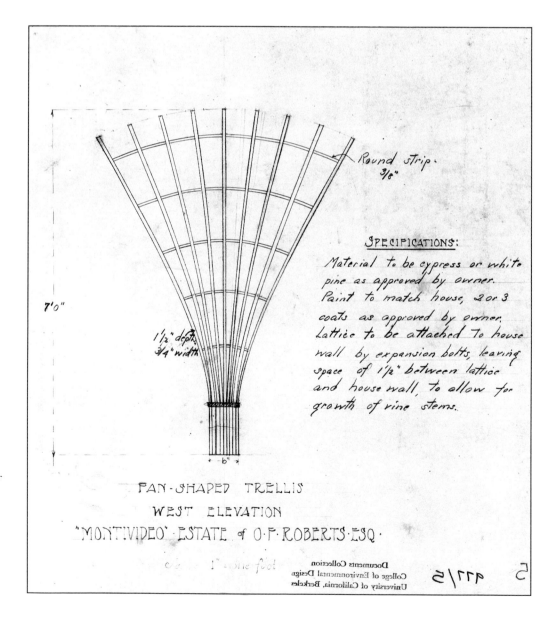

I doubt whether Beatrix had much to do with Peto himself, for he was arrogant and frosty, and not acquainted with Henry James (though the Master undoubtedly knew Daisy Warwick). James's "best of landscape gardeners and painters" was Alfred Parsons, who had settled in Broadway, the stylish Cotswold village so beloved of Americans in exile or just visiting.[35] Beatrix did rounds of Cotswold gardens under the friendly and delightful Parsons' wing; she went to Abbotswood at Stow-on-the-Wold, where Mark Fenwick was making a vast natural rock garden as a backdrop for his house and formal garden by Edwin Lutyens, she saw Court Farm in Broadway, the garden Parsons himself designed for Anthony and Mary de Navarro[36] and perhaps met the newcomer to this coterie of like minds, Lawrence Johnstone who had just moved into Hidcote Manor.

From Broadway, the scene shifts northward to Scotland and the climax of the summer, John Lambert Cadwalader's shooting party at Millden. Here Beatrix was conveniently close to Edzell, the Lindsays' early-seventeenth-century pleasance, and she saw gardens associated with Robert Lorimer, including Balcaskie and Earlshall; at Traquair House she found ogee-domed pavilions that were to reappear at Crosswicks and Dumbarton Oaks.

After all the introductions he made for her in England, it was in America that Henry James led Beatrix to her most fascinating client. In the autumn of 1904 James went to Farmington, Connecticut—"really exquisite Farmington"[37] and there met Theodate Pope for the first time. Theodate had studied architecture, and played a major role in building the house James called "a magnified Mount Vernon," called Hill-Stead, for her parents, Mr. and Mrs. Alfred Atmore Pope.[38] After a prolonged return visit by James in the spring of 1911, Beatrix and Theodate collaborated on Theodate's plans for Westover School in Middlebury, Connecticut, and she introduced Beatrix to other clients in the area.[39] Theodate became something of a legend in her own lifetime. She inherited Hill-Stead and its fabulous collection of French Impressionist paintings upon her father's death in 1913. At this time Beatrix prepared a planting scheme for the formal garden in front of Hill-Stead (which Theodate had designed herself when the house was built) with generous drifts of delphiniums, columbines, pinks, roses, iris, peonies, phlox, and silver gray lavenders and santolinas. All the flowers were in shades of pink, cream, lavender, and blue, thus avoiding Theodate's detested red and magentas.[40]

Theodate set up her own architectural practice, and it would be wonderful if further evidence of her collaboration with Beatrix came to light, for they would have been a formidable pair! Theodate survived the sinking of the *Lusitania* and then married Ambassador John Wallace Riddle in 1916.[41] She was to live her own colorful parallel to Beatrix's life for another thirty years.

Chapter 7

❧❧

THE WHITE HOUSE
CONNECTION, 1903—12

*I*n her interview in *The Outlook,* published in March 1908, Beatrix spoke with feeling about the fatigue of all the traveling necessary to her work. She knew of no one "who has not had to stop all work for a longer or shorter time as the result of a breakdown."[1] Whether she had an actual breakdown is not known, but there are several pointers to her being ill or out of sorts during her early thirties. There is a definite lull in her workload and she concentrated on writing and lecturing as alternative activities.

Shortly before her thirtieth birthday (June 19, 1902) she received $45,000 from Freddy Jones, part of his mother's legacy which he passed directly to Beatrix.[2] She was certainly in Europe that summer, but did she, out of filial duty, spend some time in Paris with her father? She spent considerable time pursuing Le Nôtre, and it would have been in character that she sought comfort in this sympathetic soul, standing by his tomb in St. Roch (near the Louvre and near Freddy's apartment) when she was in difficulties herself. She was certainly not well throughout the following spring, and this ended in an operation for appendicitis in June 1903, followed by six weeks' convalescence at The Mount, before she and her mother made their delayed departure for Europe at the end of August. There is a photograph of her at this time standing timidly beside a garden gate. She looks overweight and overdressed—too much pattern and too many flounces (so unlike her usual elegance), all topped by a ridiculous hat adorned with curly topknots with wings.

Her article "Le Nôtre and His Gardens" appeared in *Scribner's* magazine of July 1905. She had researched him thoroughly, following in his footsteps to Vaux le Vicomte, Versailles, Chantilly, and Fontainebleau and hunting the ghosts of his gardens at St. Cloud, Marly, Meudon, and Clagny. She excused his flowerless *parterres de broderie,* castigated by William Robinson for being flowerless, because there were then few glasshouses for propagating. She admired, with feeling, Le Nôtre's patience with capricious clients, and his ability to produce a stream of alternative ideas. She schooled herself in these aspects most effectively.

Her next magazine piece was thoughtful and philosophic; she called it "The Garden as a Picture" and it appeared, in *Scribner's,* in July 1907. The title came from Gertrude Jekyll: "Should it not be remembered that in setting a garden we are painting a picture?"[3] Beatrix accepted that the arts of painting and garden design were closely related, but then she analyzed the differences: a painter has a flat surface and limited palette, and while "no sane person would think of going behind a picture to see if it were equally interesting,"[4] the garden designer, governed by the context and possibilities of nature, must be prepared for criticism from any standpoint, more like a sculptor. Her experience told her that most people seemed irresistibly drawn to look at a composition from the least attractive angle.

She went on to justify the ways in which landscape appreciation could be cultivated, and always had been, by people other than painters. She felt that variations in a landscape, the lessons of the great landscape paintings, such as the differences between the rocky coast of Maine and the sleepy luxuriance of the Pennsylvania pastoral country, were equally well observed by anyone with an interest in outdoor life, wildflowers, or birds. And a "painterly" sensitivity to light and shadow was easily learned in Italian gardens, or even in misty England "where the preponderance of dark yews gives a brightness to the flowers, even on sunless days."[5] All could now be captured not only by sketching, but by pointing a camera: this she had clearly done and Henry McCarter's line illustrations were drawn from her photographs.[6]

Beatrix made her point in great detail—that to possess a landscape artist's eye one does not necessarily have to be a painter. She needed to do this because she was only too conscious that she had neither the talent nor the application to spend hours painting. She had to make her case against the interminable pleadings of Gertrude Jekyll's early books that her first love was painting, and it was her painter's education that made her into an artist-gardener. And there was Claude Monet looming to prove that a great painter could not but fail to make a marvelous garden.

There were other aspects to be tackled in this long article as well: good gardening had a strongly national character, and thus marble goddesses and fountains hauled back from Italy did not necessarily suit America (nor did the frosts of New England do them much good).[7] No collection of flowers, no matter how beautiful, made a garden either; masses of color and masses of greenery must be balanced, and to achieve perfect naturalistic harmony this needed to be done on a very large scale. Consequently, most gardens had to be artificial and were best enclosed, so that they could be kept from all pretense of being in harmony with their natural setting. This idea of a garden that suited East Coast America as an enclosed room, separate from the house, was the single most radical diversion from current English fashion when patterns and flower beds were visually and actually related to the doors and windows of the house.[8] That Beatrix realized this, when most of her contemporaries only dreamed of *copying* English gardens, was a tribute to her intelligence as well as an important step in her career.

She wrote no more long articles for magazines after this; whether she found writing too difficult or was perhaps wary of competing with her aunt Edith is not clear. Perhaps Le Nôtre and artistry in gardening had served their purposes in allowing her to refuel and renew her own professionalism by reading, thinking, and writing. "The Garden as a Picture" was converted into a lecture on the art of gardening, which she illustrated with glass slides of landscape paintings. This was her first lecture subject in a list she prepared for garden clubs and ladies' societies. At first she was shy, and her notes are nervously marked "learning how to bow," upon introduction, and hopefully upon ovation. A second lecture, "On the art of landscape gardening," was developed when she became an accomplished lecturer, and this was technical, a detailed explanation and demonstration of the planning and layout of sites. The impact of the word *landscape* made a significant difference in Beatrix's mind.

The publication of *The Outlook* piece, naming her—at thirty-six—as the doyenne of her profession, gave her confidence just the boost it needed, and from that spring of 1908 she returned to working at the frantic pace that she was to keep up for almost the rest of her life.

If her early thirties were restful years, they were certainly also highly sociable. Apart from Mary and Beatrix's usual company and the annual trips to Europe, there was for both of them, and especially for Mary, the frisson of having Theodore and Edith Roosevelt in the White House. They made several trips to Washington, sometimes to stay at the White House, and many weekend visits to Sagamore Hill.[9]

The Sagamore Hill table talk led Beatrix to work for Edward F. Whitney at Oyster Bay. She dressed up an existing walled garden with an ingenious bamboo and chestnut trellis for roses, clematis and vines, and she laid out thirty-eight small rectangular beds of summer flowers, divided by herringbone brick paths. Doing walled gardens was now easy for her, and familiarity had bred confidence. Rather more unusual, but in line with her careful enhancement of nature to make a garden, was a delicious iris dell, with drifts of tall iris species, *pallida, germanica,* and *sibirica,* their sweeping drifts defined by grass paths through a glade sheltered by lilacs, forsythia, and the native dogwood, *Cornus florida.* This pleasant job was one of the sidelines that was leading her inevitably it seemed toward one of the most important connections of her life, with Dorothy Whitney.

There were other fateful connections too. In early 1909 Beatrix designed a formal town garden, edged with masses of box, rhododendrons, deutzia, priv-

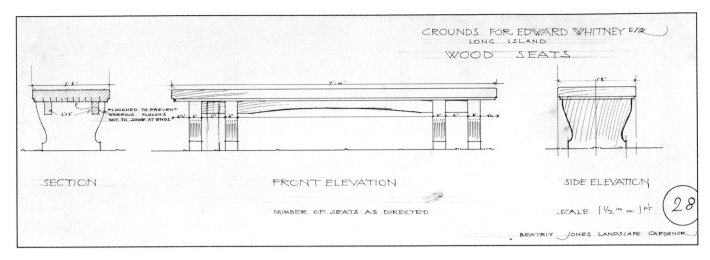

The Edward F. Whitney home, Oyster Bay, Long Island, New York, c. 1910: construction drawing for a bench seat in wood.

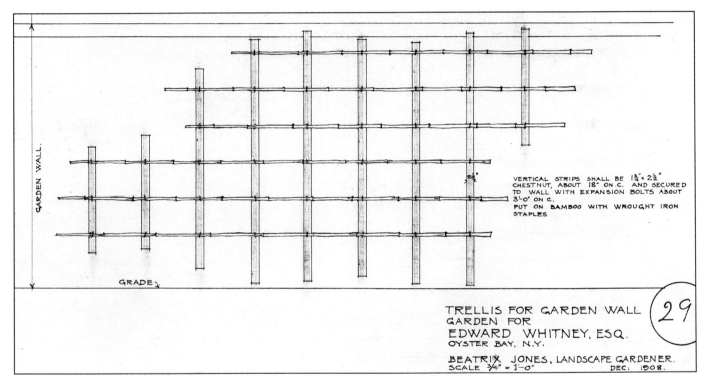

Construction detail for Mr. Whitney's wall trellis of chestnut strips bolted to the wall,
with bamboos attached with wrought-iron staples, 1908.

ets and other evergreens, underplanted with spring bulbs, for Dr. James Markoe at 20 West Fiftieth Street in Manhattan. Dr. Markoe may well have been Beatrix's own consultant, and he was certainly friend and physician to J. Pierpont Morgan, and the combination of Dr. Markoe and John Lambert Cadwalader (sometime shooting colleague of Morgan) brought her a summons early in 1913 to 219 Madison Avenue, the Morgan town house and library. Beatrix would have fitted well into that shaded West Room, with its red silk damask walls, where the aging, cigar-smoking, patience-playing Pierpont

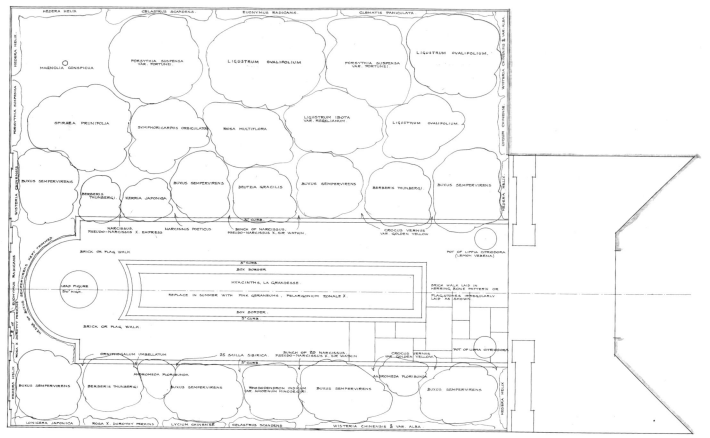

Dr. James Markoe, 20 West Fiftieth Street, New York City, commissioned a design for a town garden, 1909.
A simple, classical, evergreen garden with a "pool" of pink flowers as a brilliant variation on convention.

Morgan stared at her in the flickering firelight, and bid her design a garden for him. This was their only meeting, and her work on the formal garden for the library was mostly done during the 1920s. It was an effective demonstration of her status, and that she was noticed by some of the most powerful people of her day.[10]

She resumed work on Clement Newbold's Crosswicks at this time, which led to a string of commissions along Philadelphia's "Main Line" of prosperous suburban gardens. For Mrs. John K. Mitchell's garden on a lakeside site at Rosemont, Villanova, she drew a watercolor perspective of a long, enclosed garden with iron railings and a stepped, apsidal curving end containing a square pool. A stone-pierced pergola ran down one side, covered with roses, and the beds of the garden were filled with summer flowers.

There were other watercolors, exercises in pleasing prospective clients, which sometimes came to nothing, but there was also a very important commission, started in 1910, for Henry Frazer Harris at Harston, Chestnut Hill. In contrast to so many freestanding walled gardens Harston relates to the house in the English manner. The architects, Cope & Stewardson, had built in the manor-house style, with many gables, steep roofs, and leaded-glass windows. Philadelphia landscape architect James Bush-Brown called it "one of the finest examples of Tudor architecture to be found in this country."[11] Beatrix was

Clarence B. Newbold's Crosswicks, Jenkintown, Pennsylvania: a contemporary photograph of the main vista through the flower garden, c. 1903.

Crosswicks: a second contemporary photograph of the walls constructed to Beatrix's designs. This was her first major garden.

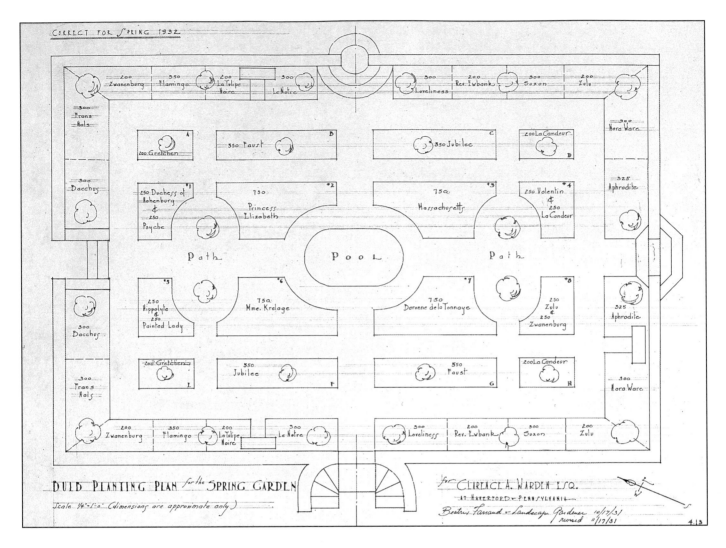

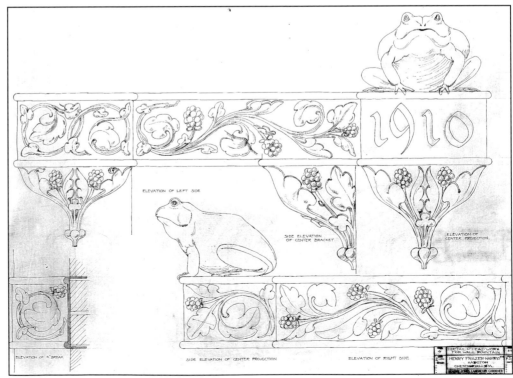

Clarence A. Warden residence, Haverford, Pennsylvania, 1932: plan for a formal spring flower garden with beds of tulips and narcissi in single varieties.

The residence of Mr. and Mrs. Henry Frazer Harris, Harston, in Chestnut Hill, Pennsylvania, 1909–11. Sketch design for leadwork to the wall fountain with foliage and toads.

presented with reams of survey plans by Franklin & Clarke of Philadelphia, and Harston's garden was clearly a triumph of teamwork. With them she achieved very clever terracing, which fitted the house into its setting. The South Garden, centered on a large, mullioned window of the Great Hall, is the most important space; immediately outside the window is a generous green terrace and a "moat," then steps descend to a rectangular sunken garden. This is a simple, serene lawn shaded by an ancient apple tree (saved on the site) and surrounded by a brick path through flower borders. Mrs. Harris was a competent gardener, a great figure in Philadelphia garden society, so the planting was definitely her care; tulips, iris, and columbines were followed by delphiniums, lilies, and thalictrums in the borders. Beatrix's contribution was the ornamentation—wall details, garden gates with ornamental hinges, the wall fountain with lead toads and leafery, and wooden pavilions and pergola. The highly critical Bush-Brown praised the garden's simplicity, consistency, and "refinement of detail": Beatrix's consistency was in the way she carried the vista from the Great Hall window through the South Garden and on down three small green lawn terraces, hedged in hemlock, to an ancient cherry tree as the finale, all with tremendous ingenuity at fitting the geometry of the site to surviving trees. There was also a small enclosed East Garden, designed by Beatrix, which Bush-Brown appreciated most of all: "The treatment is so simple that it hardly seems to have been designed at all and yet it forms a most harmonious and happy adjunct to the house. A lead-roofed shelter occupies the outer side and two arched doors lead to the service area and greenhouse. The central panel of turf is bordered by a brick path, climbing roses have been trained against the wall, and lilies have been planted at the base."[12]

The work at Harston was done mostly during 1910, and the disciplined spaces of the South and East Gardens, combined with Dr. Markoe's town garden, concentrated Beatrix's mind on this scale. Her undoubted success, and her persistent enthusiasm for trying all aspects of her profession made her decide to enter the Architectural League's competition for "An Ideal Suburban Place."[13] By this time her initial broad-minded approach to her work had been somewhat tempered by experience. The people she was most likely to meet tended to have, or want, large country gardens, and it was difficult to break into social spheres that were not her own. The flood of planned housing and industrial developments that were really geometrical puzzles were retained by their own architects and engineers. Parks, it seemed, despite her early efforts at putting forward her ideas, remained the jobs for parks men in the most prestigious offices, almost invariably the Olmsted office.[14] She did get a toehold on the famous Roland Park, Baltimore. She did a lovely, simple design for the Women's Club garden but would no doubt have greatly enjoyed more of this exciting project.

Thus, determined to keep trying to widen her field, and to break out of any even half-set mold, she designed her ideal suburban place. The lack of privacy in the burgeoning suburbs, much grumbled about in articles and exploited in advertisements of the day, motivated the competition. The

Roland Park, Baltimore: the Roland Park Women's Club, design for the garden by Beatrix Jones, April 28, 1905. (Scale: 1 in. = 10 ft.) A variation on the "suburban garden" theme using an irregular site; the club building has a large lawn with a pergola at the far end, small flower beds to the site and, in the corner of the plan, a curved arbor seat, which is outside the garden, for the benefit of passersby.

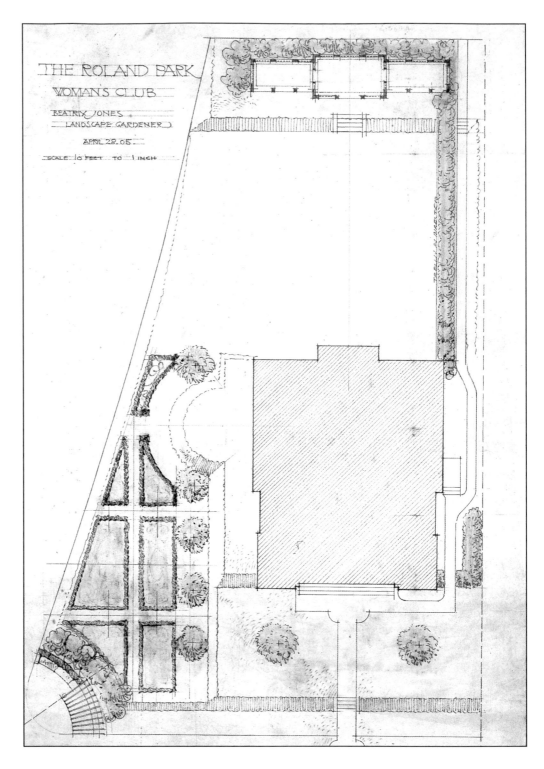

THE ROLAND PARK
WOMAN'S CLUB

BEATRIX JONES
LANDSCAPE GARDENER

APRIL 28.05

SCALE 10 FEET TO 1 INCH

FACING PAGE: *Watercolored competition design for a suburban garden by Beatrix Jones, 1910.*
TOP: *Perspective of the house and garden.*
BOTTOM LEFT: *A detail of the pergola.*
BOTTOM RIGHT: *A detail of a classical garden doorway.*

hardworking commuter needed a private garden for his weekends, and his wife and children needed somewhere to sit and sew or play all week long, somewhere to spend time in the fresh air and sunshine. This was the motive for the suburban garden in America, rather than any love of growing flowers or vegetables (as in England).

Beatrix's design was for a classic plot 125 feet in depth, with a straight frontage of 75 feet; the house is set back 20 feet, with a straight path leading to the front door, and there are clumps of lilacs, quince, and philadelphus on either side, with small lawns. The whole lot is fenced with a simple wooden paling. The back lot is largely lawn with a gravel path around it, then grass borders and the all-important hedge, of spruce, hemlock, arborvitae, beech, thorn, privet, or chaenomeles (*Pyrus japonica* to Beatrix). On one boundary was a pergola or arbor, a sitting place for the heat of the day, covered with vines, wisteria, roses, clematis, or honeysuckles. The borders on the lawn could be for annuals—heliotrope, verbena, scarlet salvias, or for the smaller perennials "of our Grandmothers' gardens," columbines, day lilies, moss pinks, campanulas, and Japanese anemones.

This ideal garden of exquisite restraint makes an interesting comparison with Gertrude Jekyll's plan for Millmead, designed some six years previously, which was also her effort, with Edwin Lutyens, to show that good design could come in fairly small parcels. Millmead's garden was on an old, longer and thinner plot (a common shape in England), but the idea of enclosure, with a sheltering pergola or summerhouse on one side, was very similar. But Miss Jekyll would not let her small gardener off with anything less than a garden full of flowers. The presentation of Beatrix's ideal suburban place was of a far more sympathetic professional standard.[15]

An antidote to this rather cerebral designing of restricted spaces, Beatrix's own hands-on gardening at Reef Point was tussling with planting around the rocks. Her passion for this ran deep, because of her childhood fascination with the island plants, and designing a tasteful rock garden, undoubtedly one of the most difficult of all garden tasks, was always to be one of her strengths. She put her passion and experience into a lecture given to her fellow practitioners of the ASLA. Her draft notes reveal her self-deprecating humor, in a dark vein, which was her defense in a daunting situation, addressing an overwhelmingly male audience who would regard themselves as experts, on a highly technical subject. "I shall probably make many statements this evening with which you may disagree, but from my first I do not believe there will be a dissenting voice—the making of a rock garden is probably the hardest problem which can be put before us."[16] She made them laugh with visions of "the Prophet's valley of dry bones," heaps of stones which looked "as if they had been hurled from the tail of a dump cart" or stones put into a bank "like raisins in a pudding." Then, seriously, she tackled the metaphysics—that the unseen, underground construction was just as important as the seen surfaces, and that the goal was the simulation of nature with "integrity of geological expression."

For the rock gardener every mountain walk becomes a thrilling expedition "as we are perpetually trying to see how the hill streams slide over the rocks, and just how nature has disposed the stones which make the little waterfall . . . and where the iris draws the line at being perpetually soaked."[17] She describes herself as a "barbarian" in digging up wild plants, only to discover that her "clumsiness had ripped apart the network of roots stretched flat between the stones like a growth of filmy sponge." Finally, she allowed herself a galaxy of plants that could be used.[18]

She finished: "Anyone who is infested with the bacillus of rock gardening may as well be given up at once as the disease will only grow worse instead of better as time goes on. Each year the victim will try to grow more capricious things, and if he succeeds in raising a new primula or establishing a plant, which according to his friends is impossible to grow, he will be as overjoyed as if he had really accomplished a great work."[19]

Beatrix's rock gardening lecture not only presages exquisite work to come at Eolia and in the wild garden at Dumbarton Oaks, showing how she practiced what she preached, it also refutes any impression that this tall, elegant, superbly and expensively dressed lady was anything less than a modest, hardworking and humorous being. These qualities, plus perhaps her patience and forbearance, were further highlighted by an experience in London in July 1910. She had been invited to speak at a Horticultural Congress organized by Frances Wolseley, who had undoubtedly heard Beatrix's name and reputation from Henry James.[20] She was to share the platform with the architect Harry Inigo Triggs, whose monumental *Formal Gardens in England and Scotland* and *Garden Design in Italy* were on her shelves at home. Triggs was speaking about design, but Beatrix stood up to hear herself being introduced to talk about American market gardening! She made a brave stab at describing how industrious Germans and Italians ran market gardens in the eastern states and how New York and other cities relied upon the South for winter vegetables. With an apologetic "at a pinch I can tell a cabbage from a beet, and no one can claim that landscape gardening is useful,"[21] she talked at greater ease on the flowering shrubs that grew so well at home, and ended with a general note about the opportunities in her profession.

The embarrassing mistake in the congress organization, which Beatrix gallantly overcame (the *Times* report shows nothing amiss), reveals that though she was careful to learn so much about English gardening, English gardening people—her hosts—had not taken the trouble to find out about her and her work. This irony was aggravated the following year, when for Christmas (1911) Professor Sargent gave her Wilhelm Miller's *What England Can Teach Us About Gardening*.[22] Beatrix must have winced when she opened this, but soon realized that its unwritten subtitle was "and what we can do better ourselves." It was an important book—it contained a great deal of what she already knew—but for the spirited Miss Beatrix it proved another spur to her finding her native voice.

In the meantime fate was conspiring to introduce her to a new field of operations which she had entirely overlooked.

It was the Roosevelt connection that brought another of her "fortunate meetings," this one with Mrs. Moses Taylor Pyne, whose husband was chairman of the Princeton Trustees' Building Committee. The philosopher and Stuart Professor of Logic, John Grier Hibben, had become president of Princeton in May 1912, and with money from the will of Isaac Wyman, the building of the Graduate College, the pet scheme of Dean Andrew Fleming West, was going ahead. West was also an old friend of Charles Sargent, who had sent two young lebanon cedars grown at the Arnold Arboretum for the new college grounds. Beatrix was asked to advise on the college landscape.

She paid her first visit in late May 1912, when Ralph Adams Cram's Gothic buildings were taking shape. On June 27, 1912, she informed the trustees of her terms: "My charges are fifty dollars a day and my travelling expenses. Work done in the office is paid for at the same rate; thus a complicated plan might require four or five days to complete and a rough sketch half a day; office expenses such as telegrams etc., and writing of specifications is charged to the client at the same rate at which I pay for it; no percentage of any kind is charged on anything."[23]

This having been approved, she got on with the real job. The crucial thing was that Cram's very lovely collegiate Gothic building, dominated by the Cleveland Tower, was sited away from the main campus, on rising land west of Alexander Street and the dinky station, overlooking Springdale golf course. Beatrix, quite naturally and professionally, could not confine her ideas to the Graduate College, but felt the linkage between campus and college was an important idea for her attention. She could see no point in stopping her planting, imposing false boundaries, when there was no need; she felt the whole experience of walking from the heart of the campus, out across Alexander Street and up the hill to the Graduate College, should be one harmonious "landscape." But, one can see how in certain Princeton gentlemen's eyes she was overstepping herself immediately, by taking this unbounded-landscape point of view. When her report was submitted, there must have been some eyebrows raised. She wanted the golf clubhouse moved (this was done), she wanted only essential roads and paths for the moment, paths especially could come later when "desire lines" had become apparent. Her main and service approaches to the Graduate College curve gracefully up the slope, with an English landscape feel, and she planted trees and shrubs—red oaks, sugar maples, buttonwood (*Platanus occidentalis*), sweet gum, tulip trees, and basswood (*Tilia americana*) with masses of native dogwood (*Cornus florida*) beside road and paths. She felt that harmonious streams of native trees (mostly deciduous) and shrubs would mark the transition from campus to Graduate College across the open landscape and rolling golf course green. At the Graduate College she trod warily, flattering Cram's buildings with modest wall plantings, various ivies, and lots of broad-leaved *Euonymous radicans* of interest through the winter when graduates were in residence. She designed an entrance court for the college, with a low stone wall that extended along the south front, making a broad terrace, from which Cleveland Tower rose. This final stroke of "interference" was too much for the "homespun feudalist"[24] from Boston, Ralph Adams Cram, who finally burst out: "I am very strongly of the opinion that the landscape treatment around a given building should be determined by the architect thereof. . . . no landscape gardener, however competent, can be expected to see the thing as he sees it . . ." especially when ". . . the landscape gardener enters the premises late in the game and can hardly do more than acquire superficial impressions." He allowed that Beatrix could prepare the soil, select trees and shrubs and arrange their planting, but in the case of *his* Graduate College he could not "approve all the details of Miss Jones's scheme." He didn't like her elegantly curving roads ("for my part I prefer straight runs"), nor her planting that accompanied their courses ("she has left no vistas through"). Finally, Cram did not appreciate Beatrix's careful channeling of the approach to the Graduate College, by planting evergreens so that little was seen of the building until one "arrived" in the forecourt. In his eyes she was "masking" the east face of the buildings, which he regarded as the most important "prospect."[25] Beatrix stood up to Cram's complaints, and President Hibben and Moses Taylor Pyne had to keep the peace between them.[26] (Beatrix was appointed the university's supervising landscape architect in 1914.)

Today, though, one's first impression of Princeton owes a great deal to her earliest work there during 1912 and 1913. On arrival at the dinky station, freshman and stranger alike find the broad stone paving gently indicating the path through to Blair Arch and the heart of the campus. Across Alexander Street, the line of the trees leads just as helpfully to the stone-paved footpath through pines and maples, dappled sun and shade, which follows the rim of the golf course, offering frequent glimpses of the Cleveland Tower and finally depositing the walker in the entrance court of the Graduate College. As one takes this walk, the landscape gives just that feeling of confidence that one is not alone, that some friendly intelligence knew exactly what such passing strangers would need, and worked it out long ago. Much of the Princeton campus is, in this remarkable way, still home to Beatrix's ghost.

On one of her visits to Princeton, probably in the spring of 1913, she went to dinner with President Hibben and found a visiting professor of history from Yale among her fellow guests. The setting was all that could be desired— the romantic Italianate Prospect House with its lovely garden—and the professor in question was very distinguished—Max Farrand, who was at the time working on his great classic, *The Framing of the Constitution*.[27] He was tall, as tall as Beatrix, broad-shouldered, and rather tweedy (so was she in winter), with a kind, open, and humorous face beneath a domed and already balding pate. He was a bachelor and forty-four years old. He was passionate about his hobbies, golf and freshwater fishing, and had almost certainly ventured to the northern borders of Maine for the Sainte-Marguerite River salmon. In Max

Farrand, Beatrix had found her "Chief," as she called him after their marriage, her Cockyolly Bird,[28] her ideal partner, a partner of brains, distinction, and kindness, with a passion for the outdoor life to equal her own.

Only one story remains from the time of their courtship that I have been able to find. The late Margaret Farrand Thorp, wife of Professor Willard Thorp of Princeton, long remembered her mother, Mrs. Livingston Farrand[29] and Max's sister-in-law, telling how she heard of the rumored romance and was determined to get a look at Beatrix without being seen herself. On a visit to Princeton, she specially went out to where "The Bush Woman" was working and watched her directing the workmen. Having seen enough, Mrs. Farrand was convinced: "If *that* lady really wants Max, she'll get him!"[30] was her verdict.

J. P. Morgan, Princeton, Max Farrand—but 1913 had not finished with Beatrix yet! She had become fairly familiar with the White House during President Roosevelt's administration, but that was now over. Roosevelt's presidency saw the dramatic, if somewhat hectic, refurbishment by McKim, Mead & White of 1902–1903, with Charles McKim's much praised balancing east and west wings, which had extended the idea that Benjamin Latrobe had brought in for President Jefferson one hundred years before. These east and west wings had created garden spaces. Edith Carow Roosevelt was a capable gardener, and though she quite possibly discussed these new gardens with Beatrix—for both Roosevelts were very proud of her profession—there is no record of a formal "job." The work at the White House was very firmly under the control of the U.S. Army *engineers,* who passed for *gardeners* in government parlance, but Ellen Axson Wilson (who moved in with her beloved Woodrow in March 1913) was a lady of courage, and asked for changes to the east and west gardens. They arrived in the form of a "design" from Colonel Spencer Colby, a layout of lozenges—"warts of flowers" as Beatrix would have dubbed them—for the East Colonial Garden, as it was now to be called. She summoned Beatrix, who responded with a lovely watercolor perspective of a simple, classical design. The East Garden was to have a central rectangular pool, 10 feet by 22 feet, edged with ivy, with four columnar Irish yews set back from the pool's corners, in line with four corner L-shaped beds edged with box and filled with flowers. Ellen Wilson was delighted and the proposal was accepted. Beatrix went home from Washington happily to work up the detailed design and prepare for her wedding in the winter of 1913.

Chapter 8

❧❧❧

BEATRIX AND THE SON
OF THE MORNING

*B*eatrix's letter to Henry James telling of her engagement brought a jubilant reply from Lamb House, Rye, dated October 24, 1913:

My dear brave Trix,

> This is a grand showing, & I am greatly touched at seeing the curtain so generously drawn for me by your fair hand. I congratulate you without reserve . . . for I think a married lady is in a much better situation even than the most free-ranging single. . . .
>
> It's jolly that you have so big & beautiful an asset as your delightful profession to contribute to the concern, & I seem to see that the union of your so perfectly individual & sovereign states will make for a tremendous strength & a most striking frontier. . . . Therefore . . . in the absence of any positive presumption that Mr Farrand will beat or otherwise mis-use you, kindly assure him, please, of my great consideration and confidence. He sounds most interesting . . . and I rejoice that you are not marrying into the banal bloated business world. I regard him thus, on your showing, as much more a son of the morning than the New York *parle* in general affects my imagination as being.[1]

He rolls on in a Masterlike way, expressing concern for Mary Cadwalader Jones's losing her companion, but equal confidence in Mary's unselfish love and his own ability to comfort her . . . "Besides, at the worst, Mummy can come over here & live with *me* as that strikes me indeed as a very natural

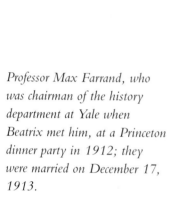

Professor Max Farrand, who
was chairman of the history
department at Yale when
Beatrix met him, at a Princeton
dinner party in 1912; they
were married on December 17,
1913.

arrangement" (which he was probably equally confident Mary would not pursue!). He continues to Beatrix ". . . so, strike out without fear & fulfill your brilliant destiny." Perhaps he felt this necessary because of Beatrix's immediate experiences. Her own parents' divorce, which she had learned to live with, had recently reverberated through the long agony of Edith's divorce from Teddy Wharton, which had finally taken place in April 1913. It was therefore very important to Beatrix that the one person who knew all these painful family details, and (unlike the chilly John Lambert Cadwalader) was unafraid of facing them, should so warmly endorse her own feelings. The Master concludes: "In short my dear Trix be assured of my thorough belief & and backing, & that I am more than ever affectionately yours Henry James."[2]

Beatrix and Max were married in Beatrix's home, at noon on December 17, 1913. Beatrix was given away by John Lambert Cadwalader and the marriage ceremony was performed by the Reverend Philip Rhinelander, bishop of Penn, assisted by the Reverend Charles Lewis Slattery, rector of Grace Church. The *Bar Harbor Record*[3] reported this good news from New York in its Christmas Eve edition, describing the quiet elegant ceremony with a few friends and relatives in the drawing room of 21 East Eleventh Street.

So, who were they, the friends and family, who found it their place to be there, the moment Beatrix passed into her second life? Her usually indomitable mother was in bed upstairs and indisposed. Max Farrand's mother was similarly absent. But Beatrix found herself with a new, warm, and affectionate family including Max's brothers Livingston and Wilson and their wives. As to her own family, besides Mr. Cadwalader and the Reverend Mr. Rhinelander there were some Newbolds, and most importantly, her aunt Edith. Edith brought with her news from Paris, that Beatrix's father, Freddy, had apparently suffered a stroke, at age sixty-seven, though Edith had not felt inclined to visit him.[4] Edith's presence—she made the crossing on the *France* especially and installed herself at the Ritz-Carlton—revealed the stoutness of her affections and best of her character.[5] On her return to 53 rue de Varenne in early January, Edith wrote immediately to Beatrix, with only a slight twinge of bitterness and a great deal of affection—"It is nice to know that somewhere in the world there is a bit of real happiness."[6]

The Farrands, as they were almost immediately dubbed—Theodore Roosevelt immediately sent his love to Mary for "the *very* nice Farrands"—or "MaxTrix," as they soon became to intimates—immediately set about organizing their lives. They set up home in New Haven, at 285 Prospect Street, the leafy, hilly road that winds up to the Divinity Schools. Beatrix made an office there, and kept a foothold at 21 East Eleventh Street, though this now became the framework of Mary Cadwalader's life on her own. Mary adapted herself particularly well to what she saw as a newfound freedom; she no longer had to keep a home for the hardworking, hard-traveling Beatrix, and she slipped into a routine of long annual trips to Europe to stay with Edith and other friends, and to be with Henry James in his last years. Mary continued to act as a kind of New York agent for Edith, reading and delivering her manuscripts to publishers and dealing with routine inquiries, a general and loving amanuensis across the ocean.

John Lambert Cadwalader died in March 1914, not long after Beatrix's wedding: he left her $20,000, which was one of his major bequests. The rest went to his already rich brother Richard, and other Cadwaladers, and to the New York Public Library and Trenton Public Library, for both of which he had worked hard during his life. The best of his collection of porcelain, bronzes, and furniture went to the Metropolitan Museum of Art. John Lambert Cadwalader's will was a final testimony to his distinguished but rather stoical existence. He had served Mary and Beatrix well, in "discreet and decent dignity" was Henry James's way of seeing his care of them, but his death undoubtedly freed both of them, and it is unlikely that his rather heavy, demanding presence was much missed. In Beatrix's life, his exit was perfectly timed.[7]

The Farrands had a working honeymoon, settling in quickly to their new life. Right from the start, Beatrix's priority was to be with her husband, especially when university society, or his many other friends, associations, and committees, demanded her presence as his partner. The journeying and juggling that this demanded was to take a lot of her energy, and though there is every evidence that Professor Farrand was equally, or almost equally, forgiving and flexible, there is no doubt that it was Beatrix's life that had to be manipulated, and her skill in this became considerable. Her bias was to be with Max in New Haven during term time as much as she could; if he traveled she almost always went with him, but when he was busy teaching it was she who made exhausting trips to New York, Washington, Princeton, or wherever, packing in as many appointments as possible in a day or two, in order to get back to New Haven. Sanity, even paradise, was regained when they went off to Reef Point, sometimes for a spring break, but always from mid-June until late September during the long vacation. Max loved Reef Point instantly. He played golf to his heart's content and Beatrix sometimes joined him. He learned to garden; the making of Reef Point's garden became their joint concern from the outset. She accompanied him north, to the Sainte-Marguerite River Fishing Club over Canadian borders in Quebec, where she took up fishing, and sometimes she worked or gardened at home while he had a fishing expedition of his own. Knowing themselves very well, they slipped efficiently—though not without mutual effort—into a life together.

Beatrix's marriage did not stop her working—she was writing letters and sending out plans nine days later, on December 27, 1913. She now had an excellent assistant, a qualified landscape gardener, Anne Baker, who worked from her own home in New York, 36 West Eleventh Street, but who eventually opened a New York office at 124 East Fortieth Street for Beatrix's work. And what glamorous work it turned out to be—the Morgan Library, the White House, the New York Botanical Garden, and a string of commissions from fashionable architects Thomas Hastings and William Adams Delano.

Immediately after her marriage, in January 1914, Beatrix began to work for Willard and Dorothy Straight at their home in Old Westbury, Long Island. They both knew Beatrix already and had many friends in common, but there was a brilliant aptness to the timing of this commission: though Dorothy was fifteen years younger than Beatrix (and had one small son, Whitney, and another child on the way, Beatrice, born in August 1914), they were both very happily married and shared a deep conviction that it was vital to live in harmony with one's natural surroundings, and that making a garden was a vivid expression of this harmony. For the first time, perhaps, Beatrix had found a client with beliefs to match her own. It wasn't a question of how large would be the commission, or how prestigious, or how much expensive stonework could be installed—it was the fact that she could supply the design skills to serve a philosophy that she shared, and so build a relationship through building a garden. Willard and Dorothy Straight knew what they wanted and would challenge her constantly in order to achieve their dreams; they were perfect clients.

The Straights had settled back in New York at the end of their diplomatic posting in Peking in the summer of 1912. Willard Straight had gone to work for J. P. Morgan & Company, for which he was particularly unsuited; he had studied architecture, "he was an artist, a knight errant and a bohemian in the best sense of the word"[8] was how Herbert Croly described him, and he soon

gave up banking. He busied himself by financing *The New Republic* (and founding the magazine *Asia*), by setting up the Straight Improvement Company to develop the sandspits of Long Beach on the Long Island south shore, and by seeing to their own houses. The Straights' Manhattan house, 1130 Fifth Avenue at East Ninety-fourth Street, was built by Delano & Aldrich between 1913 and 1915, and their country home was Elmhurst on Wheatley Hills Road in Old Westbury, a rambling, shingle-style house that had been a present from Dorothy's father, William C. Whitney.[9]

It was at Elmhurst that Willard and Dorothy decided to make a garden with traditional Chinese features. Beatrix did not know much about Chinese gardens at this time, apart from what she could find in books, so there was a learning curve for both designer and clients, learning from each other. One of the earliest surviving drawings, dated January 4, 1914, is a pencil sketch and elevation for a Chinese trellis pavilion with "not quite satisfied" penciled on it. They discussed and revised the pavilions, or playhouses, during the spring, and in the summer of 1914 Beatrix painted a watercolor perspective of what she thought they wanted—an enclosed flower garden approached by a path from the center of Elmhurst's garden facade (which already possessed a hedged lawn terrace enclosure). The garden was entered by ornamental gates and guarded by Chinese stone dogs. Beatrix's photographs of the completed garden show it to be on a much more intimate scale than her perspective implies,

The residence of Willard D. Straight, Elmhurst, Wheatley Hills, Old Westbury, Long Island, c. 1912: the garden front of the large shingle-style house where Beatrix designed a large walled "Chinese" garden. The workmen can be seen starting the path to the walled garden, which led down the steps from the lawn enclosure.

with two seasons of flowering—spring daffodils, narcissus, and pansies, with high-summer poppies, larkspur, foxgloves, sweet william, candytuft, ageratum, anchusa, and phlox in the long borders. Her pictures also show beds of columbine, peonies, lupins, delphiniums, meadowsweet, and heuchera around box circles. Beyond the flower garden were two trellis pavilions, with tip-tilted Chinese-style roofs, round "moon" doorways, ornamental bargeboards of carved and painted flowers, and musical bells. Beatrix's photos show both pavilions wreathed in wisteria. This garden sequence—the walled flower garden, pavilions, and swimming pool garden—was completed fairly quickly, perhaps by 1916, though Beatrix's photographs are not dated.

Beatrix had high hopes that her plans for the East and West gardens of the White House would be carried out, but tragedy struck early in 1914 when President Wilson's wife became seriously ill; she died in August. The president was bereft, and the garden was forgotten until it was revived in early 1916 by the second Mrs. Wilson, Edith Bolling Galt. Beatrix was summoned again and presented her planting plans, which were duly approved and most likely carried out. But the White House formal gardens have probably been worked over more times than any other plot of ground in America, and Beatrix's ideas have long since been changed.[10]

Another of her prestigious commissions has had a happier fate. In late 1915 the director of the New York Botanical Garden, Nathaniel Lord Britton, asked her to design a rose garden. This garden was an additional luxury to be added to the riches of the already popular public garden in the Bronx. Dr. Britton, inspired by a visit to Kew on his honeymoon with his wife, Elizabeth Gertrude Knight Britton, a noted specialist in mosses, had campaigned vigorously for his dream gardens, which were started in 1895. New Yorkers were quick to appreciate his efforts and within ten years he had an ever-increasing success on his hands. The papers gleefully reported that the dwellers of Manhattan's East Side tenements spent summer weekends sleeping out among the hemlocks and cherry groves along the Bronx riverbanks; but the daylight attractions were also popular, including the enormous glasshouse with winter gardens and palm court,[11] the vast lawns and flower beds, the liriodendron avenue, the lakes, and over forty acres of carefully preserved natural forest in the heart of the city.

Beatrix's design for the rose garden was spectacular. The site was roughly triangular, which dictated the geometry of the paths and beds, and its size, over two acres, allowed ninety rectangular beds, each for a different variety of rose. These were within a perimeter path, which was also flanked by long beds. The whole was enclosed—for tradition and to prevent New Yorkers from "acquiring" the roses—by lattice fencing, home to climbers and ramblers. The centerpiece was a pretty lattice arbor, with a domed roof, also covered in roses. Beatrix did a lot of work on her drawings during 1916, but the garden was not built to her plans. A scaled-down version of the idea was built in 1918, but Beatrix had nothing to do with it.

Plans for Crosswicks, the Clarence B. Newbold estate in Jenkintown, Pennsylvania, 1903: Beatrix's presentation drawing of gate and wall treatments with a half plan of paving to the exedra.

A botanical study by Mary Robeson Sargent. She collected these into albums, which she presented to her husband.

Beatrix designed the East Colonial Garden of the White House for Mrs. Woodrow Wilson, Washington, D.C., 1913.

Elmhurst: watercolored design for the walled flower garden, "Chinese"-style play pavilions, and the swimming pool designed and built before the First World War. After Willard Straight's death in 1918, and Dorothy's subsequent marriage to Leonard Elmhirst, the name of the house was changed to Apple Green and the garden was maintained under Beatrix's instructions until the late 1940s. Though the area has been built up, part of the garden remains.

Harston, Chestnut Hill,
Pennsylvania: a Garden Club
of America archive picture of
the sunken garden.

BELOW: *Wingwood House,*
Eden Street, Bar Harbor,
Maine: garden design for
Mrs. Edward T. Stotesbury.

Great Head, Ocean Drive, Bar Harbor, Maine: the Satterlee ravine garden for which the planting plans are included in chapter 9.

The Haven, Northeast Harbor, Maine: the garden made by Beatrix for her longtime patrons and friends, the Millikens.

Miss Mildred McCormick's home, The Farm House, Highbrook Road, Bar Harbor, Maine: another of the old hand-colored pictures showing the charm of Beatrix's planting of "cottage-garden" borders.

The Eyrie, Seal Harbor, Maine: the Spirit Path, a natural woodland walk made especially to hold John D. Rockefeller Jr.'s collection of Korean tomb figures.

ABOVE: *The Eyrie, Seal Harbor, Maine: the flower garden as it is today.*

RIGHT: *The Eyrie: a Garden Club of America archive photograph of the flower garden in the 1940s.*

FACING PAGE: *The Eyrie: the "bottle" gate in the wall leading from the woodland into the flower garden.*

The Eyrie: the principal entrance into the flower garden.

The Eyrie: the flower garden and pink-washed wall.

The Eyrie: the garden wall showing the Moon Gate.

Rock Creek Park, Washington, D.C.: The natural woodland that Beatrix Farrand originally designed for Dumbarton Oaks is now part of the park. The stone bridge design was inspired by a similar bridge she saw in the English Lake District in 1895 (illustrated on page 55), and the details of the watercourse design were adapted from Mediterranean gardens she had seen on her travels.

The tribute to Beatrix Farrand's friendship that Mrs. Robert Woods Bliss put in the garden at Dumbarton Oaks.

Dumbarton Oaks: the Green Garden terrace.

FACING PAGE: *Dumbarton Oaks, Washington, D.C.: the ogee-roofed pavilion inspired by those Beatrix saw at Traquair in Scotland.*

*Dumbarton Oaks: four
variations on the Wisteria
Pergola, inspired by the French
architect Jacques du Cerceau,
but also similar to Harold
Peto's work at Easton Lodge,
which Beatrix visited on her
English journeys (and illustrated on page 85).*

ABOVE: *Dumbarton Oaks: the Box Terrace.*

RIGHT: *Dumbarton Oaks: entrance facade.*

FACING PAGE: *Dumbarton Oaks: the Swimming Pool Terrace.*

Dumbarton Oaks: the Beech Terrace.

RIGHT: *The varied designs for the seats are among the most distinctive features of Dumbarton Oaks.*

Dumbarton Oaks: the terraces above the Lover's Lane Pool.

LEFT: *Dumbarton Oaks: the Path End marks the boundary of the garden that was given to Harvard University in 1940.*

OPPOSITE PAGE: *Dumbarton Oaks: the Box Walk leading to the Ellipse.*

BELOW: *Dumbarton Oaks: the North Vista.*

Dumbarton Oaks:
the Perennial Border.

Dumbarton Oaks: the Lover's
Lane Pool Terraces.

That, however, is not the end of the story. The rose garden was grassed over in 1969 and forgotten. Nearly twenty years later, Beth Straus, chairman of the Botanical Garden's Horticultural Committee, happened to see Beatrix's drawings exhibited and was so enchanted with them that she campaigned for the garden's re-creation. The funds, around a million dollars, were provided by David Rockefeller and the original plans were brought to the detailed construction stage, with careful adherence to Beatrix's original sketches, by the architect Robert E. Meadows. The lattice fencing, rose supports, and the focal arbor have all been constructed in galvanized steel and painted dark blue and the paths have been made with bluestone chippings. This triumphant re-creation of Beatrix's design now flowers as the Peggy Rockefeller Rose Garden with over 2,700 roses in over two hundred varieties.[12] Many of the varieties are those Beatrix would have included in her original scheme, had it got that far; the old hybrid perpetuals she remembered from her childhood, silvery-pink "Mrs. John Laing" and the large, crumpled and scented rich pink flowers of "Paul Neyron." There are those particular favorites of the earliest years of the twentieth century, roses repeatedly planted by Gertrude Jekyll and by Beatrix, following the English example—the incomparable white rugosa "Blanc Double de Coubert," the Bourbons, the madder-crimson "Mme. Isaac Pereire" and "Souvenir de la Malmaison," and species *Rosa moyesii, Rosa eglanteria* (sweetbriar) and *Rosa chinensis* "Viridiflora," known as the "Green Rose" and very like Miss Jekyll's favorite of all, the Old Blush China rose.

New York Botanical Garden: preliminary sketches for details of the proposed rose garden in Bronx Park, from the office of Beatrix Farrand, 1915.

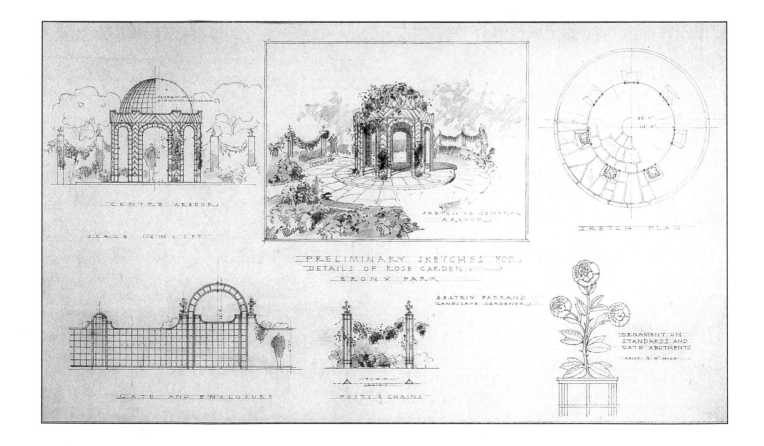

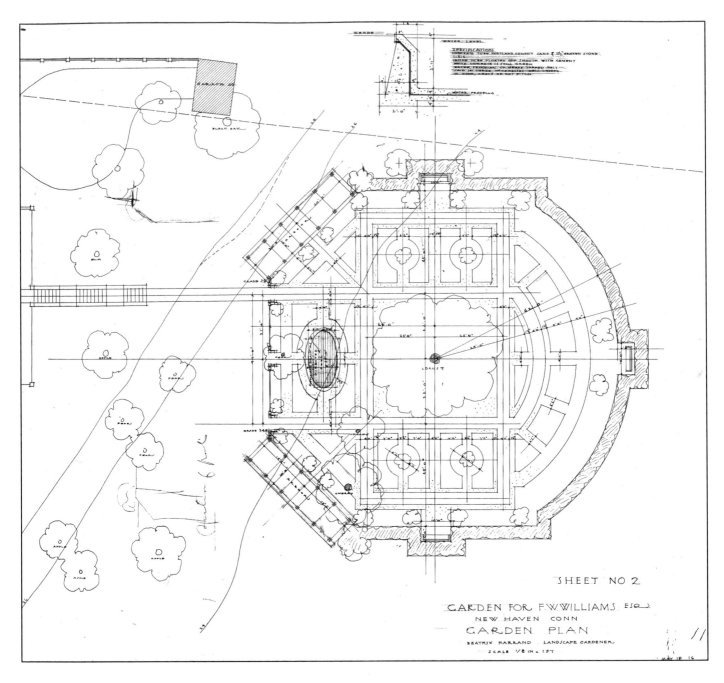

Among the climbers that now adorn the new blue lattice are several of Beatrix's favorites—"Gardenia," the yellow "Lawrence Johnstone," which she planted at Reef Point in memory of Hidcote Manor Garden, and the Bourbon of enchanting fragrance and name, the pink "Zephirine Drouhin."

Work at Princeton continued through the early years of Beatrix's marriage; her appointment as the university's supervising landscape architect put her on par with Ralph Adams Cram, and though he may have muttered disapprovals she carried on with her clear vision for giving the campus landscape "a continuity and unity of purpose."[13] Her garden for Wyman House, the residence of the Graduate College's dean, has been celebrated as one of the garden triumphs of Princeton. This garden is sheltered by walls and trees and has

Professor F. W. Williams's home on Whitney Avenue, New Haven, Connecticut: a design of the garden based upon the existence of a large honey locust tree. The area has been carefully leveled, to allow for flower beds away from the tree, in a hedged enclosure, with the idea of the "butterfly" plan introduced with the angled arbors. (Scale: ⅛ in. = 1 ft.)

the feel of a true cloistered garth; there is a lime walk, there are spring flowers, lawns for summer lounging and in autumn "tufts of yellow and Princeton orange chrysanthemums" to cheer the football visitors.[14]

Her regular visits to Princeton, averaging six a year, became part of the pattern of her life. She submitted her proposals for the whole campus soon after her marriage, and steadily put them into practice. She instituted a nursery on campus where plants could be propagated and grown to suitable size for planting out. She studied very carefully the way the campus was used, where people walked, where they needed to walk dry-shod—and the result is a beautifully convenient system of stone-flagged paths that leads one around the campus. The trees she recommended, and steadily planted through the years, sugar maples, horse chestnuts, catalpas, sweet gum, liriodendron, oaks, beeches, lindens, sassafras, and magnolias, still give the campus its elegance and serenity.

While she was working at Princeton, she was of course becoming well known in New Haven. Dinner table conversations and Max's friends brought her more jobs. For Professor Williams on Whitney Avenue she designed an elegant semicircular garden around an existing, much worshiped locust tree— she had not been able to persuade the professor to accept a "butterfly plan" garden—laid out in response to the projecting angles of the house. A further disappointment awaited her with her work on the Wallace Witt Williamson Hospital, New Haven's Tubercular Hospital on Campbell Avenue. The building of these special hospitals was a priority on both sides of the Atlantic, because of the rapid spread of tuberculosis. Beatrix had seen King Edward VII's sanatorium at Midhurst in Sussex: set high on the downs, with long wings of green-shuttered rooms with courts and sunny terraces that offered the patients every possible chance of being out-of-doors. The gardens were a charity effort, for the king, by Gertrude Jekyll, who planned them, and Frances Wolseley's Glynde School of Ladies learning to become professional gardeners, who did all the work. Miss Jekyll's courts of scented plants, the rosemary gardens, rock walls sprouting pinks, lavenders, choisya, and iris, and a liberal sprinkling of the most scented roses, especially the damask cream-flowered "Madame Plantier," was a wonderful therapeutic effort; Beatrix hoped she would be able to do a similarly satisfying job. But no; she did take a look at the shrubs up the hospital's drive, but the bulk of her involvement was with endless tracings and retracings of the design for the iron gates and railings, with the initials "WWW" enshrined in iron, and made by the faithful Anchor Post Iron Works, the company she used for so much of her garden ornament and fencing. She must have been very disappointed that her work took her no nearer to helping the hospital's patients.

It was Max Farrand who introduced her to the rich and ultraphilanthropic Edward S. Harkness, the son of Rockefeller's silent partner in Standard Oil. Harkness senior had died when his son was only fourteen; Harkness junior graduated from Yale in 1897 and, it seems, spent the rest of his life giving his money away. He gave a great deal to Yale, which would have a bear-

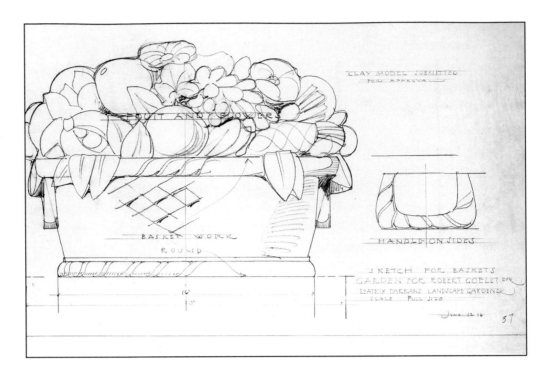

Glenmere: design drawn full size for a basket of flowers and fruit to be modeled in clay and cast for ornaments in the walled garden, June 12, 1916.

BELOW: *Glenmere, Robert Goelet's home, Goshen, New York, 1916: a detailed design of walls enclosing formal flower beds, a pergola, and a pool.*

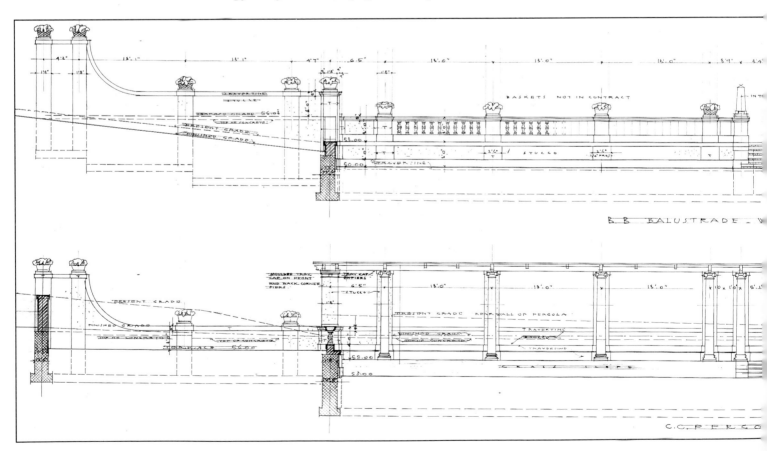

ing on Beatrix's career when she started to work for the university in the 1920s. For the moment, and the moment is late 1918, it was clearly her lyrical descriptions of drifts of flowers in soft and gentle colors that made the Harknesses think they needed her to look at their favorite garden of the several that they owned, at Eolia on Goshen Point just west of New London, Connecticut. This house of the winds has a most splendid site on its green promontory overlooking Long Island Sound. (It can still be appreciated as the estate is now a country park and much of the garden remains.) The house was built in the early 1900s by the architects Lord, Hull & Hewlett, with James Gamble Rogers brought in to design the gardens. He brought about a triumph of Beaux Arts balance and harmony, creating garden spaces on each side of the house, leaving the seaward view open. His formal West Garden with its romantic Italianate loggia springing from the house is—as can still be appreciated—especially elegant and satisfying. But, of course, the architect, Rogers, knew little about plants, so the Boston firm of Brett & Hall[15] designed the planting and put lawn tennis courts on the east side of the house and a large semicircular enclosure on the seafront, hedged with Japanese barberry and *Spirea vanhouttei* with large clumps of hydrangeas at the sides. Beyond the hedge they made an eleven-hole golf course on the sloping links to the sea. Brett & Hall's planting for the West Garden was rather more like a military set piece than anything inclined to the natural; the beds were to be filled with ranks of coreopsis, foxgloves, delphini-

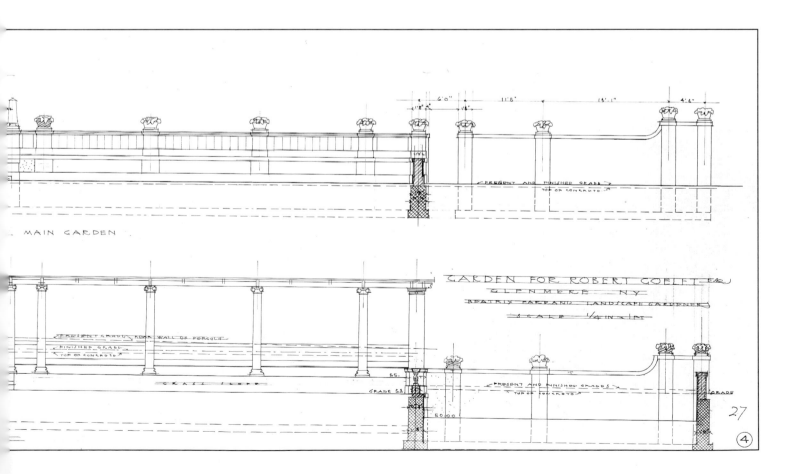

ums, tall campanulas, and tall veronicas in repetitive patterns. It is a well-known weakness in landscape gardeners to boast of outshining their predecessors on the site, but here Beatrix had a just cause. She replaced Brett & Hall's gaudy ranks with "swirled drifts of blues in expanding, loosely circular patterns," nepetas, soft blue *Salvia patens,* nigellas, including the one named "Miss Jekyll," veronicas, campanulas and many others. "The scarlet *Lobelia cardinalis* of Brett & Hall's scheme gave way to the downyleaved bright blue *Lobelia tenuior,* grown from cuttings . . . it was planted with the tiny flowered, incandescently white northern bedstraw *Galium boreale.*" Even so, "the garden was no fluffy pastel vision." Beatrix also used orange lilies, a French marigold called "Mahogany," dahlia "Black Knight," and maroon nasturtiums. The cypresses, which were focal points of the main beds, were threaded with *Tropaeolum canariense,* bright yellow-flowered climbers—a particularly fashionable device of English gardeners of the Edwardian period.[16]

Edward and Mary Harkness clearly liked the transformation of their lovely West Garden, and they became regular clients of Beatrix's.

If Eolia's drifts of blues and orange flowered in the summer of 1919 for the first time (and they were echoed far away, where Vita Sackville-West was planting this favorite color scheme in her first garden at Long Barn at the same time), then they celebrated the sixth happy summer of Max and Beatrix's marriage as well as the ending of World War I in Europe. "MaxTrix" had settled into their peaceable, affectionate companionship; they each worked while they were in New Haven, making occasional trips to New York, Washington, Philadelphia, or wherever friends or family beckoned, and they retreated gratefully to fishing, golf, and gardening at Reef Point for three months every summer. The war may have stopped them from traveling to Europe, but it was never far from their thoughts. And, as if perhaps war was not enough to remind them that the world exacted a price for such happiness as theirs, then those first six years of marriage weathered an ever mounting toll of more personal losses.

Mary Cadwalader left as usual, but alone, for her summer trip to Europe in 1914. Because of John Lambert Cadwalader's death in March there would be no Scottish shooting party, but she wanted to spend her usual time with Edith and the ailing Henry James. When war started on August 4, 1914, there was a first nagging fear for her safety. Then there was a personal battle: Max's memories of happy years in Leipzig and Heidelberg, his friends in Germany, Beatrix's thoughts of the kindness of Dr. Bolle at his island garden in the River Tegel when she went to Berlin all those years ago—how could such friends suddenly be "enemies." Although the overwhelming inclination of both of them, because of upbringing, society, and ways of thinking, was to adopt Britain and France as their "side," it was by no means easy.

They were constantly worried about Edith, who, now settled in Paris, had planned a trip to England for that August, and had rented Stocks at Tring from the Humphry Wards as the base for her "court," which included Mary Cad-

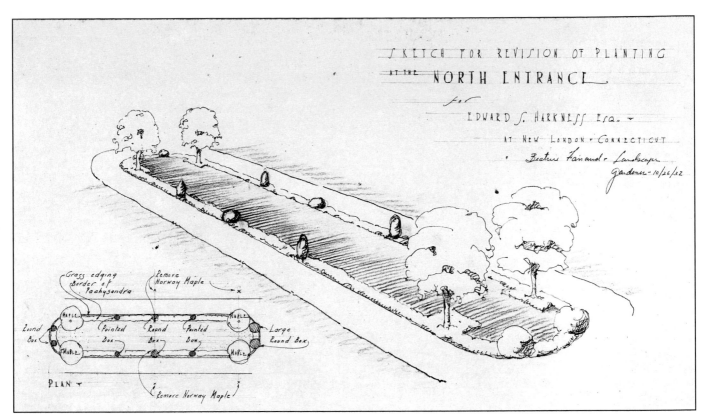

SKETCH FOR REVISION OF PLANTING
AT THE NORTH ENTRANCE
for
EDWARD S. HARKNESS ESQ.
AT NEW LONDON ~ CONNECTICUT
Beatrix Farrand ~ Landscape
Gardener — 10/26/32

Grass edging
Border of
Pachysandra

Remove
Norway Maple

Round
Box

MAPLE

Pointed
Box

Round
Box

Pointed
Box

MAPLE

Large
Round Box

PLAN

Remove Norway Maple

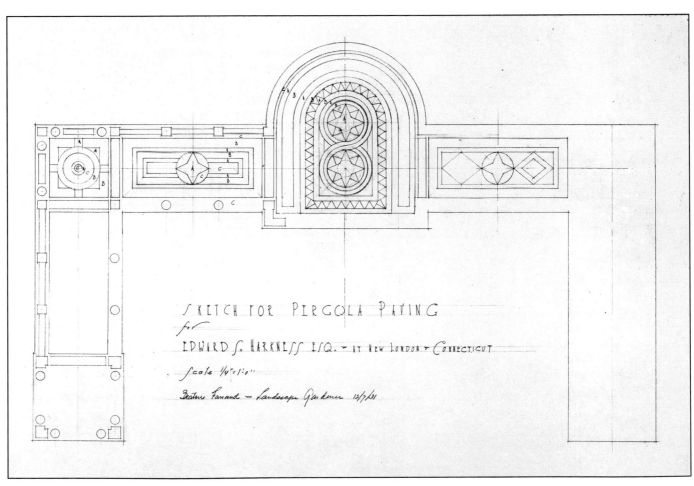

SKETCH FOR PERGOLA PAVING
for
EDWARD S. HARKNESS ESQ. ~ AT NEW LONDON ~ CONNECTICUT
Scale 1/4" = 1'0"
Beatrix Farrand ~ Landscape Gardener 12/7/31

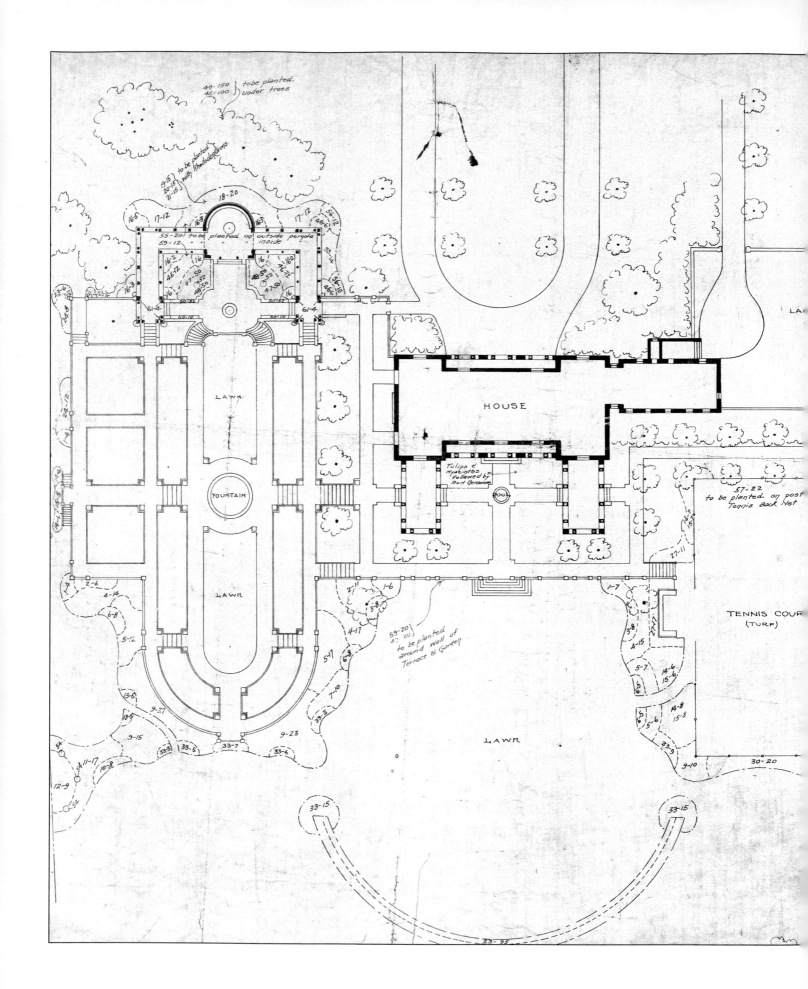

49-150 } to be planted
45-100 } under trees

19-15 } to be planted
20-15 } with Rhododendrons
21-15 }

18-20

55-20 to be planted on outside pergola
59-12   inside

LAWN

FOUNTAIN

LAWN

HOUSE

Tulips &
Hyacinths
followed by
Red Geranium

POOL

57-22
to be planted on post
Tennis Back Net

TENNIS COURT
(TURF)

59-20 }
47-20 } to be planted
around wall of
Terrace & Garden

LAWN

33-15

33-15

23-55

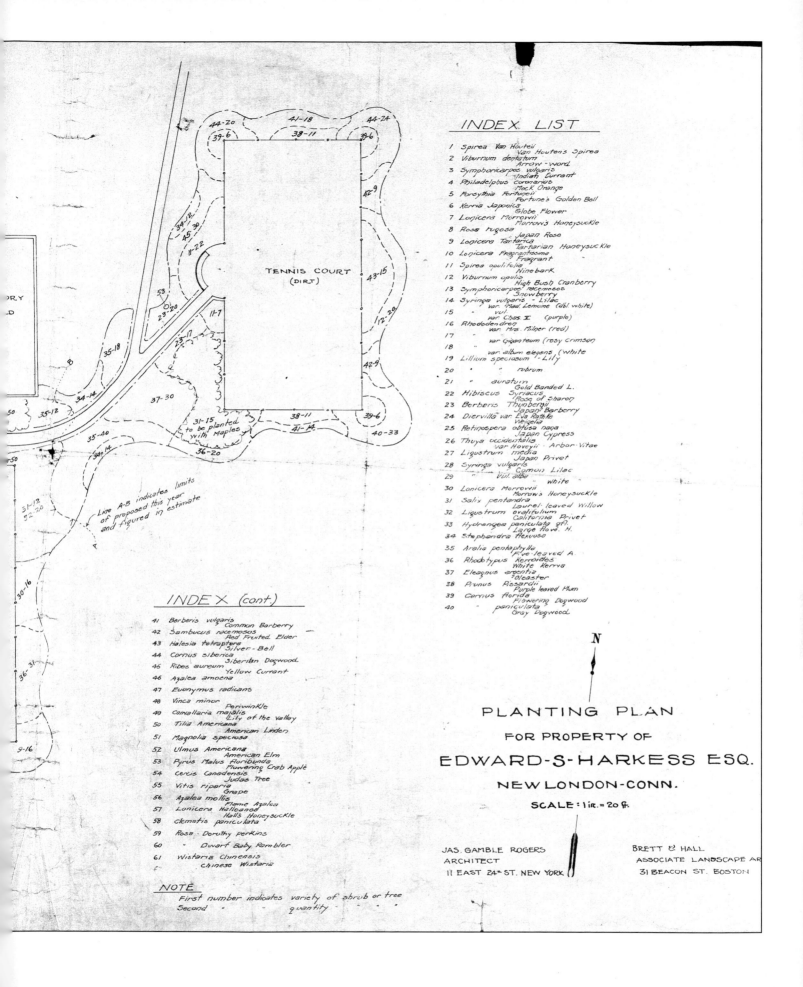

INDEX LIST

1 Spirea Van Houteii
    Van Houten's Spirea
2 Viburnum dentatum
    Arrow-wood
3 Symphoricarpos vulgaris
    Indian Currant
4 Philadelphus coronarius
    Mock Orange
5 Forsythia Fortunei
    Fortune's Golden Bell
6 Kerria Japonica
    Globe Flower
7 Lonicera Morrowii
    Morrow's Honeysuckle
8 Rosa rugosa
    Japan Rose
9 Lonicera Tartarica
    Tartarian Honeysuckle
10 Lonicera Fragrantissima
    Fragrant
11 Spirea opulifolia
    Ninebark
12 Viburnum opulis
    High Bush Cranberry
13 Symphoricarpos racemosos
    Snowberry
14 Syringa vulgaris - Lilac
    var. Mad. Lemoine (dbl. white)
15   vul.
16   var Chas. X (purple)
16 Rhododendron
    var. Mrs. Milner (red)
17
18   var Giganteum (rosy crimson)
19   var album elegans (white
19 Lillium speciosum - Lily
20   " rubrum
21   " auratum
    Gold Banded L.
22 Hibiscus Syriacus
    (Rose of Sharon)
23 Berberis Thunbergii
    Japan Barberry
24 Diervilla var. Eva Rathke
    Weigela
25 Retinospera obtusa napa
    Japan Cypress
26 Thuya occidentalis
    var Hoveyii - Arbor-Vitae
27 Ligustrum media
    Japan Privet
28 Syringa vulgaris
    Comon Lilac
29   " vul. alba white
30 Lonicera Morrowii
    Morrow's Honeysuckle
31 Salix pentandra
    Laurel-leaved Willow
32 Ligustrum ovalifolium
    California Privet
33 Hydrangea paniculata gfl.
    Large flow. H.
34 Stephandra flexuosa
35 Aralia pentaphylla
    Five-leaved A.
36 Rhodotypus Kerroides
    White Kerria
37 Eleagnus argentia
    Oleaster
38 Prunus Pissardii
    Purple leaved Plum
39 Cornus florida
    Flowering Dogwood
40   " paniculata
    Gray Dogwood

INDEX (cont.)

41 Berberis vulgaris
    Common Barberry
42 Sambucus racemosos
    Red Fruited Elder
43 Halesia tetraptera
    Silver-Bell
44 Cornus sibenica
    Siberian Dogwood
46 Ribes aureum
    Yellow Currant
46 Azalea amoena
47 Euonymus radicans
48 Vinca minor
    Periwinkle
49 Convallaria majalis
    Lily of the valley
50 Tilia Americana
    American Linden
51 Magnolia speciosa
52 Ulmus Americana
    American Elm
53 Pyrus Malus floribunda
    Flowering Crab Apple
54 Cercis Canadensis
    Judas Tree
55 Vitis riparia
    Grape
56 Azalea mollis
    Flame Azalea
57 Lonicera Halleana
    Hall's Honeysuckle
58 Clematis paniculata
59 Rosa - Dorothy Perkins
60   " Dwarf Baby Rambler
61 Wistaria Chinensis
    Chinese Wistaria

NOTE

First number indicates variety of shrub or tree
Second " " quantity

TENNIS COURT
(DIRT)

Line A-B indicates limits
of proposed this year
and figured in estimate

to be planted
with Maples

N

PLANTING PLAN
FOR PROPERTY OF
EDWARD·S·HARKESS ESQ.
NEW LONDON-CONN.
SCALE : 1 in. = 20 ft.

JAS. GAMBLE ROGERS
ARCHITECT
11 EAST 24th ST. NEW YORK

BRETT & HALL
ASSOCIATE LANDSCAPE AR
31 BEACON ST. BOSTON

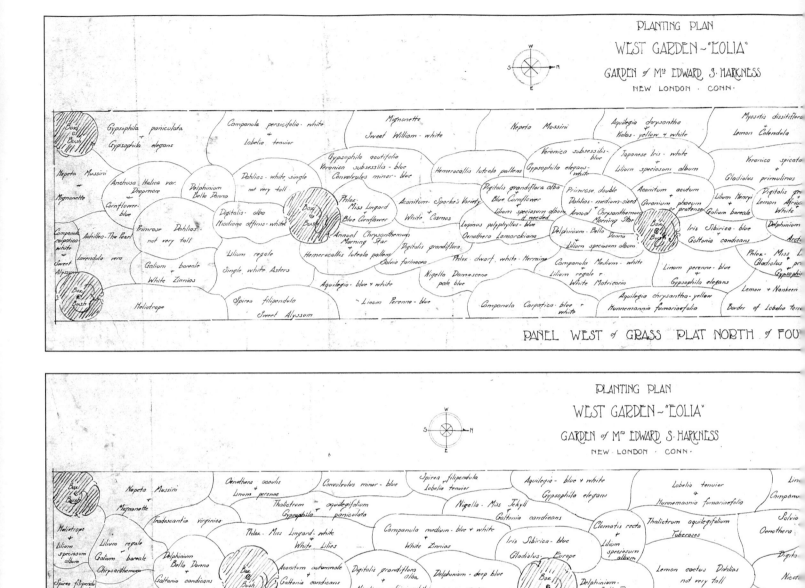

PLANTING PLAN
WEST GARDEN ~ "EOLIA"
GARDEN of Mᴿˢ EDWARD S. HARKNESS
NEW LONDON · CONN.

PANEL WEST of GRASS PLAT NORTH of FOU—

PLANTING PLAN
WEST GARDEN ~ "EOLIA"
GARDEN of Mᴿˢ EDWARD S. HARKNESS
NEW · LONDON · CONN.

PANEL EAST of GRASS PLOT NORTH of FOUNTA—

walader. But, like almost everyone else in London and Paris, Edith was in-
fected with the patriotic euphoria of a battle that would be "over by Christmas." The timeless peace of Stocks irked her, and she decamped to London
before returning to Paris at the end of September. The experience of her
beloved city, its lights dimmed, its liveliness turned to somber fortitude,
spurred Edith into a remarkable heroism. She set forth on her personal battle,
and her workshops for unemployed seamstresses, her American hostels, and
her Children of Flanders Rescue Committee were successive targets of her energies. During 1915 she motored to the war front several times; she was al-

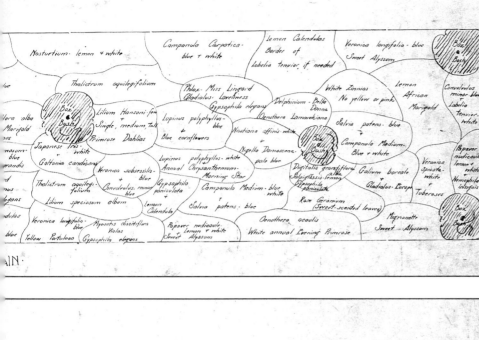

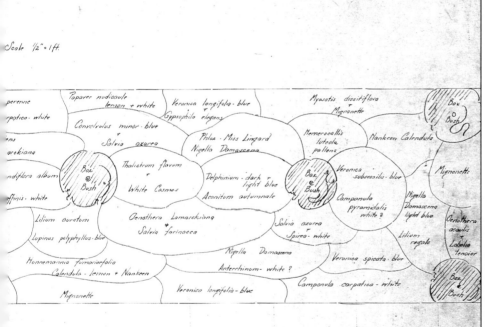

Eolia: planting plans for the east- and west-facing beds in front of the pergola in the West Garden. Beautiful schemes for loosely circular drifts of contrasting spires and domes of flowers, delphiniums with dahlias, foxgloves with nicotiana, snapdragons with nigella, all in blues, pinks, pale yellows, and a lot of white (gypsophila, lilies, white zinnias and dahlias, alyssum, lobelia, and sweet williams).

lowed to see, and report, the horrors of Ypres and the bombardments of "Cassel" and "Dunkerque." She eventually produced her book *Fighting France,* and she wrote enthusiastically on its subject to friends in America, relying on Mary to raise money in New York for her causes.

Mary Cadwalader, stalwart as ever, insisted on going to Europe again in 1915. She really wanted to see her dear old Celimare; Henry James had written of their delightful outings in that lost August of 1914—"an exquisite adventure" exploring the old Manor House at Whitton in Middlesex, and a "prowl in the City" in its Sunday desertion.[17] Of their meetings in 1915 there appears to be no record, but nothing would have stopped Mary from seeing him in London or at Rye. It was for the last time; James had a stroke in early December of 1915 and died early in the new year. His paternal wisdom and affection were gone from Beatrix's life, and she could only have felt, with deep gratitude, that these had been present when she most needed them.

But the death of Henry James was only one of the first of the black-edged letters. Beatrix found herself busy with the saddest work of all, designing the tombstones for those she knew, and who had long been part of her life. Edith's amanuensis of many years, Anna Bahlman, died from cancer in the spring of 1916, and Beatrix carefully drew out the classic lettering for her memorial. The faithful, supportive neighbor of her childhood, the lawyer and writer Frederick Wallingford Whitridge, died at the end of the year, and Beatrix again designed a tombstone for a friend.[18]

When President Wilson finally took America into the war on August 6, 1917, her young men went off with the same bravura as their European cousins, mostly now dead. They were soon brought home too, and Beatrix designed memorials for Theodore Roosevelt's son Quentin, and his friend Hamilton Coolidge in 1918. At the very end of 1918, there was the tragic death of Willard Straight in France from pneumonia, three weeks after the Armistice; Beatrix felt deeply for Dorothy, and neither had the inclination to carry on with their garden making. And then, in early 1919, came the deepest shock of all—the death in February of Theodore Roosevelt. Mary Cadwalader Jones, like so many of the intelligent lady friends who so amused the ex-president, had worshiped him as their friendship grew stronger. She had made a special effort to hear him lecture in London in the summer of 1914 so that she could report "The Lamb's" performance to Edith Roosevelt.[19] Edith and Mary spoiled and indulged him, and he loved it. Mary went to Washington to hear the tributes—"So Valiant for Truth passed over and all the trumpets sounded for him on the other side," said Senator Lodge—and Beatrix treasured the *New York Times* clipping of the occasion as something she could not throw away. Edith Roosevelt asked her to design a tombstone for them both, which is in Young's Memorial Cemetery, on Cove Road, in Oyster Bay, near Sagamore Hill. Beatrix drew out the lettering for both names, leaving only the date of Edith's death to be added.[20]

The winter of 1918–19 was that of the disastrous influenza epidemic which hit not only the cities but also the rural communities of the northeastern states. At the end of 1919 Beatrix was called to the famous Ethel Walker School in Simsbury, Connecticut. Miss Walker wanted a suitable garden for a large and comfortable Tudor-style house that had been given as a residence for senior girls in memory of the young Emily Cluett, a pupil who had died of the flu that winter. Nothing came of this, I think because at the end of 1919 the school was battling through another terrible winter, with waist-high snow drifts that did not encourage thoughts of the buried garden, and measles and mumps, plus Miss Walker's own indisposition. When they emerged into the spring, Miss Walker announced her engagement to her doctor, E. Terry Smith, and clearly had other things to think about.

It is a bitter truth that the creative, life-giving occupation of garden and landscape designing is an early casualty of a nation bent on war. Somehow it hardly seems decent to even mention such a civilizing art, such delicacy as the beauty of flowers, when people are steeling themselves to retreat into barbarism. Beatrix was supremely conscious of her potential if only she could turn her art to the wartime purpose. She was already disappointed, in 1916, that she could not give the benefit of her professional skills to help the patients of the New Haven Tubercular Hospital, and this feeling of frustration was undoubtedly aggravated as America entered the war. She knew that architects that she admired in England and Scotland, designers of wonderful houses and gardens, Edwin Lutyens, Herbert Baker, and Robert Lorimer, had turned their skills to the designing of war memorials in France.[21] Her much admired Gertrude Jekyll, having made those therapeutic scented gardens for the patients at King Edward VII's hospital, had turned her energies to the planting of the war cemeteries.[22] But, in these respects, American society was so much larger and more diverse than England's elite. For all Beatrix's connections, she had no way of influencing a national movement, particularly at short notice. Or did she?

The Garden Club of America had been founded in 1913. Beatrix was an honorary member of the Garden Club of Philadelphia (which dated from 1904), which included many people she knew, Newbold relations, and Mrs. Edgar Scott and Mrs. Henry Frazer Harris, her clients. Mrs. Bayard Henry of Germantown was a member of the Philadelphia club and secretary of the national movement. Perhaps the Garden Club of America's attitude to professionals should be categorized—at least at the outset—as wary, respectful even? They hesitated to impose upon her time, and yet needed her support; Mrs. Henry addressed Beatrix as not only our consultant, but "our Tower of Strength."[23] Beatrix was perhaps a little cool, too; she informed the New York club that she would go on their lecture list, at fifty dollars a lecture plus traveling expenses.[24] In January 1917 she became a vice president of the Society of Little Gardens, an offshoot founded in Philadelphia under the chairmanship of her relative, Miss Sophie Cadwalader, with many members of the Garden Club of Philadelphia in support, including Miss Elizabeth Leighton Lee of the School of Horticulture at Ambler. The Society of Little Gardens seemed dynamic in war initiatives, concentrating on teaching vegetable growing, beekeeping, fruit and vegetable preservation, and holding plant sales. All these were boosted in wartime—"Special War Courses" were held at the School of Horticulture and there were discussions on "Woman's Responsibilities in the Present Food Crisis" even before America officially went to war in August 1917.

This encouraged Beatrix to really try to rally the Garden Club of America. She began attending meetings of the Council of Presidents of something over thirty branches in 1917. She urged them to preserve wildflowers, by encouraging appreciation in schools and discouraging the ransacking of the wild for Christmas decorations (this was on the agenda), and mentioned her other causes. The following spring, 1918, the Garden Club asked for her advice on their wish to give "foreign relief"; the good-hearted, if misdirected, ladies thought they should help replant orchards in Picardy but as the war was far from over and the fields of France would be a long time surrendering their dead even when it was, this kind offer was gently shelved. Beatrix felt their concern was needed nearer home, and in early 1919 she told them so: "The war memorial subject is one in which I am keenly interested," she wrote to Mrs. Henry on February 3, 1919: ". . . architects and landscape architects feel that the country will be deluged by stone-cutters who have ready-made designs for war monuments."[25] She supported strongly the ASLA's propaganda on education and good design, and struck a vital chord— "As the psychology of places is as interesting and intricate as the psychology of people . . . unless people who really care about the place itself are interested in the subject, the chances are that something in-appropriate and certainly ugly will be foisted upon the community."[26] Oddly, the Garden Club of America did not feel that local war memorials were really their responsibility; that they were for individual rather than corporate involvement. They published Beatrix's recommendations though, to help spread the right idea. For war memorials involving small sums of money she suggested entrance gates, fountains, sundials, shelter houses, park colonnades, boathouses, bandstands, crosses, and groups of trees. Larger sums could be wisely spent on parks, playgrounds, playing fields, memorial highways, public squares, groves of trees, athletic grounds, and the purchase for preservation of beautiful scenery.

In early 1919 the Quarantine Regulations were also the subject of much heated discussion. It was by an act of Congress of 1912 that the proper quarantine and examination of imported nursery stock was imposed, but the Federal Horticultural Board took this further and banned the importation of a large variety of trees, shrubs, plants, and bulbs to prevent importing also their attendant insects and diseases. The nursery industry saw the emotive value of protest in 1919. A flyer from Elliott Nursery Company asked what would become of over a thousand nurseries in war-torn Belgium that had existed on this trade prior to 1914: ". . . we are obliged to say to them. . . . While we have cheerfully helped to feed and clothe you, and while our soldiers have died on the battlefield to give you freedom, we cannot buy your Azaleas, Bay Trees, rhododendrons, palms, begonias, gloxinias . . . you have our sympathy" but we are forbidden to buy your products.[27] The Garden Club of America asked Beatrix for advice. She was in no doubt, and at the January 1919 meeting at the Colony Club in New York she told them so. She was clearly in favor of the regulations which would come into force on June 1—America's soil and plant community must be protected from pests and diseases that came in unhealthy nursery stock. Also at the meeting, Miss Georgiana Sargent from the Lenox Club produced a letter from Professor Charles Sargent, who shared Beatrix's opinion (of course, she may have canvassed him on the subject), and had the last word. He knew there would be some hardship. He knew also that the inspectors of the Federal Horticultural Board were hopelessly inefficient and the dangers were great but, he thundered, ". . . it should improve American nurseries for it will compel American nurserymen to raise the plants which they have previously imported, and it will keep out of the country a lot of cheap, miserable material."[28]

Although the Garden Club of America did pass a resolution to encourage its members to keep an eye on local war memorial proposals and put forward her suggestions, Beatrix clearly felt after this brief but arduous acquaintance, that it was too unwieldy a dinosaur for her patience and limited time. She gracefully withdrew and remained a figurehead and occasional lecturer until she began to spend a lot of time at Reef Point when she became a member of the Mount Desert Island Garden Club and took her fellow members garden visiting.

As a footnote to these years which held so much sadness and frustration, there were two small commissions, which though not important in themselves, struck just that note of aptness that so often marks her career. They came out of her past, those distant days of Edith Wharton's happiness at The Mount, motoring through the countryside of remote northern Massachusetts, the countryside of *Ethan Frome* and *Summer,* out to Ashfield to see Charles Eliot Norton and to Pittsfield, where Melville had written *Moby-Dick.* In 1919 she was approached by two clients, one named Colt and one named Crane, two names that are a part of American history. For Mrs. Samuel G. Colt in Pittsfield she designed a terraced garden of rock walls, with a small garden house and a small pinetum.[29]

The more interesting garden was for Mrs. Colt's friend, Mrs. Zenas Crane of the paper-making family at nearby Dalton. Mrs. Crane was the widow of Zenas Crane Jr., the son of the founder of the paper mills, who had died in 1917. All the Crane family had, as they still have, houses dotted around Dalton. Mrs. Zenas Crane lived in Willowbrook, set in a dell by the mill pool of their first mill on the Pittsfield/Dalton boundary. From a contoured survey done in September 1919 by A. A. Forbes, engineer in Pittsfield, Beatrix sketched out a classical squared garden, with four sets of quartered flower beds surrounded by yew hedges. She designed a trellis with pineapple finials, rose arches, and highly individual iron stands for oil jars. Her planting for the beds was traditional and pretty—the square beds were edged with bergenias, lavender, and forget-me-not and filled with blocks of delicate pinks, blues, and white—scabious, lilies, and pink gladioli, or monkshood with purply echinops, campanulas, artemesias, delphiniums, pale pink lupins, *Dictamnus fraxinella,* and clouds of gypsophila, foxgloves, and pale pink snapdragons.

Around the perimeters were long borders of delphiniums, campanulas, astilbes, iris, salvia, helenium—a color scheme of orange and blue—with added polyanthus, pansies, and columbines. Of this wonderful garden, which Beatrix photographed in its prime, and its splendid nineteenth-century greenhouses, nothing remains.

*O*ne name has to be added to the litany of death in this chapter, that of Beatrix's father, Freddy Rhinelander Jones, who died in Paris on June 10, 1918, aged seventy-two. Edith conveyed the news to Mary and Beatrix, and Beatrix destroyed any letters that were written on this subject. Edith was dismissive. In a letter to Elizabeth Cameron of June 22, after polite thanks for Lizzie's sympathy, she soon turned to the subject of Harry, and his estrangement, which irked her far more. Edith continued, "Besides the real thing nowadays concerns the real people, & not the poor phantoms who have voluntarily ceased to live so long ago. Minnie and Trix make up to me for my own wretched family, & all my thoughts and interests are with them."[30]

On the seventh of July Edith wrote to Mary, who was with Max and Beatrix at Reef Point, ". . . I am so anxious to know what the financial result of Fred's death will be for you & Trix. The 'funeral' never took place—or rather it was never announced—as I told you, his death having been known here to a few of my friends, I had to go through the hollow gestures of conventional mourning."[31] This was also passed over quickly, the real point of this long letter being to describe the "matchless" celebration of the Fourth of July by the American troops in Paris.

For Beatrix and Mary the financial result of Fred's death was not great. The American property which formed their Trust Fund was left to Beatrix "his only child and sole heir and next of kin under the laws of the State of New York," but the value of this Trust had decreased over the years and the income was small. Edith had often noticed signs of Mary being short of money, and had taken to giving her generous presents of money at Christmas and whenever Mary's pride would allow. Beatrix too was self-conscious that her mother had to struggle to keep up her high standards, but Mary's pride was a great barrier; Max and Beatrix quietly managed to keep 21 East Eleventh Street going as the framework of Mary's life, but she would accept little else.[32]

Chapter 9

❧❧

BEATRIX AND THE AMERICAN
WAY OF GARDENING

*B*eatrix had her fiftieth birthday in the summer of 1922. It was celebrated happily at Reef Point, where she and Max were busily turning the house and garden into a small world of their own making. Max's presence and belongings had given Reef Point a master for the first time since those dim, sad memories of Freddy so long ago. Max enabled Beatrix to see her old home with fresh eyes, and they spent happy hours "geologising," searching the old shore rocks for clues to their history, finding the "chatter marks" left by glacial action and the hand-worked tools and clamshell deposits of a vanished Indian village. She was also able to see her beloved garden for what it was, perhaps for the first time. Years of attention and composting had built up some patches of reasonable soils where there had been little but sand and spruce roots, though there would always be that large boggy strip between the house and the sea, probably the site of a preglacial stream. Most importantly, she concluded that the acid soils were a virtue, that it was pointless to try and grow things that were unlikely to thrive, that there were "numberless" plants that would grow with enthusiasm. With Max's support and interest she set about on the grand and gradual remaking of Reef Point's garden, which formed the habit from which the eventual demonstration and teaching garden of later years would grow. This acknowledgement of working with nature, which Beatrix had perhaps known *intellectually* ever since her days at the Arnold Arboretum, was now realized in the place she loved the most. Reef Point's comfortable repertory of plants—"from the ground hugging bunchberry or dwarf cornel, bearberry and goldthread to the tallest of the rhododendron family, with heathers and huckleberries" for middle height, was identified and planted. They made the vegetable garden, which supported them from late spring until the end of October, started collecting ericas and callunas, single and semidouble roses, the scented yellow azaleas, and some surprising treasures—many clematis species, honeysuckles, and vines—which liked to grow there. In the early 1920s gardening at Reef Point was perhaps more of a pleasure than it had ever been, a companionable pastime, with discussions, for leisurely afternoons. For once Beatrix felt no pressure to prove anything, for that could be done in the outside world. It was not until the early thirties, after over a decade, that the Farrands thought seriously of turning Reef Point into a teaching garden. For the moment it was just theirs.

For Beatrix, at the opening of the 1920s, the self-indulgence so fashionable in gardening might have seemed the main threat to her well-schooled instincts for self-restraint. Wilhelm Miller was so infuriated by this indulgence that he exploded twice within five pages of *What England Can Teach Us About Gardening,* "*The supreme quality in art is self-restraint.* We overdo everything. . . . We try to snatch the best of everything in life. . . . We want a big show right off. . . . We insist on having everything we want. We crowd in every good thing we have seen on our travels. We back our taste against all the architects and landscape men, and then we wonder what is lacking and why people laugh behind our backs."[1] Nowhere was this more true than on Long Island, particularly along the fabled north shore, the Gold Coast, where the decade seemed to pass in one long Gatsby-esque party. A glance at Beatrix's list of commissions shows many of these places—Bayville, Brookeville, Syosset, Manhasset, Oyster Bay, and Great Neck; and many names of the socially prominent—Otto Kahn, Harrison Williams, Percy Pyne, a Pratt, and an Iselin.

But the list of commissions is most misleading, perhaps more so here than at any other point in her career. Beatrix did work on Long Island during the twenties, but for the most part she steered clear of the more flagrant excesses. It becomes perfectly clear that the *people* she worked for were becoming more and more important to her. She had become a fine judge of just who it was worth working for, and she certainly would have had little patience with the powerful "Mafia" of estate head gardeners which Mac Griswold identifies in *The Golden Age of American Gardens,*[2] who ruled their Long Island estates with a Kew- or Edinburgh-trained grip and imported their English/Scottish ideas wholesale.

Having lost two most precious Long Island connections with the deaths of Theodore Roosevelt and Willard Straight (if Straight had lived to develop his "Improvement Company" how different her career might have been?), she now found work through John Lambert Cadwalader's friend and shooting guest in Scotland, Thomas Hastings. Tommy Hastings had designed his own house and garden, Bagatelle (motto: *Parva sed Apta,* small yet suitable) at Roslyn. He was a fierce perfectionist where his much admired, gemlike home and garden were concerned, but it was Beatrix whom he allowed on companionable critical visits and it was Beatrix who was asked to discuss

flower borders with Helen Benedict Hastings. She also worked for the younger architects newly fledged from the Carrere & Hastings office, William Adams Delano and Chester Holmes Aldrich. She did lovely summer borders, hastily sketched on the back of another drawing in the best designer's tradition, probably as a favor, for Delano's own garden in Syosset—long drifts of lavender, poppies, thymes, columbines, lupins, hemerocallis, iris, gypsophila, foxgloves, snapdragons, eryngiums, tall dahlias, delphiniums, and Anchusa "Dropmore."

Delano and Aldrich had designed Oheka at Woodbury, Cold Spring Harbor, for Otto H. Kahn, "The King of New York." Kahn, a German Jew, had married into the banking firm Kuhn, Loeb & Company; he was fastidious, suave, and fabulously rich, but liberal in his views on social problems and he had both a sense of humor and a real love of the arts. Kahn's grand garden, acres of formal French parterres, to match his French-style château, was laid out by Olmsted Brothers, who subsequently designed a golf course and miles of parkland bridleways.

In 1920, Adele Wolff Kahn called upon Beatrix. Mrs. Kahn wanted something pretty and usable (the severe and drafty or sun-baked Olmsted parterres were visually pleasing but not suitable for sitting in), so Beatrix simply picked up the axes of the parterre design and extended them through a series of delightful rooms. There was a circular, hedged *cabinet de verdure* with four seats, and lamps and flower baskets all especially designed; an octagonal enclosure was filled with box-edged beds of annuals; and there were two circular pool gardens, the first with concentric rings of iris with lemon verbena and gladioli, and *Iris sibirica* "Snow Queen" with white cosmos, the second with pe-

Beatrix's work for Percy R. Pyne III, Roslyn, Long Island, New York: sketch perspective and elevation for the enclosed garden with a pavilion. One of 185 drawings for this project (a large garden and model farm), this sketch typifies the kind of garden enclosure, away from the house, that Americans loved and Beatrix designed so frequently, in direct contrast to contemporary English taste for a garden around the house.

onies, tulips, more iris, *Geranium fragrans,* and forget-me-not. The office had to supply drawings of how niches for statues should be cut into a hemlock hedge, and snapshots by Beatrix survive showing a unique design feature, a small, circular dished pool of Lovat cobbles seen through clear water. The cobbles were brought from Scotland.

Mrs. Kahn also had a large, circular rose garden, with curving segmental beds, a single variety of rose in each. The named roses are longtime favorites—the scented, pinky white "Pharisaer," the large flowered pinky coral "Lady Alice Stanley," coral pink "Los Angeles" and Miss Jekyll's much used cream "Viscountess Folkestone."

Beatrix's rose garden plantings were always simple, never mixing varieties in a single bed. Her knowledge of roses had developed from her childhood memories of those her grandmother had grown at Newport. Though she "borrowed" many of Miss Jekyll's favorites for a time, now she was coming to conclusions of her own, especially about roses that would do well in the harsh East Coast climate. She was steadily converting her choice from copying Gertrude Jekyll to introducing American names and associations. Her rose garden plans are usually incomplete, but a further glimpse of her choices can be seen in the designs for the Clarence A. Warden garden at Haverford, Pennsylvania. Here are rectangular beds of single varieties: her childhood favorite, bright pink tipped with orange and cream "Marie van Houtte" opposite Pernet-Ducheu's crimson "Willomere"; rose pink "Columbia" opposite pinky coral "Lady Alice Stanley"; pink "Mrs. Henry Morse" opposite the carmine pink Jekyll favorite "Lady Ashtown"; "Countess of Gosford" opposite "Koningen Carola"; "Madame Jules Bouche", white with soft pink shading, opposite "Columbia"'s daughter, "Ophelia," flesh pink; and the pure flame "Madame Edouard Herriot" opposite the deep scarlet "Château de Clos Vougeot." She learned that the only cure for rose beetle was to pick them off by hand, that bushes should not be pruned in the autumn, but that once these hybrid tea bushes were established the flowers could be cut without harm to the plant.

Through her Princeton Pyne connections Beatrix went to work for Percy R. Pyne 2d on his estate on Roslyn Road, between Glen Cove and Roslyn. The site was an old farm, with a new owner who wanted an instant transformation into a gentleman's garden. An office drawing of February 25, 1927, shows the regrading necessary for the new, large vegetable garden with details of a latticework treatment for chicken houses and the tool shed. The Pynes were difficult clients. Beatrix's assistant, Anne Baker, did endless sketches, as many as six different layouts for a given idea to try and please them. Though it is not at all clear what exactly was accomplished, there were at least two satisfactory outcomes: one, the swimming pool enclosure, hedged, with the pool ornamented with flower tubs, is shown in a snapshot, and there was also a plain rectangular lawn near the house, edged with deep borders of annuals—mignonette and pink and white linaria, godetias, and pinks, pink

Convolvulus minor and tall white snapdragons, deep carmine lupins and single pink asters with a liberal scattering of white petunias.

The most surprising of the Long Island commissions is that for Harrison Williams at Oakpoint, Bayville, on Long Island Sound. It is strange to find Beatrix connected with such flamboyance: Oakpoint was a theatrical palace, with Art Deco interiors more suited to performing than to living. Mrs. Harrison Williams, for whom it was created, "the best dressed woman in the world,"[3] apparently used a different-colored Rolls-Royce with her chauffeur in a matching livery for each day of the week.

The Williamses' garden at Oakpoint turns out to be the least well known of Beatrix's Chinese gardens, worked on between Dorothy Straight's of 1912 and Abby Aldrich Rockefeller's in the 1930s. Mrs. Williams could well have set her heart on having just what she had seen at Dorothy Straight's garden, but here there seems no sign of a serious interest in Chinese art or philosophy. According to Monica Randall the chief feature of this garden, a pool with circular tiers of rock gardens around it, cost $100,000 to build, but Mrs. Williams was not satisfied so had it leveled to the ground and rebuilt for another $100,000.[4] Whether Beatrix had to go through all this is unclear. Her snapshots show the garden being built and planted and looking fairly finished, so perhaps she was successful. The base planting was of shrubs—daphnes, androsace, cotoneaster, and viburnums with masses of iris, sedum, heathers, crocus, linaria, aubretias and pinks, columbines and phlox. There was also a garden house with a keyhole entrance, a surrounding of enchanting red Chinese latticework, along with vistas of brick paths, pools "surrounded by masses of lilac trees so high that in spring the sky seemed almost swallowed up by the fragrant purple blossoms."[5]

It was Anne Baker who did most of the endless drawings to please Mrs. Williams, as she had done for the indecisive Pynes. Much more to Beatrix's liking were the commissions for Great Neck village green and library garden. This was a case for using her beloved natives—acers, lilacs, deutzia, the flowering crab *Malus sargentii*, dogwoods, witch hazel, and crataegus made a border for the green, underplanted with polyanthus, iris, hyacinths, and the dwarf polyantha rose "Echo."

❦❦

*T*he softly raised beds with resident rocks, divided into four with grass paths, that she and Max were making the chief glory of Reef Point's summer garden, won a great deal of admiration from friends and neighbors. They were carefully cultivated, by trial and error, through the early twenties, using large Jekyllian drifts of flowers that would survive the Maine winter and yet relish the short, hot summer—drifts of *Tradescantia virgini-*

FOLLOWING PAGES: *Oakpoint, home of Mrs. Harrison Williams, Bayville, Long Island, New York: One of the most complex planting plans ever produced by Beatrix Farrand's office throughout her long career, this plan for a two-tiered rock wall garden has been reproduced in its entirety, divided into two sections. The garden was 35 feet across, with a 4-foot-diameter pool in the center. The stepping-stone paths, laced with thymes, arenarias, and other creeping rock plants, traverse the planted tiers, which are just over 4 feet deep. These tiers are filled, according to soil and aspect, with varieties of iris, primula, aquilegia, heuchera, geranium, phlox, forget-me-not, sedum, and dianthus, with occasional heathers, miniature pines, and brooms. The highest levels, which are presumably undisturbed soils, partly shaded by surrounding rhododendrons, are thickly planted with a rich and pretty spring flowering including violas, erythroniums, scillas, trillium, crocuses, gentian, muscari, and daphnes. Mrs. Harrison Williams had a reputation for her fashionable eccentricities, and it seems likely that this rather strange garden was one of them, along with her exotic outfits with their color-matched automobiles.*

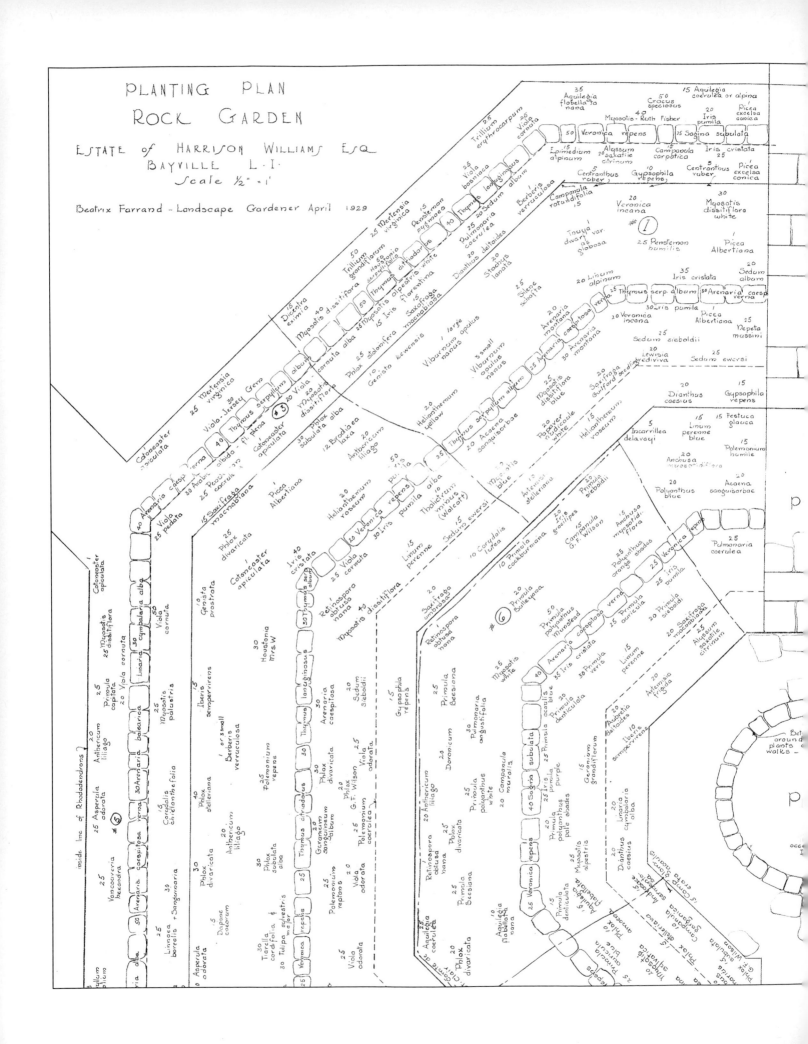

PLANTING PLAN
ROCK GARDEN

ESTATE of HARRISON WILLIAMS ESQ
BAYVILLE L.I.
Scale ½" = 1'

Beatrix Farrand — Landscape Gardener April 1929

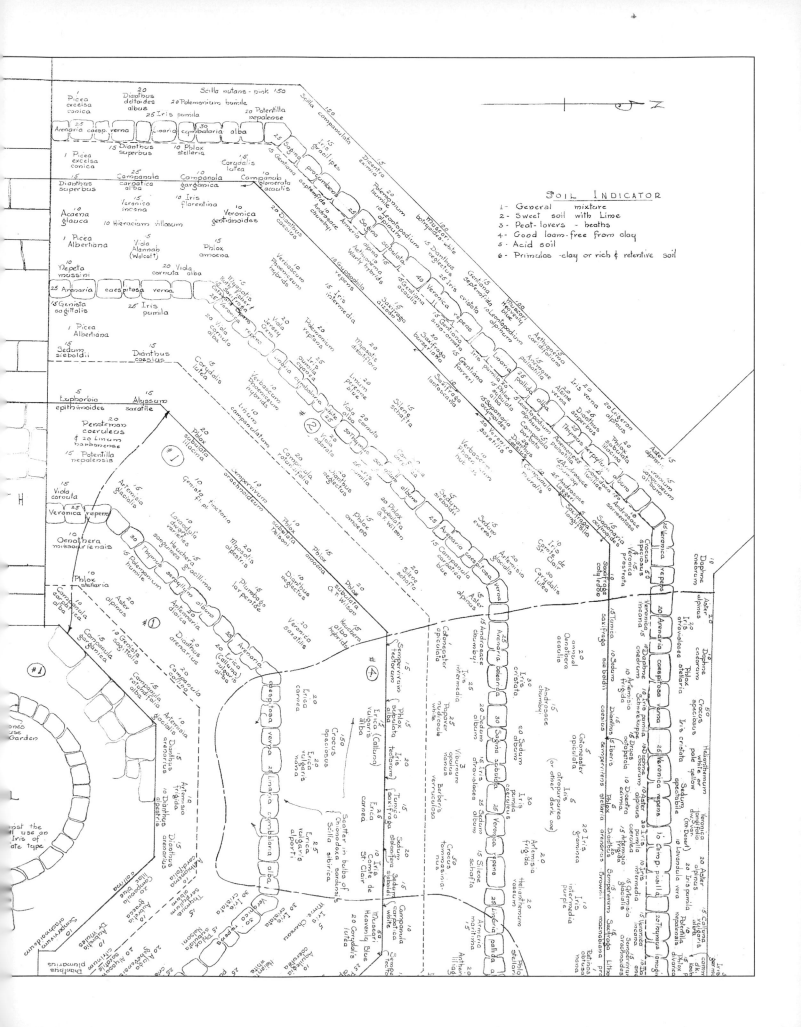

SOIL INDICATOR

1- General mixture
2- Sweet soil with Lime
3- Peat-lovers - heaths
4- Good loam-free from clay
5- Acid soil
6- Primulas -clay or rich & retentive soil

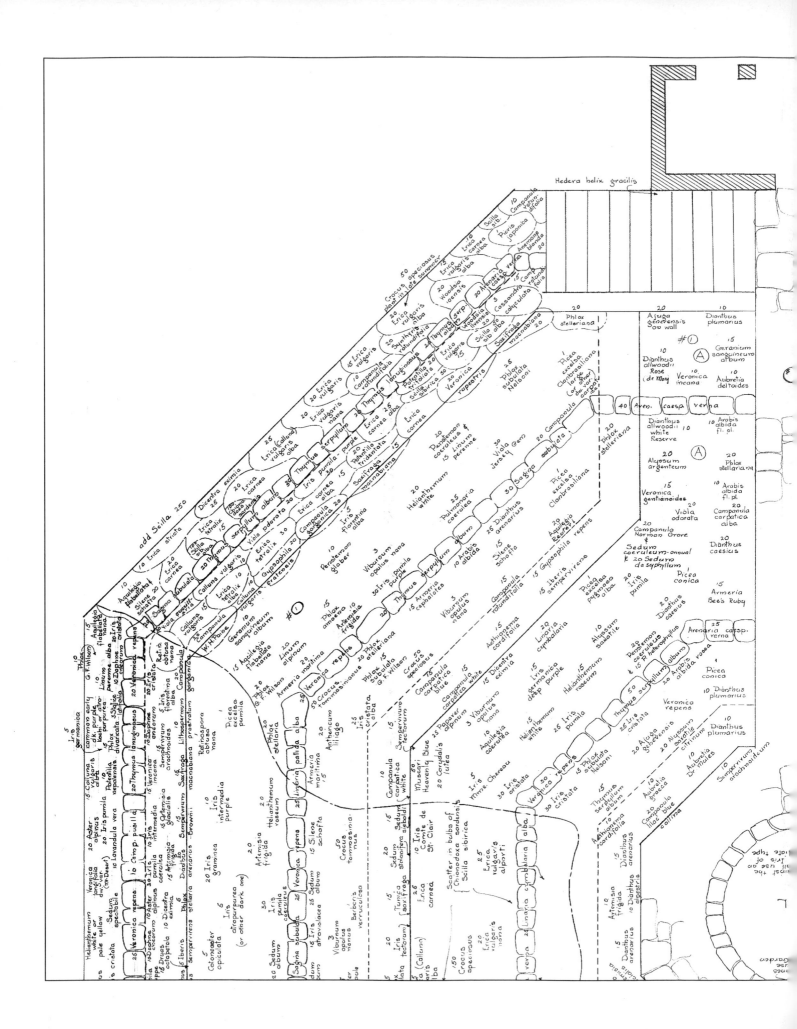

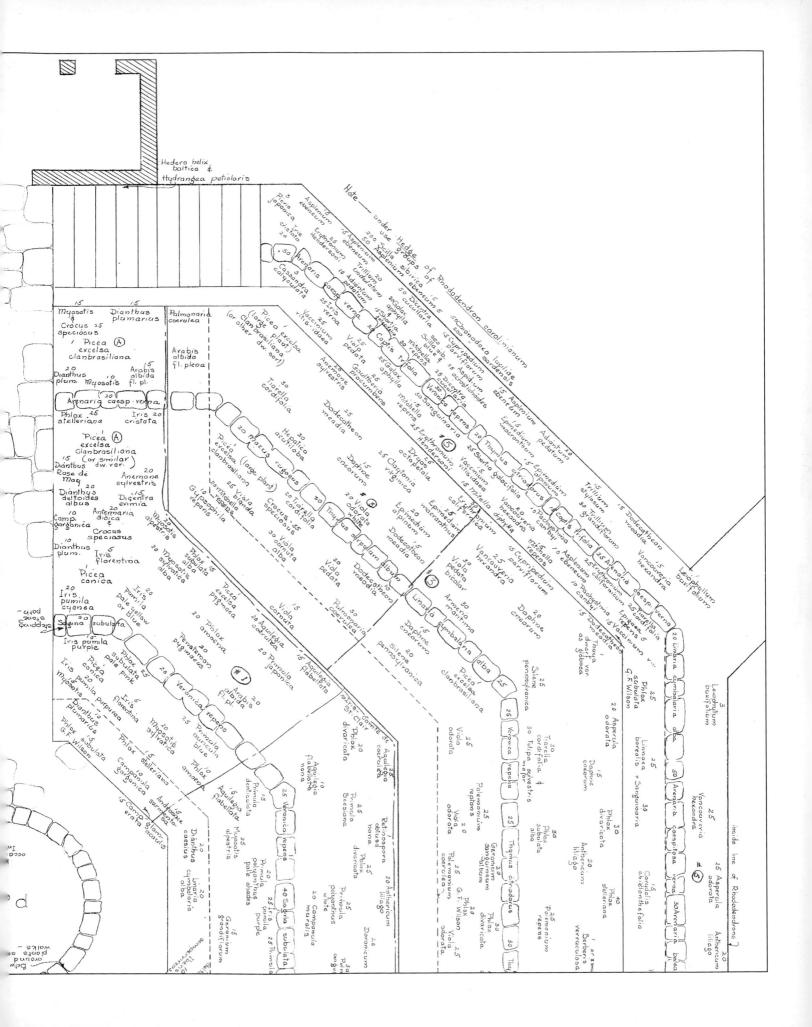

Oakpoint, April 1929:
a design for a tiered rock garden
with central pool and garden
house with a keyhole doorway.
This photograph, looking east,
was taken by Beatrix Farrand
immediately after the garden
was planted. Note the Chinese
trellis in the background.

ana, *Euphorbia correllata,* "Black Prince" iris, *Aconitum fisheri,* and *Dictamnus fraxinus alba,* with astilbes, peonies, lupins, thalictrums, campanulas, delphiniums, and phlox.

She had worked her way toward this very personal statement in a "ravine garden" for Mrs. Hanna at Seal Harbor, designed in the summer of 1920; here sandy paths wound through sweeps of hostas, forget-me-not, lilies, hermocallis, iris, oenetheras, campanulas, asters, and white valerian. And in 1925, she first planted yet another variation, one of her most justly famous island gardens, for Mrs. Herbert Satterlee at Glen Head on Ocean Drive, south of Bar Harbor. Here, on a southerly slope, with good soil and sea view, beneath a scattering of spruce and pines, she planted pansies, lilies, valerian, zinnias, coreopsis, ageratum, tagetes, and Rudbeckia "Golden Glow" (all yellows and oranges) on one side—opposed by the softer colors—lavender, stachys, *Lilium regale,* phlox "Elizabeth Campbell," pink peonies, pink linaria, and white verbena.

Beatrix seemed at last to have thrown off the habits of English traditions and to have successfully worked her way into a native, an American way of gardening. All those perennials that the English had cultivated for so long that they were called "English flowers" grew just as well and perhaps even more

ABOVE: *Oakpoint: a second photograph by Beatrix Farrand, of the pool and the enclosing Chinese Chippendale trellis, to be painted lacquer red.*

LEFT: *Oakpoint: a detail from the design drawing for the Chinese trellis.*

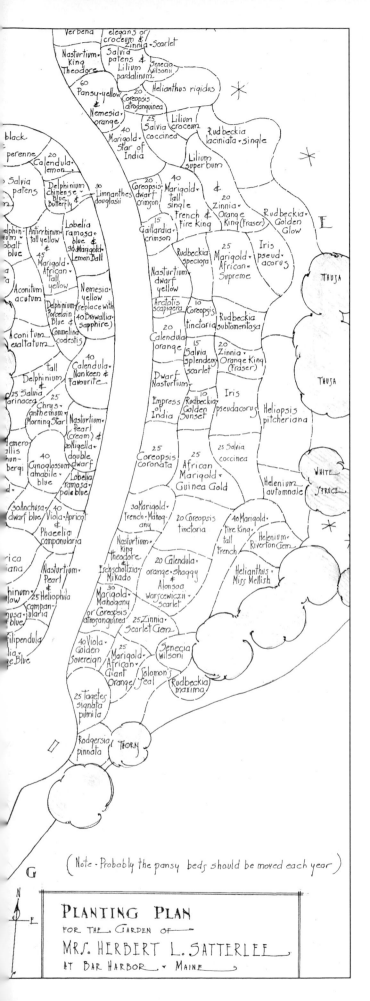

A garden for Mrs. Herbert L. Satterlee, Great Head, Bar Harbor: a most important planting plan—the essence of the gardens that basked in the sun of the brief Maine summers which Beatrix designed for her friends and herself. The garden was in a clearing sheltered by spruce and white pines, with a view to the sea at Great Head. The predominance of blue (pansies, lobelia, alyssum, ageratum, and myosotis in carpets with spires of delphiniums, salvias, and Baptisia australis) reflected the sea and sky, but there were also masses of white, with pinks and oranges carefully segregated. From the south, entering the garden, ISLAND BED F has a central mound of thuja with small sedums, lysimachia, and nemesia planted in front of a statue. Around the west side, drifts of blue (myosotis, pansies, viscaria, ageratum) are broken by silvers and gray leaves (hostas, eryngiums), and the striped Phalaris gardener's-garters support clumps of orange hemerocallis, lupins, and lilies. Across the grass path, the south end of BORDER B has the same blue carpets, generous sweeps of white astilbe, and feathery aruncus and pink flowers, with touches of dark red (Scabiosa "Black Prince" and snapdragon "Maroon King"). Farther up the central path, ISLAND BED C is of blue and white scented spires, with cloudy gypsophila and carpets of blue. A paved path crosses the bed, laced with sedums, saxifrage, and thyme. To the north of the path the colors change to mauve, violet, and soft salmon pink, with lots of silver and white. These violets and mauves respond to ISLAND BED D, where deep violet petunias and massed whites and blues have left the pinks behind in the south end of BED D. The east side of BED D has a yellow and blue planting scheme to prepare for BORDER BED E, where the oranges blaze forth.

beautifully in the clear sunlight of Maine and Long Island. The "English" roses, so called, could also be successful in America. And, at last, she was finding that other people appreciated the wonderful galaxy of hardy flowering shrubs—many of them American natives or closely allied to them—for which America could actually beat Europe soundly.

It was at this moment that her most distinguished commission arrived. It was her aunt Edith who brought Robert and Mildred Woods Bliss[6] into Beatrix's life. Edith knew them in Paris during the war; they had been stalwart supporters in her war efforts and they became close friends with many friends in common. In April 1920 Robert Bliss had been assigned to the State Department in Washington, and finding themselves at home for what seemed like a settled period, the Blisses decided to buy a house. They found The Oaks,[7] on the Rock of Dumbarton, on R Street at the highest point of Wisconsin Avenue in Georgetown, and purchased it that fall. The big, rambling house, dated from about 1800, had been the home of the Blounts since 1891.

Beatrix made her first working trip to The Oaks on June 24 and 25, 1922. She walked around with the Blisses, with Mildred, and then on her own. She found the house standing proudly on its "rock," with the Blounts' haphazard terracing on the north and east, and the land falling away all round. The whole site was dotted with lovely trees, especially oaks. She set the surveyors to work, for nothing could really be done without accurate measurements; but her enthusiasm got the better of her and she immediately dictated a six-and-a-half-page interim report of her ideas to Robert and Mildred Bliss.

First she tackled the R Street frontage: "While in no way should the planting on R Street look as though it were intended to close out people's view of the place, it should in effect do this, but by giving them interesting and pretty plants to look at, with occasional calculated glimpses of the place, arranged so that they will not rake the windows and gardens, the passers by will not feel crudely excluded." Yet privacy was assured. Thus the wily designer dealing with her clients' desire to have a country house in the heart of the city and yet not upset the neighbors, who had a traditional regard for The Oaks. With great dexterity, Beatrix went on to focus on the best things that The Oaks possessed. Mrs. Blount's collection of ancient box trees (she used to buy them up as old Georgetown gardens changed hands) would be used, and more planted, especially around the house entrance; English ivy and a smaller-leaved variety would be used on the south front of the house (these were still prominent in 1967 photographs). The famous Green Garden, an outdoor room on the north of the Orangery, was inspired by the two great oaks that were there dictating a shade-loving ground cover of periwinkle, pachysandra, hellebores, *Tiarella cordifolia,* hypericum, shortia, and Vancouveria, and spring bulbs—and not much euonymus, "rather a bristly ground cover."[8]

On the east slope there was already a rose garden, of sorts, though inadequate terracing made it seem "restless"; below it was an "uneasy" sloping herbaceous garden, and lower still, the pool. Beatrix saw immediately that "its grassy seats and slopes may be made an unusual frame for an out-of-doors picture." The pool from the start was entirely romantic. In a final long paragraph, ideas tumbling from her excited brain, she identified more pictures that have since become famous: "the brook certainly could be widened and dammed . . . used as a mirror in which to reflect large plantations of azaleas and iris"; "one ravine could be given over to a mass of azaleas, another to a plantation of magnolias and crabs"; there could be a lilac walk, all making the old-fashioned "circular walk" which was usually a part of every eighteenth-century design; a wilderness of hollies, yews, ivies, and winter-flowering shrubs; a primrose garden "possibly surrounded by a nut walk"; and "a large mass of forsythia planted on a hillside" with blue lungwort and daffodils beneath it in the grass.[9]

Mildred Bliss's reply, dated July 13, 1922, was instant and ecstatic: "Your letter and its enclosures have made us purr with contentment. You have got it exactly in every respect! and I can't be patient until you get back here and start to realise your and our mutual dream."[10] The survey of the Rock of Dumbarton reached Beatrix at Reef Point just as she was packing to leave for Europe: "To my great joy the survey has just come and I have been distracted from my morning's work. . . . the fall of the land between the Orangery and the level of the water in the pool is incredible . . . a drop of over forty feet which makes our terrace quite an amusing study. . . . a hasty glance makes me think that some of the terracing will have to be split up into two levels. . . ."[11]

Thus, almost instantaneously as a response to the site and her clients, the garden of Dumbarton Oaks was formulated. The excitement had rushed mere polite acquaintance into friendship; the letters had started politely, but soon Beatrix was writing "My very dear Mildred" and signing herself "Yours very affectionately." In January 1923 Robert Bliss was sent as minister to Sweden, and after four years there, they moved to South America. During the twenties both Dumbarton Oaks' garden and the friendship between Beatrix and the Blisses grew by the means of long letters and short meetings. Beatrix happily sent Mildred a sketch of every detail, telling her to mark it for how she wanted it, and Mildred's "sharp criticism" was a much valued spur and encouragement. On April 14, 1923, Beatrix sent a photograph of three cedars that Professor Sargent had at the Arnold Arboretum, for $300 each; they were just what the garden needed. Mildred's reply was swift, as usual: "Dearest Trix—yes, as clearly Mr Sargent loves you enough to part with them, so go ahead."[12] Her letters gave the Blisses much delight and homesickness; they were "Your devoted Blisses," and soon "MilRob," as the Farrands became "MaxTrix." Dumbarton Oaks library holds all the pieces of paper and thousands of drawings that built a garden across an ocean. They worked through every detail of

Traquair House and the seventeenth-century garden pavilions, near Peebles, Scotland. These ogee-roofed pavilions were the most distinctive that Beatrix saw on her travels, and inspired her designs for Crosswicks and Dumbarton Oaks. Photographed by Country Life *in 1906.*

the design. In the big things, the great sweeps, the levels, the actual making of the garden, they trusted Beatrix implicitly. It was in the details—with seats, tables, inscriptions, ornaments, gate hinges, all the smaller things—that the Blisses wanted endless debates upon literary connections and classical symbolism, for they were, after all, art collectors, and the garden was another part of their fabulous collection.

Mildred Bliss wrote later of Beatrix's integrity and loyalty, of her never imposing a detail, even when she was "sure" of it, if the Blisses did not quite understand. ". . . never were the owners so persuasive as to insist on a design which Mrs Farrand's inner eye could not accept. A deepening friendship born of intellectual challenges, of differing tastes and of the generous tact of her rich wisdom made the years of their close association a singularly happy and most nourishing experience. Never did Beatrix Farrand impose on the land an arbitrary concept. She 'listened' to the light and wind and grade of each area under study. The gardens grew naturally from one another. . . ."[13]

As Beatrix's first ideas were all realized through the twenties, with the addition of the kitchen garden (the twin ogee-roofed pavilions coming directly from those she had seen in Scotland, at Traquair House), the swimming pool and tennis court and Mildred Bliss's own particular idea for the North Vista, so the treasures were amassed in the house too: a sixteenth-century repoussé silver paten of the communion of the Apostles found at Riha in Syria, sixth-century Coptic tapestries, Byzantine silk fragments showing the "elephant tamer," a third-century gold necklace of forty links of paired ducks with dolphin clasp, a seventh-century Egyptian necklace of gold and lapis lazuli, and a ninth-century copper-and-gilt chalice of Grimfridus.[14] How could the garden be any less magnificent than these?

*I*n 1922 Edward Harkness insisted that Yale should make use of the woman who happened to be married to the professor of constitutional history. At the very outset, and completely in character, Beatrix instructed the university office to address her as "Beatrix Farrand," not Mrs. or Miss.

As at the Harknesses' Eolia, Beatrix followed the architect James Gamble Rogers in working on Yale's Memorial Quadrangle, between Branford, Saybrook, and Jonathan Edwards Colleges, which was paid for by Edward Harkness. She was also working on the surroundings of the Sterling Laboratory before she officially took up her post as consulting landscape gardener to Yale on January 1, 1923. She was to receive a fixed salary, not fees, and therefore she allocated her time very regularly over the next eighteen years.

She started by walking the campus and the courtyards, checking the trees, wall plantings and—most importantly—pathways worn across grass by student feet. All these things would need her attention. She went even farther, as she informed Thomas Farnam, her chief ally at Yale, on March 17, 1923: "I stopped . . . on my way back . . . to consult with Mr Klauder (the architect) with regard to the grades surrounding the new Peabody Museum. We carefully considered the whole question and we agree that the grade at the building should be forty which means a raise of two feet from the grade of thirty-eight originally proposed. I ventured to make some suggestions to Mr Klauder with regard to providing open spaces around the building and the possible re-spacing of certain areas to allow planting space at the strategic points. Mr Klauder quite saw the advisability of certain of these suggestions and kindly said he would see that these small changes were made."[15]

She also instigated the features which distinguish the older Yale colleges, their "moats," which she suggested to James Gamble Rogers. She saw the moats as "an opportunity to create a kind of planting that was protected from being trodden on and, at the same time, created a canopy for the sidewalk."[16] Crabapples, viburnums, magnolias, witch hazels, forsythias, and cherries as well as wreaths of English ivy clambered from the moats over Yale's Gothic walls.

Her Princeton experience gave her the confidence to tackle Yale in these ways, and also—right from the start—to propose a nursery, which began its life in the autumn of 1923 with fifteen hundred plants "thus getting better plants for less money and obtaining varieties not commonly available."[17] While the economics of the nursery idea pleased the university, Beatrix had formulated a wider philosophy, which Diana Balmori attributes to her Arts and Crafts beliefs, saying that buying plants from commercial nurseries was the equivalent of buying William Morris's despised mass manufactures.[18] The nursery, established with great help from Professor Sargent and seeds from the Arboretum, enabled Yale to cultivate its own plant collection. Beatrix saw the campus, as she did Princeton and would later see Chicago, as a "kind of fragmentary botanic garden," as a "small exhibition ground of certain types of trees and shrubs."[19] An extra dimension was added to the Yale challenge when Professor Othniel C. Marsh of the Botany Department donated money for a university botanic garden, which Beatrix also designed and set up, in conjunction with the nursery. Her friend, Thomas Farnam, was treasurer of the Botanical Garden, and he was the chief advocate of these schemes to the university authorities. It was hard work; university officials could be petulant and slow-witted; one, a Mr. Johnson, painstakingly wrote out the details: "I understand a nursery will be started, and that this will be under the direction of and will be operated by the Botanical Garden. That it is intended to raise at first only the more expensive types of plants. The propagating of the small plants would be done at the Botanical Garden itself; that the plants would then be moved to a nursery to develop, and I understand also that certain types of specimens might be planted about the grounds where they would serve a decorative purpose for a time, and either by thinning or removal would be transplanted later to permanent locations. Such planting about the grounds I suppose would automatically remove these plants from the care of the Botanical Garden."[20]

Such was the ruling of little empires, and Beatrix must have spent most of her Yale time, and probably much more than she was paid for, delicately dealing with the university powers—who had never had a woman in such a position of authority before—as she tried to meld a score of little worlds into a whole environment. Ironically, it was at Yale that George Perkins Marsh had written his *Man & Nature* (which inspired her as much as his contemporaries and friends F. L. Olmsted and Sargent) and at Yale there was such a chance to involve the student body, the departments of Forestry and Botany, its architects and horticulturists, into the making of a harmonious whole, the university environment. Beatrix had the vision to see such a dream; but she spent days and hours dealing with minute problems, caused by petty officialdom.

Edward Harkness, too, was a man of vision. He was so impressed by her work in his garden at Eolia, which went on through the twenties, that he had another job for her. In 1925 James Gamble Rogers designed the Harkness Mausoleum on a large plot in Woodlawn Cemetery, New York. This last residence, planned in advance, on Golden Rod Avenue, was a rectangular Romano-Gothic mausoleum, with a circular entrance court surrounded with native dogwoods, hawthorns, red cedars, and white pines, with honeysuckles and climbing hydrangeas and myrtles and a green floor of pachysandra.

At the same time, across the continent, another millionaire prepared in the same way for death. Henry E. Huntington's earthquake-proof, domed classical mausoleum in his garden at San Marino in California was designed, by John Russell Pope, to hold first the body of Mrs. Arabella Huntington, who had died in September 1924. Henry E. joined her in May 1927, having carefully prepared for his earthly belongings, which were indeed considerable, by the establishment of a deed of trust in 1919, for the establishment of the Henry E. Huntington Library and Art Gallery.

In the summer of 1927 a buzz went around the academic world, wondering just who would get the plum position as director of the library with its great collection of English and American history and literature. It was Max Farrand's old friend, the astronomer and scientist George E. Hale, who suggested that Max might like working in California, and that the Farrands should visit San Marino. Max liked what he saw; the place was magnificent, the climate was enticing, the books, pictures, and treasures that Mr. Huntington had left behind were a challenge. But what about Beatrix's very definitely East Coast career? In the late summer of 1927 at Reef Point, as she gardened ostensibly at peace with the world, her mind must have been in a turmoil. Her autumn diary was packed—a session in New Haven, to Princeton and Dumbarton Oaks, several places on Long Island to be seen, across to Eolia at New London, the shutting up of Reef Point, a dozen minor jobs, a visit to the Arnold, lectures to be given, and the indefatigable but aging Mary Cadwalader (now seventy-seven) to be cared for, let alone her beloved, unquenchable aunt Edith, still gallivanting across France like an empress.

California must have seemed the equivalent of another planet. The decision to leave the East Coast must have been a testing point of her marriage, and there was no question about it. Her priority was Max, his success, his health, welfare, and his happiness, and he wanted to be director of the Huntington Library. Somehow California would replace New Haven in their lives, their term-time home would be in San Marino, and somehow, largely by the wonder of the American railway system, Beatrix would manage three offices—one at Reef Point, one in New York, and one in San Marino, at the same time being the director's wife.

But if she counted upon work in the lush gardening climate of California as a consolation for all the effort of this transcontinental lifestyle, she was to be very disappointed. She made a marvelous job of being the director's wife, she made their home as elegant and comfortable as would have been expected, and she conscientiously played her role, often putting off her clients, especially Mildred Bliss or Dorothy Straight (Elmhirst) by explaining how a stream of visiting dignitaries to the Huntington kept her playing hostess for Max. Long-

Beatrix at her desk, a photograph probably taken in the Farrands' New Haven house c. 1925.

term planning, which had always been her forte, became necessary for survival. Her schedule for October of 1929, when she had just taken on the University of Chicago, runs thus: starting from Dumbarton Oaks on the fourth, she goes to Haverford, Pennsylvania, to see the garden and spend the night at the Wardens' Faraway Farm, on the next day to the Hill School at Pottstown where the headmaster's garden was in her care and further works were in hand. She went to her mother at 21 East Eleventh Street for the night, had a 9 A.M. appointment with Mrs. Milliken on Park Avenue, about her town garden and a 10 A.M. meeting at her trustee, Mr. Hancy's office on Wall Street; she caught the 1:30 P.M. train to Old Westbury to check over Dorothy Straight's gardens with her agent, Mr. Gorton, and returned to Manhattan for an evening with her mother. At 10 A.M. the next morning she was off to New Haven to see Mr. Cromie, Yale's superintendent, on to New London for tea with Mrs. Harkness at Eolia, then by train to Boston and Bar Harbor. From the eighth to the thirteenth she stayed at Reef Point, catching up on notes, drawings, and correspondence and undoubtedly seeing Mrs. Rockefeller's garden at The Eyrie and other local commissions, and leaving the house packed up for the winter. On the fourteenth she headed for New Haven and more work at Yale, staying at the New Haven Lawn Club, then into New York again. She allowed herself a few more days in New York, then down to Washington and another few days' hard work at Dumbarton Oaks. On the twenty-third she was en route for Chicago, spending two days getting to know yet

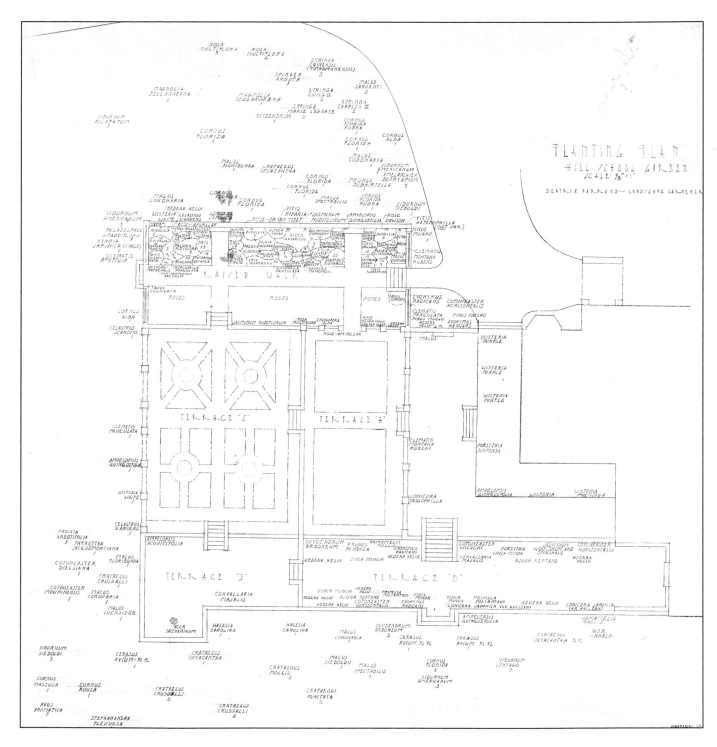

another Gothic campus and to discuss this new and important commission. On October 26, she left Chicago for California.[21]

Professionally California was a disaster. Beatrix, who was by now becoming rather used to having her own way, was completely shut out. At the Huntington she found the fabulous garden firmly in the iron and obsessive grip of William Hertrich. Hertrich, a German, had started working at "San Marino Ranch" for Henry Huntington in 1904; with a little site planning by the architect Myron Hunt, the gardens had been the sole creation of

The Hill School, Pottstown, Pennsylvania: a plan for the raised walk garden, with roses in the sunny border and peonies, irises, lilies, foxgloves, aquilegia, delphiniums, and campanula on the shadier side.

Huntington, with Hertrich following his master's directions. Hertrich had planted the first avocado orchard in 1907, and he had amassed and cared for the magnificent collections of palms and cacti. His devotion had endeared him to Henry and Arabella Huntington—he had really made their garden dreams come true. As well as roses galore and every kind of perennial, there was "a large, handsome Japanese garden bought lock, stock and barrel from a Los Angeles tea garden going out of business. The Japanese atmosphere was completed by a Japanese family . . . who had lived in the garden, celebrating their religious festivals and gardening in their kimonos. Water lily ponds had hot water piped in by the ingenious Hertrich to keep the giant *Victoria regia* blooming into January. . . ."[22] Clearly Mr. Hertrich was not going to yield an inch to anyone, let alone a woman from the chilly coast of Maine.

Outside the Huntington Library's gates, the landscape gardening was firmly in the hands of two brilliant local practitioners, Lockwood de Forest, who had set up his office in Santa Barbara in 1920, and Florence Yoch. The latter had mastered the art of giving rich refugees from the East the kind of English gardens they desired; her passion was for the English cottage garden as smartened up and finely crafted by Edwin Lutyens and Gertrude Jekyll, and her skill was in transplanting both finely crafted details and flowers to California. She and her partner, Lucille Council, did over one hundred gardens in the Pasadena area, and were famous for movie sets.[23]

So Beatrix's few California commissions came mostly from friends (the Blisses wintered in Montecito). She did George E. Hale's private Observatory grounds in Pasadena, and through him received a small commission for tree planting at Mount Palomar Observatory, where he was director. The architect Myron Hunt also involved Beatrix on his projects for Occidental College and for the California Institute of Technology, but she was never really appreciated in either place. Diana Balmori writes of Dabney Court, at the Institute of Technology in Pasadena, as "a gem set in the rest of the institute landscape. A planting of olive trees and grass, with some low plants at the edges of the courtyard, seems so simple as not to be much of a planting at all. But it is a very subtle piece of design, with low walls all round it creating a cloistered, peaceful space different from any other on the campus."[24] The olive trees were carefully shaped and pruned "into sculptures with silver leaves," and Beatrix also used eucalyptus and native palms, showing that she was perfectly willing to adjust her classical campus landscape ideas to suit Californian species. (Beatrix's only other notable Californian commission was as consultant to the Santa Barbara Botanic Garden from 1938 until her death. This was negotiated by the Blisses, Mildred's mother, Anna Blakesley Bliss, who endowed the Botanic Garden—and Beatrix's influence was mostly accidental; she had a free hand with the main report because her coconsultant, Lockwood de Forest, was in the army in 1938.)[25]

The appearance of Dorothy Straight's Old Westbury garden in Beatrix's frantic schedule of October 1929 was a hint of the future, though as yet she did not know. On her trips to Long Island during the twenties, often involved with demanding clients like the Otto Kahns or Harrison Williams, Beatrix had loyally and quietly kept an eye on the Chinese garden she had made with Willard and Dorothy Straight. She had formed a good working relationship with Harry Lee, the head gardener, and Mr. Gorton, the agent. After Willard Straight's untimely death in 1918, his widow, who was only thirty-one, had immersed herself in looking after their three small children and perpetuating Willard's memory. (As Michael Young later wrote of her, she moved in a society "made up of men and women who walked down Fifth Avenue with serious tread . . . most of them with uphill work to do."[26]) She was close to Herbert Croly and kept a controlling eye on *The New Republic.* She was president of the Association of Junior Leagues of America and staunch in her support of women's trade unions. And she was soon busy again with a group of loyal and devoted friends and suitors, and Beatrix would have encountered her regularly in New York even though their gardening relationship was shelved for the moment.

In 1920 at Cornell, where she was organizing the student union building as Willard Straight's memorial, Dorothy met an impoverished Englishman named Leonard Elmhirst, who was studying agriculture and hoped to change the world. He pursued at first her money, then Dorothy. She paid for him to go to India and learn from Rabindranath Tagore.[27] He returned with a dream of starting a progressive school (one of Willard's interests), and Dorothy was intrigued. She eventually agreed to marry Elmhirst and go to England with him to realize his dream. They were married in April 1925. A month before his marriage, Leonard had been in England, and out of forty-eight West Country estates on the market he had chosen Dartington Hall in Devon. In May he and Dorothy left for England. Her friends, including Beatrix, missed her and wondered about her. Eventually, upon inquiring about what was to happen to the Chinese garden, Beatrix received a chilly reply from Leonard, who had now taken over Dorothy's affairs: "We shall only be back for short visits during the next three years. The house will be fairly constantly occupied with convalescent people and week-end visitors. We want the ground, trees, lawns and garden to be kept up in first rate shape and a policy to be worked out looking ahead five and even ten years, so that at any time, if wanted, with the help of bedding out annuals and laying down borders, the garden could be brought into condition for our residence there."[28] Harry Lee, the head gardener, was to carry on, working with Beatrix and taking orders from her. The general idea was "to drive a middle course between extra outlay and too close a cutting down of bills," and—Leonard was an expert in forestry economics—money was to be made wherever possible.

So Beatrix kept a regular eye on Dorothy's garden. During 1927 she ordered a thinning of the hemlocks she had planted in 1914, and they were able to sell some eighty for $2,000. The garden was dug over and replanted; her earlier plantings of rhododendrons and other flowering shrubs also yielded thinnings for sale or replanting. But she seemed to be shut off from Dorothy and could only pen a note to try to get through "how much the place misses you" or "please give my best love to Dorothy" as she cared for the garden of which she had become so fond. Her stewardship continued into the early thirties; Leonard remained as stiff as ever, but at least he was satisfied with her work.[29] They hardly ever met, the Elmhirsts' rare visits to New York being short and tightly scheduled, and Beatrix invariably elsewhere. But "Apple Green," as Dorothy now called it, kept a very special place in Beatrix's heart, and soon her loyalty would be rewarded.

Chapter 10

❧❧❧

TRANSATLANTIC FELLOWS:
DUMBARTON OAKS
AND DARTINGTON HALL,
1931—37

With Max Farrand's appointment as director of the Huntington Library, Beatrix could have taken the chance to do less work: she might have been content to be just Max's wife while they were in San Marino, and with perfect justification. She would be sixty in 1932, and the constant traveling since they had moved to California took a great toll on her elegant but bony frame. If she had any thoughts of doing less, these were soon dispelled by the Crash and the arrival of the Depression years. Her mother's income had dwindled to virtually nothing, but Mary Cadwalader soldiered on; Edith was generous, but both Beatrix and Mary were far too proud to ever ask for anything. For Mary particularly there had always been plenty of money, and Beatrix carefully guarded her mother's high standards. She always gave her suitably stylish presents, as for Mary's birthday in 1930, when it was a new silver kettle on a stand, ordered from Tiffany's for $127. To keep up such standards, Beatrix kept working on every commission that came her way.

But the Depression took its toll; Yale cut its staff dramatically and Princeton had no budget for landscapes at all from 1929 to 1936. New private gardens failed to materialize, and though Dumbarton Oaks was safe and securely growing, Beatrix's garden making in the thirties was confined to Maine. It was largely because of these circumstances, as well as for friendship that she took on a major commission in England, over six thousand miles away.

Dorothy and Leonard Elmhirst had settled at Dartington. Their children, Ruth and Bill, had been born in 1926 and 1929, and Dorothy's own children had joined them. They were more than a complete family, for Leonard had drafted his own three brothers to work for the dream. "It was," wrote Michael

Young, "as if the whole family had married into the Whitney money."[1]

The plan for Dartington amounted "to nothing less than the furtherance of The Good Society—of happy, responsible, creative living—through education, the study and practice of the arts and the development of new methods of farming and industry on a sound economic basis, in a decaying rural area."[2] Their raw material was the Dartington Estate of over one thousand acres, with twenty-one acres of pleasure grounds, plus kitchen gardens and graveyard, all set in Devon hills and dales. It had been the home of the Champernownes since 1559, and had King Richard II's royal emblem, a white hart, on a ceiling boss at the entrance to the Great Hall, the Hall itself was part of a large courtyard of stone buildings. The whole place was rundown and ruinous, though Leonard assured everyone that his wife's resources "were such that I need not be frightened."[3] The Hall (which had a box tree growing through its roof) was surrounded by a tangle of brambles, rhododendrons, and laurels which obscured the medieval tiltyard and grass terraces. Twelve yews, planted in the early 1800s and inevitably named The Twelve Apostles, reared their ragged forms above the chaos, and there were also some other fine trees—sixteenth-century Spanish chestnuts, a Monterey pine (a very early Californian emigrant), and splendid nineteenth-century beeches, planes, and oaks. The head gardener, Percy Woods, spent three years just clearing rubbish, while the architect, William Weir, set to work to restore the fabric of the medieval buildings in a careful and sensitive manner.[4]

Dorothy was captivated by Dartington, by Devon, and by Englishness. The redemption and restoration of derelict manor houses was in vogue, much encouraged and illustrated in the magazine *Country Life.* The Elmhirsts chose H. Avray Tipping, one of its most distinguished contributors, who owned an exquisite antique house and lovely garden of his own in Somerset, to advise them on Dartington's garden.[5] Tipping was no professional, at least by Beatrix's standards. He was merely an English gentleman of culture and taste who knew about such things. Typically, he did not respond with enthusiasm. He was rather shocked at the Elmhirsts' airy-fairy notions on progressive education, and he could not equate their wish to own Dartington *and* make money out of it. He hesitated, but finally submitted his ideas in early 1928. He ordered the releveling of the tiltyard and renovation of its terraces, the preservation of the ruined stone arcade of the Long Gallery as a feature on the south lawn, and he planted some good yew hedges. After this he wrote to Leonard that their professional connection should be "considered closed."[6]

This chilly Englishness was unfortunately to become habitual: "The Elmhirsts liked Devon; Devon did not like the Elmhirsts."[7] At least Tipping had sent them a marvelously well qualified gardens superintendent, R. S. Lynch, who had studied in France for several years and came via Kew and Cambridge Botanic Gardens. Lynch and Leonard worked the garden, making a long Sunny Border on the south-facing terraces and constructing the open-air theater at the west end of the tiltyard.

Dorothy was dismayed at the lack of response from the English gardening world she so admired, so she sent an appeal to Beatrix. The latter replied from Bar Harbor on September 5, 1932: "Dear Dorothy, you have paid me I feel a great compliment in suggesting that you would like me to come to Dartington. . . . I should greatly like to accept."[8] Finding a time to visit England was a different matter; the Farrands went to California in October, where Dorothy's cable followed, asking for dates. Max needed Beatrix for important visitors, she had Yale, Princeton, and Chicago to catch up on, work for the Blisses who were now in Buenos Aires, and Max's brother and his wife, the Livingston Farrands, had just announced their arrival for an extended Christmas stay. It was impossible to get away before mid-January. But Julian Huxley had been visiting and he had enthused about the Dartington project and made her more keen than ever;[9] Huxley, whose mother had started her own progressive school, represented the sympathies of liberal, artistic England.

Beatrix planned to sail on the *Manhattan* on January 25, 1933. Leonard asked about her fees. She would charge $150 a day, her standard for an educational institution, and thought $1,750 would cover her work in England with $2,500 for traveling. This was agreed. She arrived in Plymouth in early February, with her itinerary planned; she spent the fourth to the seventh at Dartington, then went up to London, to Fleming's Hotel on Half Moon Street off Piccadilly, from where she wrote to Dorothy: "From the instant I saw your friendly welcoming smile at Plymouth, until yesterday when I left you on the Dartington steps, it was a real delight, an excitement, a problem and one of the keenest artistic pleasures I have ever had in my now very long working years."[10] The next day she went to Kew, to renew some English gardening contacts (with a letter of introduction from the Arnold Arboretum), then to Oxford to refresh her memory on college courtyards. She spent the weekend of February 11–12 at Douglas Freshfields' Wych Cross Place in Sussex,[11] one of Thomas Mawson's gardens, returning to London on Monday the thirteenth. The next day was spent at the Royal Horticultural Society's garden at Wisley, with another introduction from the Arnold, to renew her acquaintance with English plants, and on Wednesday she went to Cambridge, to check out the quadrangles of Trinity and King's College. Then, fortified and renewed with mental visions, she returned to Dartington for ten days' hard work, which Dorothy watched from her window: "She worked incessantly—scrutinizing every corner and angle, setting up her stakes, taking meticulous notes, planning, planning every hour of the day and night."[12] It was a remarkable example of the immersion of the artist in her work, of her getting to know the spirit of the place, of which by now she was so well practiced.

Beatrix left for France, for a "beautiful three days" at Hyeres with Edith and an "orgy of pictures" in Paris, before sailing on the *Manhattan* from Le Havre on March 9. The check for $2,500 awaited her upon arrival.

From trains and the ship a flood of notes and letters sped back to Dartington. The place was enchanting and exciting but only Dorothy's kindness and

BEATRIX

The Gardening Life of

Beatrix Jones Farrand

Dartington Hall, Devon, England: the courtyard with the Great Hall at the far end, as designed by Beatrix in her most serene campus tradition.

hospitality made this demanding, long-distance job possible. Beatrix wanted Dorothy and Leonard to see Dumbarton Oaks, and she wanted their head gardener, Stewart Lynch, to visit America. At home she worked on the intricate problems of the great medieval courtyard, which was to be her greatest gift to Dartington. It was sloping, uneven, and had a track directly across it; she drafted her idea for a gently circumnavigating stone path, every detail of paving, walls, levels, and plants devoted to making an appropriately serene setting for the magnificent Great Hall. Though this kind of intricate drafting needed to be done at home, her experience, her trips to Kew and Wisley, and the plants she had found growing happily in the soft Devon climate, had allowed her to leave instructions for a lot of planting, "backbone" planting for the spring and following autumn. Dorothy, whose gardening knowledge was still primary, wrote: "She insisted on using native material wherever possible, particularly as backbone planting—Scots pine, bays, broad-leaved hollies and beeches. Later she added ilex, deodars, libocedrus, and the two cedars on the lawn—*atlantica* and *libani*. *Magnolia grandiflora* and wisteria she ordered for the grey walls of the courtyard, and climbing roses and honeysuckle, and fifty-five camellias for the wilderness and many other small and large shrubs for that particular plantation. In a short fortnight she had shown us the way to proceed."[13] Beatrix's second great achievement for Dartington was to be the "wilderness" or woodland garden, three delicious, magical paths, the Spring, Camellia, and Rhododendron Walks, layered along the hillside to the west of the tiltyard.

After a spell at San Marino the Farrands came east in the summer of 1933. In June Beatrix, fearing that "nothing tangible has gone from me to Dartington,"[14] assured Leonard and Dorothy that they had not been out of her mind for a single day. The courtyard was gestating! She sent a draft of her plans and her senior draftswoman, Ruth Havey, who worked from the New York office, to have another look in June. Stewart Lynch made his trip—to the Arnold and Mr. Judd, to T. H. Everett at New York Botanical Garden, to Yale and Reef Point later that summer. Dorothy had seen Dumbarton Oaks on a fleeting late summer visit, but had missed Mildred Bliss: Beatrix's letter to her from Reef Point of October 3, 1933, is so typical of her level-headedness in this dizzy world of designing Dartington and Dumbarton Oaks that it is worth quoting in full:

My very dear Dorothy:

It was characteristic of you to write from Old Westbury as you did. Your writing was a real event and gave me the news of you both for which I was hungry. It is too bad that Leonard has had such a tiresome summer as arthritis is no joke, and a tonsil operation is a painful door by which to escape it. Please give him my love and tell him how sorry I am for all his discomfort and pain.

No mother ever purred more audibly with praise than I do over commendation of the joint work which Mildred and I have done at Dumbarton Oaks. Knowing her you can appreciate what a stimulating heart and soul hers is to work with and that Dumbarton Oaks has answered to her call quite as much as it has to my own. All I have done is to try to help her to dream true, as she had imagined the box ellipse when she was a child, so that its actual existence only wanted the spade and level to make it come true. I was glad you liked the sound of running water, which is never far from one during the green months at Dumbarton.

Mildred was bitterly disappointed not to see you at "The Oaks" as she had framed her whole autumn schedule on your visit and had set her heart on showing you the garden herself. Perhaps the next time you and Leonard are in this region that dream may also come true.

Thank you from my heart for what you say about my dear "Apple Green." It has always seemed to me that the place at Westbury reflects you in its quiet and beauty and charm just as Dumbarton Oaks reflects Mildred. And what has been done at "Apple Green" is only a translation of you into leaves and trees.

Thank you also for bothering about what Henry Adams called "my perishable carcass." There has been really nothing the matter except an orgy of overwork lasting too long and complicated by more years than I am ever conscious of. It has meant merely a somewhat turnip-like existence—reading, sleeping, walking and sunning and not yielding to my besetting sin of overdoing. When poor Max arrived from California he found his aged wife had given in too enthusiastically to her desire to work and so promptly and gently he has made me rest and pick up and I expect to swing back and start work again in a more moderate tempo.

If you like Dumbarton Oaks let us all three, Leonard and you and I, work to make Dartington its English fellow. Dartington is starting with infinitely more beauty and with the stimulation of you two and my enthusiasm let us do something worthy of the old place. It seems long until January.[15]

At the beginning of January 1934 she wrote again. Two months in California had "cured her aches and pains" and restored her "usual blitheness and energy." Max had found he needed to visit England, so they would be arriving in Plymouth in early February. They stayed at Dartington, Beatrix checked progress, and they had a marvelous time: Max wrote to Leonard from the Athenaeum on March 2: "It's a big thing you're attempting and thoroughly worth doing. . . ." He had wisely scouted among fellow academics for opinions of the Dartington experiment in child-centered education, coeducational learning-by-doing in a democratic, free-thinking environment. He reported great interest and enthusiasm among the younger men, but the older ones, typical of England's establishment, were just "sitting back and doing nothing."[16] This is what the Elmhirsts were up against; Max undoubtedly sensed it and expressed "nothing but admiration" for the standards they were setting. He was happy to see Dorothy looking at least ten years younger than when he had last seen her.

*D*orothy saw Dumbarton Oaks in the late summer of 1933, just as the Blisses had returned to live there full-time in retirement. Beatrix's achievement, as Walter Muir Whitehill described it, offered "an extraordinary illusion of country surroundings" in the city. "From the windows of the dining room and library on the south side of the house one looked across a broad sweep of lawns, divided by the curving driveway leading in from R Street. The north facade . . . looked onto the North Court, partly enclosed by the flanking wings of the drawing room and music room, which gave on the North Vista. There three rectangular lawns on different levels, gradually narrowing in width, led to a point of view above a steep drop, from which one saw only sky and the trees of the distant hillside."[17]

Whitehill, the doyen of Dumbarton Oaks devotees, understood the Blisses' tastes so well, and he also appreciated Beatrix's endeavors. His intelligent description of the garden in the prime of the Blisses' ownership offers a unique look backward, revealing the clever transformation of a country garden in a rural setting into a sophisticated paradise in a seemingly rural setting that was in truth the heart of Georgetown. Whitehill recognized the formal garden spaces as a series of intimate rooms—the Star Garden, north of the drawing room, with its inscription from Chaucer's translation of Boethius, "O Thou Maker of the Wheel that Bereth the Starres . . . ," and its neighboring Green Garden terrace, which overlooked the swimming pool, built on the site of the old manure pit. The poolside loggia and dressing rooms, wreathed in wisteria, replaced the cowsheds of the Blounts' time.

To the east of the house and the Green Garden terrace, a further "series of formal terraces took one down the hillside by gradual stages. Each has its distinct character. The Beech Terrace, created around a great purple beech, was made intimate and useful by the presence of pink marble benches and a table . . . ," and next came the Box or Urn Terrace, then a flight of steps led down twelve feet to the large Rose Terrace.[18] From the East the obvious direction to follow was down a double staircase to the Fountain Terrace, to the north of which was originally an herb garden, later transformed into a paved Pot Garden with a wisteria-covered arbor, built after a design of de Cerceau. From here paths curved down the hillside in various directions: "To the north . . . lay the herbaceous borders, framed in yews cut with peaked tops to avoid damage from snow, beyond which were the cutting and kitchen gardens. To the eastward another path curved to the enchanting woodland area near Lovers' Lane. . . . there in a natural glade, some 55 feet below the Beech Terrace, was Lovers' Lane Pool, approached by a winding brick path at the upper end, where a minuscule baroque amphitheatre—of bricks laid under Mrs. Farrand's personal supervision—looked down across the pool to Melisande's Alley, where a double line of silver maples . . ." led still further down the hill, following the lines of an old cow path. "Other slopes of the hillside were massed with forsythia, flowering cherries, and other delights of spring, while in the bottom of the valley were natural woodland paths, where early spring bulbs created a carpet reminiscent of a Fra Angelico celestial meadow."[19]

There were other ways through this paradise; via the neat Kitchen Garden with its ogee-roofed tool houses, to the Ellipse, "where a broad fountain was

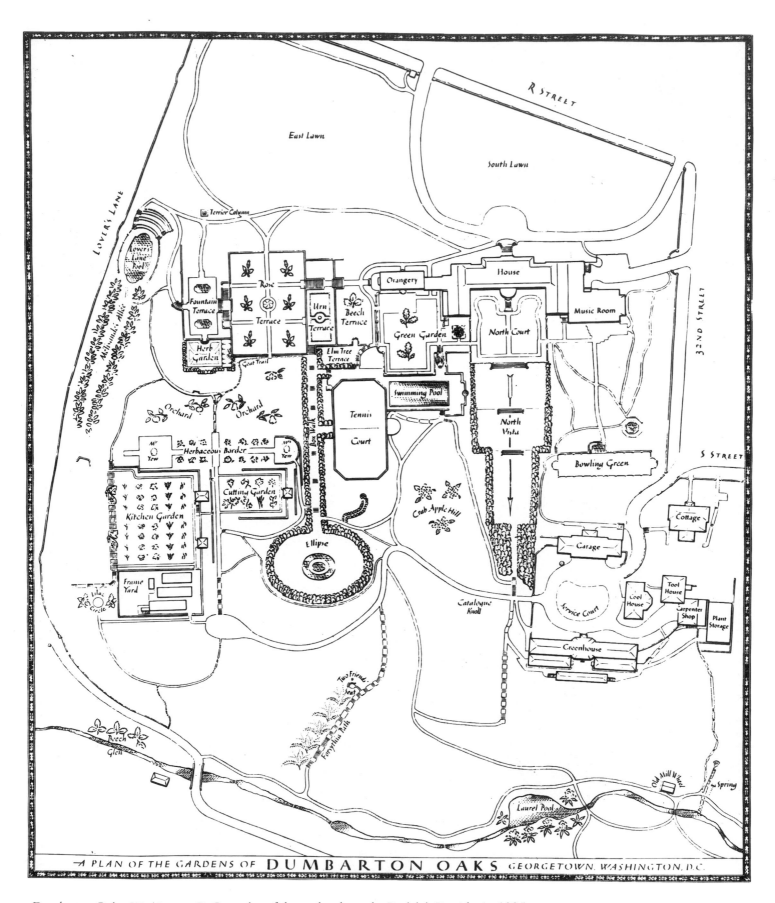

Dumbarton Oaks, Washington, D.C.: a plan of the garden drawn by Rudolph Ruzicka in 1935.

set in a vast ellipse of box"[20]—this for Mildred Bliss's childhood memory. There was a long pergola at the foot of the kitchen garden and one could walk for hours along the weaving paths through the forsythia or cherry blossom dells, which were just as Beatrix had first imagined. The garden could charm the solitary wanderer or please six hundred guests at the State Department garden party which the Blisses held each June. These were Dumbarton Oaks' finest years. The Blisses had really made their dream come true—a kind of East Coast version of Henry E. Huntington's California treasure house and garden. How strange it must have been in the Depression years of the thirties for the ever-realistic Beatrix to find that her life oscillated between them both!

But there was also Chicago, to bring her down to earth. Her first visit to the university, probably in the autumn of 1929, was something of a return journey. She found the splendid Gothic buildings rising next to the ghosts of the 1893 "White City," the World's Columbian Exposition that had so affected her choice of career. She must also have thought of her adored "Chief," Charles Sargent, who had died "in his boots" at the Arnold, aged eighty-six, on March 22, 1927; he had brought her there and made so many things possible for her since.

Her introduction to the University of Chicago came via the architect C. C. Zantzinger of Zantzinger, Borie and Medary who had worked both at Yale and Princeton. He was working on the men's halls of residence, Burton-Judson Courts, which Beatrix "furnished" with plants, but her real purpose was to review and revise the whole campus layout, which had originally been planned by John Charles Olmsted in 1902. The situation had radically changed since then. The university had amassed some very rich patrons, including John D. Rockefeller Jr. in the late twenties, and was on a building spree; great utility tunnels were being excavated across the formal lawns, and the automobile had arrived with a vengeance, invading all the walks and quadrangles to a shocking extent. Beatrix trod warily, carefully assessing what had happened to the Olmsted design and plantings through various tamperings and events. Apart from the intrusion of the motor cars, the planting was lacking in unity, with original oaks now gnarled and stunted, young trees thriving too close to buildings or sited without purpose: ". . . A still further number of discouraged and feeble trees are struggling to continue an undernourished and possibly horticulturally vitaminless existence!"[21] The chief bone of contention was Olmsted's great Circle, the focal point of the rectangular space of the main campus which had become the traditional gathering place—"something approaching a tradition, something always to be there" wrote the editor of the university magazine, just as he was about to announce that the "Circle must go"—according to the university authorities. The Circle, as a racetrack for 100-horsepower cars, was dangerous for the students, but it was also the rendezvous each noonday for the faculty wives' clubs. The ladies liked to use their cars on campus. The university stood firm: cars must go, or at any rate be rationed to one or two roadways, and be banished from the quadrangles. Beatrix now realized that *her* job was to justify this flouting of dear tradition. She quietly got on with a beautifully drawn proposal for a main campus—optimistically labeled "the university of the future" with a single crossing of motor road through allées of trees and many diagonal paved footpaths. The plan was revised and polished, drawn for publication in the university magazine and justified at great length by her skillful reasoning. "A study must be made of the past in order to understand the reason for certain conditions in the present." Two years had been spent studying campus problems, the faculty had been consulted, the staff had been well trained to look after plantings; the campus walks, she explained at great length, were designed to fulfill many purposes, all very carefully worked out, and she had a great deal of experience. She flattered the collective university consciousness by showing them Eckhart as built—bare, a "dead pile of stones"—and Eckhart as she had planted it, "a living thing."[22] The campaign went on for about four years. Beatrix achieved many of the calmly rational desire-line paths across the campus and carefully tended the planting, but she never persuaded the faculty—as opposed to the Department of Buildings and Grounds whose dictate it was—that the Circle should go. (And it is still there.)

Her less controversial work at the University of Chicago included some fine planting around the buildings and some lovely serene courtyards. The outstanding legacy is the courtyard of John D. Rockefeller Jr.'s International House, which reached the stage of final approval in March 1932. This is a small court, completely enclosed within Holabird & Root's elegant stone building. It is paved, random rectangular paving carefully specified as to color, mostly gray and green but with touches of black, mottled green and purple and red. This smooth, elegant paving is surrounded by a low wall of rough Jolley limestone, which supports the raised terrace walk around the court. In the center is an octagonal pool with a wonderful bronze fountain, the work of Jon Magnus Jonson from Indiana, a student of Larado Taft working in the finest Arts and Crafts tradition.[23]

Charles Sprague Sargent's death in March 1927 did not leave her without friends at the Arnold Arboretum but she probably did miss that direct line to her "Chief." He had undoubtedly spoiled her with plants she might not have otherwise been allowed to have—witness Mildred Bliss's astute remark about Sargent "loving her enough" to let her have three marvelous young cedars for Dumbarton Oaks—and the Arboretum supplied seed and seedlings for her campus nursery experiments in the cause of good academic cooperation. She had always used the Arnold as a living reference book—popping in whenever she was in Boston to make notes and check names. As she undoubtedly made her requests to Sargent on these occasions, and he answered them there and then, no correspondence survives to show how she softened the fearsome visage of that "autocrat of autocrats," as Ernest "Chinese" Wilson called him. With Sargent gone the hierarchy at Harvard changed: Professor Oakes Ames became the university's botany supremo with all departments in his sway and Ernest Wilson became "Keeper" of the Arnold. Beatrix only had a passing acquaintance with either of them. So, wisely, she turned to her former friend, William Henry Judd, Jackson Dawson's successor as chief propagator at the Arboretum. Judd was an Englishman, a plantsman to his fingertips, a much quieter man than Dawson, of dry humor and quick wit and impeccable manners. It was to Judd that Beatrix wrote when she needed English contacts for her work at Dartington, and when she returned home, bringing the greetings of his friends at Kew and Wisley, she invited him to visit the Huntington and Reef Point. Judd had a month off every summer to travel all over America looking at other people's gardens, so he visited both places several times during the late thirties and became a regular summer visitor at Reef Point in the early forties. Beatrix was also good friends with the remarkable Susan Delano McKelvey, sister of the architect William Adams Delano, who after a brief, unhappy spell of married life had trained herself to be useful at the Arboretum. With Sargent's encouragement, Mrs. McKelvey had become so knowledgeable about lilacs that her monograph on the genus was published in 1928; she too was a frequent visitor to Reef Point, and she rarely went empty-handed.[24]

Beatrix's surviving correspondence with William Judd reveals that Reef Point had been used as a kind of Mount Desert Island testing ground for Arnold plants, particularly clematis, honeysuckles, azaleas, Korean box, and a *Kirengeshoma palmata,* sent in the mid twenties, which spent several doubtful years before flowering creamy yellow trumpet flowers and fruiting happily in 1933 (and after). She was particularly successful with the clematis (even though winter nights could go down to 20 degrees below freezing and summer sunshine baked them at over 90 degrees), which began blooming in May with *C. montana rubens* and followed with no break in the procession: "The south window frame on which *C. montana rubens* grows with its delicate reddish shoots and soft pink flowers, looks like the frontispiece to an old gardening book."[25] Next came the faithful *C. vitalba,* followed with the hybrid "Nelly Moser" 's pale lavender flowers in profusion, then rarer species, *C. texensis* "with its attractive thick red sepals and lovely feathery seed heads . . . *C. crispa* and *C. viticella* grow well," and a later species, *C. apiifolia,* which gives a creamy mass of bloom on an eastward-facing step balustrade. A precious latecomer, *C. tangutica obtusiuscula,* with tuliplike pendant flowers—one of those clematis that look like aerial fritillaries—had iridescent seed heads as lovely as the flowers. But her prize was a species of celastrus, *Tripterygium regeli,* which Sargent sent her as one of his last offerings, in a bundle, and described as a "dud" to which Reef Point was most welcome as the Arnold could make nothing of it. Beatrix planted it on the southeast corner of the house and it had grown with "rampant cheerfulness"—sweetly scented trusses of tiny cream flowers often three feet long. ". . . and in July the whole side of the

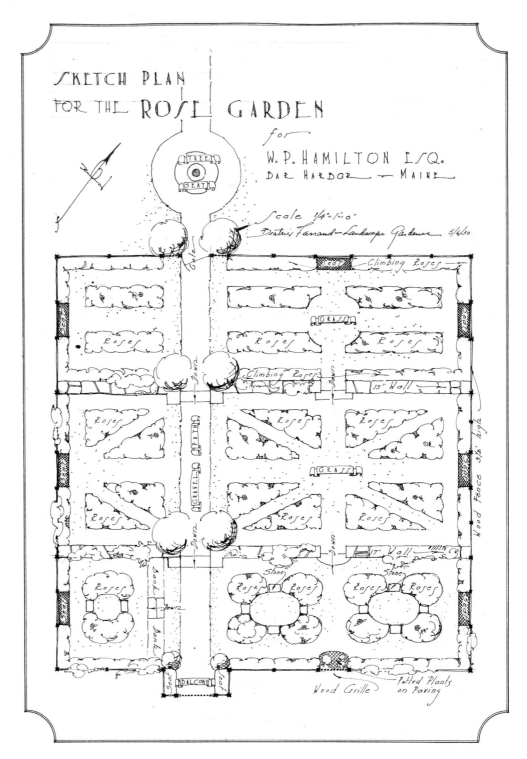

SKETCH PLAN FOR THE ROSE GARDEN for W. P. HAMILTON ESQ. BAR HARBOR — MAINE

Thirlestane, home of W. Pierson Hamilton, Eagle Lake Road, Bar Harbor, Maine: sketch layout for a garden of rose beds set in grass and enclosed by a wooden trellis fence for climbing roses, dated May 6, 1930. Thirlestane was destroyed in the 1947 fire.

house where it grows is as murmurous with bees as any English lime-tree walk."[26] She later teased Judd when the Arnold described it as a shrub—hers was well over twenty-five feet high!

The tripterygiums were presumably in full blossom in July 1934 when everything at Reef Point had been clipped and tidied for the annual meeting of the Garden Club of America on four days of talking and touring.[27] The ladies, several of them Beatrix's clients, descended upon the Malvern Hotel (in which Beatrix had a business interest) in Bar Harbor on the tenth to be docketed and labeled and introduced before they set out to see some twenty-five gardens around Bar Harbor itself, south to Great Head, with a day in Seal Harbor and another in Northeast Harbor. For Beatrix it was both an honor *and* a harrowing experience. Naturally they saw Reef Point, where the "roses and wild things naturalized" were particularly lovely according to one anonymous Garden Club lady; and a short step away, on Mount Desert Street almost opposite Saint Savior's Church, they found Miss Gertrude Sampson's enclosed and informal garden which Beatrix had been working on since 1927. The garden, so near the center of the town, was a surprise—an enclosed lawn with an irregular border of annuals, a natural flowery meadow with a path leading into a pine grove. At Tanglewold on Kebo Street, one of the resort's most colorful houses, an elaborate timber-patterned "cottage," they saw Mrs. A. Murray Young's terraced garden which Beatrix had made since 1918 "to fit the steep hillside with as little disturbance as possible." The upper terrace had a formal fountain and provided "a brilliant foreground," presumably with annuals and perennials, to the view of the distant hills, framed with clipped thuyas. Lower terraces, one of peonies and iris, one of ferns, led to the woodland path, a brook, and a pool. Farther north, on Highbrook Road, they saw Miss McCormick's old Maine farmhouse, now enlarged but rambling, keeping its homely feeling. Working with the architect, Arthur McFarland, Beatrix had made a cottage garden for vegetables and flowers "where old-fashioned borders of dahlias, delphiniums, and many-coloured annuals"[28] grew in masses of color. Still farther north, off Eden Street on the way to Hull's Cove, was the Stotesburys' Wingwood House, which was much grander: this had been remodeled in 1925 into an eighty-room classical "cottage" with a large sea-facing terrace. The locals were amazed when the Stotesburys allegedly paid Beatrix $1,500 a tree to move in ten elms to surround the terrace, as well as juggle with a hundred big pines to make the spacious, parklike setting. Mrs. Stotesbury was reputed to "shift her plants around the ground twice a week" among other excesses (apparently sending out an expedition for alligators to make up a matching set of luggage) that make up Bar Harbor's glorious past[29]—but the flowers were mostly in large containers!

South from Bar Harbor the Garden Club saw two very different gardens, proving that for every "cottager" who brought their Long Island grandeur with them, there were two who planted to enhance the very different character of northern Maine. At the Potter Palmers' Hare Forest on the road up to Schooner Head, the driveway had been carefully planned by Beatrix's friend, the conservationist George Dorr; Beatrix had added the natural planting along the drive and around the terrace which looked onto Frenchman's Bay. Farther south was the wonderful Satterlee garden at Great Head, with its magical wooded dells leading to the sea, with paths through midsummer flowers. In Northeast Harbor they visited Mrs. Charlton Yarnall at The Birches on Sargent Drive, another terraced garden with a fabulous view across Somes Sound; Beatrix planted three terraces: one of shade-loving plants under birches, the second of perennials of pink, pale blue, and white, and the third of perennials of yellows, browns, scarlet, and bright blue. Out on the South Shore Road at the entrance of Somes Sound was The Haven, the summer home of Beatrix's friend Agnes Milliken.[30] The Haven had long walks to the sea and wide views. It was such a lovely place that the most gentle enhancement was all that was necessary—clumps of lupins on rocky, juniper-covered slopes, with delphiniums and hemerocallis in large informal groups. Into this paradise Beatrix had carefully fitted a rose garden, a kitchen garden, and a tennis court, designing all the details of the seats, screens, pavings, and fences. She worked here for over twenty years, from 1925, the kind of garden and gardening friendship that she found most worthwhile. It was to be Agnes Milliken who found Gertrude Jekyll's drawings—just about to be discarded—while on a visit to England and brought them home for Beatrix.

But the adjustments of nature so carefully done for Mrs. Satterlee and Mrs. Milliken were but a preparation for Beatrix's most lovely island achievement, which undoubtedly brought gasps of delight from the Garden Club ladies. This was Abby Aldrich Rockefeller's, The Eyrie, on its bluff as its name implies, above Seal Harbor. When the Garden Club visited in July 1934 The Eyrie's garden was in its eighth summer, and perfect—indeed the designer was just about to relinquish it to the capable care of its owner.

Beatrix had known the John D. Rockefeller Jrs. for years. They had come to the island in the wake of Mrs. Rockefeller's doctor, who had insisted on his summer retreat, while she was expecting a child and did not want to be out of his reach.[31] They rented The Briars, two plots south along the Shore Path from Reef Point, where in the summer of 1908 Nelson Rockefeller was born. His parents were so captivated by the island that they decided to stay; they bought a great deal of land and built The Eyrie, a vast, rambling ragstone "cottage." For a while they had been content with the large terraces around the house, and the natural woodland that kept it secluded. It was on a trip to the Far East in the early twenties, which fueled John D. Rockefeller Jr.'s passion for Chinese porcelain, that they had collected some very fine Chinese and Korean antiques. It was to provide a setting for these that they called in Beatrix, in the autumn of 1926. Mrs. Rockefeller also wanted flower borders in the English style, so the first task was to combine two traditions separated by half a world and centuries of time.

The site for the garden, at a little distance from the house, was revealed as a patch of swampy woodland, with the usual rocky outcrops. Here it was not a problem—for reshaping the countryside, manhandling earth and rocks, was Rockefeller's passion, and almost anything Beatrix suggested he accomplished with some relish. A rectangle was cleared, and walled in pink-washed stucco, topped with glazed tiles brought from China. This walled garden was filled with summer flowers, flowers organized into tiers with low stone walls—colorful crowds of lupins, delphiniums, lilies, asters, and daisies of many kinds, eryngiums, poppies, and montbretias, all blooming in the window of Maine's high summer from July to early September. Along the walls and paths sprawled carpets of pinks, pansies, lavender, stachys, catmint, and small campanulas. The focus of these flowery paths is a round Moon Gate in the northern wall, which leads to the enchanted woodland. Here is the second, equally beautiful but contrasting part of the creation, the Spirit Path, lined with inscrutable Korean tomb figures and other sculptures of great value. The Spirit Path leads through a dappled woodland carpet—paths of raked spruce or pine needles (and they are quite separate and different in character) beneath maples, birches, and pines sheltering a green ground of mosses, lichens, ivies, cornus, and vacciniums, the most bewitching interpretation of the island's natural flora.

After the Garden Club tour, the summer at Reef Point for Max and Beatrix relapsed into the usual pleasures, before they returned to San Marino for the winter.

In early 1935 Beatrix tried to plan her year. She must fit in a trip to England as there was so much to be done. The Elmhirsts had added so many of their other projects to her work in the garden at Dartington Hall: she was designing the surroundings for the Dance Hall (to be home of Margaret Barr's dance-mime school), for the Dartington Central Office building, and layouts for various cottages and houses, and—most exciting of all—the planting for a whole village. This was a speculative development for the Dartington building company Staverton Builders, planned by Henry Wright, the "Radburn" planner, and designed by William Lescaze, the architect partner of George Howe in New York. Churston, as the village was called, was an experiment in the garden city tradition, a modern village, carefully designed to appeal to retired professional people, on the Devon coast. On top of this, Leonard Elmhirst wrote to say that he wanted to take her to Yorkshire, to see Hound Hall Farm near Barnsley, which had originally been his family home and which the family had just bought back and was restoring.

In March Edith wrote to say how much she was looking forward to Mary's visit. Mary Cadwalader, at eighty-four, had "missed" Europe the previous summer and stayed at Bar Harbor. In early April, news came that Edith had had a stroke, which had affected her sight for a while and was to give her a miserable summer. Beatrix and Mary eventually set sail in June. Beatrix arrived in England to find that her old hero William Robinson had died the previous month; she visited Gravetye and Mrs. Gilpin, his housekeeper, to hear about the wonderful tributes that had been paid to the Grand Old Man of Gardening.[32]

Beatrix went to Dartington, where the Camellia Walk had been completed; and to Yorkshire, where she gave Leonard's brother, Pom Elmhirst, some good, and free, advice. Mary went off to Edith at the end of July, but Edith was clearly irritable as an effect of the stroke—"My poor old sister in law arrives this afternoon for a fortnight. I shall be glad when that fortnight is over," she wrote from Pavillon Colombe on July 25.[33] Mary left for London in August to do some business on Edith's behalf and spend some time with friends. (Beatrix by this time was back at Reef Point.) The English weather

BEATRIX

The Gardening Life of

Beatrix Jones Farrand

Beatrix with the aged William Robinson and his cheerful nurse. Her last visit was made in the spring of 1933, when this photograph was taken. Robinson died in 1935, in his ninety-sixth year.

took a sudden turn for the worse and Mary caught a chill; she soldiered on, but the chill became pneumonia. She died at Symonds' Hotel in London, where she had been coming for forty years as a "regular," on September 22, 1935. Poor Edith, full of remorse, made herself go to London, arranged the funeral, the service, and saw to everything. Mary was buried in the little churchyard at Aldbury in Hertfordshire, where she could be with friends. It is the church nearest to Stocks, the country house of the Wards, where she had spent happy summers, and Humphry, Mary, and Arnold Ward are buried near her. Edith, exhausted, returned home to Pavillon Colombe; Bernard Berenson sent condolences, and Edith replied, "Your word of sympathy went to my heart, for I know you loved Minnie and appreciated her rare qualities."[34]

For Beatrix, who could not have got back across the Atlantic in time, there was misery and agony. "We had absolute companionship in all the big things of life . . . I must have often disappointed her . . . but she was always tolerant and kind" she wrote to Edith, and "a dozen times each hour it seems as though I must tell Mummy something."[35] She busied herself with arranging a memorial service for Mary's friends, which was held at the Church of the Ascension in New York on December 12, which would have been her mother's eighty-fifth birthday. The tributes were brave: from Florence Bayard La Farge—"She believed in breeding, in good manners, in the rules of the game and I have seen her again and again by her courtesy and her courage in speaking when no one else would, turn wrangling or a stalemate from timidity, into a valuable resolution or action"; Jane Maulsby Pindell, sometime superintendent of the New York City Training School for Nurses—"in the history of

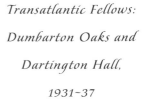

Mary Cadwalader Jones, about
70 years old.

nursing this quiet gentlewoman should rank high among the first American pioneers"; Arnold Whitridge, who had known her all his life, remembered Mary's "curiosity about life," how she had introduced him "to the talk of such different spirits as Henry James and Theodore Roosevelt" and convinced him "that here was life as it ought to be lived"; finally, Royal Cortissoz: "I feel that it is a kind of accolade to have enjoyed her confidence and her friendship . . . she loved her classics but she loved everything that was in the current . . . she was, goodness! interested in a thousand things. She was interested in every phase of life as it flowed around her . . . there was nothing that her imagination and her intelligence did not touch with a certain understanding."[36] Beatrix chose a verse from Proverbs 22:1 "A good name is rather to be chosen than great riches, and loving favour rather than silver and gold." The *Times* of London noted the passing of "a literary and artistic hostess"—"all that was best in American thought and art came into Mrs. Jones's quiet book-filled rooms"—"this gifted woman, whose quick sympathy and insight never failed . . ."[37] The front page of the *Bar Harbor Times* of Friday, September 27, recalled that Mary had come to Bar Harbor with her father in the summer of 1879, remembered her involvements and chairmanships at the Mount Desert Island Hospital and the Village Improvement Association, and that she "held an unquestioned position in the small circle of men and women who directed New York society."[38]

Beatrix had worked ceaselessly to keep 21 East Eleventh Street unaltered for the proud old lady—it was "essentially Mummy's frame and pleasure." Now she had the agonizing task of clearing out the house, and its memories.

The shabbiness of the house, its out-of-date grandeur (which Mary would not allow to be changed), as well as the pathetic relics it held brought her pain and anger, and her response was to destroy all but a few mementos. Beatrix's letters to Edith, some of which survive, are her last outbursts on Mary's behalf—of how "it seems unlikely that even you know what cruelty and injustice there was and how many efforts were made to make the trust for Mummy and me as small as possible."[39] This was her response to Edith's question as to whether Freddy's name should appear on Mary's tombstone. Beatrix was emphatic that it would not. She designed a simple stone for her mother with her name and dates. Mary had left everything to Beatrix, but when "everything" was examined it was very little; the Trust Fund when it was eventually released yielded only $1,147.18—about $200 short of the bank's fees for managing the trust, but accepted by them. Mary's house was sold to the hotel next door, who had long wanted to take it over.[40]

The crises over Edith and Mary had meant that Max and Beatrix didn't even get to Reef Point that summer of 1935, so in the following year it was very necessary. They had formulated an idea that Reef Point should be made into an educational garden, with facilities for visiting students to learn about both the wild and cultivated landscape, and the crucial relationship between the two elements of our surroundings. Beatrix was unable to get away to England in 1936, even though she had hoped to; the following January, after Leonard had sent her photographs of progress and a string of questions, a note of despair arises: "It is with some hesitation that I suggest your waiting my coming next summer," she wrote on January 29, 1937. "As the Dartington work is so intertwined with professional and personal association with you I should hate to hand it over to someone else, but I quite realize that my absence may have made my replacement necessary, in which case I accept the inevitable with as good grace as possible."[41]

The Elmhirsts did not want to lose her and she persevered. But plans for a spring 1937 trip were thrown into chaos by news of Edith's failing health. Beatrix eventually left on the *Normandie* on June 16, now determined to go to Edith and only make further plans after seeing her. Edith had been living a full life to the last; the alarums were sounded by those around her rather than herself. She had written rather wistfully to Jane Clark, after Jane reported her and Kenneth's visit to Dumbarton Oaks and the glories of the garden and Royall Tyler's collection in the house, that she "wish't she could see all that." She had been writing still—telling Bernard Berenson that she was "in the middle of the Gobi desert" of a novel, but early in 1937 three successive bouts of flu (the alarms to Beatrix) had left her "weak as a cat." She was still spirited enough, though, to be furious at only watching her garden "tuning up here & there like a symphony orchestra and suddenly bursting into a glorious 'tutti.'" This was her Sainte-Claire garden near Hyères; she planned to go north to Pavillon Colombe, and on the way she had had another stroke. By the time Beatrix arrived she had rallied and was settled in the loving care of Elisina Tyler and her own house staff, so Beatrix left for Dartington for two weeks' work, and then to set out for home. She had seen her beloved, indomitable aunt for the last time; Edith died quietly on August 11, 1937, and was buried, as she had requested, in the Cimetière des Gonards in Versailles. On August 31 Beatrix wrote to Leonard Elmhirst from Reef Point: "You and Dorothy will undoubtedly have noticed the obituary of my aunt . . . and you will know what a sorrow has come to me through her loss, the very last of my family as well as a charming companion and brilliant example. . . . You do not know with what an added glow of affection you and Dorothy and Dartington are now in my mind. . . ."[42] She felt that they were all that remained of the necessary European dimension to her life that she had grown so used to.

Those two weeks at Dartington were her last visit; her account details the work: "To professional services 15 days at Dartington July 7–21, inclusive. General consideration and details of the Great Court, Forecourt, Garden

Dartington, Devon: Dorothy Elmhirst discovered the satisfaction and joy of gardening, largely due to Beatrix's encouragement and much to her delight.

Front, Wilderness, Azaleas, Open-Air Theater, Rock Garden, Heath Garden, Kitchen Garden, Greenhouse, Flowers for cutting, loggia etc July 23–26 consultations in London with Mr Hening (on estate work and Churston). Work in American office, correspondence, notes etc. $1,000." Her expenses were another $1,000.[43]

Despite Leonard and Dorothy's worries over the rumors of war, they sent their head gardener, David Calthorpe, to America in the fall of 1938. Beatrix arranged for him to visit the Arnold, Boston parks, Yale, Dumbarton Oaks, and Mount Vernon, and she was also able to do some Dartington work with him, particularly discussing plantings. She formed a working relationship with Calthorpe and his six-monthly reports, long letters of what he had done and wanted to do were to be the chief means of contact in the future, carrying her connection with Dartington through the war years.

The gloomy outlook and what seemed like an ending to Beatrix's real role in the Dartington dream were brightened by two good prospects which were based on her hard work. Dorothy was showing signs of becoming a gardener, both at Dartington and also reviving her interest in Apple Green. In 1935 a great deal of work had been put in hand there, restoring the playhouse and the Chinese garden pavings and ornaments, and Beatrix's constant reviewing and replanting found a more enthusiastic response. A *brown* border of annuals and perennials were planned for the Chinese garden—crimson, wine, deep orange, yellow daisies of every kind, lilies, iris, nasturtiums, poppies, and dahlias.[44] Renewed interest inevitably meant a scrutiny of profits and losses and in 1937 circumstances dictated a rationalization at Apple Green. Beatrix seemed to enjoy tackling Dorothy's lawyers on the subject of the garden, and she agreed to a scheme whereby the greenhouses were scaled down, the Chinese and playhouse gardens were completely planted with perennials, most of which could be propagated from stock plants, mown lawn areas were reduced, rough grass increased. As it was chiefly necessary to lose labor, she asked for support for the head gardener, Harry Lee, in the "patient" laying off of people who had served for years. Apple Green was now used at weekends by Michael and Beatrice Straight, who had resumed American lives. Also, the Elmhirst children, Ruth and Bill, in the care of Miss Jefferies, were in New York, and at Apple Green for weekends for most of the war.

At Dartington, with England at war the artistic experiments, the gatherings of talented and beautiful people into a scene of brilliant internationalism—had all come to an abrupt end. Dorothy, bereft of all this young life and enthusiasm, and of her own children, turned to her garden. Gardening was to be the last passion of her life; she started her garden notebooks in 1942 and kept them for twenty-six years, until her death. Dartington Hall became her very own garden, and for Beatrix, an abiding symbol of friendship that would accompany her into her last lonely years.

Chapter 11

❧❧❧

MANY HAPPY AND
SAD RETURNS: 1937–59

*O*n her sixty-fifth birthday, June 19, 1937, Beatrix was beginning one of the happiest periods of her life. For the next five years all she had seemed to be working for came to what she would have called a fructuous maturity. It was a late, profound happiness, supremely well earned.

As always her life was governed by her gardens. Her most celebrated garden child, Dumbarton Oaks, was in full blooming prime, and her visits to Georgetown were joyous and exciting. The Blisses had come home at last: Robert Woods Bliss had handed in his notice to the State Department, largely because they could not bear to be away from their beautiful home any longer. Now the Oaks was filled with more treasures, more music and good conversation and laughter than perhaps it had ever known, and the garden was a perfect complement. The Farrands' winters in California were also enlivened by the Blisses' company, and the discussions over the progress and improvement of Dumbarton Oaks were not confined to the East Coast; "MaxTrix" had the support of "MilRob" in San Marino. It was Mildred Bliss who arranged for Beatrix to be a consultant at the Santa Barbara Botanic Garden, which was to be her happiest California commission. The director's house at the Huntington was now really feeling like home with all their things from New Haven settled in, and the garden that Beatrix had designed was finished and growing. It flowered in the early spring of southern California with beds of iris and wallflower edged with myrtle, followed by mixed Virginia stocks beneath standard roses. Beatrix used lots of *Lippia citrodora, Cassia artemesiades,* and hedges of leptospermum; the garden, and particularly the view from the director's office window, had an old-world serenity, a kind of mix of campus and

Robert and Mildred Woods Bliss in the music room at Dumbarton Oaks.

enclosed flower garden, a hybrid that reminded them of their East Coast homes.

For ten years Max Farrand found it congenial to work among the Huntington's treasures, and they both enjoyed the chance to escape eastern winters and build up their energies for the rest of the year. But as soon as the heat became too much they yearned to get back east, and if they could possibly manage it, they fled to Maine by the end of May and stayed through the end of October.

At first the Farrands' marriage had been a sharing of their professional lives. Max's academic steadiness provided the base for Beatrix's peripatetic profession, while she was always careful to arrange her diary so that she could be with him to play the part of director's wife when necessary. This took a great deal of organization, but then she was, or had become, the most well organized of people. As far as her personal belongings were concerned, she was ever ready to be on the move, with all her needs, cosmetic or secretarial, ready to accompany her in beautiful Italian-made boxes, folders, or cases. Her clothes conveyed the same well-ordered calm; her tall, large-boned frame was a dressmaker's delight, and she always looked marvelously and individually elegant, whether in slimly draped silks with a short velvet jacket, or in her long, vented and pleated tweed skirts and long jackets, which were her working wear. Her wardrobe was chosen and stocked with the same direct assessment of needs that she practiced on any site, for she was not one to waste precious time in changing her mind, or doubting what to wear.

This professional marriage, so well attuned over the years, was also full of affection and pleasure in each other's company. They played golf together, and Beatrix frequently accompanied Max to his much-prized Sainte-Marguerite River Salmon Club in Quebec. And they gardened together. Max Farrand had not been a gardener when he met Beatrix, but one of the greatest happinesses of their homecomings to Reef Point in their middle age, and on into their late sixties, was that he was now just as interested in the garden as she, and it was out of this shared interest that their own dream was born. With their lives so entangled with Dumbarton Oaks, Dartington Hall, and the Huntington, it might well have seemed inevitable that the Farrands too would wish to leave the fruit of their lives' work for educational purposes. But I imagine that their idea of Reef Point as "our little horticultural institution" came out of very personal beliefs, particularly Max's faith in the understanding of the past, be it the Elizabethan drama or the making of the American Constitution, which he easily translated into the civilizing of one's natural surroundings. He had always been susceptible to the beauty of nature and Beatrix had focused his ideas on the cultivated beauties in their own garden.

With backing from their local friends and professionals, they set about turning their home into an educational display garden where visitors could learn and be inspired to go home and try some of the ideas in their own gardens. From now on Reef Point had a future beyond their own. Their dreams of how it could be useful to people long after they had departed inspired the energies they poured into it. The house, their books, and especially Beatrix's collection of garden books which she had started in her teens, the vegetable and flower gardens all were no longer simply theirs, but were unselfishly steered toward a wider public. Without anywhere near the private wealth of the Huntingtons or even the Blisses, Max and Beatrix wanted to endow the future with their knowledge and experience, and it was to be all-comers in the future, not some Ivy League elite. Theirs was a generous, demanding, and difficult dream.

Though their plans for their home assumed a priority, there was still work for Beatrix, and congenial work, to be done in the outside world. Her settled happiness seemed to have perfected her judgments in so many ways, and she was able to attract the right commissions. Just as she realized that war in Europe had cut her off from Dartington, she was called to Oberlin in Ohio—a pioneer college from which so many of Dartington's progressive ideals were learned—and her last campus commission. Oberlin was liberal, coeducational, with a strong tradition of faculty self-government. Its ethnic and religious diversity and the high standards but lower costs of this midwestern campus had brought an influx of students in the late 1930s, at the end of the Depression

Max and Beatrix Farrand in their garden at Reef Point.

decade. The campus sprawled in unredeemed grid rectangles imposed on the area of former swamp, the only large and available tract of unfarmed land that the founders could use a hundred years earlier. Being farming country, care for the land and growing things had become integrated into the Oberlin philosophy. One benefactor, Charles Martin Hall (who discovered how to reduce aluminum from bauxite), who had left his fortune to Oberlin in 1914, was keen on planting trees, particularly in the large central area known as Tappan Square (from which buildings had been removed at his request), and his legacy was very evident. Olmsted Brothers had prepared a plan for a formal landscape based on Tappan Square but this had never been implemented. Beatrix was presented with a new, and third, phase of building at Oberlin in the late 1930s, but she had a firm ally in Lester Ries, the superintendent of buildings and grounds, with whom she had first worked in Chicago. Ries wrote: "It is my opinion that Mrs Farrand is the best qualified person to advise on college and university grounds of anybody in the country." And soon Beatrix was writing to Ries: "The delightful news has come from Mr Love of the appointment of a consulting landscape gardener or architect to Oberlin in the shape of your former colleague at Chicago."[1]

*Many Happy and
Sad Returns: 1937-59*

Reef Point from the air, taken in the mid-1930s, before Max and Beatrix made the alterations and added buildings for the "little horticultural institution." The Shore Path can be clearly seen along the rocks, and the buildings in the distance are on Main Street, Bar Harbor.

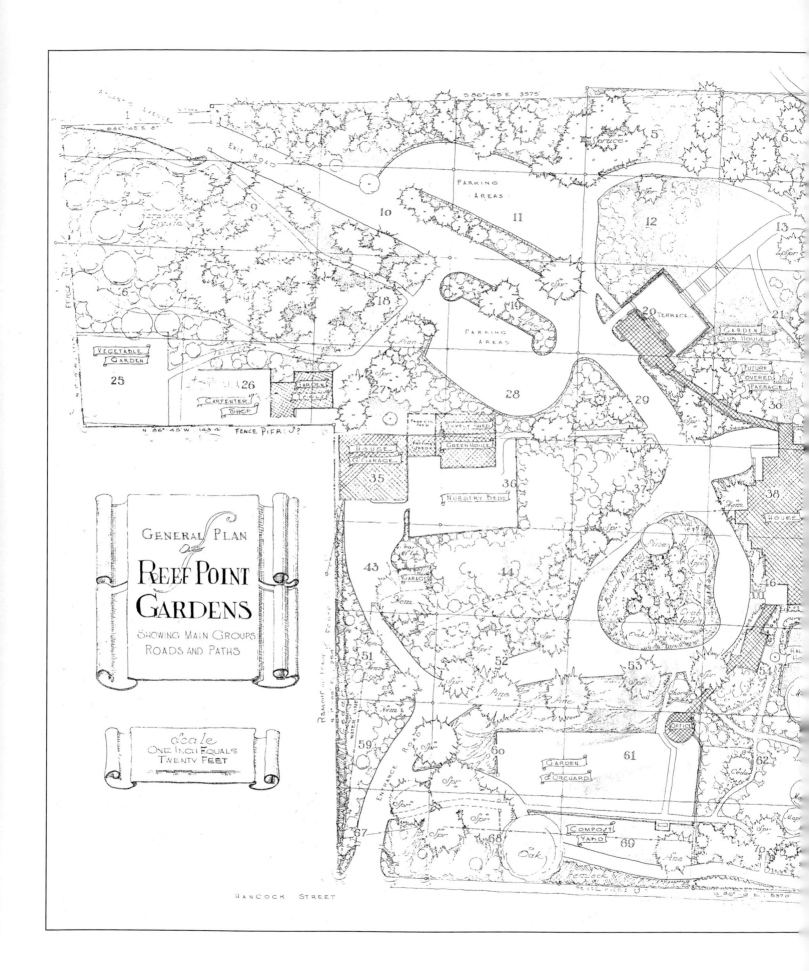

GENERAL PLAN
of
REEF POINT
GARDENS
SHOWING MAIN GROUPS
ROADS AND PATHS

Scale
ONE INCH EQUALS
TWENTY FEET

Reef Point: a general plan of its development as Reef Point Gardens Limited. Visitors entered via the original entrance from Hancock Street in the southwest corner, and new parking areas with a new exit were made to Atlantic Avenue in the northwest corner. The number 20 identifies the Garden Club House, which we would call a visitor center, that was to be linked to the main house by a covered way. Note the view lines marked through the planting to Burnt, Long, and Bald Porcupine Islands in Frenchman's Bay.

BEATRIX

The Gardening Life of

Beatrix Jones Farrand

*Beatrix Farrand, a photograph
taken in the director's house
at the Huntington Museum,
c. 1937.*

Beatrix and Ries reviewed the planting and planned work on the basis of site inspections. She created one of her Yale-style "moats" of greenery around Oberlin's Carnegie Library (built in 1908) and the administration building, giving stability and dignity, a firm base instead of a weak line of grassy bank. She introduced masses of forsythias at the corners of buildings and trained on walls, underplanted with *Vinca minor.* In fact, she gave to Oberlin that serene grounding, that linking of its buildings to their mother earth, the calming quality which she had now bestowed on so many campuses. Beatrix continued as consultant at Oberlin throughout 1940, making her regular tours of inspection with Lester Ries, carefully removing weak and ugly trees, planting new ones, trimming and tending the shrubs, pathways, and approaches to buildings, pursuing artistry in gardening on the largest scale. This lasted for two more years, until the war interfered with Oberlin's ability to pay for, or find the manpower for, tending the campus.

The Blisses, Robert and Mildred, had enjoyed a rich and active life at Dumbarton Oaks during the thirties, but now they too were working on their plans to leave it. Mildred Bliss and Beatrix had continued working happily on the garden; their letters are full of the real warmth of their well-established friendship: "Dearest Gardening Twin" from Beatrix on February 9, 1939, and "Dearest Collaborator" from Mildred.[2] On March 16, 1938, Mildred had written to Beatrix that both Harvard and Princeton universities were interested in Dumbarton Oaks, but after long discussions it was revealed that

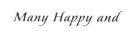
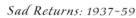

*Max Farrand, photographed in
the director's house at the
Huntington Museum,
c. 1937. He retired as director
in 1941.*

house, treasures, and garden should go to Harvard. On November 3, 1940, the *New York Times* announced the news: the house, all its contents, including the library of thousands of volumes, the new south wing, the Thirty-second Street entrance building, the gallery for the Byzantine Collection, and the garden (or most of it) would be deeded to Harvard University, as it was on November 29, 1940. On November 13 Beatrix wrote to the Blisses: "How relieved you must be to know that Dumbarton is now safely across the bridge and under the shield of permanent Harvard."[3]

Beatrix's relief was tinged with regrets. She gave her instructions to her "personal" garden for the last time that fall, and with her experience of universities and their administrators, she must have wondered what the future would hold. It was comforting that the Blisses moved to California, to their home Casa Dorinda on Hot Springs Road in Santa Barbara, where Mildred and Beatrix had already worked on the garden in readiness. "I suppose perpetual home-sickness is my self-inflicted state," was Mildred's comment on the wrench of leaving Dumbarton Oaks.[4]

In January 1941 Max Farrand made his decision to retire from the Huntington in six months' time; on January 17 Beatrix was at Dumbarton Oaks for her first meeting with Dr. John Seymour Thacher, the new executive director, who had come from the Fogg Museum in Cambridge. She liked him tremendously—it was a "poignant, interesting and we hope fructuous meeting," she reported to Mildred. Dr. Thacher also duly reported to Mildred that Beatrix's guidance would be indispensable. "So you see, my dear," wrote Mildred, "you are not rid of us, nor ever will be as long as the road lies clear."[5]

As it turned out, the road did not lie clear. Dr. Thacher had asked Beatrix for a minutely detailed report on the state of Dumbarton Oaks as they saw it in early 1941. Beatrix returned to California to organize their move from the director's house into the small "cottage" at the Valley Club of Montecito, which was now to be their winter home, and at the same time she planned how this great garden "inventory" would be taken. She went to Cambridge to lecture on the garden, telling the faculty at Harvard just what she and Mildred Bliss had tried to create; she made many visits to Dumbarton Oaks, rather daunting affairs, state progresses with a train of gardeners and survey assistants in her wake. And with her usual attention to detail, she produced her legacy to her most celebrated child, the "Dumbarton Oaks Plant Book." In the midst of all this came the Japanese attack on Pearl Harbor, and America was at war. All the treasures of Dumbarton Oaks were packed up and spirited away to a place of safety, the garden staff was cut to a minimum, dust sheets were draped in the elegant rooms, and Harvard's plans for their new acquisition were shelved for the duration of the war.

Beatrix, however, produced her manuscript of the plant book, and it is a most remarkable document.[6] She deals in detail with the philosophy of the planting for every area of the estate, for eleven enclosed gardens and the North Vista, fourteen areas of informal garden, and all the domestic and staff areas, right down to the garage court. In each case she lists the plants, describes the planting, and concisely identifies the crucial aspect of character to be maintained in each area. The main entrance steps were to be flanked with predominantly box and yew, with only the merest touch of deciduous spirea, so that the green and quiet approach was essentially the same throughout the year; the wisteria on the Orangery was to be so trained that it carried its flowers high in the air "as a floral entablature to the building over the tops of the windows."[7] The Green Garden, with its ideal carpet of periwinkle (*Vinca minor*), should only be planted with bulbs "of quite different sorts" than in other parts of the garden, to retain the very particular quality of this oak-shaded terrace. They should be small Poet's daffodils, single campernelle jonquils, and lots of white crocus. The hedge of white azalea (*Azalea indica alba*) in the Star Garden was to be carefully pruned, and would need replanting every fifteen to twenty years so that the paved star and the seats were not overshaded. In the Rose Garden the size of the box trees was of greatest importance; the large clipped mounds in the center of the garden could be allowed to be 15 feet high, but the subsidiary accent plants must be smaller, and the box edging to the rose beds must be kept very small and renewed gradually. It was all a question of balance, for the box mounds were "bad neighbours" to the roses, and yet necessary for winter interest and as a foil to the summer flowers. The roses were to be carefully placed as to colors, the pinks and salmons "together with a few of the very deep red ones, such as *Etoile de Holland* and *Ami Quinard,*" in the south portion of the garden, "salmon-colored and yellowish-pinks" in the central portion, while the northern part "was given over to yellow or predominantly yellow and orange sorts."[8]

In contrast to all these carefully regulated spaces, with restraint in flowers to give due regard to their formal design, the Fountain Terrace was designated the "real flower garden," to be packed with yellow, bronze, and orange tulips, arabis, forget-me-not, and pansies, followed by summer annuals in yellows, bronzes, and blues, and finally chrysanthemums in bronze, deep browns, and maroons.

*B*eatrix had visited Dartington Hall for the last time in the summer of 1937. She saw Dorothy Elmhirst in New York the following year and heard that a garden committee had been formed; she continued to receive long reports of Dartington's progress from David Calthorpe. Her correspondence with Dorothy had become personal and affectionate; Dorothy had become a gardener in earnest, and in the summer of 1939 she sent Beatrix a copy of Vita Sackville-West's *Some Flowers,* which they voted "a real book." Poor Dartington shuddered under the impact of the war, and Beatrix was forced to consign it to her dreams, doubting that she would ever see it again.

At the end of the winter, in early 1943, after a quiet time at Montecito, she and Max returned to Reef Point to begin another session of planning and making their own garden legacy. Soon it was impossible to avoid admitting that Max was far from well, and Beatrix insisted that he go to Boston to see his doctors. The result, which "surprised and dismayed" both of them, was that he had to have an operation for cancer of the bladder. This was duly done, and Beatrix described the progress of their summer to Dorothy and Leonard the following October. "For several weeks he was a pretty sick man, but thanks to extraordinary surgical skill and devotion on the part of his nurses he was able to leave the hospital—after the customary two or three set-backs—at the end of about seven weeks. We came home in early July, he was still pretty wretched and miserable and for the first month progress seemed so microscopic as to be almost imperceptible, but we now expect to head westward for Santa Barbara in a few days time. . . ."[9]

Through all this Beatrix herself kept fairly fit, but she was over seventy. All through that slow and painful summer and into the fall she kept working on their plans for the new buildings and the garden at Reef Point, constantly willing her frail "golden Max," as she had always thought of him, back to some kind of strength. She added a sad picture of him pottering about for a couple of hours, able to attend to some of his letters, and be more of a human being than a patient, but it was slow work. They spent a quiet winter, and from Santa Barbara on February 5, 1944, Beatrix sent her thoughts to Dorothy: "If you feel you have a phantom companion with you as you walk between the camellias, it will only be me."[10] And to Leonard, "Tell Dorothy also with my dearest love that no one ever starts gardening either too late or too early, once it gets into one's blood it can never get out (like some insidious poison) so she must resign herself for the rest of her days to be constantly struggling and constantly enjoying her garden."[11] She wrote constantly of Max, how he was progressing, putting on weight, looking rather "less like a hat-rack," and that they would stay until April, then go to Reef Point.[12]

Dorothy had now started her Garden Diary, which she would keep for the rest of her life; it was a journal of her brief observations, notes on the things she did, and the wonderment of the new-fledged gardener. "The real excitement of the past week has been the opening of *Magnolia grandiflora* . . . Jerry [Leonard Elmhirst] brought one branch actually into his study. What a flower—what utter purity!" she wrote in July 1943. "Such rhythmic curves of the petals . . . such an unearthly scent . . . How noble this flower is."[13] Part of the reason for her enthusiasm was necessity—the necessity of saving Dartington's garden from complete ruin in the face of war—everyone of working age had gone, only one elderly gardener was left, so Dorothy took to "using her spade and her trowel as a means of defeating Hitler"[14] among her other war work. But much of the credit for this late conversion must go to Beatrix and the constancy of her friendship through all those years when Dorothy's missionary zeal was turned on almost every other sphere of her life *but* her gardens. Dorothy Elmhirst was to gain great comfort from her gardening, both in wartime and long afterward, and that is a great gift to have given a friend. In turn Beatrix was to enjoy Leonard and Dorothy's affectionate consideration and understanding just when she needed it most of all.

Through the summer and into the fall of 1944 at Reef Point, Beatrix tried to keep up a semblance of normal progress on their plans and schemes for the house and gardens, but she knew that Max was failing. After spending the worst of the winter in California, they returned to beloved Reef Point in the spring, and Beatrix gardened a little and paced their days to the inevitable end.

Max, her "golden Max," a very half of MaxTrix, died peacefully two days before her seventy-third birthday, on Sunday afternoon, June 17, 1945. She was stunned, knocked completely off balance, and exhausted from the effort of keeping him going, and never letting him realize how ill he was. Being Beatrix she did not break down, but withdrew. She went through the motions, listened to the sympathies of friends and neighbors, opened all the consoling letters, was moved by some—particularly one from Dorothy Elmhirst—and she coped calmly with the funeral. Max was cremated and his ashes were scattered at Reef Point. But she later realized, and admitted to Leonard and Dorothy, that she appeared "strangely aloof and ungracious" to all around her. It was all she could do. Indeed, at the Arnold Arboretum, Chief Propagator William Judd must have slightly raised his eyebrows to find a letter from her, which she had dictated herself the day following Max's death:

Dear Mr Judd: You will have doubtless seen in this morning's *Boston Herald* a notice of the death of my husband. You do not need to be told what a heavy blow this is to me and how more and more deeply I feel that his affection for Reef Point Gardens must be one of the controlling lines in my life.[15]

All she could do was concentrate wholly on what they had been doing together, doing what Max wanted, in the hope that he would stay in her mind and her dreams. She had already asked Robert Patterson to help her plot the garden as it was at the moment Max died, and she was so set on this task as her salvation that nothing was to stand in her way. They were "bewildered" by the rhododendrons, so the flowers were picked and hastily packed to be sent by special mail to the Arnold for identification. It was to be hoped that the Arboretum wasn't having a particularly busy day, for no less than sixty-eight numbered trusses landed on the laboratory table. They were mostly species, a remarkable range with many colors of her favorite *Rhododendron (Azalea) calendulaceum*. The names were duly sent within a few days, but on June 28 she was writing again, not exactly satisfied with some, which she queried, and announcing the impending arrival of another twenty-five specimens that had now come into flower. Altogether over eighty plants were named, and she was writing gratefully on July 6: "There is no way in which you could have shown me how willing you are to help forward the work at Reef Point Gardens than by what you, Dr Rehder and Mr Wyman have done in naming our Azaleas and Rhododendrons. Probably you have given me more than you should of your over-busy days but I do want you to know that I value the help you have given me and the spirit in which it was given. . . ." She felt that 80 percent of the garden's rhododendrons now had proper names and she wondered if she should invite an "expert (so-called)" to visit. Beatrix plowed on desperately like a woman with a mission—it was the only way she could go. But she knew she was being impossible—and finished to William Judd: "I may perhaps be a nuisance to my friends in asking them to help me carry forward" now alone, what she and Max had held dear to their hearts.[16]

For the next five years it was the almost obsessive struggle with Reef Point Gardens that kept her going. The formal enterprise which she and Max had set up, the Reef Point Gardens Corporation, became the foundation for the Max Farrand Memorial Fund, in which name all her work would be done. Robert Whiteley Patterson was her architect and design consultant and Isabelle Marshall Stover was her secretary (officially the clerk). They were to be faithful supporters and stay with her until the end. In addition, she had much support from Serenus B. Rodick, Charles Kenneth Savage (a local landscape gardener), and her friend Agnes Milliken; and also from Susan Delano McKelvey from the Arnold.[17] She organized progress in her inimitable way (and she was wonderfully organized as always) by publishing a series of bulletins which were sold to visitors for ten cents. Number one appeared in August 1946, just over a year after Max's death, and it was called *The Start and the Goal*. Fourteen more followed in a steady stream over the next nine years, on all aspects of the garden; they represented Beatrix's advanced understanding of what we would call visitor interpretation, and added to the displayed aspects of the garden, the labeled plants, the small vegetable garden and orchard in production, the hardy perennials and roses, as well as the demonstration of the beauty of native plants, which made Reef Point an enterprise ahead of its time. Her garden, she wrote, was "to be useful to its community and state, and to all interested in outdoor beauty."[18] As well as Max's memorial, it was to be the summation of her life. Though many public gardens and arboreta across America can claim to give this kind of community service now, Reef Point was unique fifty years ago.

Beatrix's assault on the Arnold about her rhododendrons at least reminded them of her existence, and she was invited to be the Arboretum's landscape consultant. In writing to Dr. Paul Mangelsdorf on May 15, 1946, she accepted "in great humility of spirit and hope" that she would not be a disappointment. As her last commission it was most fitting that she should return to where she had started: "Your trust in my training is the greatest honour of my fifty years of active practice."[19] She was appointed for a year, at a fee not to exceed $2,000. But sadly, the issue of *Arnoldia* that announced her appointment also announced the sudden death of kind William Judd. She had other friends, made over the years, in Donald Wyman and Karl Sax, and she took Robert Patterson from Reef Point to help her with the strenuous surveying and staking out that were always her thorough way of tackling a job. She may have pleaded for patience and understanding of the physical limitations of her almost seventy-five-year-old frame, but it took her two short months to come up with her major recommendations for replanting along the Forest Hills entrance and on Peter's Hill, and for establishing a 25–40-acre nursery. *Arnoldia* of November 1, 1946, printed her paper on her approach to the design problems, which was a classic summation of the problems of restoration in a public garden. The passage of time, soil depletion, deterioration of soil quality, new plant introductions, visitor pressures, changes in taste, and the devastation of a hurricane in September 1938 all had to be taken into account. Her first major task, the replanting of the entrance area and drive, was marked by her piece "The Azalea Border" in *Arnoldia* of April 15, 1949. This too is a gem of landscape writing (she seems to have had a late flowering of this additional talent), a beautifully balanced treatment of the botanical versus the visual aspects of planting design.

In the fall of 1949 she explained her designs for Peter's Hill in *Arnoldia*: Professor Sargent's collection of thorns had become a thicket and a fire hazard. She rearranged them beautifully in walks and open groves which flowed with the grain of the hill form; the top of the hill, a typical New England knoll, was sensitively kept clear for its breathtaking vista of distant downtown Boston. This work was completed (much of it is still evident today) and, into her

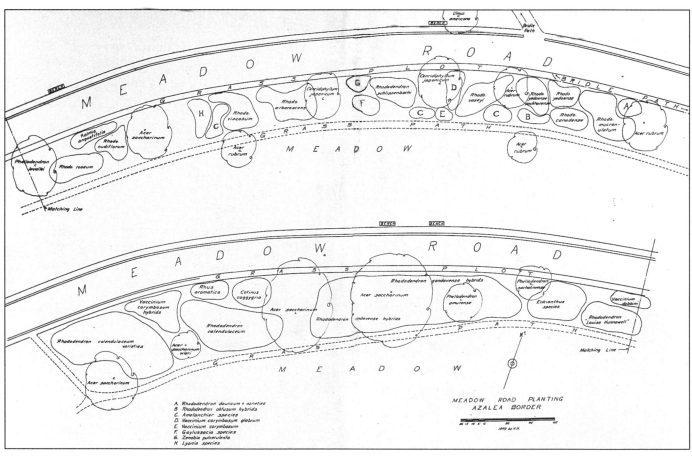

MEADOW ROAD PLANTING
AZALEA BORDER

A. Rhododendron dauricum & varieties
B. Rhododendron obtusum hybrids
C. Amelanchier species
D. Vaccinium corymbosum glabrum
E. Vaccinium corymbosum
F. Gaylussacia species
G. Zenobia pulverulenta
H. Lyonia species

fourth year of consultancy, in the fall of 1949, she was looking forward to doing more. Her time at the Arboretum had been very happy, an exhilarating chance to exercise her greatest professional skills, and it had given her a useful diversion from what was happening at home.

*T*wo years after Max's death, by the early summer of 1947, she had pulled herself back onto an even keel, and was looking forward to a busy summer of visitors. It was to be a long, hot summer in Bar Harbor, with no rain from May onward. Despite the heat, much progress was made. She planned the alterations to the house to make it into a study center, and prepared Bulletin no. 2 on how to build up soil in a garden and work within the limitations of local climate. But before it could be published, disaster struck in the most horrifying form. The Bar Harbor Fire of October 1947 was a devastation, a blow to her beloved island, from which it took a long time to recover. I do not think Beatrix ever did.

The fire started innocently enough, smoldering in the dry peat somewhere up near Eagle Lake. Though it traveled underground, it would have been well within the capabilities of the National Park firefighters, but for a sudden, hurricane-force wind that whipped the flames up into the treetops and sent the fire rolling at great speed toward Bar Harbor. The alarm bells rang all over Maine, and farther afield—to the National Coast Guard, the army, the navy in Florida. Great billows of smoke rolled out to sea between Bar Harbor and Hulls Cove, and a rescue force of fishing boats and yachts set out from Hancock Point and Sorrento across Frenchman's Bay, thinking that the sea would be the only means of escape. Suddenly the wind changed, and the fire was turned south, behind the town, through the Kebo Valley, past Champlain Mountain and the Beehive and out to sea near Great Head. It had, by some miracle, missed the town center and the shore path along Frenchman's Cove. Reef Point was safe, the loss of life was very small (only four connected deaths from heart attacks and similar tragedies), and the loss of wildlife was surprisingly low. But the damage to property, to the summer homes and estates, was devastating. Several major hotels were burned, including the Malvern, where Beatrix had spent many happy occasions and in which she had a business interest. Of her gardens, the Satterlee estate, W. P. Hamilton's Thirlestane, and Tanglewold, and many more all burned.[20]

The first reaction at Reef Point was of gratitude for survival. Bulletin no. 2 eventually appeared in November, with a note of thanks and a vow to proceed with ever-greater determination, poor Bar Harbor needing every speck of beauty and surviving attraction even more now. The following year, 1948, Bulletin no. 3 carried a detailed description of the design of the garden and reasons why, and in 1949 no. 4 was able to describe the alterations to the building, now all completed.[21] The Library had been enlarged, but kept as a memorial to Max, with his furnishings, especially the Hebridean rugs he had had made for it, which gave it warmth and comfort. It housed a collection of reference books, floras, encyclopedias, the herbarium cases, and pictures and portraits of those who had inspired the making of Reef Point Gardens, from Linnaeus and John Evelyn to Gertrude Jekyll, William Robinson, Frederick Law Olmsted, and Professor Sargent. Next to the Library, the Blue Room, decorated with Beatrix's valuable collection of prints of French gardens, and Le Nôtre's portrait, was now able to hold a hundred people for a lecture or meeting. Her whole idea was to show that an educational institution could be an elegant place to live. Upstairs, in the Morning Room, she kept her own collection of gardening and horticultural books; she had been proud of 300 volumes when she was interviewed by the *New York Sun* in 1897; now she had over 2,000, collected over years of browsing in the bookshops of London and Paris, and more recently from the catalogs sent from London dealers.

The refurbishment of Reef Point was now complete. A new entrance had been made to Atlantic Avenue, with a large, well-planted parking area for visitors. The Garden Club House, for meetings, was finished and connected to the main house by a covered way. Each summer saw a steady stream of visitors. She was able to write to Dorothy and Leonard Elmhirst on May 1, 1950, of how her "work has gone forward as well as was possible" without Max's daily advice, and she felt "the foundation is laid, and the structure is sturdy and it will last as long as it can be of use to those who care for plants, birds, the open air and outdoor beauty."[22]

The Herbarium was growing under the daily attention of Amy Magdalene Garland, and Isabelle Stover was in charge of the correspondence and kept Beatrix in touch. Beatrix could now, after five years of very hard work, afford a little rest. After all, she was nearing her eightieth birthday.

Her winter months in her little apartment at the Valley Club of Montecito were for dreaming. She realized she had neglected her friends and favorite "children" in the painful aftermath of Max's death, and now she turned to them again. Leonard and Dorothy Elmhirst responded with letters and photographs of Dartington's progress: "The hanging wood and its great beech trees, magnolias and camellias are all before me; & the sun in the great court with its silvery stone walls, paved walks & green lawn seem to be just here with me in this distant Californian room . . . the evening light on the terraces across the tilting yard & the quiet slopes on the garden side are all with me, as vividly as though we were standing together, talking of our next move . . . tell me . . ." Tell me, she wrote again and again, and her questions mounted the more photographs Leonard Elmhirst sent. Was the lovely Carpentaria still thriving? And the twelve Apostle yews? and the Sunny border? Tell me about the new farm building in the orchard. Dorothy is quite right to be ruthless, "there is no sense fiddling with an ill-tempered plant . . . has she tried *Cornus canadensis*? . . . You see what you have brought on yourselves by your letters and photographs. . . . Sometimes in the dark of night, the great court is before me, as it looked from my window, and again, from Beatrice's [Straight] window, the sward, the yews, the hanging wood and the chestnut trees are with me, and it is never far away. Such happy days they were for me, with you both, perhaps the happiest of a long working life."[23]

Beatrix was eighty on June 19, 1952. That month the bulletin from Reef Point, no. 8, by Robert Patterson, described the conifers, the white pines, white spruce, the dwarf Alberta spruce, *Picea glauca conica* that were anything but dwarf at Reef Point, and others that were such a basic virtue of the garden. The following year Beatrix concentrated on her collection of single hybrid tea roses, "now said to be the most complete group . . . in this country or abroad," with rare treasures—"the beautiful spinel coloured Armstrong Ruby, the delicate pink with red brown anthers Ellen Willmott, the deeper pink Ethel James with yellow centre, madder rose Sweet Sue and cherry coloured Colette Clement." Subsequent bulletins described the heather collection, climbing plants, and the now-so-unfashionable "foundation planting."[24]

But the flurry of bulletins in 1954 was a desperate effort, as a dying plant will do everything to produce a last seed. Beatrix and her fellow directors knew that things were not well; the visitors did not come in sufficient numbers (the island took such a long time to recover from the fire), and, perhaps even worse, remote Bar Harbor did not appeal to staff of the right caliber. The faithful Garlands needed help and none could be found. All the work, all the rebuilding of the house (which had needed serious work to the foundations for its new role), the reorganization of the garden, its documentation, the new buildings for staff and visitors, and the arrangement of the collections had eaten up two-thirds of Beatrix's remaining income. The final straw were the taxes. After the fire so many of the island's rich cottagers, summer residents, and taxpayers just did not return. The money required for recovery was enormous and the higher levy was imposed on the few who stayed. This meant an intolerable burden on Beatrix, an old resident who had seen the cost of living on the island escalate beyond her imagining.

She approached the inevitable in her usual organized way. Her ability to solve problems did not desert her, but it took every last ounce of energy and courage. She put all this in a last, well-reasoned, courageous letter of May 1955, sent to all concerned with Reef Point Gardens:

Nearly twenty years ago Max and Beatrix Farrand started on an enterprise they called Reef Point Gardens. The project was intended to commemorate their enjoyment in the house and grounds and to give others like education and pleasure. The world was different at that time, before the second great war, and life was keyed in another and quieter note. Both Farrands worked at the organization of the undertaking and since Max Farrand's death in 1945 Beatrix Farrand has made every effort to carry on the scheme. As all the Directors know, entire remodelling of the house and grounds was done and all the utilities renewed, as well as a house built for the head of the gardens, with its necessary additional tool houses. This work has entailed heavy inroad on capital and sale of many personal items of silver, jewellry, etc.

The expenses of running the house and grounds now take two-thirds of Beatrix Farrand's income not including Federal taxes and costs of administration. It must be realized by all who are interested in Reef Point Gardens that a quiet appraisal of the future is needed. Efforts have been made in the last years to find understudies for Mr. and Mrs. Garland, who could eventually take over their tasks. Boston, New York and England have been tried with no success as the region is considered remote from educational projects and well trained garden associates. Labour is unwilling to work at gardening and constant changes have to be made in the staff. All concerned in the management of Reef Point Gardens are growing older and the heavy burdens cannot be carried much longer. Mounting costs and devaluation of the dollar have added a load which Max and Beatrix Farrand had not foreseen.

The library has been built up so that it is now considered one of the best sources of the history of garden design, and reference books in several languages and volumes on architecture make a whole, not only financially valuable, but still more important, to students educated in design both in this country and over seas. There are rich collections of catalogued scraps, and drawers full of the plans and sketches of distinguished gardeners. The gardens themselves have been visited by over fifty thousand people and are recognized as one of the botanic gardens of the country.

The conditions of the present day have been considered for hours, days, weeks and months and have been the source of deep anxiety to the present owner. Her enthusiasm and desire to make the enterprise as perfect throughout has not been wisely curbed by the wisdom and far sight of Max Farrand, who would have told her, that changing times, the total change in the neighbourhood surroundings did not justify placing the amount of capital required to run the establishment. The responsibility regarding the wise use of funds seems to override personal preference and inclination. By the law of the state no promise can be given by the town assessors as to perpetual tax exemption and Federal authorities will not recognize Reef Point Gardens as an educational centre until after the death of the present owner and the foundation has been in operation for a year or more.

These conditions have been known since the start, but what has developed in the recent years makes it necessary to review the whole situation from a point of view of larger than local interests. The report of the committee last autumn was reassuring in many ways, but it took local interests more into account than the wider educational possibilities.

In order to get impersonal advice three gentlemen have been consulted who have no personal interest in the scheme. One is the respected and able head of one of the great universities of this country, another is a man in legal practice, who is highly esteemed, and the third is a trustee of a kindred foundation. Separately and together their unanimous opinion is that the situation was precarious—distance from educational centers, entire change in neighbourhood conditions, uncertainties of taxation and difficulties in recruiting labor and teaching staff.

With these opinions supporting her own anxious thought the owner of Reef Point asks the directors to meet in order to take such steps as may be legally needed to dissolve the Max Farrand Memorial and Reef Point Gardens corporations, and if possible to trace the generous donors to these, and restore to them the gifts made where this is in accordance with their wishes.

The future use of the funds available would be to found two graduate scholarships in American History to be known as the Max Farrand scholarships, and to give the library and related collections to a recognized school of landscape architecture, where students would use the books and references, and to place the collection of prints where they also would be of wider use than ever would be possible at Reef Point.

It has taken all the courage the present owner of Reef Point can muster to have arrived at this decision and to have written this letter, but it is better to "be of good courage and arise and do it" than to have to face deterioration of the gardens and waste of the resources of the library and collections.

(sgd) Beatrix Farrand

May 16, 1955.[25]

Beatrix had given a great deal of thought to what might happen. She may even, while she was in California the previous winter, have opened up the subject with the University of California, who were one of the few with a course in landscape architecture.

In characteristic fashion, once the inevitable was faced, and the directors of Reef Point agreed, the decision was taken. It was not easy. "The decision to discontinue the gardens was reached after long heart searching. Those most nearly connected . . . felt and saw their hopes and work of nearly twenty years dissolving before their eyes. Deep disappointment filled their hearts as the place they had built, and the work and effort they had given . . . were soon to come to an end." But surely it was Beatrix who added, "It would have been faint hearted to have closed their minds to a changed and ever changing situation."[26]

The library, drawings, and herbarium specimens were offered to Berkeley and Professor Leland Vaughan enthusiastically accepted. The packers arrived in the late summer of 1956, and Beatrix did not disguise the emotion of the occasion: "After several days of apparent confusion and many hurrying feet, the van drew up, and all day the book boxes and cartons of pictures were loaded into the open maw of the carrier. Finally it drove off, with its packers and load, and a little group watched with smarting eyes and tight throats as it turned into the highway on the first night of a long journey. Every precaution was taken for the safety of the cargo . . . and news of its progress was received from time to time. . . ."[27]

Though she kept a brave face for those around her, being positive in her faith for the safe future of her life's work, she accepted immediately that the purpose as well as the soul had gone from Reef Point. The house and garden were useless on their own. She then made the most remarkable decision, so unlike a garden-maker who usually is only too determined that their garden-child live on. She decided to dispose of Reef Point and destroy—perhaps dismantle would be a kinder word—her garden. No one could stop her from offering Reef Point as a development site; with the proceeds she bought the Garlands a small farm and built herself a cottage, where she would live out her days under their care. But at least one of her directors, the Bar Harbor landscape designer Charles Savage, persuaded her to let him save the garden plants. Whether she watched this second exodus is not recorded, but Savage, with financial help from John D. Rockefeller Jr., purchased all Reef Point's larger plants, mostly the rhododendrons and azaleas, and moved them carefully to his Asticou Azalea Garden in Northeast Harbor, where many flower still.[28]

Beatrix herself seemed not to have anything to do with this project. She wanted a clean break, a definite end. She had spent all her life making gardens, so there was a bitter logic in that her last task was to unmake her own. She wrote the last Reef Point bulletin, no. 17, which was to be published at her death. It was her own obituary. She never went to California again, preferring to tolerate the Bar Harbor winter, settled in the warmth of her own small world, largely of her memories and dreams, under the watchful eyes of the Garlands. She made a small garden outside her cottage, a little sunny formal garden of small beds that could be filled with her favorite summer flowers that would come to new life and beauty each year. It was a little like William Robinson's similar flower plot at Gravetye, which she remembered from so many years before. She must have spent most of her waking time wandering through those gardens of her memories, to Crosswicks, Eolia, and Hill-Stead, to Apple Green, Princeton, and Oberlin, even to The Mount, Lamb House at Rye, and her grandmother's rose garden in Newport. The Rockefellers' Eyrie was the only one she would have visited in reality.

On August 8, 1958, Isabelle Stover typed out her last letter to the Elmhirsts: she was so pleased that the taxodium in the Great Court and the magnolias were flourishing, they must be very careful with the approach to the Gate House, which was now being planned at last, for this was "as important to the whole composition as is the Inner Court." She had lost none of her judgment in her mind's eye. She mused on: how the thought of storm-damaged davidias "twisted her heart," and "Very well, if Dieramas don't fit in the Sunny Border, they should not stay—would white Watsonia like the warm shelter. . . . Ask Dorothy whether their white spires would fit in with her greys and the sages and the mulleins. . . . There is no way to learn about gardening save by trial and frequent error. . . . Would they like a *Beatrix Farrand* forsythia? . . ." And, at the end, "You and Dorothy have taught me so much that can never fade."[29]

Leonard and Dorothy now wintered in the Bahamas. By the time Leonard had scoured Dartington for the answers to all her questions and to take the photographs she loved to see, it was early 1959. His long reply, full of affection, never reached her. It was posted on February 21 and she died at the Mount Desert Island Hospital on Friday, February 27, after a brief illness. She would have been eighty-seven at her next birthday.

Being Beatrix, she wrote her own ending:

> She felt her life had been a happy one, she was grateful for what it had given her. She was ever thankful for the affection and help of her friends and associates during her long life, and attributed much to having had the privilege of their guidance.
>
>   Lux perpetua luceat eis   Finis.[30]

Chapter 12

❧❧❧

BEATRIX FARRAND, 1872–1959: HER LEGACY, AND WHAT HAS BECOME OF IT

Seven months before her death Beatrix had penned a postscript to her last letter to the Elmhirsts: "It is a great surprise finding that at 86 one has not all the strength of 26 but life is amusing and interesting."[1] She had retained her interests and sense of humor until the end, which came in the manner of her life, with serenity, even some elegance and little fuss. She collapsed from a heart attack, rallied a little in Mount Desert Island Hospital for a few days, then slipped peacefully away. She was cremated as she had wished, and there was a private funeral service at the Garland farm.

Characteristically she had left everything in good order. Isabelle Stover and Amy Magdalene Garland wrote to her friends and saw that obituary notices appeared in newspapers all over America and in the *Times* (London). Beatrix had taken the *Times* all her life to keep in touch with England, so it was particularly fitting that a long column of her achievements saluted her passing. Her honors were recited; her honorary degrees from Yale and Smith College, her medals from the Garden Club of America, the Massachusetts Horticultural Society, and the New York Botanical Garden, her honorary membership of the American Institute of Architects, and that she was the last surviving charter member of the American Society of Landscape Architects.[2] The many obituaries were followed by Robert W. Patterson's gracious and perceptive tribute in *Landscape Architecture,* and Mildred Bliss's "An Attempted Evocation of a Personality."[3] Mrs. Bliss took rather theatrical license with her stories, but she gave an important acknowledgment of Beatrix's influence on Dumbarton Oaks. A memorial tablet inscribed in Latin had already been placed over the swimming pool loggia, which reads, in translation:

May kindly stars guard the dreams born beneath
The spreading branches of Dumbarton Oaks
Dedicated to the friendship of Beatrix Farrand
and to succeeding generations of seekers after Truth.

Rather more to Beatrix's taste was Dorothy Elmhirst's note in Dartington's *News of the Day:* "No one who worked with Beatrix Farrand could fail to be impressed by her professional attitude to her job. Always the first to be out in the morning, she was the last to come in at night. Her energy seemed able to surmount any obstacle—even the worst onslaughts of rain. . . . In her tweeds and Mackintosh we could see her tall, erect figure conversing, in all weathers, with architects, builders, gardeners, tactfully collaborating with them all and slowly winning them to her ideas."[4]

Robert W. Patterson's final paragraph in *Landscape Architecture* added a prophetic note to his accolade: "It is commonplace to say that a garden is a living painting; it is not at all common to see one that has the quality of a good painting. The Beatrix Farrand gardens did have that quality, in their freedom and scale, their color, and their composition. But they were living things, and those that survive will miss the painstaking hand and the unerring eye of the artist who created them."[5]

Since he wrote that in 1959 our outlook on gardens has changed, and the idea that gardens can be restored and conserved in sympathy with their designers' intentions has become accepted. Of course "the painstaking hand and the unerring eye" can never be adequately replaced, but the form and structure, and the mood of a garden can be recalled, and given sympathetic maintenance be allowed to mature, to convey a great deal of a designer's skill and idea to new generations. We now know that we have a duty to landscape designers and garden artists of the past to conserve their works, just as we cherish the work of painters and playwrights. But to recall a living work of art successfully does require adequate instructions, as well as the survival of the site of the garden. Only those designers who have left their message clearly and in sufficient detail will be appreciated by posterity.

After Beatrix's death in 1959, her work and her gardens were quickly forgotten, just as happened to Gertrude Jekyll after her death in 1932. Beatrix's influence on the garden of the White House was swept away with the dawn of Camelot, and though her other and more substantial works were not cleared so dramatically, they slipped into obscurity, tended by newcomers who had never heard her name. But though the gardens faded, all the essential information about them rested safely and quietly in the neatly numbered folders at Berkeley. Beatrix's astute foresight in carefully saving not only her own drawings but those of Gertrude Jekyll as well is illuminated by the story of Miss Jekyll's reputation. For thirty years after her death Miss Jekyll slept in obscurity; the memories of those who had known her were gathered by Betty

Massingham for her biography, published in 1966, but Mrs. Massingham was only subsequently made aware of the Jekyll drawings surviving at Berkeley. It was the good news that she brought back from her examination of the drawings and the excitement at their contents that inspired the interest in Gertrude Jekyll and the books and exhibitions that sent her reputation soaring through the 1970s and 1980s to its present starry prominence. The survival of the drawings allowed dozens of owners in England to discover at first hand the joy of Jekyll gardening. Her legacy became immediate and specific rather than merely academic, and she has consequently found her way into thousands of gardening hearts.

So it is the Farrand drawings that now stand sentinel over Beatrix's reputation. Her collection is large (though not so large as Gertrude Jekyll's) and some information survives on almost all of the 202 commissions that are listed on pages 203–216. Simply seen as a collection, the drawings highlight and clarify some aspects of Beatrix's career. The numbers alone offer revelations: at least a dozen of the commissions were complete non-events, and no fewer than fifty-three, a quarter of the total, were for work on Mount Desert Island. She worked on eight major campuses all over the United States, as well as five smaller schools and colleges. To these must be added the "campus" of Dartington Hall in England. For many of her friends and patrons Beatrix was the ultimate designer, and she saw them to their last resting place; she designed fifteen tombstones or cemetery plots, including Theodore Roosevelt's, and she worked on three larger cemetery or churchyard layouts. In this she was following in the footsteps of William Robinson, who thought this to be an important part of the designer's work. (Robinson also advocated cremation, which probably influenced Beatrix's choice of this ending for her own mortal coil.)

Of her remaining 105 commissions there are many that were minor—the design of a seat or just a drive entrance. But there are also those of major national importance, where her work often needs much greater recognition. These include her early work on the siting of the National Cathedral in Washington, D.C., her garden for Otto H. Kahn on Long Island, now the Eastern Military Academy, her garden for the Morgan Library in New York City, her rose garden for the New York Botanical Garden, her garden for the White House, and her late restoration and replanting of the 1940s at the Arnold Arboretum of Harvard University. These are the commissions, along with Dumbarton Oaks and Dartington Hall in England, that raised Beatrix head and shoulders above many of her contemporaries, but where so much of her actual work has been disregarded or forgotten.

Further examination of her list of commissions prompts some analysis of her network of clients and patrons, essentially the social context of a designer's life. The fact that a quarter of her commissions were for work on Mount Desert Island confirms that this was her true home. She was, as I have shown, a spirited young woman of prominence in this small society of unusually prosperous and leisured persons, who were only too willing to help her in her un-

193

æ

Beatrix Farrand,

1872-1959:

Her Legacy, and What

Has Become of It

usual ambition (even if they did not always understand her capabilities). She had to prove herself, and undoubtedly did so early on, particularly in the eyes of a local civil engineer and surveyor, Edgar I. Lord, who brought her many early jobs. Landscape design is a peculiarly territorial art for most practitioners, and once Beatrix had made her name on her island, the residents remained almost exclusively loyal to her throughout her career. It is interesting to note that the only other Bar Harbor landscape designer with a list of commissions anywhere near as long as hers, Isaac N. Mitchell (1827–1901), did his last job two years before Beatrix started work properly in 1895. Her timing was excellent. From then onward she dominated her "patch" and, it is even more interesting to note from a checklist of contemporary designers in Maine, no one "poached" on her island; even the distinguished Warren H. Manning, Olmsted-trained and her fellow ASLA charter member, confined himself to Bangor and Rockport.[6]

Beatrix's immensely sociable island home base, her privileged background, and then her happy marriage to Max Farrand governed the pattern of patronage and work in her life and kept her in some professional isolation. Not for her the clubbable professionalism that architects and landscape architects seem to enjoy today; as a woman she was barred from those dinners and dining clubs that Charles Eliot and John Charles Olmsted regarded as a necessity to life. And after the founding of the ASLA in 1899 she restricted her attendance to useful lectures and the obligatory annual dinner, clearly never spending time with her fellows merely for the pleasure or enlightenment of their company. Later on, once she was well known and in demand, her contact with gardening clubs and the Garden Club of America was of a visiting nature, and though she was too tactful to say so directly, she had little patience with long afternoons of chatter.

Her professional isolation was also the product of her time and society. Even if there had been a course of study in landscape design available to her in the early 1890s, she would have been unlikely to have participated. The code of her old New York upbringing forbade such fraternizing for a woman, and before her were shining examples of how a woman could win great distinction on her own merits and efforts—that of her aunt, Edith Wharton, and Mrs. Schuyler van Rensselaer. Their way of succeeding, though it was far from easy, would also be hers. Beatrix's society and her personality gave her access to her heroes (Frederick Law Olmsted, William Robinson, and Gertrude Jekyll) under the wings of her eminent mentors (Charles Sprague Sargent, Henry James, and Theodore Roosevelt), and thus to her most powerful patrons (Edward S. Harkness, John D. Rockefeller Jr., and Robert Woods Bliss). Her passion for her work brought her all the friends—notably Mildred Bliss, Agnes Milliken, and Dorothy Straight Elmhirst—that she needed outside her family life.

But her social advantages and her independence may have given her a professional isolation that worked against her interests, especially in terms of her posthumous reputation. The historians of the women's movement prefer those designers who stormed the bastions of male education, Beatrix's contemporaries Marian Cruger Coffin[7] and Annette Hoyt Flanders,[8] or those who came from poor beginnings, like Ellen Biddle Shipman,[9] or those who pioneered the schools for women, Lowthorpe School at Groton, founded in 1901, and the Cambridge School of Architectural and Landscape Design, founded in 1915.[10] Although she may have been seen as an inspiration, there is no evidence that Beatrix either supported or joined what some modern writers perceive as a feminist struggle. But whenever she lectured on landscape design as a likely career, Beatrix laid careful emphasis on the hard work and dedication that was required. The physical effort was something she learned to live with, and must never be underestimated.

Territory, however, must not be forgotten in the landscape world; its dominance in America, only emphasized by climate and social history, is demonstrated by Mac Griswold and Eleanor Weller's encyclopedic volume *The Golden Age of American Gardens*. Beatrix's contemporaries can be traced within carefully maintained geographical limits, for the most part: Ellen Biddle Shipman was prominent in the South (she worked most notably for Mrs. Ralph Hanes in Winston-Salem and at Longue Vue Gardens, New Orleans) and in Texas. Marian Cruger Coffin worked at Winterthur in Delaware, and though Beatrix did only one garden south of the Delaware (Dumbarton Oaks), they both had plenty of scope on Long Island, where nine hundred commissions were to be picked up between 1865 and 1940. It was when Beatrix moved to southern California that she came up against a barrier, such as any of her competitors would have found crossing to Mount Desert Island. In 1927 she undoubtedly assumed that her reputation would open Californian doors, but even the influence of Mildred Bliss failed to do this. Florence Yoch and Lucille Counsel and Lockwood de Forest were in firm control. Yoch was making mock-English gardens that were a remarkable achievement, considering the differences in climates, and she was most famous for her film sets and gardens for movie moguls.[11] It was the loyalty of the Huntingtons' architect Myron Hunt and Lockwood de Forest's call to service in the war that really enabled Beatrix to have any Californian jobs at all. But her heart was not really in it, and—with the one notable exception of the Santa Barbara Botanic Garden, where the Blisses were both instrumental and influential—she was not enthusiastic for the flora of a climate so very different from her own.

As a footnote to the subject of territory it is worth noting that the Olmsted firm was the only exception to this rule. They worked on ten sites that also appear in Beatrix's list, but thoughts of collaboration or influence can be dismissed. They were but passing coincidences; Beatrix was either working years later, or she was called in to do something completely different, as with the Kahn garden, Woodbury, where the Olmsteds made vast French parterres and golf courses and Beatrix was asked for a series of elegant garden rooms where Mrs. Kahn could spend her time.[12]

No correspondence survives that shows any continuing relationship between Beatrix and the Olmsted office; it seems that from those early days when John Charles Olmsted and Warren Manning corresponded over their doubts about letting women into the ASLA and their ignorance of Miss Jones's abilities, they had gone their separate ways. Beatrix's way was, it must be admitted, a progressively independent road. After her attempts to achieve professional design standards for the First World War memorials, she devoted her energies to her own busy career rather than battling with her fellow professionals. In the Depression era her life was an anachronism, divided between the treasure houses of Dumbarton Oaks and the Huntington Museum and her private paradise on Mount Desert Island. The Second World War brought her despair, a final separation from her beloved England and Dartington Hall; Max Farrand's death in 1945 brought her desolation. By the time she had regained her equilibrium, the world was changing. At the moment she left California the star of Thomas Church was rising (he designed the Donnell garden at Sonoma in 1948), and during the 1950s when Beatrix was ordering her legacy, the new age of Kevin Lynch, Garrett Eckbo, and Ian McHarg was being born.[13]

There was no little irony in the fact that at the moment of her death in 1959, all the things she had believed in—working with nature, with regard to tradition, and above all for the benefit of humankind in the landscape—found its apotheosis in the work of these new designers and planners in America, and the old tide of European influence had turned at last.

But, for Beatrix in her last years, it was the fate of her beloved island, the disastrous fire and its consequences, the decline in summer visitors and the lack of young and energetic people to carry on her work at Reef Point that finally brought her to the decision to dismantle her garden. She even sent the nameplate from the gate to California with her books, drawings, and prints. Reef Point cannot be recalled, but now the island is popular again, and, some thirty years after the death of Mount Desert's distinguished daughter, the revival of many of Beatrix's island gardens is being brought about by the island-born, Harvard-educated landscape architect Patrick Chassé. The beacon of hope for him and for Beatrix's island reputation is the Rockefellers' Eyrie garden at Seal Harbor, which is exquisitely maintained, as it always has been, by the family.[14]

And what of Dartington Hall in Devon, where Beatrix returned in her last daydreams and where she wrote that her heart would reside "as long as life lasts"?[15] Leonard and Dorothy Elmhirst had told her that—on Constance Spry's advice—they appointed Percy Cane as consultant to Dartington after the neglect of wartime. Cane was self-educated, an aesthete, finding his design inspiration in the music of Wagner or Mozart, according to scale—rather prissy, but hardworking and eager to please. Beatrix, in the early 1950s, recorded her high opinion of him; Cane never acknowledged that Beatrix had even been at Dartington, let alone paid tribute to her work. Cane won the

Elmhirsts' confidence and he worked at Dartington until the end of Dorothy's life. At least they never let him touch Beatrix's great Courtyard, and the Spring, Camellia, and Rhododendron Walks are also places where her ghost may happily linger. Almost everything else is Cane's work, but always done in closest consultation with Dorothy. He was undoubtedly talented—most evidently in his elegant flight of the Azalea Steps through massed shrubs (including great swaths of *Juniperus pfitzeriana,* his favorite, but definitely *not* Beatrix's), and less so in some fine design drawings for unexecuted features that remain in the Dartington archives. At least, at Dartington, the record has been clearly set straight and the credits apportioned in a recent book, *From the Bare Stem: The Making of Dorothy Elmhirst's Garden at Dartington Hall,* by Reginald Snell.[16]

At Dartington, the Elmhirsts (Dorothy died in 1968, aged eighty-one; Leonard in 1974, aged eighty) are a legend. The once-famous school has closed, but the Hall survives in an appropriate role as an arts education center.[17] Many of the enterprises, the Dartington glassworks and tweeds, have become commercial successes and the whole area a tourist center. Fortunately, with time, Dorothy's garden—never perhaps really accepted by the English when she was alive, despite her efforts to bring it to the attention of Vita Sackville-West, Lanning Roper, and Russell Page—is now more appreciated.

And what of Beatrix's other favorite child, Dumbarton Oaks? First it must be noted that "permanent Harvard," the safe haven as she thought it to be, did not take all of her garden. The magical woodland acres below and beyond the Lover's Lane Pool were excluded from the garden, and left outside in Rock Creek Park, where they will be found in sometimes lovely but mainly sad ruin. A short walk down Lover's Lane along the stream (an anything but romantic venture in urban Washington) will reveal the pebbled water courses, the waterfalls and stone bridges (miniatures of that bridge Beatrix saw in the English Lake District in 1896) and the wildflower meadow, all so sensitively designed to blend with nature, now almost completely reclaimed by it.[18]

Inside the Harvard fence Beatrix had no official role after 1955 when the Garden Advisory Committee took over. In practice this committee veered farther and farther toward its academic duties and was mostly concerned with lectureships and fellowships in landscape history research, where Dumbarton Oaks' reputation remains supreme. The redesign of the Urn Terrace and the making of the Pebble Garden are the two most obvious changes from these years when Beatrix's restraining hand was removed. The Garden Library was completed in 1963, and from that time the garden research took equal place with the departments of Byzantine and pre-Columbian studies, making up the present triumvirate of Dumbarton Oaks. Academically, Dumbarton Oaks has been supremely loyal to Beatrix, and has played a crucial role in the revival of her reputation, particularly with a symposium on her work held in 1982.

The garden is almost always open to the public and it is Beatrix's most important memorial. During my many visits I have always found it interesting, and it is often enchanting, but I do not think it is fittingly maintained. I suspect that the denizens of the Garden Library, in stretching their minds across the world to Renaissance châteaus or the planting for the Agora, find it difficult to accept the essential part of their department, the real, earthy, sometimes dripping, sometimes frosted but always demanding garden outside their windows. I am forced to wonder why so many Americans make pilgrimages of adoration to Sissinghurst Castle, and yet have never heard of, or visited, Dumbarton Oaks. For Dumbarton Oaks is a far, far superior garden in design to either Sissinghurst Castle or Hidcote Manor, and it ranks (as they cannot) with the greatest gardens in the world, such as Villa d'Este or Vaux-le-Vicomte. All the instructions exist, notably in the "Dumbarton Oaks Plant Book," for it to be planted and maintained as a garden work of art, and it should dazzle and delight all who see it, as one of Harvard's greatest treasures. To suggest that the expertise to do this in America may be lacking is untrue, for look at the brilliance of Filoli in California or the Wave Hill Gardens in New York.

Unlike Gertrude Jekyll, Beatrix did not leave her legacy in books she had written. Any appreciation of her artistry and her gift to America depends upon winning hearts for her gardens by explaining how they were made, which is something I have tried to do. Their revival and restoration is up to others, and there are many places where this awareness is growing and the work is in hand. I have one final task on Beatrix's behalf, and that is to put into words my reasons for believing that her reputation has not been best served by those who owed her most, and that if her loyalty to some of her most powerful and influential clients had been returned, her fragile legacy would be more greatly valued.

For every English person who asks why Gertrude Jekyll's drawings are in America there is an American who asks why Beatrix Farrand's drawings are on the West Coast. Why are the gardens and the essential information about them a continent apart? California was the place that rejected Beatrix in her lifetime, the climate is alien to her work, and this is a considerable, albeit subtle, barrier. The answer seems to lie in a sequence of unhappy events and personal difficulties that were aggravated by much larger tragedies. I cannot claim to have solved all the mystery as to why there is no Beatrix Farrand School of Environmental Research and Design anywhere. I can only offer the following calendar of Beatrix's last unhappiness and seeming betrayal.

In June 1936 she was given an honorary degree, a Doctorate of Letters, in the Commencement Day ceremony at Smith College. Smith wished to recognize the work of Mrs. Max Farrand, as she was styled, and also honor the profession of landscape architecture. It had recently been affiliated with the pioneering Cambridge School of Architecture and Landscape Architecture for the purposes of graduating women. A Cambridge School graduate, Dorothy May Anderson, who had also worked with Ellen Biddle Shipman, was appointed landscape architect to Smith College, and she was to teach and redesign the campus: the future looked hopeful. On the strength of this Beatrix decided that Smith could make good use of the books she no longer needed, and she duly packed some up and sent them to Dorothy Anderson in the late summer of 1941.

Then came the Japanese attack on Pearl Harbor, which brought America into the war. Early casualties were landscape architecture and the Cambridge School; the latter was closed and it was announced that the few women who required graduate study facilities would be admitted to the Harvard Graduate School for the duration. Undeterred, Beatrix offered Smith more books in the fall of 1942. These were precious source books that she had had the wit and money to collect in her youth, such as the original editions of Percier & Fontaine, William Shenstone, and Gilpin's *Travels in Search of the Picturesque,* extreme rarities in America. Dorothy Anderson agreed that these treasures would be kept in Smith's new rare-book room, and she undoubtedly urged President Herbert Davis to be duly appreciative of the gift. In return Beatrix replied in a letter of September 1, 1942, that she and Max had decided that her entire collection should go to Smith after her death. At that point Dorothy Anderson's post at Smith became a casualty of wartime economies, and though Beatrix's books were carefully and safely housed, a careless reply to Beatrix's request for a valuation of her gift—set at $363, or $1 a book— undoubtedly led her to think that no one at Smith was capable of appreciating her generosity. Her reply was coldly polite. No further books would come Smith's way and the spare bookplates were duly returned as she requested.[19]

The "valuation" and Beatrix's frosty response are dated January and February 1943, just at the time she was coming to terms with Max Farrand's illness and impending operation. She needed all her concentration to muster her support and care for him, and maintain her cheerful and bantering exterior, and this was to occupy her totally for two and a half years, until Max's death in June 1945. The shock of his death stunned her; as she later confessed to the Elmhirsts, she became intolerable, rude, and impatient, and ultra-demanding of all those around her and everyone with whom she came into contact.

Smith College was clearly dismissed for past misdemeanors. We know that her relationship with the Elmhirsts survived and she explained herself to them, but what of Mildred and Robert Woods Bliss? They had been so close, Mil-Rob and MaxTrix, but was Mildred Bliss the kind to cope when Beatrix was in difficulties? I suspect not. Though she had written that Beatrix would always be needed at Dumbarton Oaks "as long as the road lies clear," this was not the case when the Blisses returned to their Georgetown home after the war so that they could keep a close eye on their bequest to Harvard. Beatrix offered her resignation on March 21, 1947, and after that the previously effusive correspondence sputters and fades. Mildred Bliss and Ruth Havey, Beatrix's former chief assistant and a graduate from the Cambridge School, set about a postwar revival and reorganization of the garden, adding baroque touches—most notably the Pebble Garden—of which Beatrix would never have approved. Three years after she offered to step down as consultant, Beatrix announced that she was sending all her papers and plans about the making of the garden to the Dumbarton Oaks library, so that the complete story could be told to future students of landscape architecture. This was in the spring of 1950. Is it not strange that in the following months and years, when Mildred Bliss was collecting books for the Garden Library at Dumbarton Oaks, she did not see fit to offer a home to Beatrix's already complete library? Or, when Beatrix was in real difficulties in 1955, Dumbarton Oaks did not come to the rescue? I suspect that the answer lies in the pride of two distinguished and elderly ladies, who had *once* been such close friends with a "garden child" in common, but now wished to leave individual legacies. But it is very sad that no kind mediator was at hand.

Though Beatrix's relationship with Dumbarton Oaks faded, she may have had hopes of another Harvard institution. She regarded her appointment as consultant landscape architect to the Arnold Arboretum as the "greatest honour" of her fifty years of professional work. This was a return to her alma mater, and she could pay tribute to her adored Professor Sargent by restoring some of his ideas to his Arboretum. She did this with great skill and distinction, despite her seventy-five-plus years, between the summer of 1946 and the fall of 1949.[20] She was full of plans to continue: "It looks as though our next big job were the re-arrangement of the shrubs in the present shrub collecting area," she wrote to Dr. Karl Sax, promising to visit at the end of November so that the work could be done through the winter. Perhaps she was also contemplating offering the Arnold her books and drawings, for there would have seemed a logic in that.

Once again fate intervened. The distinguished plantsmen at the Arnold did not want any designer, however distinguished, interfering with their collections, and the mounting criticism from the dyed-in-the-wool conservatives who wanted no changes at all at the Arboretum were growing louder. As a final straw, Dr. Sax found himself embroiled in the bitter controversy over the removal of some of the Arboretum staff, its herbarium, and precious library from the Arborway into Cambridge, and Beatrix would have realized that the moment was far from right to mention any concerns of her own. Thus there was another parting of the ways. Though there was no formal break, she was consultant no longer, her "greatest honour" had fizzled out, and her library still had no future home. Thus she came to face the dismantling of Reef Point alone. With hindsight, it does seem that those to whom she had given so much during her working life failed her when she needed help most.

Was it any wonder when Professor Leland Vaughan, chairman of the Department of Landscape Architecture at Berkeley, came a-courting her collection, that she felt relieved that someone appreciated her legacy after all? Her books, her drawings, Miss Jekyll's drawings, the herbarium specimens, everything was dispatched across a continent to reside in a climate where neither her gardens nor most of their plants could survive. They came to rest in brilliant but alien company, with the works of Bernard Maybeck, Greene &

Greene, Julia Morgan, and (now less irrelevantly) Kevin Lynch. There Beatrix's belongings were filed away until travelers from the east, from the old world, found them.[21]

I am not suggesting that Beatrix's drawings should be recalled from the Berkeley campus, because they have rested safely there for a long time now. But it is time that Beatrix herself was exhumed and appreciated for the great American heroine she was. She was far, far more perceptive and talented a gardener than Gertrude Jekyll, and in her own way she achieved every bit as much as did her distinguished aunt, Edith Wharton. She gave America a very precious gift: In an age when most of her contemporaries were pandering to a taste for copying European fashions, Beatrix was being truly creative, and absorbing the best of the old traditions but converting them into something of her own, into places that America could call its own, original and lovely gardens. She gave most eastern and mid-continental climatic zones a workable style and tradition in garden and landscape design, equally beautiful in the smallest scale or spreading campus, and all in a sustainable tradition that made best use of precious natural resources. In recent years the people of America have discovered the pleasures of gardening as an effective antidote to our time, and they have become enormously interested in America's rich heritage of wonderful gardens. At the last, as I have promised, I offer them a heroine in their gardens, Beatrix Jones Farrand, a heroine to inspire and to love.

LIST OF COMMISSIONS

*T*he Reef Point Gardens Collection of Beatrix Farrand's drawings, owned by the College of Environmental Design at the University of California's Berkeley campus, is catalogued in alphabetical order by name of client, and each client is given a file number. The first accession number is 820 and the numbering runs consecutively to 833, then from 853 to 1031, for a total of 192 folders, including a miscellaneous folder.

The cataloguing of these drawings has been a considerable achievement, first by Marlene Salon, then by Meredith Shedd, as described by Michael Laurie in his paper on the collection to the Eighth Dumbarton Oaks Colloquium (1982), which was a tribute to Beatrix Farrand's life and work.

In addition to the Reef Point Gardens catalogue, there is a list of works drawn up by Beatrix Farrand in "about 1950," a copy of which was given to me by Scott Marshall at Edith Wharton Restoration Inc., The Mount, Lenox, Massachusetts. This list is also in alphabetical order by clients, but there are variations between the two lists. I have combined both in order to make what follows the most comprehensive list of Beatrix Farrand's commissions. Places where Beatrix Farrand's work survives and can be seen are indicated with an asterisk.

CALIFORNIA

Mrs. Robert Woods Bliss, Casa Dorinda, Santa Barbara
"Occasional consultant," including design of parking-lot area and a garden wall, 1936.

Mrs. William H. Bliss, El Montecito
>   Brief query about the garden, 1925.

California Institute of Technology, Pasadena
>   Consultant, 1928–38, for planting of Dabney Hall, Gates Hall, Crelling Hall, and the Hall of Humanities.

Professor Max Farrand, Director's House, Huntington Library and Museum, San Marino
>   Design and planting for the garden, 1930–35.

Dr. George E. Hale, Solar Observatory, Pasadena
>   Design of garden for this private observatory, 1928.

Mount Palomar Observatory (California Institute of Technology)
>   Brief advice about trees on the site when Dr. Hale was director, 1938.

Occidental College, Los Angeles
>   Consultant, 1937–48, with Myron Hunt, architect, for central quadrangle; Thorne, Wylie, and Haines halls; and the Men's Dormitories.

Robert I. Rogers, Beverly Hills
>   Design for a garden, 1929, including walls, seat, pavilion, and steps. No planting.

CONNECTICUT

Mrs. Gordon Bell, Ridgefield
>   Design for a seat, 1901. Mrs. Bell was a friend of Edith Wharton.

★Thomas W. Farnam, 328 Temple Street, New Haven
>   Advice given on his garden, which is now Farnam Park, c. 1922. He was treasurer of the Yale Botanic Garden trustees.

Mrs. Samuel H. Fisher, Litchfield
>   Garden design with details for grape arbor, rose trellis, gates, fences, and a tennis stool for Mr. Fisher, 1922–29.

Greenfield Hill Schoolhouse, Greenfield Hill
>   Shrub planting around the schoolhouse and on the green, 1898.

★Mr. and Mrs. Edward S. Harkness, Eolia, New London
>   Consultant for replanting of West Garden, design and planting of rock garden walk, box garden, and ornamental details, 1918–24.

Miss Mary Robbins Hilliard, Westover School, Farmington
>   Planting advice for the garden of the school built by Theodate Pope Riddle, 1912.

Gerrish H. Milliken, Greenwich
>   Design for farm layout (next to Yale Farms property), 1937.

New Haven Parks Department, Edgewood Park, New Haven
>   Brief advice on azalea planting, 1937.

New Haven Hospital, New Haven
>   Design for drive, railings, and gates for Wallace Witt Williamson building for tuberculosis patients, 1915–16.

Dr. Frederick Peterson, Three Rivers Farm, Shepaug
>   Sketch design of grounds for Dr. Markoe's partner. (*See* New York.)

The Phelps Association, New Haven
  Brief planting advice to architects Cram & Goodhue, 1923.
★Mrs. J. W. Riddle, Hill-Stead, Farmington
  Planting plan for enclosed flower garden designed by Theodate Pope Riddle, 1913. The Hill-Stead Museum and garden are beautifully restored.
Owen F. Roberts, Montevideo, Simsbury
  Design for "Chinese" lattice and planting for mixed border, 1920.
Anson Phelps Stokes, Brick House, Noroton Point, Darien
  Design for the garden, 1902.
Ethel Walker School, Simsbury
  Consultant for planting to Emily Cluett House, 1919. Nothing done.
Henry Whitfield State Historical Museum, Guilford
  Sketch design for grape arbor, 1932. Nothing remains of this.
Professor F. W. Williams, Whitney Avenue, New Haven
  Design for the garden, 1915–16.
Nathaniel Witherell, Belle-Haven, Greenwich
  Design for a garden with dovecot and sundial, 1899–1900.
★Yale University, New Haven
  Consultant landscape gardener for twenty-three years. Areas of design include the Marsh Botanic Garden, Sterling Library court, Pierson-Sage, Sloane Laboratory, the Divinity School, Calhoun, Trumbull, the Sterling Hall of Medicine, Silliman College, the Harkness Memorial Quadrangle (Jonathan Edwards College and Library Walk).

ILLINOIS

★University of Chicago, Chicago
  Landscape consultant, 1929–43. Her work includes the courtyard of International House; the Oriental Institute Garden; alterations to the design of the main quadrangle, including The Circle; the Women's Residence; Eckhardt, Blaine, and Ida Noyes halls; Yerkes Observatory; and Sunny Gymnasium. For the Yerkes Observatory, Beatrix also advised on some planting at Green Bay, Wisconsin.

MAINE

Dr. Robert Abbe, Brook End, Bar Harbor
  Driveway and bridging of Duck Brook designed c. 1901, and natural garden planted. Abbe was a New York surgeon, amateur archeologist, and distinguished Bar Harbor resident. Brook End was demolished in the early 1960s.
William F. Apthorpe, Hull's Cove
  Only plan from Edgar I. Lord, civil engineer, and no eventual work by Beatrix Jones, 1906.
Augusta, Maine, the State Park
  There is one undated blueprint with notes on planting. Beatrix referred to this in correspondence with W. H. Judd at the Arnold Arboretum, July 12, 1932. Dr.

R. H. Pierson, state entomologist, had asked for advice on native Maine trees on the capitol grounds.

Mrs. Walter Ayer, Bar Harbor

Design for garden and trellis, seat and doorway details, 1924–25.

Bar Harbor Village Green and Athletic Club

Plan for walks across the green and planting, and planting for the athletic field, 1922.

Mrs. W. Gerrish Beale, Bar Harbor

Planting for bed under a window, 1926.

Mrs. William H. Bliss, Bar Harbor

Beatrix's first job, drainage of a field, was done for Robert Woods Bliss's mother, c. 1896, and recalled in a letter to Mildred Bliss, July 7, 1922.

E. C. Bodman, Seal Harbor

Contour plan of site, 1900. No work done.

George S. Bowdoin, La Rochelle, West Street, Bar Harbor

Sketch design for fence, 1902, but see chapter 5, page 50. Now the Sea Coast Mission.

Robert P. Bowler, Bar Harbor

Brief consultation over driveway, with architects Jacques & Rantoul, c. 1901.

Eugene S. Bristol, Bar Harbor

One blueprint of summerhouse, c. 1901. No work by Beatrix Jones.

Mrs. James Byrne, Bar Harbor

Design for a garden, 1928, with planting, spring 1929.

Mrs. Alfred Coats, Tanglewold, Kebo Street, Bar Harbor

Design for a garden, 1906; also a garden at Newport, Rhode Island, for Mrs. Coats, but there are no drawings.

Mrs. Edwin Corning, Stoney Point, Northeast Harbor

Architects' drawings of the house, c. 1938, but no work by Beatrix Farrand.

Parker Corning, Bar Harbor

Design of a garden with sunken court, terrace, trellis, steps, flower boxes, and gates, 1923–25.

Henry D. Dakin, Seal Harbor

Sketch layout for cemetery plot.

Jacob S. Disston, Northeast Harbor

Planting for a house by Tilden, Register & Pepper, 1926.

Dr. and Mrs. Edward K. Dunham, Keewaydin, Sea Cliff Drive, Seal Harbor

Perennial borders on either side of a path, small garden, c. 1900, for Dr. Dunham, a family friend and founder of Mount Desert Island Hospital.

Mrs. Gano Dunn, Sutton's Island

One sketch plan for flower beds, 1929. (*See* New York.)

W. Barton Eddison, Northeast Harbor

Brief advice on grading of site, 1930.

Mrs. Ernesto Fabbri, Buonriposo, Eden Street, Bar Harbor

Design discussions with Edgar I. Lord, engineer, 1904.

Mrs. Bradford Fraley, Northeast Harbor

Designs for garden house, fences, gates, seats, iris garden, for architects Tilden, Register & Pepper.

Miss Lucy Frelinghuysen, Northeast Harbor

Advice on garden. No drawings.

William Pierson Hamilton, Thirlestane, Eagle Lake Road, Bar Harbor

Hamilton was J. P. Morgan's son-in-law; he bought the house in 1926 and Beatrix designed the garden including pavilion, pools, fences, gates, walls, and ironwork for elaborate terraces, and a patchwork quilt garden in diamond shapes. Thirlestone burned in the 1947 fire but there are remains on Hamilton Hill. *See also* New York.

Mrs. Marcus Hanna, Seal Harbor

Ravine garden with mixed planting and lovely details, 1920.

Harry G. Haskell, Arnold House, Northeast Harbor

Terraces and drive designed with architect Arthur McFarland, 1931.

Henry Hatfield, Bar Harbor

Designs for driveway and avenues, c. 1900.

Mrs. Morris Hawkes, Bar Harbor

Design for planting, 1928.

Edward Cairns Henderson, Bar Harbor

Design for a headstone, undated.

Dr. and Mrs. C. A. Herter, Seal Harbor

Design for garden to house by Grover Atterbury, 1904.

Richard M. Hoe, Eastholme, Seal Harbor

Design and planting of garden, 1921–24.

Mrs. John Innes Kane, Bar Harbor

Design for Kane Memorial Bridge in Acadia National Park, 1928.

Miss Mildred McCormick, The Farm House, Highbrook Road, Bar Harbor

Kitchen and flower garden to suit old Maine farmhouse (enlarged by architect Arthur McFarland), including fences, gates, paving, "cottage" flower borders, and "martin house," mid-1920s.

Mrs. Robert McCormick, Bournemouth, Bar Harbor

Brief planting advice; gate and trellis design, 1936.

Mrs. Vance McCormick, Northeast Harbor

Design and details for bluestone terrace and steps, and border planting, 1927–35.

Mr. and Mrs. Gerrish H. Milliken, The Haven, Northeast Harbor

Constant designs for and alterations to terraces, fences, arbors, trellis, flower tubs, gates, "martin house," etc., and planting plans for a rose garden, phlox garden, and borders for twenty years, 1924–45, with three architects: Arthur McFarland, J. F. Kelly, and Robert W. Patterson. The Gerrish Millikens were close friends and business partners. *See also* New York and Connecticut.

Dr. James F. Mitchell, Bar Harbor

Undated design for a garden. No drawings.

William S. Moore, Woodlands, Bar Harbor

Undated design for flower garden planting for Mrs. Moore, who was Edith Pulitzer. Woodlands was destroyed by the 1947 fire.

Henry Morgenthau, Bar Harbor

Undated design for a garden. No drawings.

Mrs. Dave Hennen Morris, Bogue Chitto, Bar Harbor

Brief advice on planting, 1919. House demolished. *See also* New York.

Mount Desert Island Hospital, Bar Harbor

Advice on alterations to the hospital with Arthur McFarland.

Mrs. James Murphy, Seal Harbor

Undated design for a garden. No drawings.

Northeast Harbor Tennis Club, Northeast Harbor

Design for a tennis shelter, 1934.

Mrs. Potter Palmer, Hare Forest, Schooner Head Road, Bar Harbor

Garden designed after Arthur McFarland's extension to the house, 1926; includes terraces and tool house, but mainly natural planting to enhance sea views. Planting to driveway with George Dorr.

Mrs. Charles T. Pike, Bar Harbor

Garden consultant for several years. No drawings.

Mr. and Mrs. Henry Rawle, Northeast Harbor

Design advice for grounds to house by Arthur McFarland, 1929–30.

Mrs. F. B. Richards, Scrivelsby, Blue Hill

Planting for courtyard garden, 1919.

David Rockefeller, Seal Harbor

Design for proposed terrace and fences; layout for guest house by Arthur McFarland, 1949.

★John D. Rockefeller Jr., Seal Harbor

Planting design for Beaver Pool on Rockefeller Road, and also in connection with Brown Mountain Gate Lodge and Jordan Pond Gate Lodge (both lodges by Grover Atterbury and John Tompkins, architects) in Acadia National Park, c. 1930.

Mr. and Mrs. John D. Rockefeller Jr., The Eyrie, Seal Harbor

Complete design for the walled flower garden and Spirit Path woodland from 1926, including moon gate, bottle gate, tool house, pool, seats, walls, steps, gate piers, incense burner, and ironwork—136 construction details and planting plans. The garden was completed by 1935, when Mrs. Rockefeller assumed the care of it herself, with occasional design help from Duncan Candler and Robert W. Patterson.

Mrs. Frank B. Rowell, Bar Harbor

Design for grounds. No drawings. (Baker, Andrews, Rantoul & Jones, architects)

Charles E. and Miss Gertrude Sampson, Rockhurst, Mt. Desert Street, Bar Harbor

Design for small informal garden with irregular beds of annuals and perennials, leading to natural meadow and pine grove, 1927.

Mrs. Herbert L. Satterlee, Great Head, Ocean Drive, Bar Harbor

Like the Sampsons, large beds of annuals and perennials with careful color harmonies for a natural seaside garden. Destroyed in 1947 fire.

Edgar T. Scott, Chiltern, Bar Harbor

Design of driveway and bridge over Cromwell Brook, 1896, followed by designs for informal flower garden, 1909–12.

Seal Harbor Cemetery, Seal Harbor

Design for lych-gate, 1897.

Seal Harbor Green, Seal Harbor
Relocation of drinking fountain and design of seats and walls, after alterations to Steamboat Wharf Road, 1924.

Charles and Mary Dow Stebbins, Bar Harbor
Headstone design with flowers for Charles Stebbins, who died on May 4, 1898, and Mary Stebbins, who died on October 2, 1909.

Mrs. Edward T. Stotesbury, Wingwood House, Eden Street, Bar Harbor
Design of garden after the architects Magaziner, Eberhard & Harris had created an eighty-room, "classical" cottage. Designs include fences, gates, garden pavilion, enclosed garden with pool, 1928–31.

Roland Taylor, Northeast Harbor
Undated design for grounds and gardens. No drawings.

Mrs. Archibald Gourlay Thatcher, Bar Harbor
Brief design advice. No date.

Mrs. Charlton Yarnall, Northeast Harbor
Designs for terrace, steps, gate, and fence, and shrub planting and flower borders for a kitchen garden, 1926–27.

Mrs. A. Murray Young, Tanglewold, Kebo Street, Bar Harbor
Design and layout for three terraces on this steep site, and a woodland path, pool, and kitchen garden, from 1918. Tanglewold burned in 1947.

*Marie Hunt Young Memorial, St. Saviour's Church, Bar Harbor
Design for a tablet, bench, and table, 1944.

MARYLAND

Mrs. Elliott, Ruxton Park
No drawings.

Roland Park Women's Club, Baltimore
Design for garden with teahouse and corner seat beneath arbor, 1905.

MASSACHUSETTS

*The Arnold Arboretum of Harvard University, Jamaica Plain
Landscape design consultant to the arboreteum, 1946–50. Beatrix Farrand wrote about her work in *Arnoldia,* volume 9, no. 2 (April 1949), pp. 6–7, and volume 9, no. 9 (October 1949). The drawings are in the Arnold Arboretum archives.

Cortlandt F. Bishop, The Winter Palace, Lenox
More than one hundred drawings from Beatrix Farrand's office of designs for driveway, gates, terraces, arbors, basin, and paving with bronze mythological and classical figures, 1924–25. Nothing of this garden survives.

*Mrs. Samuel G. Colt, Pittsfield
Garden designed and constructed, 1919–24. House demolished in the 1960s but part of the garden survives at the Knessas Israel Synagogue, Colt Road, Pittsfield.

Mrs. Zenas Crane Jr., Willowbrook, Dalton

Design for a large flower garden with arbors, trellis, pineapple finials, oil jars, etc., all photographed by Beatrix Farrand, 1919–24. The house has been demolished and the site redeveloped.

Harris Fahnestock, Eastover, Lenox

Details and planting design for house by Francis L. Hoppin, 1910–14.

Giraud Foster, Bellefontaine, Lenox

Minor suggestions for softening of planting in formal garden by Carrere & Hastings, c. 1905. The structure of this garden is preserved.

Mrs. Henry Cabot Lodge, Nahant

Design for playground fence and planting, 1910–11.

C. M. Perry, Cambridge

Sketch drawings for tree planting, c. 1895 (probably the early job found by Professor Charles Sprague Sargent).

Mrs. John T. Phillips, North Beverly

Brief consultation over water garden, undated.

Miss Alice Sargent, Holm Lea, Brookline

Brief advice about lattice on house walls for Professor Sargent's spinster daughter, 1930. Sargent had died in 1927.

Mrs. J. Montgomery Sears, Southborough

Design for a tennis shelter, 1913.

William Douglas Sloane, Elmcourt, Lenox

Large, many-bedded flower garden for Mrs. Emily Vanderbilt Sloane, 1908.

★Mr. and Mrs. Edward Wharton, The Mount, Lenox

Designs for entrance drive and kitchen garden and suggested layout of formal garden, 1901. The latter was done by the Whartons themselves.

NEW JERSEY

Lawrenceville Cemetery, Mercer County

Design of fence and gates, 1928.

Emma J. Martin, Spring Lake

Plan of a garden, undated.

★Princeton University, Princeton

Design and planting of the grounds of the Graduate College, 1913, then consultant to the university for twenty-eight years: the best surviving areas are the garden of Wyman House, the walk from the dinky station through Henry, Foulkes, Blair, Joline, the Chapel, the chemical and engineering laboratories, Macmillan, and the garden of Prospect House.

Mrs. Moses Taylor Pyne, Princeton

Design for features and a cutting garden, 1914.

Mr. and Mrs. Henry Rawle, Morristown

Brief planting advice, undated.

The Rockefeller Institute for Medical Research, Plainsboro

Advice on planting to buildings by Coolidge & Shattuck, c. 1917.

Dr. J. C. Ayer, Glen Cove, Long Island
Design for a garden, undated.

Percy Chubb, Dosoris, Long Island
Design for a rose arbor, water rill, and planting, 1900.

Thomas Condon, Tuxedo Park
Terrace design. No details.

William Adams Delano, Syosset, Long Island
Design of flower borders for the architect's garden, 1921.

Mrs. Richard Derby, The Old Adam House, Oyster Bay, Long Island
Sketch for entrance for President Theodore Roosevelt's daughter, 1921.

Dr. C. Dunham, Irvington-on-Hudson
Garden with arbor and planting details, 1899–1900.

Mrs. Gano Dunn, White Plains
Sketch design for plot in White Plains Cemetery, c. 1929.

Mrs. Roswell Eldridge, Great Neck, Long Island
Sixty-plus drawings from the office for alternative designs for an oval enclosed garden, but all were unconvincing and it is unlikely that much was done. Drawings are dated 1924–30.

Sherman Flint, Islip, Long Island
Only a 1912 map of property. No work by Beatrix Farrand.

William R. Garrison, Plot No. 1., West Lake Road, Tuxedo Park
Beaux-Arts house by William A. Bates, for which Beatrix Jones designed drive planting, planting around the house, and a natural garden layout, 1896–99.

Robert Goelet, Glenmere, Goshen
Elaborate rectangular garden, pools, green garden, box-edged beds, pergola, gardens for annuals and bulbs, and rose garden, 1920s.

Great Neck Green, Great Neck, Long Island
Enclosed garden with flowering shrubs and underplanting of spring bulbs, 1922–32.

★Great Neck Library, Great Neck, Long Island
Shrub planting around building and in courtyard, 1925.

William Pierson Hamilton, Table Rock, Sterlington
Advice given on planting for large terrace, c. 1926.

★Hamilton College, Clinton
Advice given by request of Elihu Root on planting around the buildings of the central quadrangle, 1924.

Edward J. Hancy, Tuxedo Park
Sketches for rose trellis and planting, 1927. (Mr. Hancy was Beatrix's trustee at the Bank of New York.)

Mrs. Edward S. Harkness, Manhasset, Long Island
Brief advice on a garden, 1921.

Mrs. Edward S. Harkness, Woodlawn Cemetery
Design and planting of shrubs and trees around James Gamble Rogers's Romano-Gothic mausoleum for Edward Harkness, 1925.

Thomas Hastings, Bagatelle, Roslyn, Long Island

Advice on border planting to Helen Benedict Hastings, 1915.

C. Oliver Iselin, Locust Valley, Brookville, Long Island

Design of drive and garden, including rose garden, 1914.

Mr. and Mrs. Otto H. Kahn, Oheka, Woodbury, Cold Spring Harbor, Long Island

Series of garden rooms for Mrs. Kahn, 1919, including a *cabinet de verdure*, rose garden, pool gardens with circles of planting, a Lovat cobbled pool, octagon garden, and Dutch garden, all complete with planting schemes and details. Olmsted Bros. had established the overall large-scale design prior to Beatrix Farrand's appointment. The site remains as part of the Eastern Military Academy.

Mrs. Francis P. Kinnicutt, Woodlawn Cemetery

Memorial stone and planting for Francis P. Kinnicutt, professor of clinical medicine at the College of Physicians and Surgeons of New York, and his wife, Eleanor Kissel Kinnicutt, 1913.

Mrs. Thomas Lamont, New York City

Advice given on a town garden on Park Avenue (next to Milliken, no. 723), undated.

Mrs. Philip W. Livermore, Jericho, Long Island

Brief design and planting advice, 1911.

Mrs. Alfred T. Mahan, Quogue, Long Island

Plan of grounds, with trellis, steps, and fence details, 1908.

S. Vernon Mann, Grove Point, Great Neck, Long Island

Two hundred thirty-four drawings for garden design, with many details including a knot garden, rose garden, arbors, fences, gates, a boat house, shell basin, fountain, seats, trellis, vases, urns, and a bird bath. Planting designs for a lilac walk, rose garden, tulip and evergreen gardens, 1920–30.

H. E. Manville, Pleasantville

Design for a new garden with many details but unfinished planting, 1927–28.

Gerrish H. Milliken, 723 Park Avenue, New York City

Design for a town garden with paving and planting, 1923–30.

Mrs. Gerrish H. Milliken, Sterling Falls, Armonk

A tulip garden, c. 1949, designed for the widowed Mrs. Milliken.

Mrs. Gerrish H. Milliken, Woodlawn Cemetery

Headstone for Gerrish Milliken and planting for plot, 1949.

★J. P. Morgan Sr. and J. P. Morgan Jr., Morgan Library, Madison Avenue, New York City

J. P. Morgan originally commissioned Beatrix Jones to plant his town garden, but this turned into a long period of consultancy to the Morgan Library (which opened in 1924), from 1913 to 1943.

Mrs. Dave Hennen Morris, Glen Head, Long Island

Brief advice on screen planting and layout of the estate, 1925.

★New York Botanical Garden, Bronx, New York City

Complete first design for the layout, fencing, and arbor of the Rose Garden, 1915–16, which was never fully implemented. Restoration has been based on the Farrand designs. Now the Peggy Rockefeller Rose Garden.

New York Zoological Society Garden, Central Park, New York City
Preliminary advice given. No drawings, no date.

Thomas Newbold, Hyde Park
Brief garden advice including design for a summerhouse, 1912.

Mrs. Douglas W. Paige, Bellport, Long Island
Two sketch planting plans for flower borders, undated.

Trenor L. Park, Harrison
Very early designs by Beatrix Jones for terrace details, a berceau, balustrade, and some planting, probably as a result of drawing lessons at Columbia College, 1897–98.

Dr. F. Peterson and Dr. James Markoe, 20 West Fiftieth Street, New York City
Design for a town garden, 1909.

Mrs. George D. Pratt, Killenworth, Glen Cove, Long Island
Plan of garden with summerhouse and tennis court, 1914.

Percy R. Pyne III, Roslyn, Long Island
One hundred eighty-five drawings for design of a garden and model farm, 1926–29. This seems to have been more design than substance (though parts were photographed complete) but designs include an annual garden, swimming pool, fencing, and trellis screenings for cart sheds, etc., designs for a weather vane, finials, pot stands, a sundial, and box plantings for the forecourt.

William A. Read, Hillcrest, Harrison
Garden design in two stages: 1909–11, terrace, balustrades, arbor, and pool with color-graded border planting, including a white border, a pink border, and a blush, cream, and silver scheme. In 1927 the planting was revised and more work carried out.

Mrs. Geraldyne Redmond, Tivoli-on-Hudson
Brief design advice given for terrace, gates, and gate to churchyard, undated.

John D. Rockefeller Jr., Pocantico Hills
One drawing for summer border planting, 1906.

*Mrs. Theodore Roosevelt, Sagamore Hill, Oyster Bay, Long Island
Designs for the headstones for Quentin Roosevelt and Hamilton Coolidge, both killed in France, 1918. Beatrix Farrand also designed the gravestone in Oyster Bay Cemetery for President Theodore Roosevelt, who died on January 6, 1919.

*Saint Paul's Church, Red Hook
Complete layout around church and planting of paths through the churchyard, 1912. The church is now St. Paul's (Zion's) Evangelical Lutheran Church, and car parking has destroyed its surroundings, but much of the character of the churchyard planting remains. Many graves of Rocks and Fellers.

Mr. and Mrs. Willard Straight, Old Westbury, Long Island
Design for a walled "Chinese" garden and playhouses with swimming pool for the house Elmhurst, 1913–18. After the death of Willard Straight in 1918 and Dorothy's subsequent marriage to Leonard Elmhirst, the name was changed to Apple Green, and the garden was maintained by Beatrix as consultant until the late 1940s. Part of the garden survives. The papers are in the Elmhirst Centre Archive at Dartington Hall in Devon, England.

Charles Edward Strong, Woodlawn Cemetery
Monument with floral motif to John Lambert Cadwalader's partner in the law firm of Strong & Cadwalader, 1909.

Mrs. J. C. Thaw, Southampton, Long Island
Brief design for shrubs and spring flowers along driveway to house by Grover Atterbury, 1914.

★Tuxedo Village
Early commission for entrance planting and screening for station and cottages, 1896.

★Vassar College, Poughkeepsie
Consultant, 1926–27, on the layout and planting of the forecourt, the planting for Kendrick House and other faculty houses along Raymond Avenue, and the new science quadrangle. Not well preserved.

Paul Moritz Warburg, Sleepy Hollow Cemetery
Design of tombstone and plot, 1932.

Edward F. Whitney, Oyster Bay, Long Island
Thirty-five drawings between 1906 and 1914 of designs including drive planting, fountains, rose trellis, seats, arbor, a walled flower garden, and an informal iris garden.

Mrs. Frederick Wallingford Whitridge, East Eleventh Street, New York City
Headstone for Frederick Wallingford Whitridge, who died on December 30, 1916.

Mrs. Harrison Williams, Oakpoint, Bayville, Long Island
Layout and planting for Willow Garden, tiered rock wall garden, with lovely Chinese lattice fencing and pool garden, 1920s.

Nelson B. Williams, Bedford
Notes on map of the property, 1923. Nothing done.

OHIO

★Oberlin College, Oberlin
Consultant landscape gardener, 1939–48, but actually little work was done after 1942. Design and planting of Tappan Square, Cox Administration Building, and Carnegie Library.

PENNSYLVANIA

John F. Braun, Merion
Entrance, driveway, grounds, and garden design, 1916–17.

Mr. and Mrs. Henry Frazer Harris, Harston, Chestnut Hill
Large garden designed and made, 1909–11. Walls, gates, balusters, trellis, tool house, finials, and fountains.

The Hill School, Pottstown
Design of headmaster's garden and consultant to the school, 1922–34.

Merion Cricket Club and Golf Association, Merion

Planting design. Undated.

Mrs. John Kearsley Mitchell, Rosemont, Villanova

Design for walled garden and terraces overlooking the lake, with Cope & Stewardson, architects, 1911–12.

Robert L. Montgomery, Ardrossan, Villanova

Sketch design for road and garden layout, 1912

Mr. and Mrs. Clement B. Newbold, Crosswicks and The Gate Farm, Jenkintown

One hundred thirty-five drawings, including exhibition watercolors, of design for a large garden, walls, gates, tool house, exedra, steps, pool, finials, and planting plans for rock, rhododendron, and evergreen gardens, 1901–16. There are large photographs of the finished garden.

Pennsylvania School of Horticulture for Women, Ambler

Peony and rose garden with twin arbors and pool, in memory of Jane Linn Irwin Bright, 1931–32.

Edgar T. Scott, Woodburne, Lansdowne

Large rectangular flower garden with fifty-two beds of mixed spring and summer planting, rose planting, and wall, gate, arbor, and ironwork details, 1908–09.

Clarence Warden, Haverford

Design for gardens and grounds, 1925–32, including screen planting for a tennis court, spring flowers and roses, and details for terrace, steps, seats, paving, trellis, swimming pool, and yew terrace.

Charles Wheeler, Radnor House, Bryn Mawr

Terraces with pool, doorway, trellis details, but only outline planting ideas. House by architects Walker & Gillette, 1926.

RHODE ISLAND

Mrs. Elizabeth Hope Slater, Bellevue Avenue (?), Newport

Early (1898) design for Beaux-Arts pergola with exedra and seat.

Mrs. Rush Sturges, Shepherd's Run, near Providence

Sketch design for a garden, 1934–36, and design details for garden of a house on Power Street, Providence, 1923.

J. J. Van Alen, Wakehurst, Ochre Point Avenue, Newport

Design for a garden, c. 1900. The Van Alens were friends of Edith Wharton.

WASHINGTON, D.C.

*Mr. and Mrs. Robert Woods Bliss, Dumbarton Oaks, R and Thirty-first Streets, Georgetown NW

Complete design and planting of garden and grounds, 1922–40, with additional consultancy to Harvard University as the owners from 1940. More than two thousand drawings and the relevant correspondence are in the Garden Library at Dumbarton Oaks.

National Cathedral
Preliminary consultation on site and planting to Bishop Satterlee, 1899.

Mrs. Woodrow Wilson, The White House
Design for the East Colonial Garden and sketch design for the West Garden, 1913–16. (Work completed for the second Mrs. Wilson.)

UNLOCATED COMMISSIONS

1. Headstone for Anna Bahlmann, who became Edith Wharton's secretary and literary assistant in 1902 and died in 1916. The stone was commissioned by Mrs. Wharton, and though Miss Bahlmann died in Kansas City, its whereabouts is not known. It reads, "Anna Bahlmann/born March 5 1849 died April 15 1916/In Loving Remembrance of her Goodness/her Patience and her Courage/This stone is placed here by/her friend & pupil Edith Wharton."
2. Miss Charlotte Baker: planting plan for a garden, 1923.
3. Albert Craisse: planting for a flower bed.
4. William Bayard Cutting and Cutting Animal Cemetery: nothing more is evident than the names. W. B. Cutting was a friend of the Whartons.
5. J. Ramsay Hunt, no date, Reef Point Gardens file number 915.
6. ? Mann Jr., "King's Point," Reef Point Gardens file number 928.
7. Reef Point Gardens file number 999 is labeled "Stillman" (the family name of Mrs. Edward S. Harkness).
8. Reef Point Gardens file number 1002 is in the name of Michael Straight, the son of Willard Straight.

COMMISSIONS OUTSIDE THE UNITED STATES

Churston Development Company, Dartington Hall, Devon, England
Consultant, 1934, with architect William Lescaze and planner William Wright for a retirement village of which six houses were built.

Mr. and Mrs. Leonard K. Elmhirst, Dartington Hall, Devon, England
Consultant for the restoration of the landscape of Dartington Hall, and for the making of the woodland garden, the Sunny Border, etc., from 1932. Advice also given for the planting around the Dance School, Warren Cottage, Jooss House, the boarding houses, and the central offices of Dartington Hall Ltd., in the village.

Mrs. Mary Cadwalader Jones, Saint John the Baptist Church, Aldbury, Hertfordshire, England
Tombstone for Beatrix's mother inscribed "Mary Cadwalader Jones/daughter of William Henry/Rawle and Mary Binney Cadwalader/born Philadelphia December 12 1850/Died London September 22 1935."

Sainte Marguerite Salmon Club, Riviere Sainte Marguerite, Tadousac, Quebec, Canada
Brief garden advice and planting for a small garden for the fishing club of which Max Farrand was a member, 1932.

APPENDIX A

The following is a reprinting of Reef Point Gardens Bulletin no. 10, originally published in June 1953.

THE TWENTY BEST ROSES AT REEF POINT GARDENS

The names and numbers of colors are taken from "Horticultural Colour Chart,"
Charts I and II, issued by The British Colour Council in collaboration with
The Royal Horticultural Society

NAME	PETAL COLOR	CHARACTER OF BUSH	COMMENTS
1. Ami Quinard	828 Garnet Lake	Strong.	Fragrant.
2. Armstrong Ruby No. 40080-8	724 Rose Red	Strong, foliage good.	Fragrant. Petals rather loose.
3. Armstrong Seedling No. 41160–8	3 Aureolin center. Outer two-thirds 622 Camellia Rose. Backs pale in both colors, more yellow than pink.	Strong, foliage good.	Very fragrant. Stamens hidden. Back of center petals visible. Does not last well when cut.
4. Cecil	2/2 Canary Yellow	Fairly strong.	Flat, slightly recurved.

NAME	PETAL COLOR	CHARACTER OF BUSH	COMMENTS
5. Colette Clément	722/3 Cherry. 4/1 Lemon Yellow center, small.	Strong, good foliage.	Fragrant.
6. Dainty Bess	523/1 Dawn Pink	Strong.	Flat, open bloom.
7. Ellen Willmott	White. 527/1 Rhodamine Pink tips.	Strong.	Fragrant. Flat, cup-shaped bloom.
8. Ethel James	25/2 Rose Bengal. 2/2 Canary Yellow center.	Strong.	Fragrant.
9. Innocence	White. Edge of petals tinged with 629/2 Roseline Purple.	Strong.	Flat, open bloom.
10. Irish Beauty	White	Fairly strong.	Fragrant.
11. Irish Elegance	2/2 Canary Yellow center, shading to 22/3 Crimson.	Fairly strong.	Fragrant. Pale yellow center shading to pale rose. Open.
12. Irish Fireflame	2/1 Canary Yellow center, to 4/3 Lemon Yellow, to 20/2 Geranium Lake.	Rather weak.	Fragrant. General effect: single, recurved, pale ochre-ish center shading to Rose edges. Lasts fairly well when cut.
13. Isobel	724/3 Rose Red. 3/1 Aureolin center.	Fairly strong.	Flat, open bloom.
14. Kitchener of Khartoum	724 Rose Red, dark.	Fairly strong.	
15. La Nigrotte	1030 Maroon	Rather weak.	
16. Memory	24/3 Tyrian Rose	Strong.	Fairly fragrant. Rather curly.
17. Simplicity	White, with very faint yellow tinge in center.	Strong.	Fragrant, small cup-shaped bloom.

Appendix A

NAME	PETAL COLOR	CHARACTER OF BUSH	COMMENTS
18. Sweet Sue	23/1 Rose Madder, shading to small very pale yellowish center.	Strong, good foliage.	Slightly fragrant, petals long, convex.
19. Vesuvius	824 Chrysanthemum Crimson	Weak.	Flat, very slightly recurved.
20. White Wings	White. Tips very faintly tinged with 24/3 Tyrian Rose.	Rather weak.	Fragrant.

❦❧

APPENDIX B

Extract from Professor H. Leland Vaughan's 1955 report on Beatrix Farrand's library gift to the Department of Landscape Architecture, University of California at Berkeley:

It gives me immeasurable satisfaction to report in more detail than has heretofore been possible Beatrix Farrand's gift of the Reef Point landscape art library to the Department of Landscape Architecture. The collection is one of the best groups ever given to the University of California, and it comes to a department suffering from the lack of an adequate library. I cannot hope to express the extent of the stimulation and gain to study and teaching which it brings.

Mrs. Farrand's gift consists of books, prints, working drawings, plans, and an herbarium. Many rare volumes are included in the library of approximately 2700 books covering every phase of landscape design, together with books of reference, travel, and other allied subjects. These books, acquired slowly over a long lifetime, begin with the earliest approaches to horticulture through the herbals of England. There are Gerard, Parkinson, Markham, and Worlidge, all forerunners of the first books on gardening in English. *The Gardener's Labyrinth* by D. M., an abbreviation of Didymus Mountaine, a whimsical Elizabethan rendering of his name, Thomas Hill. A few are more ambitious works, some with hand-colored engravings, such as Furber's *Flower Garden*, Rea's *Flora*, and others.

The Continent contributed its authors, Mollet, De La Quintinye, Louis Liger, Audot, and Krafft from France, Hirschfeld from Germany, and many others. When formal landscape design reached its greatest era in the Renaissance and in the seventeenth and eighteenth centuries, it was magnificently shown in the splended folios of Kip, Rademaker, Visscher, Falda, Zocchi, Dahlberg, Pieter van den Berge, and other artists, whose engravings show great technical achievement as well as recording vanished splendor. The royal houses and large chateaux are depicted by Silvestre, Merigot, Perelle, and the later Italian ones by Percier and Fontaine. Architectural volumes include Vitruvius, du Cerceau, Boyceau, Galimard, and Blondel's two-volume *De La Distribution des Maisons de Plaisance*. However, one of the chief treasures is a complete set of cahiers of Georges Louis Le Rouge. Twenty of the twenty-one oblong folio cahiers are bound in their original blue paper covers, while No. 5 is the bound volume of a French translation of William Chambers's *Designs of Chinese Buildings*, translated under the title of *Desseins des Edifices, Meubles, Habits, Machines of Ustenciles des Chinois*. According to French bibliographers, Chambers takes the place of the fifth cahier as there is no record of No. 5. The cahiers consist of engravings by Le Rouge of designs of contemporary and older gardens. The whole set takes its title from the second cahier, *Jardins Anglois-Chinois a la Mode*, and publication probably began before 1776, the date of Cahier 4, and continued through 1788, the date of Cahier 20, and includes 500 plates.

Of local interest to California is an early atlas by Pietro Goos, with colored engravings, *L'Atlas de la Mer ou Monde aquaticous representant Toutes tres necessaire et commode pour tous Pilotes, Maistres de Navire et Marchands,* published in Amsterdam in 1667. California is shown as an island.

As gardens became more elegant, the trend was reflected in literature, in Batty Langley, Sir William Chambers Papworth, John Evelyn, Whatley, and Overton.

The intense interest in gardening in England in the eighteenth century is reflected in writings on gardens by Horace Walpole and printed at Strawberry Hill. Then follow the classic volumes by Repton, and the romantic descriptions of Gilpin, Brown, Knight, and Shenstone. The nineteenth century is represented not only by the complete writings of William Robinson and Gertrude Jekyll, but Miss Jekyll's entire collection of plans for gardens made during her long professional life. William Robinson and Gertrude Jekyll (1843–1932) were leaders in the reaction against the formal style in gardening and restored old-fashioned and neglected plants to their honored place in gardens. They have been called the first impressionist gardeners in England.

The development and growth of landscape gardening in the United States is marked by the books of Downing, Sargent, and Olmsted, whose work and writings date from the middle of the nineteenth century. There are also records of the park movement in this country, monographs on individual species of plants, and books by later authors associated with the art of landscape design. Bound sets of periodicals on landscape architecture and horticulture are included in the library, representing journals published in both the United States and England.

Notes

Introduction

1. Mac Griswold and Eleanor Weller, *The Golden Age of American Gardens: Proud Owners, Private Estates, 1890–1940* (New York: Abrams, 1991).

2. Edwin Lutyens and Gertrude Jekyll, *Gardens of a Golden Afternoon: The Story of a Partnership* (London: Allen Lane, 1982; Penguin rev. ed., 1994).

3. The Wave Hill American Garden and Landscape History Program is proving an important pioneer. It has spawned the *Catalog of Landscape Records in the United States,* and is the place to refer to if any reader has anything of documentary interest to report.

4. Jane Brown, *Lanning Roper and His Gardens* (London: Weidenfeld & Nicolson, 1987; New York: Rizzoli, 1987).

5. Laura Wood Roper, *FLO: A Biography of Frederick Law Olmsted* (Baltimore and London: Johns Hopkins University Press, 1973).

6. See "The Feminist Takeover of Edith Wharton," James W. Tuttleton, *The New Criterion,* March 1989.

7. Robert Grant Irving, *Indian Summer: The Making of New Delhi* (New Haven: Yale University Press, 1981).

8. Mary Cadwalader Rawle had a younger brother, William, who died in childhood. See chapter 1, page 14.

9. Reef Point Bulletin no. 17 was written by Beatrix in 1956 and intended to be published only on her death, as it was in 1959. Reef Point Gardens Collection.

10. For a full description of the gift to the library see Professor H. Leland Vaughan's descriptive paper, reprinted as Appendix B. The College of Environmental Design Library has a list of "Drawing Room Books," many of which are kept in their Rare Book Room, but has no overall catalog of the books given; the ones

that are not in the Rare Book Room have been dispersed into the general collection. The Herbarium Gift is recorded in the University Herbarium Collection Book as follows: 19 February 1957, Lot 5453, Gift from Beatrix Farrand, Reef Point Gardens Horticultural Collection M 66138-M67098-961 (14 ferns, 947 spermatophytes). The boxes of miscellaneous uncataloged material are accessible only through the Documents Collection, College of Environmental Design.

11. To the extent that when Beatrix announced her engagement, James suggested that Mary should come to Lamb House and live with him, if she would be otherwise lonely. He probably knew her well enough to know that she was unlikely to accept!

CHAPTER 1. THE ELUSIVE FREDDY AND THE SPIRITED MARY

1. Apart from Beatrix's birth certificate, there is a reference to Fred's "grand Miscellaneous Shop" in Edith Jones's letter to Pauline Foster du Pont, September 23, 1874, in R. W. B. Lewis and Nancy Lewis, eds., *The Letters of Edith Wharton* (New York: Scribner's, 1989), 30.

2. Beatrix is the name of the heroine in *The History of Henry Esmond, Esquire* (1852), and also appears in *The Virginians* (1859), by William Makepeace Thackeray.

3. Reef Point Bulletin no. 17. Reef Point Gardens Collection.

4. "Marie van Houtte," a scented cream old tea rose; "Baroness Rothschild," a rose pink hybrid perpetual. Harriet Jackson Phelps, *Newport in Flower* (Newport, R.I.: Preservation Society of Newport, 1979), 138, mentions the Jones's "gentleman's farm" at Pencraig, which was bought by Mr. and Mrs. Hamilton Fish Webster who covered the site with formal house and garden, subsequently destroyed.

5. From Edith Wharton, *A Backward Glance* (London: Century, 1987), 14–17.

6. Edith Wharton, "False Dawn," in *Old New York* (New York: Appleton, 1924).

7. Wharton, *A Backward Glance,* 19.

8. Almost everything on the Jones family comes via Edith's *A Backward Glance,* her letters, or books written about her. Appropriate references are given in this book's bibliography.

9. I searched exhaustively in class lists, dining club registers of the 1860s, etc., for any mention of Frederic Rhinelander Jones as a Harvard student, but found nothing. The records for the period are notoriously poor, which is why I feel he must be given the benefit of the doubt.

10. Henry James, *Notes of a Son and a Brother,* ed. F. T. Dupee (1914; London: W. H. Allen, 1956), 533–34.

11. October 19, 1781, Cornwallis was taken after the Battle of Yorktown. Mary Cadwalader Jones, *Lantern Slides* (Boston: Merrymount Press, 1937), 3.

12. Now the University of Pennsylvania.

13. Mary and Beatrix eventually visited St. Juliot on one of their excursions in England in the early 1900s. By that time it had been made famous by Thomas Hardy, who worked on the restoration of the church and met and married the rector's sister-in-law Emma. The countryside is described in Hardy's *A Pair of Blue Eyes.*

14. Delaware was then part of Pennsylvania.
15. Mary Cadwalader Jones, *Lantern Slides,* 3–51.
16. Colonel Cadwalader's duel figures in *The Virginians.*
17. Mary eventually wrote her version of these two adventures: "Memories of Fort Sumter" and "From Charleston to Havana," *The Bookman,* March and April 1924.
18. Mary Cadwalader Jones, *Lantern Slides,* 99.
19. Ibid., 113.
20. Ibid., 113.
21. Ibid., 117.
22. Sir Richard Owen, KCB, 1804–92, obituary *British Medical Journal* (December 24, 1892); founder of South Kensington Natural History Museum, presented 360 papers to the Royal Society; also his garden at Sheen Lodge described by William Robinson, ed., *The English Flower Garden* (1893; rev. ed., London: John Murray, 1893), 33.
23. Mary Cadwalader Jones, *Lantern Slides,* 121.
24. Ibid., 121–22.
25. Ibid., 129.

CHAPTER 2. DIVORCE! AND SOLACE IN AN EARTHLY PARADISE

1. Although 21 East Eleventh Street was sold to the adjoining hotel after Mary's death in 1935, it is now a residence again and part of the Greenwich Village Historic District. It was unusually conservative for the young Joneses to choose to be so far downtown in 1870 when the tide of fashion was running uptown. The elder Joneses lived on West Twenty-third Street and Lucretia moved only two blocks north after her husband's death in 1882. But others—the Roosevelt Seniors moved from East Twentieth to West Fifty-seventh Street in 1873—kept uptown of commercial bustle. At the city bicentennial in 1874 it was frequently noted that the city below Fourteenth Street was teeming with immigrants. Of course Edith Wharton's gesture of revolt against her family was to move up to Seventy-eighth and Park Avenue in 1891.
2. Millicent Bell, *Edith Wharton and Henry James: The Story of Their Friendship* (London: Peter Owen, 1966), 52.
3. Since 1828 the hospital, asylums, and corrective centers had been together on Blackwell's Island, so that the sick in body and mind were kept together in what were then quite normal but terrible conditions.
4. Florence Lockwood's daughter, Florence Bayard La Farge, at Mary's memorial service, December 12, 1935. Reef Point Gardens Collection.
5. Arthur Rotch, son of Benjamin Rotch, one of the founders of Boston's Museum of Fine Arts, and in practice with George Tilden at 85 Devonshire Street, Boston. He was a summer resident of Bar Harbor and built twenty other cottages and Saint Saviour's Church before his untimely death in 1894. Ref. Harry L. Katz, *A Continental Eye: The Art and Architecture of Arthur Rotch* (Boston: Boston Athenaeum, 1985).
6. F. R. Jones bought the property from Christine K. Griffin by deed of warranty dated October 23, 1882; he transferred the deed to George V. N. Baldwin, his

solicitor, on March 23, 1883, who passed it to Mary Cadwalader Jones on the same day. Reef Point Gardens Collection.

7. Beatrix Farrand to Mrs. Lee Abbott, August 28, 1944. Bar Harbor Museum.

8. George Frederic Jones's will. R. W. B. Lewis, *Edith Wharton: A Biography* (New York: Harper & Row, 1975), 47.

9. Lewis, 51.

10. Lewis, 101.

11. Edith Wharton, *The Age of Innocence* (1920), 38.

12. Freddy and Mary's divorce papers. Reef Point Gardens Collection.

13. I found only one reference. In a long and painful letter to Edith after her mother's death Beatrix explained why she would allow no mention of Freddy's name on her tombstone. "It seems unlikely that even you know what cruelty and injustice there was and how many efforts were made to make the amount of the trust for Mummy and me as small as possible." May 18, 1936, Beatrix Farrand to Edith Wharton. Beinecke Library.

14. Leon Edel and Lyall H. Powers, eds., *The Complete Notebooks of Henry James* (Oxford and New York: Oxford University Press, 1987), 340.

15. Charles E. Strong was the survivor of the Strong family firm, which had been in existence since 1806 and included George Templeton Strong, who died in 1875.

16. John Lambert Cadwalader, born November 17, 1836. Graduated from Princeton and Harvard Law School and practiced at the New York Bar. Assistant secretary of state to Hamilton Fish, 1874–77, then a world tour and partnership with Strong in 1878. He commissioned the New York Public Library from Carrère & Hastings and was president of the board until his death in 1914. He was also involved with the Metropolitan Museum of Art, the American Museum of Natural History, and the New York Zoological Society. Refs. include *Memoir of J.L.C.* in H. W. Taft, *A Century and a Half at the New York Bar* (New York: privately published, 1938), 274.

17. Taft, ibid., also thought JLC's expectations to be ambassador at the Court of St. James did not materialize because of those less-pleasant characteristics.

18. Jane Maulsby Pindell, MCJ's memorial service, December 12, 1935. Reef Point Gardens Collection. A story was related of her, by Jane Maulsby Pindell, sometime superintendent of the City Nursing School, that was typical of Mary's devotion to her cause. "A small steam launch setting out for Blackwell's Island on New Year's Day, 1888. Snow is falling and a deck hand stands in the bow to push back the high blocks of ice that bar progress. In the open boat are three women: the newly appointed Superintendent of Nurses; her Assistant, and Mrs. Cadwalader Jones, whose indomitable spirit was not content to select the women who were to take charge of the nurses at Charity Hospital, but who felt it her duty to face with them the rigours of their installation."

19. From Maud Howe Elliott, *My Cousin F. Marion Crawford* (New York: Macmillan, 1934).

20. Beatrix designed the headstone for Frederick Wallingford Whitridge, who died on December 30, 1916.

21. Arnold Whitridge, memorial service to MCJ, December 12, 1935. Reef Point Gardens Collection.

22. Elliott, *F. Marion Crawford,* 260–61.

23. M. G. van Renssalaer, "American Country Dwellings," *Century Magazine,* no. 3 (July 1886).

24. Reef Point Bulletin 1, no. 3 (September 1948). Reef Point Gardens Collection.

25. F. Marion Crawford, *Love in Idleness: A Bar Harbor Tale* (New York and London: Macmillan, 1894), 9.

26. Ibid., 11.

27. Ibid., 13–16.

28. Ibid., 25.

29. Mariana Griswold van Renssalaer (1851–1934) was the contemporary and friend of Mary Cadwalader Jones and knew John Lambert Cadwalader. She had married Schuyler van Renssalaer in 1873 and their son George Griswold was born in 1875; Schuyler died 1884, George died 1894. She devoted her life to writing, especially on architecture, and traveling, and in the late 1880s had turned her interest to landscape gardening. At the time she influenced Beatrix's choice of career she was working on *Art Out of Doors: Hints on Good Taste in Gardening* (New York: Scribner's, 1893).

30. *New York Sun* interview, October 31, 1897.

31. Beatrix Jones draft, "Art of Landscape Gardening for Women." Reef Point Gardens Collection.

32. All quotes from Beatrix's 1893 notebook. Reef Point Gardens Collection.

33. George Bucknam Dorr (1853–1944). His life and fortune were devoted to the creation of Acadia National Park. Sargent F. Collier, *Mount Desert Island and Acadia National Park: An Informal History* (Camden, Maine: Down East Books, 1978).

34. From a printed handout of Frederick Law Olmsted's *Six Principles of Landscape Design,* Frederick Law Olmsted National Historic Site, Brookline, Mass.

35. All notes on Dorr estate, etc., from Beatrix's 1893 notebook. Reef Point Gardens Collection.

36. Ibid.

CHAPTER 3. BEATRIX AND THE BRAHMINS

1. Charles Eliot (1834–1926) summered on Mount Desert and was always supportive of the environmental sciences, especially when his son Charles (1859–97) decided to be a landscape architect.

2. Professor Francis Parkman (1823–1893) was still working on his history of the Quebec campaign and accepted appointment as professor of horticulture as recognition of his passion for his garden.

3. Andrew Jackson Downing, *The Theory and Practice of Landscape Gardening* (1841; 6th ed., New York: Moore & Co., 1859), 38, continues (on Colonel Perkins, Pine Bank): "the natural surface of the ground is exceedingly flowing and graceful, and it is varied by two or three singular little *dimples* or hollows, which add to its effect." . . . On the other side of the lake the cottage of Thomas Lee Esq., who is "enthusiastically fond of botany and gardening in all its departments."

4. Stephen A. Spongberg, "C. S. Sargent: Seeing the Forest and the Trees," *Orion* (New York), Autumn 1984: 5–11.

5. Stephanie Sutton, *Charles Sprague Sargent and the Arnold Arboretum* (Cambridge: Harvard University Press, 1970), ch. 1, "The Importance of Being Sargent."

6. Spongberg, "C. S. Sargent," 6.

7. Stephanie Sutton, *Arnold Arboretum: The First Century* (Cambridge: Harvard University Press, 1971), 15.

8. Ibid., 29.

9. Sutton, *Charles Sprague Sargent*, 6.

10. Ibid.

11. The firm's office until 1979, 99 Warren Street, is now the Frederick Law Olmsted National Historic Site and open to the public. The fascinating story of the Arnold Arboretum and its worldwide connections is told by Spongberg in *A Reunion of Trees* (Cambridge: Harvard University Press, 1990).

12. From *Garden & Forest,* no. 204 (January 20, 1892). The magazine was begun in 1888.

13. From Beatrix's 1893–94 notebook (Reef Point Gardens Collection). We now know that Professor Sargent did not succeed in stopping the road along the shore, and visitors to Jamaica Pond today can only imagine that it must have been once lovely.

14. Sutton, *Charles Sprague Sargent,* ch. 1.

15. From Beatrix's 1893–94 notebook. At the time of writing the Hunnewell Laboratory is the Visitor Center of the Arboretum.

16. Sheila Connor Geary and B. June Hutchinson, "Mr. Dawson, Plantsman," *Arnoldia* 40, no. 2 (1980).

17. Mariana van Renssalaer on Holm Lea, referred to as "the most beautiful suburban country place that I know." *Century Magazine,* May 1897.

18. This collection, paid for by the president of the American Museum of Natural History in New York, F. Morris Jesup, was of over 500 tree-trunk sections more than 5 feet long, and the illustrations were exhibited at the museum in 1893 where Beatrix could have seen them at her leisure. There was a controversy over payment to the Sargents, and the illustrations by Mary have since disappeared.

19. Hollis Hunnewell, ed., *Life, Letters & Diary of H. H. Hunnewell (1810–1902)* (Boston: privately printed, 1906).

20. For the full details of Olmsted and the 1893 Exposition see Laura Wood Roper, *FLO,* 425–33.

21. J. B. Campbell, *The World's Columbian Exposition Illustrated,* vol. 2 (Chicago: n.p., 1893).

22. Beatrix's 1893–94 notebook continues, "a strange looking thing, two long bare sticks about 3½ feet high bearing at the top a curious pendulous twig of the pine (*P. densiflora*) the only thing which had leaves on it." For the Larz Anderson Collection, see Peter del Tredici, *Early American Bonsai* (Cambridge: Harvard University Press, 1989).

23. For Olmsted and the Chicago Exposition, see also Melvin Kalfus, *Frederick Law Olmsted: The Passion of a Public Artist* (New York: New York University Press, 1990), 303–308.

24. Roper, *FLO,* 417.

25. Clive Aslet, *The American Country House* (New Haven: Yale University Press, 1990), 3 and 3–17 for full description.

26. As U.S. ambassador in Italy, Marsh had come to this conclusion, quoted in Max Nicholson, *The Environmental Revolution* (London: Hodder & Stoughton, 1970), 194.

27. Roper, *FLO,* 455 n.

28. Beatrix's 1893–94 notebook.

29. Ibid.

30. Ibid.

31. Ibid.

32. *Charles Eliot, Landscape Architect: A Lover of Nature* (Cambridge: Harvard University Press, 1902), 36. Although there is no formal authorship of the book, it was written by Charles Eliot's father, President Eliot: "For the dear son who died in his bright prime/From the Father."

33. Roper, *FLO,* 421, on Olmsted's support of Elizabeth Bullard to take over from her father on the park at Bridgeport, Connecticut.

34. Beatrix's 1893–94 notebook. Reef Point Gardens Collection.

CHAPTER 4. THE HUNT FOR BEAUTY: EUROPE, 1895

1. This sounds rather too catholic for Sargent and more likely to have been the advice of John L. Cadwalader or F. Marion Crawford. Quoted in Reef Point Bulletin no. 17.

2. F. L. Olmsted to William Platt, February 1, 1892. Roper, *FLO,* 433–34.

3. They saw twenty-five gardens that interested Charles, who painted them, though the trip had been made for William's education as a landscape architect. When William drowned, in July 1892, his brother vowed to record their journey and take up designing in his stead. For Charles Platt's career, see Keith Morgan, *The Artist as Architect* (New York: Architectural History Foundation; Cambridge: MIT Press, 1985).

4. Charles Platt's book, *Italian Gardens* (New York: Harper Bros., 1894), was reviewed in *Garden & Forest.* See Morgan, *The Artist as Architect,* 45.

5. Platt, *Italian Gardens,* conclusion.

6. Ibid.

7. William Robinson (1838–1935) had started his *Garden* magazine in 1871; his *The English Flower Garden,* first published in 1883, had become a popular classic on both sides of the Atlantic. He is the subject of a biography, *William Robinson,* by Mea Allan (London: Faber & Faber, 1982).

8. Mrs. Earle had written for the *Garden* and *Country Life* magazines but became most famous for her potpourri books, *Pot Pourri from a Surrey Garden* (1892), sequels in 1899 and 1903, and her *Memoir and Memories,* 1911.

9. Gertrude Jekyll was known for her pieces in the *Garden* and *Country Life* when Beatrix first met her; she had written regularly for the *Garden* since 1881. A bibliography of her articles is in Michael J. Tooley, ed., *Gertrude Jekyll* (Durham, England: Michaelmas Books, 1984), 139–51.

10. The details of Beatrix and Mary's grand tour of 1895 are recorded by Beatrix in her notebook to May 31, 1895, and in Mary's diaries and notes in the Reef Point Gardens Collection.

11. Ibid.

12. Ibid.

13. Ibid.

14. Georgina Masson, *Italian Gardens* (London: Thames & Hudson, 1966), 133.

15. Charles Percier and Pierre Fontaine, *Choix de plus célèbres maisons de plaisance de Rome et ses environs* (Paris, 1809), which was not highly regarded by the landscape school nor did it figure in Harry S. Codman's 1890 list of required books. But Beatrix soon acquired a copy, possibly in Italy, to study the plans.

16. Among the cardboard-boxed remnants of her papers in the Reef Point Gardens Collection is a folder of these (professional) photographs of lightly dressed waifs posing as statuettes.

17. See note 10 above.

18. Sir George Sitwell, *On the Making of Gardens* (London: John Murray, 1909), 14–15.

19. Ibid.

20. Beatrix's notebook. Reef Point Gardens Collection.

21. Ibid.

22. Ibid.

23. Ibid.

24. Sitwell, *On the Making of Gardens*, 15–16.

25. Beatrix's notebook. Reef Point Gardens Collection.

26. Beatrix was seeing the Grosser Garten at one of its greatest moments, for it was severely damaged during the Second World War.

27. Beatrix's notebook. Reef Point Gardens Collection.

28. Ibid.

29. Bicycles were not allowed in the royal parks.

30. Amabel Williams-Ellis, who was Amabel Strachey and a child at Newlands Corner in *All the Stracheys Are Cousins* (London: Weidenfeld & Nicolson, 1983), describes her home and how visitors, however distinguished, were often brought up from the station in the baker's cart; the explorers Mary Kingsley and Gertrude Bell, Kipling and Theodore Roosevelt were not immune from this; Beatrix also may have arrived this way.

31. Gertrude Jekyll, *Wood and Garden* (London: Longman, Green & Co., 1899), 130.

32. Ibid., 138–39.

33. Ibid., 133.

34. Born Maria Theresa Villiers (1836–1925), Mrs. Earle was married to Captain Charles Earle. Her niece, Emily Lytton, was to meet Edwin Lutyens in 1896 and marry him in 1897.

35. Just one book, *The English Flower Garden,* first published in 1883 (London: John Murray), went through fifteen editions in his lifetime, and there were his many other books and the *Garden* weekly, started in 1871.

36. Reginald Blomfield, *The Formal Garden in England* (1892; facsimile ed., London: Waterstones, 1985), 72.

37. "Bridge Over the Kent at Levens Hall," *Garden & Forest,* January 15, 1896.

38. Beatrix Jones, "Le Nôtre and His Gardens," *Scribner's* magazine, July 1905, 44.

39. Ibid.

40. These designers have never been given full acclaim for their works.

41. Blomfield, *The Formal Garden in England*, 58–59.

42. William Robinson's *Gleanings From French Gardens* (London, 1868), and *The Parks, Promenades and Gardens of Paris* (London, 1869).

43. Jean Pierre Barillet-Deschamps, 1824–75, French landscape architect from Bordeaux who became chief gardener in Paris in 1860. He designed the gardens of the Champs-Elysées and the Parc Monceau.

44. Jean-Charles-Adolphe Alphand (1817–91), engineer and landscape architect, largely responsible for the Bois de Boulogne present layout, establishing nurseries and greenhouses there and for many parks and boulevards of Paris.

45. *Oxford Companion to Gardens* (New York: Oxford University Press, 1986), 421.

46. *Municipal Affairs,* December 1899, 687–90.

47. Edith Wharton, *Italian Villas and Their Gardens* (London: John Lane, 1904), 157.

48. Beatrix Jones, "Le Nôtre and His Gardens," 43.

49. President Seth Low of Columbia was a Bar Harbor summer resident and she would have been supported by John Lambert Cadwalader's partner George Strong, let alone her own family, Joneses and Schermerhorns, who were Columbia's great benefactors.

50. Charles A. Harriman was the instructor in architectural drawing and Charles P. Warren tutor in construction. It is also interesting to note that Thomas Hastings started in 1895 and she may have first met him there. The architecture course became the School of Architecture in May 1896 and moved to Morningside Heights the following year. Ref. T. K. Rohdenburg, *A History of the School of Architecture, Columbia University* (New York: Columbia University Press, 1954).

CHAPTER 5. EARLY WORK AND A PLACE IN HER PROFESSION

1. The *New York Sun,* October 31, 1897. Reef Point Gardens Collection.

2. This early patronage was acknowledged when she started Dumbarton Oaks, in a letter to Mildred Bliss of July 7, 1922. Dumbarton Oaks Library.

3. *New York Sun,* October 31, 1897. Reef Point Gardens Collection.

4. Beatrix Jones, "The Garden in Relation to the House," *Garden & Forest,* April 7, 1897.

5. Ibid.

6. Ibid.

7. Ibid.

8. Augusta (Maine) State Park: The surviving plan is for advice given in 1932. Nothing presumably came of her earlier approach.

9. *Municipal Affairs,* December 1899. Olmsted Collection, Loeb Library.

10. Olmsted's concept for the New York parks system. See Roper, *FLO,* 294.

11. Samuel Parsons Jr. was the son of the Long Island nurseryman who had supplied the trees and shrubs to Central Park almost forty years earlier.

12. Roper, "Afterword," in *FLO,* 475.

13. Roper, *FLO,* 462.

14. McLean Hospital, Waverley, Massachusetts. Roper, 474, quoting Olmsted: "They didn't carry out my plans, confound them!" He died at the end of August 1903.

15. Roper, *FLO,* 463.

16. Roper, *FLO,* 462.

17. John Charles Olmsted to his wife. Olmsted Collection, Loeb Library.

18. Transactions of the American Society of Landscape Architects, vol. 1, 1899–1908. Loeb Library.

19. Robert W. Patterson, "Beatrix Farrand, 1872–1959: An Appreciation of a Great Landscape Designer," *Landscape Architecture,* summer 1959.

20. See Roper, *FLO,* 420–21, on Miss Bullard and Olmsted's attitude toward women in landscape architecture, plus LWR's letter to the author, November 15, 1991, emphasizing Olmsted's lack of male chauvinism which was ahead of his time. This and LWR, 455 and 455 n. explains that Olmsted's impression of Beatrix at Biltmore was that she was not serious; she probably looked just too svelte and smart!

21. The Olmsteds and Warren Manning were members of the Repton Club, which existed until 1905, and also kept in touch with Harvard's elite Toparian Club.

22. Warren Manning (1860–1938)—his "territorial" limitations illustrate the nature of the landscape professional. Only the Olmsted office drew commissions from all over America.

23. For a published description of the founding members of the American Society of Landscape Architects, see Norman K. Newton, *Design on the Land: The Development of Landscape Architecture* (Cambridge: Harvard University Press, Belknap Press, 1971).

24. For Barrett's work see Griswold and Weller, *The Golden Age of American Gardens,* 57, 123.

25. "History of the Cathedral of Saint Peter and Saint Paul," Private Record of Henry Y. Satterlee, p. 25. Washington Cathedral Archives. Unpublished typescript.

26. Biographical details in *Municipal Affairs,* December 1899.

27. Clipping from the *Newburgh Daily News,* January 23, 1900. Reef Point Gardens Collection.

28. Roper, *FLO,* 292.

29. T. H. D. Turner, "The Scottish Origins of 'Landscape Architecture,' " *Landscape Architecture,* May 1982.

30. Jane Brown, *Art & Architecture of English Gardens* (London: Weidenfeld & Nicolson, 1989), 103. Queen Victoria dismissed the scheme, preferring to see the trees in St. James's Park.

31. An arrangement that lasted for only two years because of Downing's tragic death in 1852.

32. Calvert Vaux to Olmsted, June 3, 1865. Roper, *FLO,* 292.

33. Olmsted to Calvert Vaux, August 1, 1865. Ibid.

34. Jones, "The Garden in Relation to the House."

CHAPTER 6. AUNT PUSSY, MISS NIMROD, AND OLD CELIMARE

1. Henry James to Edith Wharton, September 19, 1911, from Millden Lodge, Forfarshire. Houghton Library.

2. Douglas Sladen, *Sicily: The New Winter Resort* (London: Methuen, 1905).

3. Maud Howe, *Sicily in Shadow and Sun* (London: Stanley Paul, 1911), 404.

4. See note 1, chapter 4, Sargent's advice in Reef Point Bulletin no. 17.

5. All quotes from Mary Cadwalader Jones, diary 1899. Reef Point Gardens Collection.

6. Suzanne K. Miller, letter to the author, November 7, 1991.

7. Henry Yates Satterlee of Calvary Church, New York City, was appointed first bishop of Washington in 1895. The Glastonbury stones, twenty-three cubes 18 inches or 20 inches, arrived in June; they were built into the Glastonbury Cathedra, designed by Robert W. Gibson, made by C. Flannery, stonemason, in 1901, when the Cathedra was placed in the Little Sanctuary (and eventually moved into the Sanctuary). Ibid.

8. Quotes from "History of the Cathedral of Saint Peter and Saint Paul," Private Record of Henry Y. Satterlee, pp. 25–26. Washington Cathedral Archives.

9. In 1906 Bishop Satterlee appointed a heavyweight committee, including Charles F. McKim and Professor Charles F. Moore, Harvard professor of Gothic architecture, who moved the site of the cathedral northward, and the Olmsted brothers were appointed in 1907. The bishop died in 1908 and Beatrix's connection with the cathedral almost certainly ceased abruptly.

10. The family of Gifford Pinchot, the Yale-educated forestry expert who worked with F. L. Olmsted and George Vanderbilt at Biltmore.

11. Bell, *Edith Wharton and Henry James*, 51.

12. This was the summer of 1898 after "Souls Belated" and "The Muse's Tragedy," the moment dubbed by Professor Lewis as the true beginning of her "sustained literary career." She was, he adds, so unsettled and seemed "not to have been entirely in her proper mind" while with Mary, until Dr. Mitchell took over. Lewis, *Edith Wharton*, 81–82.

13. Beatrix painted a vivid watercolor showing this French-style treillage as the centerpiece of The Mount's terrace, but later photographs show it down in the garden. Reef Point Gardens Collection.

14. It was Ogden Codman's idea to use Belton as a model. See Clive Aslet, *The American Country House* (New Haven: Yale University Press, 1990), 164.

15. The kitchen garden disappeared in the 1940s when the area was turned into a riding paddock for Foxhollow School. Ref. C. Palermo-Schulze, *Guide to The Mount* (Lenox, Mass.: Edith Wharton Restoration Inc., 1989). The quote is from a letter to Sara Norton, June 7, 1902, in Lewis and Lewis, eds., *The Letters of Edith Wharton*, 66.

16. Letter, October 10, 1902, ibid., 73. She wrote to Gilder about the articles that were eventually published in book form, 1904.

17. Percy Lubbock, *Portrait of Edith Wharton* (London: Jonathan Cape, 1947), 28.

18. Ibid., 29.

19. Wharton, *A Backward Glance,* 125.

20. Eastover was soon spoiled and was a cheap hotel in the 1940s; nothing now remains of the garden.

21. Henry James to Mary Cadwalader Jones, May 7, 1908. Houghton Library.

22. Leon Edel, *Henry James,* vol. 2, *The Conquest of London,* 188–89.

23. Henry James to MCJ, July 1901. Houghton Library.

24. Leon Edel, *Henry James,* vol. 5, *The Master, 1900–16* (London: Hart-Davies, 1972), 27–28.

25. Edwin Lutyens had built one of his earliest houses, the Red House, at Effingham in Surrey for Miss Muir-Mackenzie after Gertrude Jekyll had introduced them. She was part of the circle that met at Barbara Bodichon's home, Scalands, near Robertsbridge, not far from Rye, which is how James met her. He called her "Hereditary Grand Governess of the Garden," "Dear Friend Florist," and "Our Lady of Tobacco" when she planted nicotiana for him. Ref. Edel, n. 24 above.

26. Edel, ibid.

27. Edel, *The Master*, 273. "Mrs Jones had a pet name for James out of a French farce by Labiche—Celimare—perhaps because the central character . . . inspires universal affection [he carries on love affairs with two ladies whose husbands also dote on him, and manages to keep their love when he marries a young woman half his age]. James was not capable of the comedy . . . but he seems to have been the centre at Mrs Jones's of an adoring circle."

28. Gertrude Jekyll became intensely annoyed by intrusions at Munstead Wood as her garden became more well known—"visititis," as she called it (see Sally Festing, *Gertrude Jekyll: A Biography* [London: Viking, 1991], 188–89), so visiting other Jekyll gardens was a good idea, and Beatrix visited Hall Place, Shackelford (now Aldro School), and Little Tangley (and also Great Tangley, where there was a magnificent water garden and a large rocky dell filled with alpines and rock plants).

29. For more on Sturgis see Miranda Seymour, *A Ring of Conspirators: Henry James and His Literary Circle, 1895–1915* (Boston: Houghton Mifflin, 1988).

30. Cliveden's planting described by Brent Elliott, *Victorian Gardens* (London: Batsford, 1986), 136–38, and the bedding traditions established by John Fleming, head gardener until his death in 1883.

31. See John Sutherland, *Mrs. Humphry Ward, Eminent Victorian, Pre-Eminent Edwardian* (Oxford: Oxford University Press, 1990).

32. Danesfield was created for the son of a Victorian soap magnate: Romaine-Walker's "eclecticism and pastiche" illustrated an element of Edwardian gardening that was akin to popular American taste but in England was frowned upon and "caused his name to be erased from all historical accounts of the period." David Ottewill, *The Edwardian Garden* (New Haven and London: Yale University Press, 1989), 165–70.

33. Harold Ainsworth Peto (1854–1933), English architect who turned to garden design, strongly influenced by his love of Italian art and architecture.

34. Ottewill, *The Edwardian Garden*, 152.

35. For the story of Broadway's rise to fame see my essay "The Henry James Americans" in *Eminent Gardeners* (London and New York: Viking, 1990), which traces the connection from John Singer Sargent's painting *Carnation Lily, Lily Rose* to the making of Hidcote Manor garden.

36. John Lambert Cadwalader left both Navarros $5,000 each in his will.

37. Henry James to Edith Wharton, October 4, 1904, in Lyall H. Powers, ed., *Henry James and Edith Wharton: Letters 1900–1915* (London: Weidenfeld & Nicolson, 1990), 39.

38. Edel and Powers, eds., *The Complete Notebooks of Henry James*, 335–37.

39. Theodate Pope Riddle (1868–1946). See *My Godmother* by Phyllis Fenn Cunningham (Canaan, N.H.: Phoenix Publishing, 1983). Miss Mary Robbins

Hilliard, Theodate's former teacher at Miss Porter's School, became headmistress of Westover School.

40. This planting scheme has been restored by New Haven landscape architect Shavaun Towers for the Garden Club of Hartford and Connecticut Valley Garden Club.

41. Apart from Westover, Beatrix also worked briefly for Owen F. Roberts at Montevideo, Simsbury; see list of commissions. J. W. Riddle was sometime ambassador to Montevideo.

CHAPTER 7. THE WHITE HOUSE CONNECTION, 1903–12

1. *The Outlook,* March 28, 1908, 695–704.

2. Freddy Rhinelander Jones kept $50,000 of his mother's legacy for himself. According to Edith Wharton, he married for a second time; perhaps his generosity to Beatrix was in discharge of his paternal duty in advance of his remarriage?

3. Gertrude Jekyll's first published writing on this subject appeared in her contribution "Color in the Flower Garden" in William Robinson, ed., *The English Flower Garden,* 1st ed. (London: John Murray, 1883). My quote is taken from 3rd ed. (1893), 193.

4. "The Garden as a Picture," *Scribner's* magazine, July 1907.

5. Ibid.

6. The illustrations were: the parterre of Villa Castello which "vibrates with light" until the eye settles on the curtain of water falling from the Hercules and Antaeus fountain; Shasta daisies of "perfectly untranslucent white" in a border at Drummond Castle; Moorish fragments used as ornament at Villa Reed; the pond garden, Hampton Court; and three unnamed natural water garden pictures which are probably of Reef Point.

7. Cf. Edith Wharton, *Italian Villas and Their Gardens,* "a marble sarcophagus and a dozen twisted columns will not make an Italian garden," 12.

8. A concept revived from pre-Victorian England and emphasized as the first premise of the first edition of Robinson's *The English Flower Garden* (1883), that the garden should no longer be set apart from the house, limited by soil and aspect and only to be visited.

9. Some evidence of the friendship between Roosevelt and Mary Cadwalader Jones is in their surviving correspondence (Houghton Library, Theodore Roosevelt Collection).

10. Eleanor McPeck's researches have revealed that the commission came from Morgan himself, although the work was not carried out until the 1920s. This meeting must have been early in 1913, for Morgan went abroad, and died in Rome, on March 31 of that year.

11. Louise and James Bush-Brown, *Portraits of Philadelphia Gardens* (Philadelphia: Dorrance & Co., 1929), 91.

12. Ibid., 96.

13. The "Ideal Suburban Place" competition was publicized in *Country Life in America* in March 1910. For context and background, see John R. Stilgoe, *Borderland: Origins of the American Suburb, 1820–1939* (New Haven: Yale University Press, 1988).

14. Comparisons of lists of works reveals eleven sites where Beatrix and the Olmsted office both worked, but closer examination reveals that there was no passing on of work to her, and any work in the same places was purely coincidental. There is also no evidence to show that Beatrix benefited anything at all from her colleagues on the ASLA.

15. For a comparison with Beatrix's drawings see chapter 1, "Millmead," in Miss Jekyll's *Gardens for Small Country Houses* (1912; facsimile reprint, Woodbridge, Suffolk: Antique Collectors' Club, 1981), but the garden was designed in 1904.

16. Manuscript "Rock Gardening." Reef Point Gardens Collection.

17. Ibid.

18. Ibid. Her plants: "violas, cypripediums (slipper orchids), Androsace and campanulas, primulas, meconopsis, dryas (mountain avens), erigeron, ranunculus, veronicas, saxifrages, sempervirens; the great race of Dianthus and Lychnis and our old friends Myosotis; Dorinicum and gypsophila are only the names of the heads of clans where almost every individual is interesting. Then we have armies of bulbs: crocuses of many species, tulips too frail for the beds of the garden, dodecatheons (shooting stars), Iris, alliums, colchicums, galanthus, and here again I become conscious of neglected races like the epimediums, the drabas, the lobelias, the aquilegias, the ericas . . . the daphnes (for those brave enough) . . . the phyteumas with their queer little pointed closed blossoms, the gorgeous Incarvilleas, the Onosmas, the mertensias and the aubretias that reproach one for leaving them out."

19. Ibid.

20. For Frances Wolseley's pioneering work in gardening for women, see my essay in *Eminent Gardeners* (London: Viking, 1990); the Congress was reported in the *Times* (London), July 6, 1910.

21. Beatrix Jones's draft notes for speaking to London Horticultural Congress, 1910. Reef Point Gardens Collection.

22. Probably also because Holm Lea was highly praised in it! Wilhelm Miller, *What England Can Teach Us About Gardening* (New York: Doubleday, 1911).

23. Diana Balmori, "Campus Work and Public Landscape," quoting correspondence in Princeton University archives, in Diana Balmori, Diane Kostial McGuire, and Eleanor M. McPeak, *Beatrix Farrand's American Landscapes: Her Gardens and Campuses* (Sagaponack, N.Y.: Sagapress, 1985), 151.

24. Edward Tenner, "Yankee Feudalist, Collegiate Gothic Architect, Ralph Adams Cram," *Princeton Alumni Weekly,* January 15, 1986.

25. Balmori et al., *Beatrix Farrand's American Landscapes,* 158–59.

26. See also Ann Waldron, "Landscaping the Campus," *Princeton Alumni Weekly,* January 15, 1986.

27. Max Farrand was born on March 29, 1869, the youngest of the four sons of the headmaster of Newark Academy, New Jersey. He graduated from Princeton in 1892 with a degree in biology, but changed to history and studied at Heidelberg and Leipzig universities, earning his Ph.D. in 1896. Returning to America, he taught first at Wesleyan University in Connecticut, then in 1901 was appointed head of the history department at Stanford; after the 1906 earthquake he left for Cornell. In 1908 he was appointed Harkness Professor in history at Yale. His books include *The Records of the Federal Convention of 1787* (1911), *The Framing of the Constitution* (1913), and *Fathers of the Constitution* (1921).

28. The Cockyolly Bird was the subject of a rhyme, on paper tied with red ribbon, that she treasured all her life. It runs thus:

> Behold a Cockyolly Bird!
> I come from Labrador
> And you can bet your life I'm glad
> To find a warmer shore!
> I doubt if I'm of any use,
> Nor can I beauty claim,
> But since you know by whom I'm sent
> You'll love me all the same
> I am Ho-tei, the god of luck,
> And Happiness I also bring;
> (It's well I make myself of use
> For I am not a pretty thing.)
> And now I laugh and shout and cry
> On notes too high for mortal ear
> That you may have all kinds of luck
> And happiness throughout the year.

29. Livingston Farrand, born in 1867, was president of Cornell, 1921–37; he married Daisy Carlton of New York (1879–1957), who was a good gardener and has a peony named for her. She restored the President's Garden at Cornell.

30. This story comes from correspondence at Princeton, corroborated by Livingston Farrand's descendants to the author.

CHAPTER 8. BEATRIX AND THE SON OF THE MORNING

1. Henry James to Beatrix Jones, October 24, 1913. Houghton Library.
2. Ibid.
3. *Bar Harbor Record,* clipping in Reef Point Gardens Collection.
4. Lewis, *Edith Wharton,* 331. She also brought news of a rift with Harry, now rather stout and living in fine style in Paris and wanting to marry a countess of Russian extraction named Tecla. Edith's lack of appreciation, though she hardly knew her, of the countess and need of help over her divorce from Teddy Wharton had, unaccountably in Edith's eyes, infuriated Harry, so they weren't on good terms at the moment.
5. Edith Wharton, letter to Bernard Berenson, January 30, 1914, in Lewis and Lewis, *Letters,* 312. She was at her most imperious; she swept around Europe and into New York as a kind of royal progress; she was prepared to look askance on the world that she had left—"a kind of nightmare chess without rules or issue" was her verdict to Bernard Berenson on New York society. Henry James, however, knew her best and in between the literary word-games he softly praised the generosity of her making the effort to be at Beatrix's wedding.
6. Edith Wharton to Beatrix Farrand, January 3, 1914. Beinecke Library.
7. Will of John Lambert Cadwalader supplied by Cadwalader, Wickersham & Taft of New York.

8. Herbert Croly, *Willard Straight* (New York: Macmillan, 1924), 552–53.

9. It seems the name Elmhurst was chosen for the house when it was built; after Willard Straight's death when Dorothy met and decided to marry Leonard Elmhirst, she changed the name to Apple Green, as it appears in most of Beatrix's papers. The house and Chinese garden survive, though some parts of the garden have been built on.

10. Perhaps something of hers remains in the present planting of the fountain garden on the north front, which in 1991 was splendidly dressed with red tulips and blue forget-me-not; Beatrix suggested "Pride of Harlem" and "Clara Butt" tulips, great favorites in the early years of this century, as they still are.

11. The original palm court is now restored as the Enid A. Haupt Conservatory. See *New York Botanical Garden Guide,* 1986 edition.

12. Paula Deitz, "Beauty and the Bronx," *House & Garden* (New York), October 1990.

13. Diana Balmori, "Campus Work and Public Landscape," in Diana Balmori et al., *Beatrix Farrand's American Landscapes,* 157.

14. John T. Faris, *Old Gardens in and about Philadelphia* (Indianapolis: Bobbs-Merrill Co., 1932).

15. Franklin Brett, graduated MIT in 1887 and worked for Olmsted and Charles Platt; George D. Hall, graduate of Harvard landscape course, 1902.

16. Griswold and Weller, *The Golden Age of American Gardens,* 67.

17. Henry James to Mary Cadwalader Jones, last surviving letters, dated 1914. Houghton Library.

18. F. W. Whitridge lived on East Eleventh Street; was a partner in Cary & Whitridge, lawyers; and was married to Lucy Arnold, daughter of Matthew Arnold and therefore Mary and Beatrix's connection with the Arnolds, Wards, etc., in England.

19. Mary Cadwalader Jones to Edith Kermit Roosevelt, June 16, 1914. Theodore Roosevelt Collection, Houghton Library.

20. Edith Kermit Roosevelt died in 1948.

21. Gavin Stamp, *Silent Cities:* An exhibition of the Memorial and Cemetery Architecture of the Great War. Royal Institute of British Architects, London 1977.

22. See Jane Brown, *Gardens of a Golden Afternoon* (London: Penguin Books, 1982), 136–38.

23. Mrs. Bayard Henry to Beatrix Farrand, March 5, 1918. Garden Club of America file, Reef Point Gardens Collection.

24. Her list of lectures in a letter dated January 26, 1917, was: Roses, Le Nôtre & His Gardens, Evergreens, Spring Gardens, Autumn Gardens, Rock, Wall & Water Gardens, Garden Flowers Old & New, Roses & Peonies, and A Garden Sermon on Composition & Design. Reef Point Gardens Collection.

25. Beatrix Farrand to Mrs. Henry, February 3, 1919. Garden Club of America file, Reef Point Gardens Collections.

26. Ibid.

27. "Regulation v. Strangulation," the Elliott Nursery Company paper in Reef Point Gardens Collection.

28. Record of Garden Club meeting, January 1919. Reef Point Gardens Collection.

29. The pines are now outgrown, but a little of the garden survives (steps, rock walls,

a pool now filled with flowers and the garden house). The fragments of the Colt gardens are cared for by Knessas Israel Synagogue, 16 Colt Road, Pittsfield, Mass. The house was pulled down in the 1960s.

30. Edith Wharton to Elizabeth Cameron, June 22, 1918. Lewis and Lewis, *Letters,* 405.

31. Edith Wharton to Mary Cadwalader Jones, July 7, 1918. Lewis and Lewis, *Letters,* 407.

32. Also, Mary had finally made Reef Point over to Beatrix in 1917. Information from Trust deed dated April 1894. Copy from Cadwalader, Wickersham & Taft of New York to the author, 1991.

CHAPTER 9. BEATRIX AND THE AMERICAN WAY OF GARDENING

1. Wilhelm Miller, *What England Can Teach Us About Gardening* (New York: Doubleday, 1911), 9 and 14.

2. Griswold and Weller, *The Golden Age of American Gardens,* 100.

3. Monica Randall, *The Mansions of Long Island's Gold Coast* (New York: Rizzoli, 1987), 238.

4. Ibid.

5. Ibid., and information from snapshots in Beatrix Farrand's Reef Point Gardens Collection.

6. Mildred Barnes Bliss was the daughter of the congressman for Ohio, Demas Barnes: born in 1879, she married Robert Woods Bliss, diplomat, in 1908. He was at the Paris embassy during the war and she worked tirelessly for the Red Cross, so this was how Edith knew them.

7. See Walter Muir Whitehill, *Dumbarton Oaks: The History of a Georgetown House and Garden* (Cambridge: Harvard University Press, Belknap Press, 1967).

8. Beatrix Farrand to Mildred and Robert Woods Bliss, report dated July 1922 in Dumbarton Oaks Library.

9. Ibid.

10. Mildred Bliss to Beatrix Farrand, July 13, 1922. Dumbarton Oaks Library.

11. Beatrix Farrand to Mildred Bliss, July 1922. Dumbarton Oaks Library.

12. Mildred Bliss to Beatrix Farrand, April 1923. Dumbarton Oaks Library.

13. Whitehill, *Dumbarton Oaks,* 67.

14. Whitehill, *Dumbarton Oaks,* 69–70.

15. Balmori et al., *Beatrix Farrand's American Landscapes,* 139.

16. Julie B. Ovine, "Pleasures of Landscape," in *Yale Alumni Weekly* (1980), 26.

17. Balmori et al., *Beatrix Farrand's American Landscapes,* 140.

18. Ibid.

19. Ovine, "Pleasures of Landscape," 25.

20. Balmori et al., *Beatrix Farrand's American Landscapes,* 169.

21. Schedule in Reef Point Gardens Collection, uncataloged.

22. Griswold and Weller, *Golden Age,* 340.

23. Ibid., 342; and James J. Yoch, *Landscaping the American Dream: The Gardens and Film Sets of Florence Yoch 1890–1972* (New York: Sagapress/Abrams, 1989).

24. Balmori et al., *Beatrix Farrand's American Landscapes,* 181.

25. Beatrix also designed Anna Blakesley Bliss's garden, Casa Dorinda.
26. Michael Young, *The Elmhirsts of Dartington: The Creation of a Utopian Community* (Boston: Routledge & Kegan Paul, 1982), 71.
27. Rabindranath Tagore, poet, teacher and mystic, winner of the Nobel Prize in literature, 1913, was setting up a school at Santiniketan in West Bengal. Leonard Elmhirst went there to help with agricultural reconstruction and the revival of crafts. Tagore was to be very influential on the Dartington project. See Michael Young, *The Elmhirsts,* 63–84, for this aspect of Leonard's courtship of Dorothy.
28. Leonard Elmhirst to Beatrix Farrand, May 4, 1927. Elmhirst Centre Archive.
29. The correspondence on Apple Green from 1925 is in the Elmhirst Centre Archive.

Chapter 10. Transatlantic Fellows: Dumbarton Oaks and Dartington Hall, 1931–37

1. Michael Young, *The Elmhirsts of Dartington,* 110.
2. Reginald Snell, *From the Bare Stem: The Making of Dorothy Elmhirst's Garden at Dartington Hall* (Exeter, Devon: Devon Books, 1989), 17.
3. Young, *The Elmhirsts,* 106.
4. William Weir had previously worked on Penshurst Place in Kent. He was a pupil of Philip Webb, William Morris's architect. His work on the medieval fabric of Dartington can hardly be faulted, even by modern conservationists. See Reginald Snell, *William Weir and Dartington Hall* (Exeter, Devon: Devon Books, 1987).
5. H. Avray Tipping contributed the articles to *Country Life,* which were subsequently published as *English Homes* (eight volumes). He lived at Mathern Court in Somerset.
6. Snell, *From the Bare Stem,* 25.
7. Young, *The Elmhirsts,* 122.
8. Beatrix Farrand to Dorothy Elmhirst, September 5, 1932. Elmhirst Centre Archive.
9. Julian Huxley (1887–1975), the biologist and conservationist, was a friend and colleague of Leonard Elmhirst. He was probably in California visiting his brother Aldous, the novelist, who had settled there in 1938.
10. Ibid. Beatrix wrote nine notes in nine days she was so euphoric about her introduction to Dartington.
11. Douglas Freshfield was Mary Cadwalader Jones's friend, at Wych Cross Place, Forest Row, Sussex, built 1900–1903 by the architect Edmund Fisher, with large formal garden by Thomas Mawson.
12. Dorothy Elmhirst, writing in Dartington's "News of the Day," reporting Beatrix's death, no. 2056 (March 13, 1959). Elmhirst Centre Archive.
13. Ibid.
14. Beatrix Farrand to Leonard Elmhirst, June 1933. Elmhirst Centre Archive.
15. Beatrix Farrand to Dorothy Elmhirst, October 1933. Elmhirst Centre Archive.
16. Max Farrand to Leonard Elmhirst, March 2, 1934, from the Athenaeum, Pall Mall. Elmhirst Centre Archive.

17. This and ensuing description from Walter Muir Whitehill, *Dumbarton Oaks.*

18. Ibid.

19. Ibid.

20. Ibid.

21. Beatrix Farrand, "Squaring the Circle: A Study of Campus Development," *University of Chicago Magazine,* June 1936.

22. Ibid.

23. Jon Magnus Jonson (1893–1947), sculptor of the fountain; information on the courtyard and symbolism of carvings, etc., from International House, University of Chicago.

24. Edmund A. Schofield, "A Life Redeemed: Susan Delano McKelvey," *Arnoldia* 47, no. 4 (Fall 1987). Also S. D. McKelvey, *The Lilac: A Monograph* (New York: Macmillan, 1928).

25. Beatrix Farrand, "Climbing Plants in Eastern Maine," *Plants and Gardens,* Spring 1954 (Brooklyn Botanic Garden), 44.

26. Ibid.

27. Garden Club of Mount Desert, Annual Meeting of the Garden Club of America, July 11–13, 1934. Program in Reef Point Gardens Collection.

28. Ibid.

29. G. W. Helfrich and Gladys O'Neil, *Lost Bar Harbor* (Camden, Maine: Down East Books, 1982), 74.

30. Mrs. Gerrish H. Milliken, for whom the 723 Park Avenue town garden was also done.

31. Letter from John D. Rockefeller, May 1, 1941. Bar Harbor Museum.

32. At his funeral service at Saint Margaret's, West Hoathly, they had sung "Abide With Me" and played the "Londonderry Air." William Robinson, Order of Service for Funeral, Saint Margaret's. Reef Point Gardens Collection.

33. Edith Wharton to John Hugh Smith. Lewis and Lewis, *Letters,* 587.

34. Edith Wharton to Bernard Berenson. Lewis and Lewis, *Letters,* 590.

35. Beatrix Farrand to Edith Wharton, May 18, 1936. Beinecke Library.

36. Typed manuscript of tributes at memorial service for Mary Cadwalader Jones, December 12, 1935. Reef Point Gardens Collection.

37. "Mrs. Cadwalader Jones, A Literary Hostess," *Times* (London), September 26, 1935.

38. *Bar Harbor Times,* Friday, September 27, 1935, tribute on the front page. Clipping in Bar Harbor Museum.

39. Beatrix Farrand to Edith Wharton, May 18, 1936. Beinecke Library.

40. Trust Deed released March 20, 1939, copy to author from Cadwalader, Wickersham & Taft, New York.

41. Beatrix Farrand to Leonard Elmhirst, January 29, 1937. Elmhirst Centre Archive.

42. Beatrix Farrand to Leonard Elmhirst, August 31, 1937. Elmhirst Centre Archive.

43. Note on fees and expenses, Elmhirst Centre Archive.

44. A brown border for the Chinese garden. The list of "brown" annuals and perennials for the Chinese garden beds included: orange, bronze, and yellow violas; orange and yellow wallflowers; yellow and orange Iceland poppies; rudbeckia "Golden Sunset"; yellow and orange *Nemesia strumosa;* gaillardia "Crimson Glow" or other deep red; helichrysum "Golden Glow" (tall for border); *Dimor-*

photeca aurantiaca "Star of the Veldt" are all oranges and deep pinks; erysimum "Golden Gem"; *Coreopsis astrosanguinea* and var. "Dark Crimson"; *Cheiranthus allioni* (Siberian wallflower), orange; *Chrysanthemum atrococcinium;* arctotis (African daisy), crimson, bronze, orange, and wine shades; calendulas; single French marigolds and African marigolds (tagetes), tall varieties; *Cosmos sulphurea* "Orange Ruffles."

N.B. The list is obviously of suggestions rather than definite planting plans; presumably helianthus, zinnias, and heleniums could also be included with appropriate sedums, euphorbias, peony "lutea" hybrids, and hemerocallis to add foliage interest.

CHAPTER 11. MANY HAPPY AND SAD RETURNS, 1937–59

1. Paul Solyn, *Oberlin Observer,* April 11, 1985, 6.
2. Correspondence. Dumbarton Oaks Library.
3. Beatrix Farrand to Mildred Bliss, November 13, 1940. Dumbarton Oaks Library.
4. As it turned out, it was not for long: Robert Woods Bliss felt "constitutionally unable, after a third of a century of public service, to eat lotus in wartime," and they returned to Georgetown in 1942. Walter Muir Whitehill, *Dumbarton Oaks,* 89. The Blisses bought 1537 Twenty-eighth Street NW as their last home.
5. Beatrix Farrand to Mildred Bliss and reply, January 1941. Dumbarton Oaks Library.
6. Manuscript for *Plant Book* in Dumbarton Oaks Library; published version, edited by Diane Kostial McGuire, Washington, D.C.: Dumbarton Oaks, 1980.
7. McGuire, ed., *Plant Book,* 9.
8. Ibid., 63–64.
9. Beatrix Farrand to Leonard and Dorothy Elmhirst, October 22, 1943. Elmhirst Centre Archive.
10. Ibid., February 5, 1944.
11. Ibid.
12. Ibid.
13. Reginald Snell, *From the Bare Stem,* 77.
14. Ibid., 48.
15. Beatrix Farrand to William Judd, June 18, 1945. Arnold Arboretum Library.
16. Beatrix Farrand to William Judd, July 6, 1945. Arnold Arboretum Library.
17. In the aftermath of Max's death, Beatrix wanted everything to be done in the name of the Max Farrand Memorial Fund; all the Reef Point Bulletins were published by this fund. But in 1947 her business partners persuaded her to set up the Reef Point Gardens Corporation: of this she was the president, Albert Hall Cunningham was treasurer, and Mrs. Stover was the clerk. Robert Whitely Patterson was the consultant, and the members were Roger Clapp, A. H. Cunningham, Beatrix Farrand, Susan D. McKelvey, Agnes Milliken, Lawrence Morris, Joseph Magee Murray, R. W. Patterson, Serenus Burleigh Rodick, Charles K. Savage, Mrs. Stover, and Robert Amory Thorndike. There were in addition directors (Cunningham, Farrand, Morris, Rodick, and Savage). This was the corporation that was eventually wound up, by mutual consent, in 1955.

18. Reef Point Bulletin no. 1, August 1946. Reef Point Gardens Collection.

19. Beatrix Farrand to Dr. Paul Mangelsdorf, Arnold Arboretum Library. Also Jane Brown, "The Lady as Landscape Gardener: Beatrix Farrand at the Arnold Arboretum," part 2, *Arnoldia* 52, no. 1 (spring 1992).

20. Sargent F. Collier, *Mount Desert Island and Acadia National Park;* for chapter on Bar Harbor fire, 75–87.

21. List of Reef Point Bulletins: Reef Point Gardens Collection. Reef Point Gardens Bulletin published by the Max Farrand Memorial Fund, Bar Harbor.

   1. The Start & the Goal, August 1946
   2. Past Present & Future, November 1947
   3. The Plan of the Grounds, September 1948
   4. The Buildings, August 1949
   5. The Max Farrand Library, July 1950
   6. A Visit to Reef Point Gardens, August 1950
   7. Reef Point Gardens Herbarium, August 1951
   8. Conifers at Reef Point Gardens, June 1952
   9. Maintenance, January 1953
  10. Roses including the 20 best roses at Reef Point, June 1953
  11. Climbing Plants in Eastern Maine, June 1954
  12. Heaths, July 1954
  13. Simple Foundation Planting in Eastern Coastal Maine, August 1954
  14. Prints at Reef Point, August 1955
  15, 16 (not published)
  17. Beatrix Farrand, 1872–1959

22. Beatrix Farrand to Leonard and Dorothy Elmhirst, May 1, 1950. Elmhirst Centre Archive.

23. Ibid., December 13, 1956. Elmhirst Centre Archive.

24. See note 21.

25. Copy of letter of May 16, 1955, sent to Elmhirsts. Elmhirst Centre Archive.

26. Letter of December 13, 1956, and attached note. Elmhirst Centre Archive.

27. Ibid.

28. Patrick Chassé, "A Dream Transplanted (The Story of the Asticon Azalea Garden)," in *Garden Design* (Washington, D.C.), spring 1988.

29. Last letter to "Dear, dear Leonard and Dorothy," August 8, 1958. Elmhirst Centre Archive.

30. Reef Point Gardens Bulletin no. 17. Reef Point Gardens Collection.

CHAPTER 12. BEATRIX FARRAND, 1872–1959: HER LEGACY, AND WHAT HAS BECOME OF IT

1. Footnote to letter, Beatrix Farrand to Leonard and Dorothy Elmhirst, August 8, 1958. Elmhirst Centre Archive.

2. *Times* (London) clipping and related correspondence, Elmhirst Centre Archive.

3. Robert W. Patterson, "Beatrix Farrand, 1872–1959, An Appreciation of a Great Landscape Gardener," *Landscape Architecture,* summer 1959. And Mildred B. Bliss,

"An Attempted Evocation of a Personality," *Landscape Architecture,* summer 1959, 218–24.

4. "News of the Day," Dartington, March 13, 1959. Elmhirst Centre Archive.

5. Patterson, "Beatrix Farrand."

6. A Preliminary Historical Checklist of Landscape Architects in Maine. Earle G. Shettleworth Jr., 1987. Loeb Library.

7. Marian Cruger Coffin (1876–1957) graduated from MIT, 1904.

8. Annette Hoyt Flanders (1887–1946) studied landscape architecture at the University of Illinois.

9. Ellen Biddle Shipman (1869–1950) went to Radcliffe.

10. Cambridge School.

11. James J. Yoch, *Landscaping the American Dream: The Gardens and Film Sets of Florence Yoch 1890–1972* (New York: Sagapress/Abrams, 1989).

12. I am grateful to Cynthia Zaitzevsky for her list of sites, which are common to both the Olmsted and Farrand lists of commissions. The clients are as follows, with the date of the Olmsted work in parentheses: Dr. C. Dunham, Irvington, N.Y. (1903–14); W. D. Sloane, Shadowbrook, Lenox, Mass. (1885–99); William Bayard Cutting (1886–94); J. Montgomery Sears, Southborough, Mass. (1889); C. Oliver Iselin (1925–46); Otto H. Kahn, (1917); Mrs. Phillips, North Beverly, Mass. (1881); John D. Rockefeller Jr., Pocantico Hills, New York (1895–1939).

13. Garrett Eckbo's *Landscape for Living* was first published in 1950, Thomas Church's *Gardens Are for People* in 1955; these were the harbingers of the new thought in garden and landscape design. It is irresistible to suggest that if only Beatrix had been in San Francisco instead of San Marino in her Californian years, she would have encountered Thomas Church and seen how he was taking forward the best of her own beliefs.

14. To a great extent the island's summer popularity is now restored; a best-seller to tourists is Helfrich and O'Neil, *Lost Bar Harbor.*

15. Beatrix Farrand to Leonard and Dorothy Elmhirst, May 1, 1950. Elmhirst Centre Archive.

16. Snell, *From the Bare Stem*, 48–60.

17. Michael Young, *The Elmhirsts of Dartington,* tells the story up until 1982 with the closure of the school.

18. At the time of this writing, spring 1994, there are plans for restoration.

19. I am grateful to Paula Deitz for bringing the Smith College correspondence to my notice. All the letters are in the Smith College Archives, Northampton, Mass.

20. Jane Brown, "The Lady as Landscape Gardener: Beatrix Farrand at the Arnold Arboretum," part 2, *Arnoldia* 52, no. 1 (spring 1992), 9–17.

21. Michael Laurie, a Scot migrated to California, relates the story of the collection in California in his paper to the Eighth Dumbarton Oaks Colloquium, "The Reef Point Collection at the University of California, 1982."

Sources

Primary Sources

Dartington Hall, Totnes, Devon, England, the Elmhirst Centre Archive: correspondence between Beatrix Farrand and Dorothy Whitney Straight, later Elmhirst, and Leonard Elmhirst, concerning Apple Green, Long Island, and Dartington Hall.

Harvard University, Cambridge, Massachusetts, Library of the Arnold Arboretum: Beatrix Farrand's correspondence with William Judd and others.

Harvard University, Houghton Library: letters of Mary Cadwalader Jones and Beatrix Jones Farrand, and letters of Mary Cadwalader Jones to Eleanor K. Roosevelt. (Derby papers kindly provided for me by Mr. W. K. Finlay.)

Harvard University, Graduate School of Design, Frances Loeb Library, the John Charles Olmsted Collection, and proceedings of the American Society of Landscape Architects (also Frances Loeb Library).

Oberlin College Archives, Oberlin, Ohio.

Smith College, Northampton, Massachusetts, William Allan Neilson Library, Rare Book Room, Beatrix Farrand Collection.

University of California at Berkeley, College of Environmental Design, Beatrix Farrand/Reef Point Gardens Collection: all drawings, correspondence, photographs, and books.

University of Chicago, Chicago, Illinois, Library, Buildings and Grounds Records. Richard C. Bumstead, university landscape architect, kindly provided additional material. Also, Library of International House.

Yale University, New Haven, Connecticut, Beinecke Rare Book and Manuscript Library, Yale Collection of American Literature, Edith Wharton Collection.

Balmori, Diana, Diane Kostial McGuire, and Eleanor M. McPeck. *Beatrix Farrand's American Landscapes: Her Gardens and Campuses.* Sagaponack, N.Y.: Sagapress, 1985.

Berkeley, Ellen Perry, ed. *Architecture: A Place for Women.* Washington, D.C.: Smithsonian Institution Press, 1989.

Block, Jean F. *The Uses of Gothic Planning and Building the Campus of the University of Chicago, 1892–1932.* Chicago: University of Chicago Press, 1983.

Collier, Sargent F. *Mount Desert Island and Acadia National Park: An Informal History.* Camden, Me.: Down East Books, 1978.

Griswold, Mac, and Eleanor Weller. *The Golden Age of American Gardens: Proud Owners, Private Estates, 1890–1940.* New York: Abrams, 1991.

Laurie, Michael. *An Introduction to Landscape Architecture.* London: Pittman, 1976.

Lewis, R. W. B. *Edith Wharton: A Biography.* New York: Harper & Row, 1975; Fromm International, 1985.

Lewis, R. W. B., and Nancy Lewis, eds. *The Letters of Edith Wharton.* New York: Scribner's, 1989.

McGuire, Diane Kostial, ed. *Beatrix Farrand's Plant Book for Dumbarton Oaks.* Washington, D.C.: Dumbarton Oaks Trustees for Harvard University, 1980.

McPeck, Eleanor. "Beatrix Farrand." In Barbara Sicherman and Carol Hurd Green, eds., *Notable American Women.* Cambridge: Harvard University Press, Belknap Press, 1980.

Ottewill, David. *The Edwardian Garden.* New Haven: Yale University Press, 1989.

Roper, Laura Wood. *FLO: A Biography of Frederick Law Olmsted.* Baltimore and London: The Johns Hopkins University Press, 1973.

Seymour, Miranda. *A Ring of Conspirators: Henry James and His Literary Circle, 1895–1915.* Boston: Houghton Mifflin, 1989.

Spongberg, Stephen A. *A Reunion of Trees: The Discovery of Exotic Plants and Their Introduction into North American and European Landscapes.* Cambridge: Harvard University Press, 1990.

Stilgoe, John R. *Borderland Origins of the American Suburb, 1820–1939.* New Haven: Yale University Press, 1988.

Turner, Paul Venable. *Campus: An American Planning Tradition.* New York: Architectural History Foundation of New York, 1987; Cambridge: The MIT Press, 1987.

Wharton, Edith. *A Backward Glance.* London: Century, 1987.

Whitehill, Walter Muir. *Dumbarton Oaks: The History of a Georgetown House and Garden, 1800–1966.* Cambridge: Harvard University Press, Belknap Press, 1967.

Young, Michael. *The Elmhirsts of Dartington: The Creation of an Utopian Community.* Boston: Routledge & Kegan Paul, 1982.

INDEX

Abbe, Dr. Robert, 63
Adams, Brooks, 18
Adams, Henry, 18, 154
Age of Innocence, The (Wharton), 22
Aldrich, Chester Holmes, 127
Alphand, Jean-Charles-Adolphe, 56
American Architect & Building News, 82
American Institute of Architects, 191
American Society of Landscape Architects, 68–72, 74, 98–99, 122, 194, 196
Ames, Oakes, 159
Anchor Post Iron Works, 111
Anderson, Dorothy May, 198–99
Anderson, Larz, 41
Apple Green, *see* Elmhurst
Architectural League, "An Ideal Suburban Place" competition, 95–98
Arnold, James, 33
Arnold Arboretum, 5, 33–37, 77, 100, 139, 151, 153, 158–60, 168, 181
 Beatrix as consultant for, 182–84, 193, 200
 Beatrix's studying at, 4, 26, 34, 35–37
 Olmsted and, 34
 Sargent as director of, 33–34
Arnoldia, 182, 183
Art and Practice of Landscape Gardening, The (Milner), 65

Astor, Caroline Schermerhorn, 8
Astor, Lady, 84
Augusta State Park, 67
Austin, Mr. and Mrs. Stanley, 76

Backward Glance, A (Wharton), 80
Bacon, Sir Francis, 84, 86
Bahlman, Anna, 120
Baker, Ann, 106, 128, 129
Baker, Herbert, 3, 121
Baldwin, George V. N., 22
Balmori, Diana, 2, 142, 146
Bar Harbor, Maine, 19, 24–30, 42, 62–65, 77–78, 160–61, 165, 194
 Beatrix's last years in, 189–190
 Fire of October 1947, 184, 186, 196
 social life of, 25, 77
Bar Harbor Record, 104
Bar Harbor Times, 165
Barillet-Deschamps, Jean Pierre, 56
Barr, Margaret, 163
Barrett, Nathan Franklin, 69–70
Bates, William A., 60
Battersea Park, London, 51
Beatrix Farrand's American Landscapes: Her Gardens and Campuses, 2
Bell, Mrs. Gordon, 80
Bellefontaine (Foster home), 82
Berenson, Bernard, 164, 166

Biltmore (Vanderbilt home), 42, 65, 69
Birch Point, 28–29
Black, Eliza, 13
Bliss, Mildred Barnes, 3, 59, 70, 138–41, 143, 146, 153–55, 157, 158, 169, 170, 176–78, 191, 194, 195, 199–200
Bliss, Robert Woods, 3, 138–40, 146, 154–55, 157, 169, 170, 176–77, 194, 195
Blomfield, Reginald, 47, 54, 56
Boboli Gardens, Florence, 49
Bolle, Dr. Carl, 50, 114
Book of Roses, The (Parkman), 31
Booth, John Wilkes, 14
Borghese gardens, Rome, 50
Boston City Council, 34
Bouche, Carl F., 50
Bowditch, Ernest W., 59
Bowdoin, George S., 64–65
Bowler, Robert P., 65
Brett & Hall, 113–14, 116–17
Brick House (Stokes home), 72, 82, 83
Britton, Elizabeth Gertrude Knight, 108
Britton, Nathaniel Lord, 108
Bullard, Elizabeth, 69
Buonriposo (Fabbri home), 64
Burnham, Daniel, 41
Bush-Brown, James, 92, 95
Bussey Institution, 31, 33, 37
Buttes-Chaumont, Paris, 56

Cadwalader, Elizabeth, 12
Cadwalader, General George, 14
Cadwalader, Hannah Lambert, 12
Cadwalader, John, 12
Cadwalader, John Lambert, 12, 23, 26, 46, 55, 78, 87, 91, 104, 105, 114, 126
Cadwalader, Lambert, 12
Cadwalader, Mary Binney, 12
Cadwalader, Richard, 105
Cadwalader, Sophie, 121
Cadwalader, Dr. Thomas, 11–12
Cadwalader, William, 13
California Institute of Technology, 146
Calthorpe, David, 168, 179
Cameron, Elisabeth, 124
Cane, Percy, 196–97
Carrere & Hastings, 82, 127
Casa Dorinda (Bliss home), 177
Casa Respiglia, Rome, 48
Cathedral Park Board, 77
Cathedral School for Girls, 77
Central Park, New York City, 40, 67, 68
Century, 79
Chantilly, France, 75
Chassé, Patrick, 196
Chatwold (Bowler home), 65
Chemical Bank of New York, 22
Chiltern (Scott home), 63, 78
Choate, Joseph H., 70, 80
Church, Thomas, 196
"City Parks," 56–57
Civil War, 10, 14
Clark, Jane, 166
Codman, Harry Sargent, 40, 45, 67
Codman, Ogden, 57, 79
Coffin, Marian Cruger, 195
Colby, Colonel Spencer, 102
Colour Schemes for the Flower Garden (Jekyll), 44
Colt, Mrs. Samuel G., 123
Columbia University, 9, 58
Coolidge, Hamilton, 120
Cope and Stewardson, 92
Correvon, M., 75
Cortissoz, Royal, 165
Council, Lucille, 146, 195
Country Life, 150
Cram, Ralph Adams, 100, 101, 110
Crane, Mrs. Zena, 123–24
Crawford, Francis Marion, 23–24, 25–26, 46
Crawford, Thomas, 23
Croly, Herbert, 106, 147
Crosswicks (Newbold home), 70–71, 72, 80, 87, 92, 93, 140, 189
Crucial Instances (Wharton), 82

Daisy, Countess of Warwick, 86, 87

Danesfield, Buckinghamshire, 85
Dartington Hall (Elmhirst home), 5, 147, 149–52, 163–64, 167–68, 171, 179, 190, 193
under Percy Cane, 196–97
News of the Day, 192
Davis, Herbert, 199
Dawson, Jackson Thornton, 36–37, 159
Decoration of Houses, The (Wharton and Codman), 57, 79
de Fiori, Mario, 48
de Forest, Lockwood, 146, 195
Delano, William Adams, 106, 127, 159
Delano & Aldrich, 107
de Navarro, Anthony and Mary, 87
Dixwell, Mr., 33
Dorr, Charles F., 27, 77
Dorr, George Bucknam, 27, 63, 161
Dorr, Mary Ward, 27, 28, 77
Downing, Andrew Jackson, 31–33, 72
Dumbarton Oaks (Bliss home), 1, 3, 87, 99, 138–41, 144, 149, 152–58, 168–70, 191–92, 193, 196–200
deeded to Harvard, 176–78, 197
plan of garden, 156
Plant Book, 178–79, 198
Dunham, Dr. Edward K., 63

Earle, Theresa, 47, 53
Easton Lodge (Countess of Warwick's home), 85–86
Eastover (Fahnestock home), 81–82
Eckbo, Garrett, 196
Eliot, Charles William, 31, 34, 44–47, 50, 51, 56, 65, 68, 69
Elliott, Maud Howe, 24
Elm Court (Sloane home), 81
Elmhirst, Dorothy Whitney, 5, 90, 106–8, 120, 129, 143, 144, 147–54, 163, 166–68, 179–80, 185–86, 190, 192, 194, 196–97
interest in gardening, 167, 168, 179, 180
Elmhirst, Leonard, 147–50, 153, 154, 163, 166, 167, 168, 180, 185–86, 190, 196–97
Elmhirst, Pom, 163
Elmhurst (Straight home) (renamed Apple Green), 106–8, 168, 189
English Flower Garden, The (Robinson), 44
Eolia (Harkness home), 99, 113–19, 142, 144, 189

Ethel Walker School, 120–21
European Travel for Women (Jones), 76
Evelyn, John, 49, 185
Exotics, 28, 75
Eyrie, The (Rockefeller home), 162–63, 190, 196

Fabbri, Ernesto, 64
Fahnestock, Harris C., 82
Fairstead (Olmsted home and office), 42–45
"False Dawn," 9
Farnam, Thomas, 141, 142
Farrand, Beatrix Jones:
ancestry, xvi–xvii, 8–14
appearance, 7, 99, 149, 170–71
Arnold Arboretum consultancy, 182–84, 193, 200
Arnold Arboretum training, 4, 26, 34, 35–37
baptism, 7
birth, 7
California move, 143–46
childhood, 7, 17, 24–26
choice of career, 26, 30
commissions, list of, 203–216
courtship, 102
death, 190, 191
destruction of family papers by, 4, 124
drawing ability, 57–58
early work, 59–65
European study tours, 45–58, 74–76
European travel for social and cultural purposes, 74, 83–87
finances, 105, 124, 149
forsythia named for, 34
health, 88, 179
as landscape "gardener," 72, 73
legacy of, 191–200
marriage, 3, 102–6, 114, 143, 170–71
naming of, 7
obituaries, 191–92
Olmsted offices, visit to, 42–45
personality, 67, 99
photographs of, ii, 19, 32, 60, 144, 164, 172, 176
place in her profession, 65–73, 192–201
portrait, 18
tombstones designed by, 66, 120, 193
Farrand, Livingston, 105, 151
Farrand, Mrs. Livingston, 102, 104–5, 151
Farrand, Max (husband), 3, 104, 124, 151, 153, 154, 163, 172, 177, 179–80, 184–85
Beatrix's clients and, 111
courtship of Beatrix, 102
death, 180–81, 196, 199

Farrand, Max, (husband) (*cont.*)
  described, 101–2
  as director of Huntington
    Library and Art Gallery,
    143, 144, 149, 169–70,
    177
  marriage, 3, 102–6, 114, 143,
    170–71
  Reef Point gardens and,
    125–26, 129
Farrand, Mrs. Wilson, 105
Farrand, Wilson, 105
Fenwick, Mark, 85
Fighting France (Wharton), 119
Flanders, Annette Hoyt, 195
Fleming, Dean Andrew, 100
Formal Garden in England, The
  (Blomfield), 47, 54
*Formal Gardens in England and
  Scotland* (Triggs), 99
Foster, Giraud, 82
Framing of the Constitution, The
  (Farrand), 101
Franklin, Benjamin, 11–12
Franklin & Clarke, 95
Freshfield, Douglas, 151
*From the Bare Stem: The Making
  of Dorothy Elmhirst's
  Garden at Dartington
  Hall* (Snell), 197

Gammon, George, 83
Garden (magazine), 47
Garden & Forest, 34, 41, 47, 55,
  65, 66, 68, 73
"Garden as a Picture," 89–90
Garden Club of America,
  121–23, 160–63, 191,
  194
Garden Club of Philadelphia,
  121
Garden Craft Old and New
  (Sedding), 47
Garden Design in Italy (Triggs),
  99
Gardens of a Golden Afternoon
  (Brown), 1–2
Garland, Amy Magdalene, 185,
  191
Garlands (Farrand home), 189
Garrison, William R., 60–61,
  62
George, Sir Ernest, 85
Gettysburg, Battle of, 14
Gibson, Robert W., 77
Gilder, Richard Watson, 79
Gilman, Daniel, 65
Glastonbury Abbey, 76
Glenmere (Goelet home),
  112–13
Goelet, Robert, 112–13
*Golden Age of American Gardens,
  The* (Griswold and
  Weller), 126, 195
Gorhambury (Bacon home), 84
Gorton, Mr. (agent), 144, 147
Gravetye Manor (Robinson
  estate), 53–54, 163, 189
Gray, Asa, 33
Great Neck, New York, village

green and library garden,
  129
Greene & Greene, 200–1
Greenfield, Connecticut,
  Village Improvement
  Association, 61, 70
Griswold, Mac, 1, 126, 195
Grosser Garten, Dresden, 50
Gutheim, Frederick A., 2

Hadrian's villa, 50
Hale, George E., 143, 146
Hall, Charles Martin, 173
Hamilton, W. Pierson, 160, 184
Hanna, Mrs., 134
Hardy, Alpheus, 28
Haring, James Smith, 59
Harkness, Edward S., 111–14,
  141, 142, 144, 194
Harkness, Mary, 114
Harkness Mausoleum, 142–
  143
Harris, Henry Frazer, 92, 94
Harris, Mrs. Henry Frazier, 95,
  121
Harrison, George, 61
Harston (Harris home), 92–95
Harvard University, 10, 31, 33,
  69, 159
  Dumbarton Oaks deeded to,
    176–78, 197
Hastings, Helen Benedict, 127
Hastings, Thomas, 82, 106,
  126–27
Haven, The (Milliken home),
  162
Havey, Ruth, 19, 153
Hearst, Mrs. William
  Randolph, 77
Henry, Mrs. Bayard, 121
Hertrich, William, 145–46
Hibben, John Grier, 100, 101
Hill School, Pottstown, 144,
  145
Hill-Stead (Pope home), 87,
  189
Holabird & Root, 158
Holm Lea (Sargent home), 31,
  33, 37–40, 42, 45, 77
  gardens at, 37–40
Hoppin, Francis L., 79, 82
Hoppin & Koen, 82
Horticultural Congress, 99
Howe, George, 163
Howe, Maud, 75
Howelles & Stokes, 82
Hunnewell, Horatio, 33, 36
Hunt, Myron, 146, 195
Hunt, Richard Morris, 42
Huntington, Arabella, 143,
  146
Huntington, Henry E., 143,
  145–46
Huntington Library and Art
  Gallery, Henry E., 143–
  146, 149, 169–70, 196
Huxley, Julian, 151

Indian Summer (Irving), 3
Irving, Robert Grant, 3

Isola Bella, 50
Italian Villas and Their Gardens
  (Wharton), 47, 48

Jamaica Plain gardens, 45
James, Henry, 4, 5, 10–11, 17,
  19, 42, 74, 82–84, 87,
  194
  Beatrix and, 83–84, 87, 99,
    103–4, 120
  death, 120
  friendship with Mary Jones,
    11, 82–83, 103–4, 105,
    114–20
Jardin d'Essai, Algiers, 48
Jekyll, Gertrude, 1, 2, 44, 47,
  52, 84, 89, 109, 111, 121,
  128, 185, 192–93, 194
  Beatrix's meeting with, on
    European tour, 51–53
  drawings of, 3–4, 162, 192,
    193, 198, 200
  plan for Millmead, 98
Johnstone, Lawrence, 87
Jones, Edward, 9
Jones, Edward Renshaw, 9
Jones, Elizabeth Schermerhorn,
  9
Jones, Frederic Rhinelander
  (father), 8–11, 75, 88,
  105, 166
  death, 124
  divorce, 4, 19–22, 55–56
  finances, 21–22
  marriage, 7, 15–19
  mistress, 21, 22
  occupation, 7, 17, 19
Jones, George Frederic (grandfather), 7–8, 9–10, 21
Jones, Henry Edward (Harry)
  (uncle), 78, 124
  birth, 8, 10
  finances, 21, 22
Jones, Joshua, 22
Jones, Lucretia Rhinelander
  (grandmother), 8–9, 19,
  22, 78
  birth, 8
  death, 22
  finances, 21
  as gardener, 8, 10, 19, 128,
    189–90
  marriage, 9
  New York society and, 8, 10
Jones, Mary Cadwalader
  (Minnie) (mother), 17, 25,
  62, 65, 77, 78, 82, 105,
  124, 143, 144
  as an author, 13, 14, 76
  appearance, 13
  birth, 13
  charity work, 17–18, 19, 23,
    25, 164–65
  childhood, 13, 14–15
  death, 4, 164–66
  divorce, 4, 19–22, 55–56
  on European study tours
    with Beatrix, 46–58,
    74–77
  first trip to Europe, 14–15

Henry James and, 11, 82–83,
103–4, 114–20
as literary hostess, 19, 23–24
marriage, 7, 15–19
in 1930s, 149, 163–64, 165
personality, 11, 18–19
Roosevelts and, 90, 105,
120
Jonson, Jon Magnus, 158
*Journal of the Committee of
Municipal Administration*,
67
Judd, William Henry, 153, 159,
160, 180–81, 182

Kahn, Adele Wolff, 127–28,
195
Kahn, Otto, 126, 127, 193
Kent, William, 57
Knole (Sackville home), 51

La Farge, Florence Bayard, 164
La Farge, John, 24, 46, 77
La Favorita, Sicily, 75
Lamb House (James home), 83,
84, 189
Landscape Architecture, 191, 192
Land's End (Wharton home),
78
Langston, Daniel W., 69
Lanning Roper and His Gardens
(Brown), 2
Lantern Slides (Jones), 13, 14
La Rochelle (Bowdoin home),
64–65
Lee, Elizabeth Leighton, 121
Lee, Harry, 147, 168
Lee, Thomas, 31
Le Nôtre, 56, 58, 88, 185
"Le Nôtre and His Gardens,"
88–89
Lescaze, William, 163
Levens Hall, Cumbria, 54–55
Lincoln, Abraham, 14
Lindsay garden, Edzell Castle,
55
Lockwood, Florence, 18–19
Lodge, Henry Cabot, 18
Long Barn (Sackville-West
home), 114
Lord, Edgar I., 63–64, 194
Lord, Hull & Hewlett, 113
Lorillard, Pierre, 59
Lorimer, Robert, 87, 121
Loseley, 53
Loudon, John Claudius, 72
*Love in Idleness: A Bar Harbor
Tale* (Crawford), 25–26
Low, Seth, 65
Lowrie, Charles Nassau, 69
Luton Hoo (Wernher home),
85
Lutyens, Edwin, 2, 3, 51, 87,
98, 121
Lynch, Kevin, 196, 201
Lynch, R. S., 150
Lynch, Stewart, 152, 153

McAllister, Ward, 8
McCarter, Henry, 89

McCormick farmhouse, Bar
Harbor, 161
McFarland, Arthur, 161
McGuire, Diane Kostial, 2
McHarg, Ian, 196
McKelvey, Susan Delano, 159,
181
McPeck, Eleanor, 2
Macray, Ngaere, 2
Man and Nature (Marsh), 42
Mangelsdorf, Dr. Paul, 182
Manning, Warren, 68, 69, 194,
196
Markoe, Dr. James, 91, 92, 95
Marsh, George Perkins, 42, 142
Marsh, Othniel C., 142
Massachusetts Horticultural
Society, 191
Massingham, Betty, 192–93
Masson, Georgina, 48
Mawson, Thomas, 151
Max Farrand Memorial Fund,
181, 188
Maybeck, Bernard, 200
Meadows, Robert E., 109
Meason, Gilbert Laing, 72
Miller, Wilhelm, 99, 126
Milliken, Agnes, 162, 181, 194
Millmead, Jekyll plan for, 98
Milner, Henry Ernest, 65–66
Mitchell, Isaac N., 194
Mitchell, Dr. Silas Weir, 65, 78
Monreale Cathedral, 75
Morgan, J. Pierpont, 65, 91–
92
Morgan, Julia, 201
Morgan Library, 106, 193
Morrill family garden, 28
Mount, The (Wharton home),
57, 78–80, 81, 88, 189
gardens at, 79–80, 81
Mount Desert Island Garden
Club, 123
Mount Palomar Observatory,
146
Mount Vernon, 168
Muir-Mackenzie, Susan, 83,
84
Municipal Affairs, 56–57, 71
Munstead Wood (Jekyll
garden), 51–53, 84

National Cathedral, Wash-
ington, 76, 77, 193
Nesfield, William Andrews,
72
Newbold, Clement B., 80, 92,
93
Newbold, Tom, 80
Newbold family, 10, 15, 70, 80,
105, 121
New York Botanical Garden,
106, 108–10, 153, 191,
193
New York City Hospital
school, 17
New York Parks Department,
67
New York Sun, 26, 59, 61, 64,
185

New York Times, 120, 177
Norton, Sara, 79
Nymphaeum, 48–49
Nymphenburg, 50

Oakpoint (Williams home),
129–35
Oberlin College, 171–73, 176,
189
Occidental College, 146
Oheka (Kahn home), 127–28
Oldfarm, 27–28, 77
Olmsted, Fidie, 68, 69
Olmsted, Frederick Law, 2, 28,
34, 57, 67–68, 72, 73, 194
on Italian gardening, 46
World's Columbian Exposi-
tion in Chicago and,
40–41
Olmsted, Frederick Law, Jr., 68,
69, 81, 95, 142, 185
Olmsted, John Charles, 42, 68,
69, 157, 196
Olmsted Brothers, 127, 173,
195
*On the Landscape of Architecture
of the Great Painters of Italy*
(Meason), 72
Outlook, The, 88, 90

Page, Russell, 197
Palazzo Colonna, Rome, 48
Palazzo Reale at Caserta, 50
Palermo Botanic Garden, 75
Palmer, Potter, 161
Parc Mondeau, Paris, 56
Parco Aumale, 75
Park, Trenor L., 62
Parkman, Francis, 31, 33, 35,
37
Parsons, Alfred, 87
Parsons, Samuel, Jr., 67, 68,
69
Parsons, Shepard & Ogden, 22
Patterson, Robert, 69, 181,
182, 186, 191, 192
Peabody & Stearns, 81
Pencraig, 7, 10, 19, 78
rose garden, 8, 128, 189–90
Pentecost, George F., 69
Perkins, Colonel, 31
Perry, C. M., 59
Peto, Harold Ainsworth, 85–87
Pinchot, Amos, 77
Pinchot, Gifford, 42, 77
Pindell, Jane Maulby, 164–65
Platt, Charles, 46–47, 85
Platt, William, 46
Point d'Acadie (Vanderbilt
estate), 42
Pope, John Russell, 143
Pope, Theodate, 87
Pot-Pourri from a Surrey Garden
(Earle), 53
Price, Bruce, 60
Princeton University, 100–2,
110–11, 151, 189
Wyman House garden,
110–11
Pulitzer, Joseph, 65

Pyne, Mrs. Moses Taylor, 100, 101
Pyne, Percy R., II, 126, 127, 128–29

Quincy, Mrs. Harry, 77

Randall, Monica, 129
Rawle, Emily Cadwalader, 14, 15, 19
Rawle, Francis, 12
Rawle, Martha Turner, 12
Rawle, Mary Cadwalader (grandmother), 12, 13–14
Rawle, William (uncle), 13–14
Rawle, William Henry (grandfather), 12, 13, 14–15, 19
Rawle family, xvii, 12–13
Reef Point (Farrand home), 20–21, 24, 26, 78, 106, 114, 123, 125, 144, 153, 159, 163, 196
  building of, 19
  bulletins, 181–82, 184, 186, 189, 217–19
  early planting plan, 29–30
  garden at, 25, 28, 29, 45, 98, 106, 125–26, 129–34, 143, 159–60, 179, 180, 189
  Garden Club of America's visit to, 160–61
  sale of, 189
  as teaching garden, 125, 126, 166, 171, 172–75, 181–82, 184–85, 186–89, 196
Reef Point Gardens Corporation, 181
  dissolving of, 186–88, 196
Repton, Humphrey, 57, 72
Rhinelander, Frederic William, 8
Rhinelander, Reverend Philip, 104, 105
Richardson, H. H., 34
Riddle, John Wallace, 87
Ries, Lester, 173, 176
Robbins, Mrs. J. H., 34–35
Robinson, William, 44, 47, 53, 56, 75, 89, 185, 189, 193, 194
  Beatrix's visits with, 53–54, 164
  death, 163, 164
Rockefeller, Abby Aldrich, 129, 162
Rockefeller, David, 109
Rockefeller, John D., Jr., 65, 157, 158, 162, 189, 190, 194, 196
Rodick, Serenus B., 181
Rogers, James Gamble, 113, 114, 141, 142
Roland Park Women's Club, 95, 96
Roosevelt, Edith, 90, 102
Roosevelt, Mrs. Theodore, Sr., 78
Roosevelt, Theodore, 18, 65, 90, 100, 105, 120, 126, 193, 194

Roosevelt, Theodore, Sr., 18
Roper, Lanning, 197
Roper, Laura Wood, 2
Rotch, Arthur, 19, 24
Royal Horticultural Society, 151
Rutherford, Lewis, 9
Ruzicka, Rudolph, 156

Sackville-West, Vita, 51, 114, 179, 197
Saint-Gaudens, Augustus, 24
Sampson, Gertrude, 161
Santa Barbara Botanic Garden, 146, 169, 195
Sargent, Charles Sprague, 30, 31, 33, 35, 38, 40, 42, 50, 56, 75, 77, 99, 100, 123, 139, 142, 157, 185, 194, 200
  Beatrix's studying at Arnold Arboretum and, 4, 26, 36
  death, 158
  as director of Arnold Arboretum, 33–34
Sargent, Georgiana, 123
Sargent, Henry, 33
Sargent, John Singer, 23, 24, 33, 34
Sargent, Mary Robeson, 26, 33, 37, 38, 42, 77
Satterlee, Constance, 77
Satterlee, Bishop Henry Yates, 71, 76, 77
Satterlee, Mrs. Herbert, 134, 136–37, 161, 184
Savage, Charles Kenneth, 181, 189
Sax, Dr. Karl, 182, 200
Schwarfenberg, River Tegel, 50
Sckell, F. L., 50
Scott, Edgar T., 63, 64, 77–78
Scott, Mrs. Edgar T., 77–78, 121
Scribner's, 88, 89
Seal Harbor Cemetary, 59, 70
Sedding, John Dando, 47
Shipman, Ellen Biddle, 195, 198
Simmonds, Ossian Cole, 70
Sitwell, George, 49
Slader, Douglas, 74
Slater, Elizabeth Hope, 78
Slattery, Reverend Charles Lewis, 104
Sloane, Emily Vanderbilt, 80–81
Smith College, 191, 198–99
Society of Little Gardens, 121
Some Flowers (Sackville-West), 179
Spring-Rice, Cecil, 51
Spry, Constance, 196
Starke, Mariana, 47
Staverton Builders, 163
Stevens, General Ebenezer, 8
Stevens, Mary Lucretia Lucy, 8
Stiles, William A., 68
Stokes, Anson Phelps, 72, 82, 83

Stoppard, Albert, 75
Stotesbury, Mr. and Mrs., 161
Stover, Isabelle Marshall, 181, 185, 190, 191
Strachey, St. Loe, 51
Straight, Dorothy, *see* Elmhirst, Dorothy Whitney
Straight, Willard, 106–8, 120, 126, 147
Straus, Beth, 109
Strong, Charles E., 23
Strong, George Templeton, 9
Sturgis, Howard, 84
Subtropical Garden, The (Robinson), 75
Sutton, Stephanie, 34

Taft, Larado, 158
Thacher, Dr. John Seymour, 177–78
Thackeray, William Makepeace, 13
Thirlestane (Hamilton home), 160, 184
Thomas, F. Inigo, 54
Thorp, Margaret Farrand, 102
Tiergarten, Berlin, 50
Times of London, 99, 165, 191
Tipping, H. Avary, 150
Touchstone, The (Wharton), 82
Traquair House, Scotland, 140
Travels in Europe (Starke), 47
Triggs, Harry Inigo, 99
Tuxedo Park, 59–61, 70
Tyler, Elisina, 66
Tyler, Royall, 166

University of California at Berkeley, 1–4, 189, 193, 200–1, 220–21
University of Chicago, 144, 145, 151, 157–58
Updike, Berkeley, 78

van Alen, Mr. and Mrs. J. J., 78
Vanderbilt, George Washington, 42
van Renssalaer, Mariana, 24, 26, 30, 194
Vatican gardens, 49
Vaughan, Leland, 189, 200, 220–21
Vaux, Calvert, 67–68, 72–73
Vaux, Downing, 69
Versailles, 56, 75
Villa Albani, Rome, 75
Villa Aldobrandini, 48
Villa Carlotta, Lake Como, 50
Villa d'Este, 50
Villa Gamberaia, Florence, 49–50
Villa Giulia, Palermo, 75
Villa Lancelotti, Frascati, 49
Villa Lante, Viterbo, 49
Villa Madama, Rome, 75
Villa Medici, Rome, 48
Villa Odescalchi, Rome, 75
Villa Ruffinello, Frascati, 48, 49
Villa Tasca, Sicily, 75
Villa Torlonia, Frascati, 48

Walker, Ethel, 120–21
Wallace Witt Williamson
    Hospital, 111
Ward, Arnold, 164
Ward, Humphry, 84, 104, 164
Ward, Louisa, 23
Ward, Mary Augusta, 84, 114,
    164
Warden, Clarence A., 94, 128
Ware, William, 58
Wave Hill Amerian Garden
    History Program, 2
Weir, William, 150
Weller, Eleanor, 1, 195
Wernher, Julius, 85
Westover School, 87
Wharton, Edith (née Jones)
    (aunt), 4, 9, 15, 46, 48,
    57, 74, 82, 105, 124, 138,
    151, 166–67, 194
  Berkshire home, see Mount,
    The
  birth of, 8, 10
  closeness with Beatrix, 7, 24,
    105, 143
  death, 167
  divorce, 104
  finances, 21, 22, 149
  as gardener and writer about
    gardens, 8, 47, 48, 79–80,
    166

Henry James and, 82–83
  marriage, 22, 78
  novels, 22
  strokes suffered by, 163, 166
  during World War I, 114–19,
    138
Wharton, Teddy, 24, 48, 78
  Berkshire home and, 78–80,
    81
  divorce, 104
  marriage, 22, 78
What England Can Teach Us
    About Gardening (Miller),
    99, 126
Whitehall, Walter Muir,
    154–55
White House, 90, 102, 106,
    108, 192, 193
Whitney, Dorothy, see Elmhirst,
    Dorothy Whitney
Whitney, Edward F., 90, 91
Whitney, William C., 107
Whitridge, Arnold, 24, 165
Whitridge, Frederick Walling-
    ford, 24, 120
Whitridge, Lucy, 24
Whittaker family gardens,
    74–75
Williams, F. W., 110, 111
Williams, Mr. and Mrs.
    Harrison, 126, 129

Wilson, Edith, 108
Wilson, E. H., 33
Wilson, Ellen Axson, 102, 108
Wilson, Ernest "Chinese," 159
Wolseley, Frances, 99
Wood & Garden, 52
Woodburne (Scott home), 64,
    78
Woodbury (Kahn garden), 195
Woods, Percy, 150
World's Columbian Exposition
    at Chicago, 1893, 4,
    40–41
World War I, 14–19, 120,
    121–23, 138
World War II, 168, 171, 178,
    179, 196, 199
Wright, Henry, 163
Wyman, Donald, 181, 182
Wyman, Isaac, 100

Yale University, 105, 111–13,
    151, 153, 168, 191
  Beatrix's work at, 141–42,
    144, 149
Yarnall, Mrs. Charlton, 161
Yoch, Florence, 146, 195
Young, Mrs. A. Murray, 161
Young, Michael, 147, 149–50

Zantzinger, C. C., 157

JUN 16 1995	**DATE DUE**	
JUL 21 1995	FEB 15 1998	
JUL 31 1995		
OCT 12 1995		
NOV 3 1995		
NOV 24 1995		
JAN 24 1996		
JUL 2 1997		

Cold Spring Harbor Library
Cold Spring Harbor, NY 11724